Innovation and Small Enterprises in the Third World

NEW HORIZONS IN THE ECONOMICS OF INNOVATION

General Editor: Christopher Freeman, *Emeritus Professor of Science Policy, SPRU – Science and Technology Policy Research, University of Sussex, UK*

Technical innovation is vital to the competitive performance of firms and of nations and for the sustained growth of the world economy. The economics of innovation is an area that has expanded dramatically in recent years and this major series, edited by one of the most distinguished scholars in the field, contributes to the debate and advances in research in this most important area.

The main emphasis is on the development and application of new ideas. The series provides a forum for original research in technology, innovation systems and management, industrial organization, technological collaboration, knowledge and innovation, research and development, evolutionary theory and industrial strategy. International in its approach, the series includes some of the best theoretical and empirical work from both well-established researchers and the new generation of scholars.

Innovation and Small Enterprises in the Third World

Edited by

Meine Pieter van Dijk

*Professor of Urban Management in Emerging Economics,
Faculty of Economics, Erasmus University, and
Senior Economist, Institute for Housing and
Urban Studies (IHS), Rotterdam, The Netherlands*

Henry Sandee

*Lecturer, Department of Development Economics, and
Senior Research Fellow, Economic and Social Institute,
Vrije Universiteit Amsterdam, The Netherlands*

NEW HORIZONS IN THE ECONOMICS OF INNOVATION

Edward Elgar

Cheltenham, UK • Northampton MA, USA

Published by
Edward Elgar Publishing Limited
Glensanda House
Montpellier Parade
Cheltenham
Glos GL50 1UA
UK

Edward Elgar Publishing, Inc.
136 West Street
Suite 202
Northampton
Massachusetts 01060
USA

A catalogue record for this book
is available from the British Library

ISBN 1 84064 914 3

Printed and bound in Great Britain by MPG Books Ltd, Bodmin, Cornwall

Contents

Figures

Tables

Contributors

Manuel Albaladejo is an industrial economist at the International Development Centre of the University of Oxford. His areas of interest include technological capability development, clustering, and business development services for small enterprise development. His recent publications include a study on enhancing the competitiveness of small firms in Africa, and on East Asian Exports.

Rosemary Atieno is an economist, with research interests in rural and agricultural development issues, focusing on rural finance and food security. She is currently a research fellow at the Institute for Development Studies, University of Nairobi, Kenya.

Bert Bongenaar studied for his Masters degree at the Eindhoven University of Technology. Within the framework of his studies he carried out eight months' field study in Tanzania on government agencies involved in small firm development.

Joy Clancy is a Senior Lecturer with the Technology and Development Group, University of Twente, The Netherlands. She teaches Technology Transfer. She has a first degree in Chemistry (University of London) and a PhD in Engineering (University of Reading). Her research interests cover the use of renewable energy resources and energy management in developing countries.

Meine Pieter van Dijk is Professor at the Economic Faculty of the Erasmus University in Rotterdam and at the Institute for Housing and Urban Studies in Rotterdam. He is author of *Burkina-Faso: Le Secteur Informal de Ouagadogou*. He edited *Enterprise Clusters and Networks* (with R. Rabelotti). He recently published *Local Economies in Turmoil* (Macmillan 2000) and *Developing Female Entrepreneurship in Zimbabwe* (Shaker 2000). His research interests include enterprise clusters, the problems of women entrepreneurs, private–public partnerships in development, and the development of urban infrastructure.

Bert Helmsing is a Professor in Local and Regional Development at the Institute of Social Studies, The Hague, The Netherlands. His research interests include small enterprise development, regional development, and local governance. His PhD research was on regional development in Zimbabwe. He is co-editor of *Small Enterprises and Changing Policies: Structural Adjustment, Financial Policy, and Assistance Programmes in Africa* (IT Publications).

Peter Knorringa is a Senior Lecturer in Local and Regional Development at the Institute of Social Studies in The Hague. He works on global value chains, fair trade, small-scale enterprise, clustering, and the role of trust in economic relationships. He has a PhD in Development Economics (Vrije Universiteit Amsterdam).

Dorothy McCormick is a Senior Research Fellow at the Institute of Development Studies, University of Nairobi, where she has been involved in teaching and research since 1988. She holds a PhD degree from The Johns Hopkins University. Her current research interests are in the areas of small enterprise development, industrialization, entrepreneurship, and the impact of gender on access to resources.

Davide Parrilli is a PhD student at the Birmingham Business School. He has a Masters degree in Development Studies at the University of Sussex. He has been working at the Universidad Centroamericana in Nicaragua during 1996–2000 as research coordinator.

Regine Qualmann is a fellow at the German Development Institute in Bonn. She has long-term research experience in West Africa on the impact of structural adjustment programs on small firm development. Her current research interests include labour and small firm development.

Henny Romijn is a Lecturer in Technology and Development in the MSc programme on Technology and Innovation Policy at Eindhoven University of Technology. Before joining that university, she worked at the University of Oxford, the Institute of Social Studies in The Hague, and projects of the International Labour Organisation in East Africa and India. Her work has focused on industrialization and technological development. Her PhD entitled *Acquisition of Technological Capability by Small Firms in Developing Countries* was written at Tilburg University, and published by Macmillan and St Martin's Press in 1999.

Henry Sandee is a Senior Research Fellow at the Department of Development Economics, Vrije Universiteit Amsterdam. He has a long-term interest in small enterprise development in Southeast Asia. He is involved in research and consultancies on small enterprise development in Indonesia, Vietnam, and Sri Lanka. Presently, he is studying exports from small enterprise clusters in Indonesia.

Adam Szirmai is a Professor in Technology and Development at Eindhoven University of Technology. He is also director of the Eindhoven Centre for Innovation Studies. His research interests include industrialization and technological development in China and Indonesia. He has published a textbook on *Economic and Social Development* in the Third World.

Árni Sverrisson is Assistant Professor at the Department of Sociology, University of Stockholm. He is author of *Evolutionary Technical Change and Flexible Mechanisation in Kenya and Zimbabwe*. His research interests include technological change in small enterprise networks, sustainable technology and social network theory.

1. Innovation and small enterprise development in developing countries

Meine Pieter van Dijk and Henry Sandee

Innovation is crucial for small enterprises to become and remain competitive in a global economy. It contributes to the process of industrialization and economic development. It is essentially a strategy to stay on board and accommodate changes in the behaviour of technology buyers. An innovation in a small enterprise in a developing country may not be new to the world, in the sense that the entrepreneurs produce new products that have not seen the light of day before. Rather the innovation adoption by small enterprises concerns imitation of production processes that have already been adopted elsewhere in the country or region. Although not new to the world it may be a novelty in the local milieu.

Technological change implies four stages, starting with the introduction of the new technology. In a second stage local producers may try to imitate the technology. Subsequently efforts will be made to adapt the technology to the local circumstances. Finally innovation may take place when local producers manage to develop it further.

Evidence will be presented on the factors that foster or inhibit innovation adoption by small enterprises in developing countries. Innovation is virtually synonymous with technological change, as it refers to the first practical use of a new, more productive, technique. A distinction can be made between product and process innovation. Process innovation concerns changes in the amount, combination, quality or types of inputs required to produce the same kind of output. Product innovations refer to changes in the nature of output and, in principle, this may come about without changes in the process of production, although most of the time process and product innovations occur simultaneously (Stoneman, 1983). In this book evidence will be presented on product and process innovation in small-scale manufacturing. To some extent the distinction between product and process innovation coincides with the distinction between radical versus incremental innovations.

Innovation at the level of the firm is in the first place the outcome of a cumulative process. It is cumulative in the sense that technologies of production used today influence learning processes and the nature of accumulated

1

experiences. Calbrese and Rolfo (1992) found that the introduction of process and product innovations in small firms takes place in such a way that they conclude that the factors which condition the innovative processes in firms change through time. Firms at different technological levels and with different organizational and management structures appear to react differently to similar external stimuli.

The various case studies in this book make clear that innovation adoption doesn't come about by itself. Innovation adoption may be viewed as the outcome of decisions taken by various actors. It is the outcome of a process, and the actors involved may be viewed as a network that does not have a boundary, but rather a focus, namely innovation (Sverrisson in Chapter 13). The various case studies show that it is possible to distinguish between leaders and followers in innovation adoption processes and between producer-, consumer- and institution-driven innovations.

Producer-driven innovations are cases where it appears that the producers themselves are the main actors in process innovation. Small entrepreneurs turn out to be very capable of continuously upgrading production processes. Learning by doing and social learning are key instruments by means of which small entrepreneurs are constantly trying to improve the way they do things.

Buyer-driven innovations are those innovations for which traders, industrialists and other intermediaries play an important role in fostering innovations in small-scale enterprises. It appears that buyers are most prominent in stimulating product innovations. Frequently, buyers have better insights into consumers' preferences than small producers, and they may be in a good position to encourage these producers to manufacture improved or new products. There is also evidence of buyers financing part of the technological change process by small firms. Large-scale manufacturing firms are likely to take an interest in financing technological upgrading by their small-scale subcontractors.

Institution-driven innovations are important because stimulating techno-logical change by small-scale producers is high on the agenda of government agencies and NGOs. Fostering innovation adoption is regarded as important for strengthening the role played by small firms in employment creation strategies (for example, Bongenaar and Szirmai in Chapter 12). Such institutional interventions are often justified by pointing at the existence of market failures that hamper private initiatives to bring about innovation adoption in the small firm sector.

In reality there are several actors involved in technological change processes in the small firm sector, and it may not always be easy to determine who are the key agents of change. Innovation adoption in small-scale enterprises does not necessarily lead to upgrading of their technological capabilities. The latter may be defined as the ability to make independent technological choices, to adapt and improve upon chosen techniques and products and eventually to generate new technology, endogenously. These are essential parts of the process of development (Stewart, 1981: 80). It is argued that without development of technological capabilities, innovation adoption by small producers may not contribute much to the long-term development of their firms. The reason is that innovation adoption will not set in motion learning processes that make small firms stronger and that make it increasingly likely that small entrepreneurs manage subsequent innovations on their own.

The European Association of Development and Training Institutes (EADI) Working group on industrialization strategies in the third world focused on technology development and innovation diffusion: how this process works and how it affects small enterprises.[1] It is known that innovation adoption does not always lead to enhancement of technological capabilities in small enterprises. For this reason the issue of developing local technological capabilities will also receive attention. In the last decade the Working group has concentrated its work on the role played by clusters and networks of small enterprises. There is growing evidence that collaboration between small enterprises, either in clusters or in networks, makes individual small firms stronger. Understanding the characteristics of collaboration may well be of great importance when we want to understand why many small firms appear to be doing well during periods of economic growth and crisis.

This book continues the debate on the development of small enterprises by focusing on technology development and innovation diffusion. The key question is how this process works and how it affects small enterprises. We do not exclusively concentrate on innovation adoption in clustered enterprises or in networks, but we also look at the role of flexible specialization for fostering the development of small firms in developing countries. Does flexible specialization lead to innovation?

According to the flexible specialization concept (Pedersen *et al.*, 1994), first, the innovative mentality of the entrepreneur and the skill level of the workers are important factors in the competitiveness of small and medium enterprises (SMEs). This is partly the learning-by-doing aspect of the endogenous growth theory. Secondly, flexible specialization stresses the importance of factors like clusters and networks (Van Dijk and Rabellotti, eds, 1997). The idea is that innovation would take place more easily in networks and clusters, hence special attention will be paid in this book to the role of clusters for innovation and small enterprise development.

The various contributions to this book also shed light on the question of whether clusters are important for innovation adoption in small enterprises. Innovation adoption in clusters does not occur massively during the early phases. Frequently, there are pioneers who are able and willing to take more risks than other entrepreneurs. The latter may simply wait and see whether adopters do better after innovation adoption or not. It is relevant here to distinguish between producer-driven, buyer-driven and institution-driven change processes.

A WORKING DEFINITION OF INNOVATION

What can be considered an innovation? The disadvantages of taking patent statistics are well known.[2] Three types of innovation can be distinguished: basic research, invention and development. Innovations are again related to learning. It is well known from, for example, computer programs that users gradually master the possibilities of these technologies.[3] Finally it should be noted that at present some very new production technologies are available, using advanced electronics, new materials or allowing efficiency at smaller scales of production. These may have substantial effects in improving the productivity of SMEs. It may make technology development and adaptation in third world countries more difficult in the future.

In this book a broad definition of innovation will be used. It was found that in the African case studies, everything the researcher did not expect, given the traditional context and way of doing things can be called an innovation in this local context. This means making a different product or a product of slightly better quality. 'Innovation' would include all the following: using different raw materials or economizing on the use of raw materials or energy; improving the design or introducing a new way to finance, distribute or stock products and changing the management of a small business. Koot *et al.* (eds, 1996), based on Wittgenstein, call 'something surprising' a broad definition of a paradox and as such a good point of departure for research, trying to explain the surprising phenomenon that traditional and small enterprises can be very modern and big in coming up with and implementing new ideas.

A great deal of research concerns the mechanisms of innovation diffusion. The following factors seem to influence a small entrepreneur willing to learn from others:

- travelling around the region
- special demands from customers
- the potential of a niche market
- the use of different marketing techniques and
- being part of a cluster or network

Three levels of analysis for studying innovation can be distinguished:

1. The macro or policy level, promoting (or discouraging) innovation and innovation diffusion
2. The meso level or the level of the business support system and how technological development and innovation is influenced at that level
3. The level of the enterprise or a cluster of enterprises where the actual development and diffusion will take place.

Most studies in this book concentrate on studying innovation at the meso and enterprise level. However, the interaction between these three levels is also important. The second and the third level together could be called the technological capability or local technological capacity and it is important to explain why this capacity is developing in certain cities and countries and lacking in others.

The role of intermediary organizations in the business support system also requires attention. For that reason the chapters of this book have been grouped under four different headings. First, theoretical papers are presented in Part I, to understand the importance of innovation and mechanisms for innovation diffusion for small enterprises. Secondly, a number of case studies will be presented, ranging from countries as different as India and Zimbabwe and for sectors like furniture and brick making. In Part III innovation in a time of crisis will be discussed, continuing in Part IV with some specific mechanisms which seem to promote innovation and technology diffusion. In the final part some theoretical and practical conclusions will be drawn.

PRODUCER-DRIVEN, BUYER-DRIVEN AND INSTITUTION-DRIVEN INNOVATION IN CLUSTERS

There is evidence that innovation adoption takes place more easily in clusters and networks. Various explanations may be brought forward while referring to the distinction between producer-, buyer-, and institution-driven technological change. Producer clusters may have comparative advantages in innovation adoption as there are good opportunities to share costs and risks associated with innovation adoption. This is particularly relevant when innovation concerns the adoption of technological indivisibilities. In clusters and networks, adoption may take place through collaboration among adopters, where producers work together to render innovation adoption profitable. Buyers may give preference to fostering innovation adoption in clustered enterprises because it brings down the transaction costs of collecting and marketing new output.

Development of technological capabilities is most likely to succeed when small producers are the main actors in innovation adoption. In other cases it appears to be less certain whether innovation adoption will lead to increases in technological capabilities. In clusters it is very likely that there will be differences among producers with regard to the development of technological capabilities, depending whether they are part of a producer-driven, buyer-driven or institution-driven innovation process. Pioneers and early adopters are expected to be in the best position to upgrade their technological capabilities. Later adopters and laggards may adopt because they have been inspired by the experiences of others, and their process of technological change may lack the learning-by-doing elements that are crucial for the development of technological capabilities. Secondly, it seems that differences in development of technological capabilities among clustered producers are not necessarily a problem. Technological change may lead to growth of income and new employment opportunities in the cluster, while only a limited group of the clustered producers increase their technological capabilities. This suggests that development of technological capabilities is important but it is not always a prerequisite for growth of income and employment in small clustered enterprises.

In clusters and networks, firms are linked horizontally and vertically to other entities. Collaboration among small firms and subcontracting are good examples of, respectively, horizontal and vertical linkages. McCormick argues in Chapter 11 of this book that these linkages deserve our attention because their nature may influence the performance of individual firms as well as their ability to innovate or their technological capabilities.

Finally for both government agencies and NGOs, it makes sense to concentrate innovation adoption efforts on clustered enterprises, as learning and diffusion processes are facilitated when small producers operate close to each other and there are patterns of interfirm collaboration. Various case studies in the book show that small enterprises do not operate in isolation. There is ample evidence of networking and collaboration among small enterprises. This draws our attention to a methodological issue, namely to what extent is the individual small firm an adequate unit of analysis when discussing the importance of innovation for small enterprise development. It seems that, at least, it takes two to tango (Helmsing in Chapter 5 of this book) and that there are virtually no examples of small entrepreneurs who adopt innovations totally on their own. Innovation decisions are frequently made by those other than the small producers themselves.

THE STRUCTURE OF THE BOOK

Henny Romijn in Chapter 2 deals with the issue of acquisition of technological capability or innovation. She argues that there is a difference for small enterprises in the third world, where 'doing new things usually means the adoption of a new machine, product design or manufacturing technique invented elsewhere'. An innovation would be the inhouse development of fundamentally new things. Doing new things requires technological capability and she focuses on the acquisition of this technological capability.

For small firms the key challenge is not innovation, but rather the acquisition of technological capabilities, or the capacity to innovate. What do we know about technological capabilities? First that we can distinguish production, innovation and investment capability; secondly that capabilities are built up over time. The question then becomes how they are built up, which factors influence the process and how the process can be reinforced.

Subsequently Romijn reviews indicators of capability increase and determines to what extent this increase has taken place according to a number of case studies in different parts of the world. At the end of her contribution she indicates what makes firms learn and finds that capability building takes place in particular in the metalwork sector and among capital goods producers.

In the third chapter on cluster trajectories in developing countries, Peter Knorringa aims to identify in which types of cluster one is more likely to find endogenous upgrading capabilities. He distinguishes three cluster trajectories, coined the Italianate, the satellite and the hub-and-spoke trajectory. He concludes that the latter provides the best opportunity for endogenous upgrading of technologies used by SMEs.

The second part of the book brings together a number of case studies. The first one concerns the small-scale industry sector in India (Joy Clancy in Chapter 4) and in particular briquette making. She also uses a broad definition of innovation as 'creating adjustments to produce efficiency improvements'. The focus is on the innovative capabilities of briquette producers rather than the equipment producers, but like Henny Romijn she tries to identify whether there are constraints hindering technological capability development.

Clancy finds that weaknesses in investment capabilities often lead to problems in production capabilities. These weaknesses and the resulting inability to innovate are linked to factors such as lack of basic business skills, lack of organizational skills and derived knowledge. Also poor communication with suppliers and customers inhibits innovation. Finally the technology discussed was not yet mature and the institutional support has been found to be weak. Clancy also discusses policy-induced constraints and concludes that all these factors (and in particular those relating to the environment of the enterprise) make the acquisition of technological capabilities a slow process.

Two chapters deal with innovation in the formal and the informal sector in African countries. Bert Helmsing in Chapter 5 discusses innovation in the formal manufacturing sector in Zimbabwe. In this sector innovations are considered 'a critical element in maintaining competitiveness'. Most firms he studied in Bulawayo, the second city of the country, show a defensive response to the changes imposed by the structural adjustment programmes in the country, which started in the 1990s. Only a few formal sector enterprises are innovative in the sense of developing products, integrating production, improving marketing and sales or introducing other management improvements. At present an 'innovative milieu' is very much missing for these formal sector enterprises in this Zimbabwean city.

Innovation in the informal sector in Ghana, Burkina Faso and Zimbabwe is the subject of Meine Pieter van Dijk's Chapter 6. His contribution focuses on technology capacity building in these African countries and the importance of enterprise clusters and cooperation. He starts with a very broad definition of innovation (everything which the researcher did not expect) and concludes that indeed the networks and clusters in these African countries contribute to a number of unexpected results. Many of these 'innovations' could be qualified as 'embodied learning'.

In part III the question is asked whether an economic crisis would contribute to or hinder innovation in small enterprises. Mario Davide Parrilli studies in Chapter 7 the innovation and competitiveness within the small furniture industry in Nicaragua, a country that has gone through a prolonged economic and political crisis. Given the present results of the firms, which are mostly not very profitable, he feels that despite many of them being organized in clusters the furniture industry is not successful. Institutional support would be critical and the industry may have to be treated as an 'infant industry' for some time.

He argues against the so-called low road to industrialization, where industrial development is based on producing low-priced poor-quality products. Using the flexible specialization paradigm, first, he argues that a combination of clustering, an innovative mentality and skilled labour can bring about the required innovation in the sector. Secondly, export-orientation would be required. Finally, he analyses to what extent innovation is currently taking place at the intrafirm level, between firms (the interfirm level) or due to the existing support system. At all these levels improvements are suggested to make the furniture sector more competitive. Parrilli sees an important role for local government in creating the right kind of conditions for this development.

Why do(n't) small (and medium in this case) enterprises innovate? Regine

Qualmann explains in Chapter 8 diverse SME adjustment strategies in Africa. She concludes that the SMEs she studied in Senegal did not show the dynamic response after a major shift in incentives as a result of structural adjustment. She explains that the transaction costs are high in an environment of uncertainty and much depends on the learning capabilities of the firm which are the result of the past.

In Chapter 9 Henry Sandee studied the same question in Indonesia. The aim of his contribution is to assess the impact of the crisis on selected clusters on Java. His follow-up study was inspired by the impression that small-scale enterprises have been weathering the crisis better than larger companies because they are less reliant on formal markets, and less reliant on far more costly borrowed funds. Indeed clustered small enterprises appear to have been weathering the crisis better than their dispersed counterparts, pointing at a different kind of dynamics.

The advantages associated with clustering are substantial. In the clusters Sandee studied it meant the adoption of specific technologies that could not have been adopted in a profitable way by individual enterprises. The cluster promoted innovation adoption, which contributed significantly to growth of smaller enterprises in the clusters. Sandee notes that development in dynamic clusters is often buyer driven. Traders link small firms to distant markets, while technological upgrading has allowed small producers to adjust to changes in demand.

Finally three papers are ranged under the heading: Mechanisms for Innovation Diffusion. Manuel Albaladejo discusses in Chapter 10 the service centre approach to SME development in Spain when drawing policy lessons for developing countries. He shows service centres can play a role, but it would be difficult to transplant them. They are the result of concrete historical, cultural, social and economic circumstances. The lessons learnt are that the service centres should be located close to the industry they serve and should benefit SMEs more than large firms. He also concludes that although horizontally oriented institutions are of great importance, sectorally dedicated institutions can be crucial for particular industrial sectors. The service centres should be run on a business-like and demand-led basis and their effectiveness also depends upon the existence of a wider institutional framework.

Dorothy McCormick and Rosemary Atieno look in Chapter 11 at linkages between small and large firms in the Kenyan food processing sector. They conclude that firms in the food processing sector in Kenya are not well linked. Certain types of relations did show a relation with firm growth. Technological linkages offering opportunities for improving technological capacity of the enterprises were missing in their sample of enterprises, but could be promoted. However, subcontracting, one of the possible mechanisms for technological capacity development, was discouraged by a number of factors in the current economic situation. The authors feel more research is necessary to confirm their insights. They add that supplementing basic surveys with more qualitative information would provide a better picture of the local situation.

The role of a Research and Development institute in the development and diffusion of technology in Tanzania was taken up by Bongenaar and Adam Szirmai in Chapter 12. The Research and Development organization is rather successful in developing technologies, but not in large-scale diffusion of these innovations. The analysis provides insights in the factors explaining the success and failure of the organization.

Árni Sverrisson finally looks in Chapter 13 at social capital and technological innovation processes in the South. He defines social capital as useful social connectivity and wants to determine its potential for understanding technological developments and innovation diffusion in small enterprise clusters in the South. After reviewing the work of Fukuyama, Burt and Bourdieu on this subject he defines his task as determining in which way social capital facilitates or hinders innovation. He concludes that social capital influences innovation by facilitating particular network constellations, which may be conducive to or obstacles to innovation processes. He concludes that it is the structure of social capital that is important, rather than its presence or absence, and provides a number of examples to illustrate this. The conclusion is that the local network of proprietors and technical personnel is the main source of information and inspiration to adopt a technical novelty. Trustful relations will help and the presence of the characteristics of flexible specialization may also facilitate technology adaptation: multi-purpose equipment, skilled labour and an innovative mentality!

At the end Meine Pieter van Dijk and Henry Sandee draws some conclusions. Innovation doesn't come by itself. One needs an enabling environment and the right chemistry between people with complementary, but also overlapping specialization. A topic to deal with would be the nursing of technology-based enterprises and the development of flexible specialization or industrial parks. They look in particular at enterprise co-operation, technology partnerships and the importance of science and technology policies in developing countries for stimulating innovation for SMEs.

NOTES

1. A joint initiative of the EADI Working group on industrialization strategies, the Institute of Social Studies and the Free University at the ISS in the Hague on 18 and 19 September, 1998.
2. Kamien and Schwartz (1982: 50) formulate three arguments against this approach.
3. They may start with 20 per cent use of the functions of the program and finish after some years mastering about 80 per cent of the potential of this particular software.

REFERENCES

Calbrese, G. and S. Rolfo (1992), 'Factors leading to the introduction of products and process innovations in small firms', EARIE conference, Stuttgart.

Castells, M. and P. Hall (1994), *Technopoles of the World*, London: Routledge.

Dijk, M.P. van (1994), 'The interrelations between industrial districts and technological capabilities development', in UNCTAD (1994).

Dijk, M.P. van (1996), 'Learning from technology partnerships', in UN (1996), pp. 87–99.

Dijk, M.P. van and R. Rabellotti (1997), *Enterprise Clusters and Networks in Developing Countries*, London: F. Cass.

Dijk, M.P. van and S. Sideri (1996), *Multilateralism versus Regionalism: Trade Issues after the Uruguay Round*, London: F. Cass.

Florax, R. (1992), *The University: A Regional Booster?* Aldershot: Ashgate.

Hayden, F.G. (1992), 'Corporate networks: a US case study', Rotterdam: Erasmus University, Conference on the dynamics of the firm.

Jacobs, D., P. Boekholt and W. Zegveld (1990), *De Economische Kracht van Nederland*, The Hague: SMO.

Kamien, M.I. and N.L. Schwartz (1982), *Market Structure and Innovation*, Cambridge: Cambridge University Press.

Koot, W., I. Sabelis and S. Ybema (eds, 1996), *Contradictions in Context*, Amsterdam: VU UP.

Pedersen, P.O., A. Sverrisson and M.P. van Dijk (1994), *Flexible Specialisation, the Dynamics of Small-scale Industries in the South*, London: Intermediate Technology Publication.

Porter, M.P. (1990), *The Competitive Advantage of Nations*, New York: The Free Press.

Reich, R.B. (1991), *The Work of Nations, Preparing Ourselves for the 21st Century Capitalism*, New York: Vintage Books.

Schumpeter, J.A. (1942), *Capitalism, Socialism and Democracy*, New York: Harper.

Solow, R. (1957), 'Technical change and the aggregate production function', *Review of Economics and Statistics*, No. 39, pp. 312–20.

Stewart, F. (1981), 'International technology transfer, issues and policy options', in P. Streeten and R. Jolly (eds), *Recent Issues in World Development*, Oxford: Pergamon.

Stoneman, P. (1983), *The Economic Analysis of Technical Change*, Oxford: Oxford University Press.

Tsipouri L.J. (1991), 'The transfer of technology issue revisited: Some evidence from Greece', *Entrepreneurship and Regional Development*, **3**, pp. 145–57.

UN (1996), *Exchanging Experiences of Technology Partnerships*, Geneva: UNCTAD.

UNCTAD (1994), *Technological Dynamism in Industrial Districts*, Geneva.

UNCTAD (1995), *Technological Capacity Building and Technology Partnership*, Geneva.

PART I

Framework for Understanding Innovation
Diffusion

2. Small enterprise development in developing countries: innovation or acquisition of technological capability?[1]

Henny Romijn

The need to create remunerative employment opportunities in small-scale industries in low-income countries has already occupied the attention of researchers and policy makers for quite some time. The urgency is clear. *Registered* small-scale firms[2] generate an estimated 63 per cent of manufacturing employment in countries with incomes between US$ 500 and 1000 per capita, and close to 40 per cent in countries with incomes between US$ 1000 and 2000 (Gillis *et al.*, 1996:4 96). These percentages would be much higher still if we could give estimates that also include the countless unregistered activities that typify the small-scale manufacturing sector in developing countries.

A plethora of policies and programmes have been mounted to improve the income conditions in these enterprises since the early 1970s, and an almost boundless literature documenting these efforts is now available. Yet, the importance of small firms' technological performance is hardly discussed in this literature. This is peculiar, because one might expect that improvements in products, processes and production organization would be crucial for their sustained competitiveness, and thus for their income-generation potential. This would seem to be especially vital in a context of economic liberalization and increasing global integration, where many developing country markets – even traditional ones – are undergoing fast change. In this environment, lack of adaptation and upgrading spells defeat, while firms that keep up or even initiate their own original improvements can be expected to perform well. More knowledge about technological improvement in small enterprises is therefore badly needed.

Nevertheless, a focus on 'innovation' is not the most convenient analytical starting point for such research. In small firms in developing countries, 'doing new things' consists predominantly of the adoption of a new machine, product design or manufacturing technique which has been invented and developed elsewhere, rather than the development of fundamentally new things in-house. This is not to dispute the notion that the adoption of an innovation does to some extent constitute an act of creativity, and that it can be viewed as an innovation within the particular local context within which it is newly introduced (Rogers, 1983). Yet, this chapter claims it is useful to employ a conceptual framework that enables us to make a much clearer distinction between these fundamentally different notions of 'innovation' – between efforts to advance the technological frontier, on the one hand, and efforts to catch up or crawl along at some considerable distance, on the other.

The literature about technology and development provides such a framework. It starts from the premise that successful technical change depends on the presence of relevant skills and knowledge that enables people to do new things – *technological capability* for short. Even if technical change consists of the mere adoption of an externally developed innovation, a modicum of such skills will generally be required to be able to assimilate that innovation and to get the maximum benefit out of it in a new setting. However, the skills needed for successful adoption of given innovations will generally be less demanding than those required for internal generation of completely new technologies, or even for making substantial improvements to given technologies. They may also differ to some extent in nature, and in how they are acquired. Accordingly, different concepts are used to denote these fundamentally different kinds of capabilities.

A focus on technological capabilities has another, more fundamental advantage. The benefits of acquiring technological capabilities extend far beyond the benefits associated with the introduction and diffusion of specific new artefacts. This is because capabilities equip enterprises with valuable potential for participating in, and modestly shaping, technological change processes in the local economy *on an ongoing basis*. A focus on capabilities, therefore, is consistent with Sen's criticism of what he calls 'a commodity-centred approach' to development. The quality of human life, he says, is determined not by the commodities which people are instrumental in producing, nor by the goods that they receive (for example, as part of a basic needs package), rather, what matters is what people are capable of being or doing with the goods that they have access to (Sen, 1985). The aim of this chapter, then, is to explore what we know about technological capabilities in small manufacturing firms in developing countries.

CONCEPTS AND QUESTIONS

The concept of technological capability is well established in the literature about technology and development. In 1981 Frances Stewart pointed out that:

> the ability to make independent technological choices, to adapt and improve upon chosen techniques and products, and eventually to generate new technology endogenously are essential aspects of the process of development. The process may be described as the accumulation of technological capacity; it is at least as important to economic development as the accumulation of capital (Stewart, 1981: 80).

The significance of this statement, written at a time when very little empirical evidence was available to support it, has since been borne out by a wealth of (mostly firm-level) case studies carried out in several different developing countries since the late 1970s (see, for example, Katz, 1987; Lall, 1987; Amsden, 1989; Westphal *et al.*, 1984; Fransman and King, 1984; Stewart *et al.*, 1992; Hobday, 1995; Biggs *et al.*, 1995; and Lall *et al.*, 1994). These studies showed that an increase in hardware capacity through import of new technology – whether in the form of actual physical plant and machinery or documentation and blueprints – is by itself insufficient for enhancing efficiency and inducing a self-sustaining industrialization process; that is because mere access to technology does not imply *mastery* over it (Dahlman and Westphal, 1981).

There are two main reasons why mastery of new technology is needed (Evenson and Westphal, 1994). First, knowledge tends to be partly *tacit*. Transfer of a technology from one party to another is never effortless and instantaneous, not even if both operate in the same environment. Its underlying principles can only be fully understood through first-hand practical experience. Secondly, technology has *environment-specific* elements. It is always a product of the economic, climatic, social and cultural context within which it was designed. Efficient use in an environment that is different from the one in which the technology was developed will generally call for modifications.

Overcoming tacitness and making environmental adaptations will thus generally entail the need for new or enhanced technological skills and knowledge to assimilate technology effectively, adapt it to local conditions, improve upon it and (ultimately) create new technology locally. Acquisition of *technological capabilities* requires effort. Only limited capabilities accumulate costlessly and automatically over time as a result of 'doing production' (Arrow, 1962). More complex capabilities will require *technological effort* – a purposive commitment of time and human and physical resources to activities that lead to technological learning (Dahlman and Westphal, 1981).

Three types of capabilities have been distinguished in the capability literature (Lall, 1992):

- *Production capability* – the skills and knowledge required to run a given existing production technology efficiently. This includes from the ability to make minor adaptations aimed at overcoming bottlenecks to the smooth efficient functioning of existing technology that emanates, for example, from use in an environment that is different from the context in which the technology was designed originally.
- *Innovation capability* – the skills and knowledge required to substantially improve and modify existing technology and to create original innovations (that is to create new technology)
- *Investment capability* – the skills and knowledge required to choose and install new technology that is in harmony with local factor endowments and is in a more general sense suited to the local environment in which it has to function.

Unfortunately, the capability literature has had very little to say about capability building in small firms specifically. In fact, its focus has been predominantly on the large-scale modern industrial sector of developing countries.[3] Whatever the precise reasons for this neglect, the upshot is that capability building in small enterprises has not been studied systematically. While the capability literature has more or less left out small firms, the small enterprise literature has largely neglected the issue of capability building.

The purpose of the review in this chapter is to shed light on this apparent gap in the literature, using the conceptual tool kit of the capability literature. It addresses four basic questions:

1. What kinds of capabilities do small manufacturing firms in developing countries acquire, how advanced are these capabilities, how widespread is the learning process, and which categories of firms stand out? This will help us to shed light on the issue raised in the introduction, in what sense and to what extent small enterprises actually 'innovate'.
2. How are those capabilities built up?
3. What important factors induce, facilitate and hinder the process?
4. What are the main socioeconomic effects of the process?

The main focus of the review is on the individual small firm. While innovations (in the form of new artefacts, blueprints, and so on) quite often emanate from outside the small enterprise unit, the learning associated with the adoption, assimilation, reproduction, adaptation and improvement of those innovations takes place within that unit, and is to a degree controlled and directed by it. In a fundamental sense, the firm is a central actor in processes of technological change. However, firms interact with their socioeconomic environment, and this may stimulate, facilitate or hold back their learning processes. In this connection, it is important to note that several studies for the EADI Working group on industrialization strategies as well as others have put forward arguments that networks of geographically clustered producers in developing countries may facilitate the adoption of innovations in various ways (see, especially, Van Dijk and Rabellotti, 1997; Sverrisson, 1997; Sandee, 1994; and Stewart and Ghani, 1991). Although the technological learning associated with such innovation adoption is not discussed systematically in these studies, there will often be a close link.

The link runs in two directions. First, by facilitating innovation adoption (for example, through pooling of resources and investment risk, or through opportunities for investment arising from advanced interfirm division of labour), clustering may promote technological learning among small producers. The acts of acquiring a new technology, product design or quality control technique puts pressure on a firm to make efforts to put them to good use, and the teething problems that are likely to emerge in the process of the first-time application set in motion technological efforts to overcome them, which are in turn valuable sources of experience-based learning.

Secondly, clustering of enterprises may directly facilitate acquisition of technological capabilities among small firms (for example, through information diffusion arising from interfirm movement of labour, demonstration effects, visits from traders attracted by a large clientele, or purposive interfirm co-operation). Such learning may facilitate subsequent innovation. This link from learning to innovation is perhaps even more crucial than the link from innovation to learning: firms need to possess certain capabilities in order to adopt innovations successfully. They have to have some basic knowledge about how to make the right choice from among available alternative technologies, for mastering the operation of a new technique and for its basic maintenance and repair, and for dealing with adjustment problems emanating from its use in a new environment. In view of the dearth of empirical information on the relationship between small-firm clustering and technological learning its treatment in this review has to be cursory. A detailed and more systematic discussion of these issues requires significant new research, and is clearly beyond the scope of this chapter.

INTRODUCING THE STUDIES IN THE REVIEW

The materials discussed in this chapter were drawn from many different bodies of research.[4] They differ widely in focus. This is important because there is a relationship between the focus of the studies and the nature and extent of information that they yield about capability building. The studies can be classified by main focus into the following four main groups:

1. Studies that focus on successful new products or processes (that is innovations) and how they were developed.
2. Studies that focus on the historical development of one or a few individual firms.
3. Studies that focus on the historical development of entire sectors of small-scale industry.
4. Studies that focus on the extent to which small firms are 'technologically active or adaptable'.

Table 2.1 lists the studies contained in the review, and summarizes how their respective foci affect the extent and nature of the information that one can derive from them. We have somewhat less information about the increase in capabilities and its effects (column 2) than about the learning that was required for these capabilities to emerge and the factors promoting that learning (column 3). The studies in row 1, which focus on successful innovations, have very little to say about capability increase in (and hence also about its impact on) firms, while the studies in row 4, which focus on the technological activities of firms, have nothing at all to say about it.

Table 2.1   Information about capability increase and technological learning from the review

The studies and their main focus	Capability increase and its impact	The learning process and its impact
1) Development of (appropriate) innovations. De la Puente (1989), Juma (1989), Basant (1990) and Sansom (1969).	*A little information* One can infer something about capability *level* from the technological complexity and superior performance characteristics of the product. However, not much information about whether the innovation was part of an ongoing process of capability *increase* in firms. Also no information about impact.	*Considerable information* Interesting information is given about the types and sequencing of activities involved in developing and perfecting an innovation and various factors that induce and facilitate these. However, one does not know whether these activities actually led to increased capabilities.
2) Historical development of one or a few individual firms. Moulik and Purushotham (1986), Mingsarn (1986), Watanabe (1987), Girvan	*Considerable information* Information is sufficient to get some idea of whether capabilities in a firm increased in the course of its existence.	*Considerable information* Considerable detail is given about the nature and sequencing of activities undertaken and the factors that induced

The studies and their main focus	Capability increase and its impact	The learning process and its impact
and Marcelle (1990), Alänge (1987), King (1974 and 1976), Malgavkar (1976), Powell (1991, 1995), Smillie (1991), Basant and Subrahmamian (1990) Fransman (1982) Gupta (1994).	Some studies provide data about economic effects. The disadvantage is that one cannot judge whether the firms were isolated success stories or their capability building was part of a broader sectoral process.	them, as well as how those activities led to increased technological capability.
3) Historical development of entire sectors. Mahjoub (1985) and Bouchrara (1985), Cortes *et al.* (1987), Dawson (1988), Nabi (1988), Child and Kaneda (1975), Aftab and Rahim (1986, 1989), Mishra (1985), Ishikawa (1981, 1985), Chudnovsky and Nagao (1983), Cortes (1979), King (1996 and 1997) and Johnston and Kilby (1975).	*Considerable information* Information is sufficient to get a rough idea of whether capabilities increased in firms over time, but the data are less precise than in the studies in row 2 because they pertain to many firms. The advantage is that one can get an idea of the degree to which the process was widespread in a sector. A few studies provide interesting data on overall impact.	*Considerable information* As above, but some studies are less detailed on activities within the firms because they are more concerned with growth at the sectoral level. In addition, some studies are useful for information about knowledge-diffusion mechanisms between firms.
4) Technological change-related activities in groups of firms (cross-section studies). Sethuraman (1989), Nurul Amin (1989), Khundker (1989), Chávez (1989), Capt (1987), Farrell (1989), Barampara (1987), Nowshirwani (1977), Ahmad *et al.* (1984), and Kirloskar Consultants (1985).[a]	*No information at all* One can infer something about capability *level* from the technological activities that firms undertake, although usually there is not enough technical detail to assess how complex the tasks are. No information at all about whether these activities are part of an ongoing process of capability *increase* in firms. Hence, there is also no information about impact.	*Considerable information* Information on entire range of strictly intrafirm technological activities and factors that induce those. No information on other possible learning mechanisms (e.g. external information search, user–producer interactions, and training). Also no information whether documented activities led to increased capabilities.

Note: [a] Somewhat abbreviated versions of the first seven studies in this group are also published in Maldonado and Sethuraman (1992). The study by Kirloskar Consultants does not fit entirely into the group, because it concentrates more on knowledge and skill levels than on the technological activities that firms undertake. However, like the other studies in this group, it is based on cross-section survey data.

The more substantive insights into capability increase and its various effects come from the studies that trace the historical development of firms (row 2) and sectors (row 3). Only in these studies can we compare a beginning state of (lower) capabilities with an end state of (higher) capabilities. All studies contain considerable evidence about the nature of the learning process and the factors that promote it. However, in some studies (notably type 4 and to some extent type 1) we do have information about the sort of processes that can without any doubt be identified as mechanisms of technological learning, but we lack concrete information about whether these processes actually did lead to more advanced capabilities.

Although the different types of studies are rather dissimilar, they have been grouped together as much as possible for the purpose of presentation and because there are gains from merging information that is to some degree complementary. In fact, it is only by combining all the diverse and fragmentary information that one can get a reasonably complete overall picture of the nature and extent of capability development and the forms of technological learning.

CAPABILITY BUILDING IN SMALL FIRMS: A REVIEW OF INDICATORS OF CAPABILITY INCREASE

Even though very few studies in the review focus explicitly on the subject of capability building, they do contain a surprisingly large number of capability indicators. While only a few studies employed one or more *explicit* indicators to assess technological capacity[5] (see Cortes, 1979; Aftab and Rahim, 1989; Chudnovsky and Nagao, 1983; Fransman, 1982; and Ishikawa, 1985), it is possible to extract from each study at least one *implicit* indicator of capabilities increasing over time. A total of seven indicators were found in the studies (number of studies in parentheses):

1. Increasing range and complexity of output over time (25).
2. Introduction of new, more advanced machinery (15).
3. Development of internal design skills (19).
4. Adoption of scientific production methods (6).
5. Increasing division of labour (2).
6. Choice and successful installation of appropriate technology (2).
7. Increased mastery of a given production technology (4).

The first five indicators are especially relevant to capability development in the small-scale metalwork sector, whereas the remaining two were found primarily in non-metalwork firms. The fact that most indicators refer to capability development in the metalwork sector is significant. Firstly, it reflects the fact that capability development in this sector is more multidimensional than for example process industries. The type and range of products to be made, the complexity of the product designs and their manufacture, and the production technology itself are important variables in addition to product quality and process efficiency. Secondly, it reflects that the bulk of the evidence about capability increase in this review comes from metalwork firms, who usually produce capital goods. This is highly significant in view of the vital role played by the capital goods sector in the development of national capacity to generate indigenous technical progress, and its scope for long-term productivity enhancement in other sectors (Chudnovsky and Nagao, 1983; Stewart, 1978).

The prevalence of capability building in small-scale metalwork shows its higher potential for evolutionary growth and associated technological development than other small-scale activities because of the divisibility of the production process into a number of discrete operations, which allows firms to start off with very modest levels of skills and capital and then expand gradually. Unlike the enterprises in some other industrial sectors, metalwork firms do not face the requirement of lumpy investments that might pose serious hurdles to growth. The resource requirements in this sector are relatively low. This is also because they have the sort of machine tools with which they can self-construct machinery for their own use, or upgrade and recondition second-hand machinery.

In addition, metal workshops are highly flexible and often located close to the users of their products, as a result of which they are generally good at catering to idiosyncratic requirements of customers and can adapt very quickly and easily to changes in market demand. These close user–producer linkages create valuable opportunities for technological learning. Together with the fact that economies of scale do not generally play an important role in the sector, this enables a remarkably sound competitive position for small metalwork firms in developing economies. The number of studies that have documented evidence of capability development in industries other than metalwork is limited. For this reason, and in view of the special importance of the metalwork sector in economic development, the discussion below will be confined to the first five indicators.

Indicator 1: Increasing Range and Complexity of Output

The upgrading of the composition of a firm's outputs in a technological sense is by far the most prevalent indicator of capability increase in the small-scale sector. The importance of this indicator lies in the fact that metalwork firms can make (and repair) a vast number of products with the same basic production technology, and that these products tend to vary in terms of the technical skills and knowledge required for their manufacture. Hence, evidence of 'upward diversification' or 'upward substitution', in the sense of an increase in the manufacturing complexity of a firm's products over time, indicates that the firm in question must have mastered more-advanced technical skills and knowledge even if its set of machinery and equipment remained essentially unchanged.

The best documentation on upward diversification or substitution is found in the studies in group 2 in Table 2.1, because they provide detailed insights into firm-level progress over time. A representative case is a Brazilian firm described in Gupta (1994) which started out in 1920 by making simple agricultural implements, undertaking repairs for small sugar-processing mills and making spare parts for trolleys, carts, and so on. Subsequently the workshop started to make simple equipment required in small sugar mills. Gradually new types of equipment were added to the range, and manufacture of equipment of larger capacity was also introduced. Then a new firm was spun off to produce equipment for the alcohol industry and yet another firm was founded to make metallurgical products. By the end of the 1940s, the group had emerged as a major contender in Brazil's heavy industry.

Eight Zimbabwean firms described by Watanabe (1987) went through a very similar process. One started out with a small cupola and foundry to service gold mines in 1929. It became involved in the repair and later the manufacture of concrete mixers and other machinery such as light mining machines and electrical travelling cranes. By the early 1980s the firm had diversified into precision diesel engines for railways and trucks, and components of agricultural implements and tractors.[6] Another good example is a producer of rice-milling equipment described in Mingsarn (1986), that started as a small casting workshop in 1945. The firm gradually became involved in making small adaptations to imported rice-milling equipment. In the next stage it started to undertake the production of such equipment itself. Until 1984, its main line was production of conventional rice-milling equipment which required only traditional technology and skills. Subsequently the enterprise took on more ambitious work, including an improved version of a rubber-roll huller originally imported from Japan. The company now makes all types of rice-milling machinery and spare parts for it. It has also constructed a number of its own machine tools. Many other illustrative examples can be found in the case studies in the review.

Indicator 2: Introduction of New Machinery

Investment in machinery with which technologically more complex or higher-precision tasks can be performed has received emphasis in about half of the studies included in this part of the review. Acquisition of new machinery by itself does not convey acquisition of the new skills with which that machinery can be used efficiently, but it may nevertheless be an important dimension of capability increase when combined with additional information on how it led to the learning of new skills. In the metalwork sector, such additional information consists primarily of evidence of increasing product complexity with which the acquisition of more machinery and equipment seems to be intimately bound up. Apparently, a firm can advance up to a certain point by increasing the complexity of its products with an unchanging set of basic equipment (that is by increasing the degree of user-capability of its existing machinery), but at a certain stage continued upward diversification or substitution evidently makes it expedient to invest in machines and equipment to carry out operations inhouse that were until then supplied by specialized outsiders, such as forging, advanced machining and heat treatment.

For example, a group of Nairobi artisans described in King (1974 and 1976) progressed from making handtools to the production of maize-stalk cutters and nail-making machines after they had introduced simple (self-made) bending, cutting, punching and shearing machinery. A more recent study by the same author features two informal sector entrepreneurs who managed to start threading plastic, metal and aluminium pipes after they acquired an old lathe that they adapted for the purpose. Several other artisans progressively graduated to the production of 'zero-grazers', maize mills and wood lathes after years of very basic metalwork, when they obtained access to various power tools (King, 1996). Indian farm equipment producers in rural Gujarat, described in Basant (1990), shifted out of the production of traditional handtools and into increasingly complex (mostly animal-drawn) farm equipment after they acquired basic power-operated machinery such as lathes, welding sets, drills and grinders. In the example of the Brazilian producer already mentioned above, production of farm implements was initiated after the establishment of a foundry and a mechanical section in the workshop; and in the Zimbabwean firm described above, CNC lathes were acquired for new work on precision items.

Indicator 3: Development of Internal Design Skills

Cortes (1979), Ishikawa (1985) and Chudnovsky and Nagao (1983) are the three studies in which the development of internal design skills in firms is analysed most systematically, but it is possible to recognize bits and pieces of similar information in many other studies in the review. Usually the development of internal design skills starts with simple repair of imported machinery, followed by crude duplication through the physical dismantling and examination of a prototype, a process known as reverse engineering. At this stage, firms have no internal sources of design. Any minor design changes that do occur are generally simplifications necessitated more by the inability of the manufacturers to reproduce the complexity of the original model than by an innovative response to local user requirements. Quality also commonly suffers at this stage due to use of inferior raw materials. Substantial price reductions are often achieved, but it is unclear to what extent they are engineered deliberately by the manufacturers in order to make the equipment financially accessible to low-income users and attractive to middle-income buyers. This stage is quite characteristic of the capital goods sector in African countries. For example, a study of a number of (predominantly small-scale) capital goods enterprises in Tanzania found them to be operating at this level (Chudnovsky and Nagao, 1983).

However, in a number of Asian and Latin American countries firms have progressed beyond the crude copying stage. In countries such as Colombia, Peru, Argentina, Thailand, Hong Kong and China, small-scale metalwork enterprises reportedly incorporate small changes into the copied designs. This level has been called the adaptive imitation phase in order to emphasize the fact that the changes entail small improvements that spring from local innovative skill rather than from the lack of local capability. The more advanced adapters even start making blueprints using their own specifications.

Some firms in these countries have reached a yet more advanced level of design skills, making major modifications and proper innovations. According to Cortes (1979), at this level the design skills have reached the point where a firm can incorporate into its outputs technical features that cannot be easily copied without understanding the scientific principles involved. The main difference between this level and the imitation stage is the employment of qualified design engineers.

Indicator 4: Adoption of Scientific Production Methods

Information about the adoption of modern production methods such as heat treatment, quality control methods, batch production and precision measuring instruments is found only in a few studies in the review (see, especially, Juma, 1989; Cortes, 1979; and Johnston and Kilby, 1975).[7] However, those studies do suggest that these methods can be very interesting and relevant indicators of capability increase.

While adoption of machinery (indicator 2) only tells us that a new machine has come into use, information about the adoption of more advanced production methods lets us know *how* the firm's machines or materials are being used. Generally, production methods have an important bearing on product quality. This is important because it is possible for a firm to have diversified upwards, to have invested in more equipment and to have evolved from crude copying to adaptive imitation without having made much headway with raising the general quality of its products.

The adoption of modern production methods spans several dimensions. The use of heat treatment to harden steels is an important dimension because it presupposes some knowledge of the composition of different metals and how they perform under various stresses. Heat treatment of parts that are subjected to much wear and tear can prolong the life of a product considerably and reduces the need for frequent repairs. Another important production method is the use of jigs, fixtures[8] and various types of measuring instruments in both the actual manufacturing process and quality control. The use of such tools is necessary to achieve some degree of standardization of parts within the firm. Testing of products is also an important form of quality control. For example, the introduction of simple thermodynamic tests generated vital information that led to improvements in fuel efficiency and lengthening of the life of the ceramic lining in the Kenya ceramic *jiko* (charcoal stove) (Juma, 1989).

Indicator 5: Increasing Division of Labour

Even though the emergence of more complex production organization is noted in only two studies (Cortes, 1979; and Johnston and Kilby, 1975), this sort of information would appear to be quite relevant to an assessment of capability increase. The study by Cortes discusses increasing division of labour *between* firms, whereas Johnston and Kilby refer to division of labour *within* firms.

As far as interfirm specialization is concerned, the emergence of separate parts' and components' suppliers and heat treatment services, as noted by Cortes in Argentina, reveals that the size of the market was increasing, and that the industry had achieved certain minimal quality standards. A substantial network of parts' and components' suppliers can develop only when a large number of firms make their parts and products to the same specifications.[9] Likewise, the emergence of specialized heat treatment facilities is evidence that several producers must have developed at least some basic knowledge about the properties of metals and their effect on product quality. In the same vein, the introduction of intrafirm specialization noted by Johnston and Kilby denotes a shift away from the one-by-one production method which is common in traditional blacksmithing activities, and towards production in batches or in series which characterizes production in small workshops. This shift requires at least some degree of internal standardization of parts.

Recapitulation

It seems justifiable to conclude that small firms considered in this review did indeed develop capabilities. The evidence further suggests that capability development in small metalwork firms predominantly takes the form of increasing *production capability* rather than innovation capability or investment capability. Indeed, all five indicators describe different aspects of production capability. Even the development of internal design skills is essentially evidence of production capability as well. The sort of adaptive imitation that the small firms in this review were involved in primarily still suggests an assimilating and reproducing external technology rather than the ability to come up with true innovations.

THE EXTENT OF CAPABILITY INCREASE

Using the indicators of capability increase discussed above, we shall now address the question of how widespread the phenomenon has been in the small-scale metalwork sector in poor countries. We shall then discuss the evidence of the degree to which capabilities developed *within* these firms.

Numbers of Firms Involved in Capability Building

An indication which suggests that the phenomenon is not limited to a few incidental cases is provided by the remarkable geographical spread of the evidence. Asian, Latin American and African countries are represented more or less equally in the review. Moreover, the countries are at widely differing levels of industrial development. Countries such as Argentina and Brazil have a much longer industrialization experience and are technologically considerably more advanced than countries like Kenya and Ghana.

Secondly, there are many studies in group 3 in Table 2.1, which means that the development of capabilities has not been limited to a few isolated cases. Even though four of those studies pertain to the same case (namely the farm equipment sector in the Pakistan Punjab), there are enough sources for other locations to enable us to conclude that the phenomenon has occurred in a considerable number of metalwork firms in several different countries. One can infer from the sample sizes that the populations of firms in Argentina, Colombia, Kenya, Ghana, Pakistan and India must have been at least 100, and possibly much larger.

Thirdly, capability development has not been limited to a particular segment of the small-scale metalwork industry. It has occurred in what we could call small modern factories, in small metal workshops and even among the very smallest and most primitive enterprises – the truly informal self-employment activities and tiny family businesses with a traditional blacksmithing background. The survey does not support the idea that small-scale enterprises, other than small factories that are started with a substantial input of formal technical knowledge and modern machinery, would be too primitive and resource-poor to develop higher technological capabilities. In fact, several small- and medium-sized factories evolved from very modest repair workshops.

Extent of Capability Development Within Firms

The review contains several interesting cases of firms that made the transition from small workshops to modern factories (Watanabe, 1987; Gupta, 1994; Cortes, 1979; and Ishikawa, 1985). This is evident primarily from the phenomenal increase in the manufacturing complexity of the outputs (indicator 1) of these firms. The most dramatic cases started as small repair and servicing outfits employing – aside from one or two owners – only a few apprentices. They gradually moved into the manufacture of simple mechanical machinery, and from there into the manufacture of high-precision machinery, such as CNC lathes. The next step was the successful production of entire plants. For example, one producer of textile machinery in China, which started in 1902 as a workshop undertaking repairs to ships and making cotton-gins and flour mills, evolved into a leading producer of spinning machines. In the 1930s it managed to produce an entire plant of cotton-spinning machines by imitating various foreign machines (Ishikawa, 1985). In the same way, an Indian hand-made paper entrepreneur managed over time to manufacture an entire plant in which several machines were self-designed or improved models of traditional hand-made paper making machinery. He started to deliver turnkey services to aspiring entrepreneurs in the area (Moulik and Purushotham, 1986). A few firms have even developed the capability to export complete knock-down kits for assembly under licence by less-advanced producers in neighbouring countries, or even to deliver entire plants to other countries on a turnkey basis (Cortes, 1979).

We are obviously not talking about large numbers here, but these cases are important because the firms grew so dramatically that they had a notable beneficial influence in their industry, especially in terms of employment generation and the provision of training to people who could subsequently start their own small enterprises. For instance, the Zimbabwean, Brazilian and some of the Chinese firms grew spectacularly. When they started as small jobbing enterprises for the mines, railways or agricultural estates, they employed at the most a handful of people. Now they employ several hundreds of people each. Some even have a workforce of more than 1000 (Watanabe, 1987; Gupta, 1994; and Ishikawa, 1985).

More commonly, however, the capabilities developed have not been that dramatic.[10] This can be seen especially from the studies in group 3 in Table 2.1. In particular, the development of local design skills and the consequent application of high-precision techniques and other quality-enhancing methods, such as rigorous testing and proper heat treatment, seem to develop relatively slowly. Apparently, progress in the initial stages of learning is concentrated more in the area of straightforward replication of increasingly complex technology and learning of new skills through investment in machinery with which new operations can be carried out in the workshop.

For example, Mahjoub (1985) reports that the informal sector in Tunisian towns still lacks scientific calculation and product testing in spite of the considerable evidence of indigenous innovations and adaptations that resulted in higher efficiency, increased safety, better labour force utilization and lighter and more compact designs. Internal design capacity is often weak, with the clients being the main source of ideas for improvements. In other words, Mahjoub's firms would not score highly on our indicators 3 and 4. Likewise, Mishra (1985) observes that product innovation and scientific testing and quality control facilities (indicators 3 and 4) are not found among the small-scale farm machinery producers in Uttar Pradesh (India), except among pumpset producers who have been under a great deal of competitive pressure from large firms. In Ghana's informal metalwork sector, firms also score low on indicator 4. It is reported that there is seldom any standardization in the use of materials and tools. Product specification is rough and does not assume interchangeability of parts (Dawson, 1988). Cortes *et al.* (1987) observed about the design skills of the Colombian metalwork firms (indicator 3):

> Small entrepreneurs are doing what their counterparts in more advanced semi-industrialized countries such as Argentina did ten or fifteen years ago. In most Colombian SMIs, design changes are made by entrepreneurs themselves without help from technicians experienced in design; it is relatively rare for these changes to be systematically transferred to blueprints. In the case of agricultural implements and stoves, an entrepreneur's design ability seems to be the result of practical experience rather than theoretical knowledge (1987: 193–4).

In fact, even in Argentina most machine-tool makers were still at the adaptive imitation stage at the end of the 1970s. Only a few firms carried out stringent quality tests at every stage of the production process and had fully equipped laboratories for that purpose (indicator 3). The majority of firms still relied heavily on eye-inspection of the final product and a 'dry-run' in the workshop (Cortes, 1979).

ECONOMIC IMPACT

Modest capability growth in many firms should not be taken to imply that the phenomenon has been economically insignificant. Even a very modest rise in capabilities can make the difference between abject poverty and a respectable income that allows the satisfaction of basic minimum needs. The best example in this respect is furnished by the informal sector artisans in Nairobi, who in the early 1970s began to manufacture basic hand-operated machine tools with which they started to make maize-stalk cutters, bicycle stands, and so on. They reportedly made an average net monthly profit of 500 Kenyan shillings, more than twice the legal urban minimum wage at the time and a vast improvement on their earlier precarious income position. It was also three times the level that the ILO mission to Kenya felt might be the average income of self-employed workers in Nairobi. Further evidence of accumulation among them is provided by the fact that some of the entrepreneurs diversified into land ownership and managed to establish more permanent, formal workshops, while previously they had operated by the roadside and had been forced to move frequently from place to place (King, 1974). By the mid 1990s, the effects of capability building among these artisans had become even more dramatic, especially when compared with a group of tin-lamp makers who were roughly in the same economic situation in the early 1970s but had experienced technological stagnation since then. According to King, there is now a huge gap between the incomes of the most successful metalworkers and the subsistence earnings of the candlemakers (1996).

The dispersed impact on a developing economy of the simultaneous emergence of a large number of such local producers can be as spectacular as the effect of one firm that grows to be a technological leader and begins to compete in world markets. This is most clearly illustrated in the case of small-scale farm implements manufacturing in Argentina. Already in 1968, when the industry was still at a low technological level, local production was already covering 94 per cent of local demand. From 1966 onwards, exports (then US$ 633 000) began to exceed imports until they reached more than US$ 12 million per annum in the mid 1970s. More than 100 small producers together generated US$ 42 million in output by 1970 (Cortes, 1979). The combined efforts of these small firms made a respectable contribution to the Argentinean economy, even without taking into account the productivity increase in agriculture which must have occurred as a result of the widespread adoption and use of their farm equipment.

Another interesting example of the economic impact of a modest capability development among many small producers comes from the farm equipment sector in Pakistan's Punjab Province. Farm equipment was initially supplied by foreign firms and then by a handful of large- and medium-scale firms in Pakistan itself, but their market was gradually taken over by approximately 600 small workshops which emerged in the early 1960s. The small enterprises were better able to service and repair the equipment due to their proximity to farmers. Even though the products were lower in quality, they were also substantially cheaper, which brought them within the financial reach of a large number of farmers with limited financial means who found them adequate for their needs (Aftab and Rahim, 1986). Some interesting estimates of the aggregate quantitative impact of the emergence of these Punjab workshops were made on the basis of a rather exhaustive survey of the industry in the late 1960s. The industry was found to employ around 6500 people and to generate Rs 80 million in output per year, which was as much as 3.6 per cent of the reported share of small-scale industries in Pakistan's national product (Child and Kaneda, 1975).

A similar process of gradual 'second-stage import substitution' was reported in the Colombian farm equipment sector by Cortes *et al.* (1987) and in Kenya's informal sector by King (1996) who speaks of a moving technological frontier. Product by product, small enterprises slowly made their way into a domain hitherto dominated by the modern sector. Apparently, in these cases the small-scale units were also more active in making relevant local adaptations than were the larger firms who had initially dominated the industry. These examples show that small-scale metal workshops can actually have a comparative advantage over large-scale modern factories in the production of relatively simple products whose manufacture does not require a high degree of precision.

HOW FIRMS LEARN

If we go by the frequency with which replication of new, increasingly complex products (including machine-tools for own use) is mentioned in the literature, it is clear that this is the primary means through which new technological knowledge is assimilated by small firms. *Tacitness* in small firms manifests itself primarily in the need to master the embodied technology. Even though the technology incorporated in products such as basic, general-purpose machine tools and farm equipment is generally freely available and has been in existence for many years, the knowledge required for the successful replication of such products is not gained automatically, costlessly and instantaneously. It is for this reason that evidence of 'upward diversification' or 'upward substitution' is such an important indicator of capability increase in small metalwork firms.

Many studies in the review also mention the need for local adaptations due to *environmental specificity*, and describe appropriate responses by small firms to meet this need. As a matter of fact, there is some evidence that small workshops are more active than large firms in this respect. And, even if large producers initiate adaptations to certain products, small producers often improve significantly upon these because their production technology is more flexible and they are better informed about user needs due to their proximity to the customers (Cortes *et al.*, 1987; Cortes, 1979; Nowshirwani, 1977; Ahmad *et al.*, 1984). The evidence is overwhelmingly of *product* adaptations rather than process adaptations. Such product adaptations are especially prevalent in the farm equipment industry because farming practices, climate and soil conditions tend to vary across regions.

Both the need to master the manufacture of new products and the need to make appropriate product adaptations give rise to the need for technological learning and result in higher capabilities in small firms. The firms under review basically seem to employ three different mechanisms to enhance their capabilities. The first mechanism is what we could call 'internal technological activity'. It consists of a variety of activities that take place *within* the enterprise. They are aimed at effectively using, copying, adapting or improving technology and at innovating. From the fact that virtually all the studies in the review make mention of such activities it would appear that this mechanism is indeed very essential to capability building. A second group of activities, identified in 20 studies, consists of the search for technological information and communication using sources *outside* the enterprise. A third learning mechanism, found in seven studies, consists of skill training and technical education of people who are already working in the enterprise, and/or hiring of new people with higher technical qualifications.

Internal Technological Activity

The transformation from small repair-based activities to full-fledged workshops (or even factories) capable of manufacturing, adapting and even improving a range of capital goods of considerable complexity seems to be a step-by-step process. Learning is based on practical experience and involves a great deal of effort. Firms often start with repair, maintenance and reconditioning of existing equipment and with the manufacture of spare parts, and only gradually evolve into manufacturing proper. Production starts with relatively simple equipment. The changeover to more complex outputs can take years, sometimes decades (Ishikawa, 1985).

Initial assimilation and adaptation efforts entirely take the form of hands-on trial and error on the shop floor. Access to a physical prototype, or at least a visual representation, is a must for the replication of new products, because in the absence of formal technical knowledge this is the only channel through which new technology can be assimilated. The capabilities in the machine-tool firms in Brazil, Hong Kong and Zimbabwe, the machine tools and farm implements sectors in Argentina, the metalwork sector in Colombia, the farm equipment sector in India's Uttar Pradesh and the Pakistan Punjab, the power tiller manufacturers in Thailand, and the capital goods sector in Peru, to mention just a subset of the evidence, all evolved entirely from experience gained through observation, reverse engineering and practical rule-of-thumb experimentation uninformed by any formal scientific knowledge. Experience-based learning is very effort-intensive, because many resources are wasted in unsystematic trial and error by untrained labour and inexperienced managers (Nabi, 1988; Cortes *et al.*, 1987: 179).

When firms advance somewhat and a basic level of formal technical knowledge is achieved (see below), trial-and-error becomes transformed into some sort of practical (but still shop floor-based) search and development. There is still no separate R&D department, but experimentation begins to become a systematic activity incorporating scientific principles. Copying is done not just from prototypes but also from blueprints, and it is preceded by drawing and pattern making. Changing designs also involves making one's own technical drawings. The more advanced Argentinean firms, the Zimbabwean firms and the Brazilian firms discussed in Cortes (1979), Watanabe (1987) and Gupta (1994) have reached this stage by now.

Information Search and Communication

A vital input at all stages of the learning process is new information from outside the firm. Its role is to spark off the sort of internal assimilation and adaptation activities described above and to give direction to these efforts. In small workshops and artisanal activities with limited resources, information search is rather *ad hoc*, and more passive forms of information collection are also important. Active information search becomes very important for capability building when firms start to outgrow the small workshop phase. It then becomes a systematic, ongoing activity (see, for example, Mingsarn, 1986). Some studies in the review suggest that there is an important correlation between successful capability building and active search efforts (Watanabe, 1987; Girvan and Marcelle, 1990; Moulik and Purushotham, 1986).

Relevant external information includes sources of new technology and unmet market demand for new technology, and feedback on the firm's efforts to meet these market needs. In the studies that document the evolution of successful innovations (group 1 in Table 4.1), such as the ceramic *jiko* and the multipurpose tool bar, it is shown that these information flows give rise to active iterative user–producer interactions that are vital for achieving the ultimate success of an innovation through continuous incremental improvement. These constitute an important source of learning for the producers.

The information flow typically starts with the exposure of the small entrepreneur to new technology. Irrespective of the specific information transfer mechanism, it seems that most of this new technology is originally from other countries. Sometimes small firms acquire it directly, but more commonly production starts in large firms in the modern sector, from where it gradually diffuses to the small-scale sector. This occurs, for example, through previous working experience in a larger firm that manufactures the relevant equipment. This particular mechanism played an important role among the small producers of farm equipment in the Pakistan Punjab and Colombia. Several *jua kali* artisans in Nairobi also learnt from employment in Asian workshops and on European coffee farms where various agricultural implements were designed and repaired.

Another, perhaps more common mechanism for the transfer of information about new technology is direct contact between producers and users of non-traditional technology. Customers may bring in a machine for repair, come with a broken-down imported prototype or describe a new machine that they have spotted somewhere in the market (Nowshirwani, 1977; Ahmad *et al.*, 1984). In Hong Kong, users of machinery repair and maintenance workshops frequently induced first-time manufacturing efforts by specifically requesting that a copy of an imported machine be made or that a new machine be designed to serve specific purposes (Fransman, 1982). In other cases, customers may demand local spare parts to replace imported ones when they find the latter too expensive or difficult to obtain due to import restrictions (Dawson, 1988). In this connection, subcontracting of parts and components to small firms by larger ones seems to be an occasional source of relevant technological information when the parent firm hands over a prototype and supervises the manufacturing process (Nabi, 1988).

Users also help to develop technological capability by transmitting specific wishes and ideas about adjustment or improvement of components and equipment already in use, and by giving feedback on the performance of products to which adaptations have been made. In the early stages of the development of the Argentine machine-tool industry, customer industries (mainly the automobile sector) played an important developmental role by demanding components and machinery of growing precision and scope (Cortes, 1979). If the users are farmers, they are important sources of information about farming practices, soil conditions and climatic peculiarities, which is essential for successful improvement of farm equipment. In addition, farmers may be able to specify the required characteristics of the wood or steel to be used and they might have specific requirements regarding the size and weight of the implements (Basant and Subrahmamian, 1990). Customer feedback on improved or adapted products is especially important when workshops are very small, in which case they do not have any internal way of generating product-performance related information through scientific testing (Juma, 1989).

Agents other than users, such as die makers or machinery suppliers, can also be important sources of significant technical information, whether about new products or useful adaptations to products (Kirloskar Consultants, 1985; Dawson, 1988; Malgavkar, 1976), or by assisting private producers with research and testing facilities to improve their products (Juma, 1989; Basant, 1990). Visits to trade fairs, observation of competitors and travel to other areas have also been important sources of technological information (Juma, 1989; Cortes, 1979; Mingsarn, 1986; Watanabe, 1987; Moulik and Purushotham, 1986; Nowshirwani, 1977; Girvan and Marcelle, 1990; Nabi, 1988).

Direct Human Capital Building

The effectiveness with which information search externally and technological efforts to assimilate and adapt technology internally are undertaken is overwhelmingly dependent on the quality of the human resource base of a firm at any one time. In particular, formal technical education widens the channels through which information can be obtained and it makes internal efforts more efficient. Whereas an illiterate artisan has to remain dependent on copying physical prototypes, an educated entrepreneur can also search out relevant information from technical textbooks and use blueprints (Mingsarn, 1986). An educated person can also design a system for generating internal performance feedback by keeping systematic records of experimentation and test results (Girvan and Marcelle, 1990). The studies in Colombia, Argentina and Hong Kong, in particular, show that firms can only go so far with experience-based learning-by-doing. When firms attempted to move into higher-income markets where improved product quality required relatively sophisticated design work and more advanced production methods, the skills learnt through learning-by-doing proved to be insufficient (Cortes *et al.*, 1987; Cortes, 1979 and Fransman, 1982). Similarly in the Pakistan Punjab, a leading farm machinery producer identified the absence of technically qualified people in the firm as his most important current handicap: 'We now have to consult engineers to understand complicated drawings – we would be able to develop a machine in weeks that presently takes us months if we could comprehend engineering drawings' (Nabi, 1988: 149).

For this reason, direct human-resource development is of paramount importance in small firms. It can take several forms, such as informal staff training through internal apprenticeship, sending workers to formal training courses, attracting expertise from outside the firm on an *ad hoc* basis to impart training and give advice, attending in-plant training in bigger companies, and attracting workers with relevant technical skills. Especially important is investment in the engineering education of a junior family member of the entrepreneur since small firms cannot usually offer attractive enough pay and working conditions to retain a highly qualified outsider.

Establishing a human scientific and engineering foundation is essential for making a technological breakthrough. One of the rice-milling equipment producers described in Mingsarn (1986) made a quantum leap in terms of the complexity of its products and processes and its innovations after a son with an engineering degree joined the firm. In another firm in this sector, success in capability building could be attributed largely to its hiring policies. At the time of the interview, this firm employed two mechanical engineers with MSc degrees, ten engineers with BSc degrees and 20 vocational school graduates. Similar development patterns can be observed in the Zimbabwean, Argentinean and Hong Kong firms in the review (Watanabe, 1987; Cortes, 1979; Fransman, 1982).

To summarize, the main conclusion from this section is that capability building apparently requires considerable purposive dedication of time and other resources by firms. Although we cannot discount the importance of passive learning-by-doing or absorption of information from external sources and diffusion of skills from the large-scale modern sector, on the whole the survey results support the contention in the large-firm capability literature about the importance of indigenous 'technological effort' in the development of technological capabilities.

WHAT MAKES FIRMS LEARN

The vital importance of purposive investment in technological learning for the development of capabilities raises the question of what factors induce small firms to devote their time and other resources to such investment, and what factors facilitate and constrain their efforts.

Factors that Induce Learning

The existence or emergence of a certain (usually externally induced) stimulus to the small firm to introduce new products or adapt existing ones in order to ensure continued survival or to take advantage of new growth opportunities has been central in all cases covered by this review.[11] Several different stimuli were found in the survey, but two in particular appear to have played a major role.

The first stimulus is the *emergence of demand for new or improved products*. Usually this took the form of a demand for new types of farm equipment as a result of the adoption of yield-raising agricultural practices such as irrigation and commercial fertilizer. These practices give rise to seasonal labour bottlenecks and, at the same time, the consequent productivity increases ease the purchasing power constraint on farmers. These two effects together have induced rapid mechanization in several places. For example, in the case of Gujarat (India), the introduction of Green Revolution cultivation practices and seeds gave rise to the need for new implements. In addition, some of the new implements were not compatible with the traditional ones and thus investment in a new full range of equipment was required, which was very costly for farmers. It was this cost factor which gave rise to the demand for a multipurpose tool bar (Basant, 1990). In the case of Iran, the increased use of tractors gave rise to demand for complementary farm equipment (Nowshirwani, 1977). In the case of Pakistan, a sudden, fast growth in the demand for tubewells emerged due to a change in government policy towards agriculture, involving relaxation of controls and significant incentives for increased production (Aftab and Rahim, 1986).[12]

The second important external stimulus has *been a change in macro-economic policy towards import substitution*, leading to a shift from demand for imported products to demand for equivalent domestic products. Sometimes this policy has also created a need to adapt to changes in raw material supply. For example, in Ghana the collapse of the formal economy and an acute foreign exchange constraint led to import restrictions in 1972. Many basic products and spare parts for which there was a ready demand became unavailable (Dawson, 1988; Powell, 1991; and Smillie, 1991). In the case of Colombia, government restrictions on imports in the late 1950s as a result of balance of payments difficulties led to a demand for local production of farm equipment and a variety of other metal products (Cortes *et al.*, 1987). In Argentina, the machine-tools industry emerged during the 1940s and early 1950s as a result of restrictions on the importation of machinery and parts during World War II and its aftermath. Production of agricultural equipment started in the early 1920s in response to demand generated by the early mechanization of agriculture. The sector developed further during the 1940s as a result of the restrictions imposed on imports during World War II. Moreover, local production was stimulated by modest levels of local protection (Cortes, 1979). Rhodesia's unilateral declaration of independence in 1965, which led to UN sanctions, put local firms under similar pressures (Watanabe, 1987). Finally, in the case of India, considerable unmet demand existed for specialized industrial equipment that could not be satisfied from abroad due to strict import restrictions (Malgavkar, 1976).

This evidence suggests that investments in technological learning activities are most likely to be made in a climate in which some protection is given to domestic manufacturers. The same conclusion has also been drawn from the large-firm capability studies (Lall, 1992). However, the evidence presented here is too limited for definite policy conclusions. In fact, there is also one study in the review (about the machine-tools sector in Hong Kong) where a free trade environment was apparently condusive to the emergence of capabilities (Fransman, 1982).

Whether capability building could be associated with import-substitution policies or with free trade, it is clear that technological efforts in small firms were often undertaken in response to market opportunities created through particular economic policies. At the same time, it is quite remarkable that *not once* were these policies actually aimed at inducing capability building in the small-scale sector. They invariably had other objectives, especially improvement of productivity in agriculture or saving of foreign exchange through import restriction. Capability increase in small firms has been an unanticipated side effect. In fact, it has been noted that in some places small firms progressed in spite of a very unfavourable policy environment which actively discriminated against them (Child and Kaneda, 1975). However, even in those cases where specific support programmes for small firms were implemented, they were rarely aimed at improving technological capabilities (Massaquoi, 1995).

Factors that Facilitate or Constrain Learning

While the existence of stimuli seems to be a prerequisite for investing in the sort of learning activities described above, whether or not they will actually have an effect depends on a host of facilitating and constraining factors within the firms and in their environment. The existing resource base of the firm, especially the stock of technical skills and knowledge already developed and its ability to attract external sources of finance, has been mentioned in almost all the studies under review as being of considerable importance. Other important factors mentioned in the studies are the availability of the right type of external support, the ease with which a novel feature can be copied by competitors, labour conditions and personal factors, such as entrepreneurial attitude and motivation.[13]

To summarize, there can be no straightforward explanation for the extent to which small firms engage in technological effort. Some types of 'carrots' or 'sticks' are apparently essential to induce such effort, but whether or not those will actually lead to a learning response depends on the complex interplay of a host of factors within firms and their environment.

CONCLUSIONS

The great majority of studies in this review did not focus explicitly on capability building in small firms. Nevertheless, they contain considerable information, suggesting that capabilities are indeed built up in the small-firm sector, and that the phenomenon has not been limited to a few isolated success stories. The evidence of economic impact is fairly limited, but whatever information we have suggests that it may have considerable favourable economic effects on the firms in which the capabilities were developed as well as on other actors in the economy. Capability building seems to occur predominantly in the metalwork sector. Many of the firms covered in this review were in fact capital goods producers. This is a significant finding in view of the importance of the small-scale capital goods sector in bringing about an indigenous process of technological change in developing countries.

The studies also yielded a set of potentially quite useful indicators that could be used for a more systematic assessment of capability increase in small metalwork firms than has been undertaken so far. These indicators suggest that capability building in firms is overwhelmingly a matter of the development of production capability, in some cases combined with some simple imitative adaptation capability. Unlike in developed countries, small manufacturing enterprises in low-income countries do not generally derive their competitiveness from their ability to create fundamentally new technology, but rather from their ability to re-create, adapt and widely diffuse technologies that already exist elsewhere in the local economy or abroad. They are innovators only in the sense that they adopt, assimilate and perhaps incrementally adapt known technologies. But in this area they do make a crucial and unique contribution to technological advance in developing countries, by bringing manifold useful products and types of equipment within reach of large numbers of customers with limited financial means, while at the same time enhancing their appropriateness.

The capability indicators discussed in the chapter also suggest that production capability itself is to some extent multidimensional. One requires several different indicators to obtain a full picture of how far firms have progressed in each of these different dimensions. Each of the indicators found in the studies under review conveys some unique information. For instance, the first indicator tells us something about a firm's ability to replicate product technology of a given complexity. The second indicator tells us about the degree of user capability of a given machinery and equipment; the third indicator tells us about the extent to which firms are able to make useful adaptations; and the fourth and fifth indicators are informative about product quality and standardization.

The learning process by which these capabilities are attained is driven by tacitness and environmental specificities. It is an incremental and evolutionary process in which internal efforts to master the production of, to adapt, repair and recondition machinery and equipment, to search for relevant technical information, and to direct involvement in the upgradation of the human resource base of the firm through training and education play an important part. Such learning results from a very complex interplay of a large number of inducing, facilitating and constraining factors that emanate from within firms and their environment.

The findings from this review need to be supported by more rigorous and systematic research before definite and detailed policy conclusions can be drawn.[14] In particular, it is premature to decide which macroeconomic environment would be best suited to the acquisition of capabilities in small firms. However, the results do point towards the need to incorporate the notion of technological learning in the design and implementation of small business support programmes. Most importantly, initiatives aimed at developing new or improved technology for this target group should to some extent get away from the notion that such technology has to be fully appropriate in the conventional static sense of the word (that is that it fits in with local needs and conditions). Above all, new technology must be designed to function as an agent for change, sparking continuous learning processes and contributing to an enhanced capacity for undertaking technological assimilation, adaptation and quality upgrading in the target enterprises on an ongoing basis. Essentially, this means that a limited degree of *inappropriateness* would be a desirable feature in a technology support project, since when a new technique is not completely suited to local conditions, it affords opportunities for technological learning through efforts to achieve a better fit.[15] On the other hand, the degree of unfitness should not be so large as to discourage such efforts. There are many examples of the latter, especially from projects in Africa.

Another ingredient of assistance that is likely to enhance or facilitate technological learning could be the facilitation of applied technical training and in-firm consulting, aimed at helping producers to overcome the concrete bottlenecks they face in the course of trying to meet customers' needs. Finally, the findings of this review suggest the potential usefulness of assistance aimed at organizing support for producers to gain access to information about new products, improved techniques, materials and production processes, and facilitating improved communication with agents in the firms' environment who could be potentially important sources of new ideas and information.

Evidence is beginning to emerge that approaches that target groups of clustered small enterprises and that are at the same time strongly market-driven can generate good results in these areas (see, for example, Tendler and Amorim, 1996; and Tanburn, 1996). However, much more detailed research is still needed before general lessons for best practice can be drawn in this area. In particular, a better conceptualization of the mechanisms through which networking and clustering influence the acquisition of technological capabilities, and more factual evidence about how those processes operate, are needed before we can hope to arrive at a better understanding about how technological learning in small enterprises can be influenced through policy interventions.

NOTES

1. This chapter draws substantially on Romijn (1999).
2. Defined as enterprises with fewer than 100 employees.
3. Perhaps there was a (tacit) assumption that this is the sector where advanced capabilities are most likely to be needed because its new technologies are complex. Also, the technological efforts that these firms make are easier to study than the very incremental shop-floor types of activities that small firms would be undertaking. Another reason may be an overriding concern with the question as to how poor countries could overcome the international technology gap with more advanced countries, at the expense of the question as to how countries could overcome their *internal* technological dualism. Small enterprises could not be expected to make a notable contribution to the first objective, although they are crucial for the latter.
4. No particular restrictive definition of firm size was imposed when collecting materials for the review, since one of the purposes was precisely to determine in which segments of the small-enterprise sector capabilities would develop most often and what differences (if any) in the nature of the learning process might be seen between these segments. The question is *which* small firms build capabilities, and whether there are enough of those around so as to make some, however modest, positive contribution to overall income generation and technical progress in poor countries. Hence, only a rough upper limit was set in order to exclude the sort of large modern firms that were the main focus of the capability literature. A few medium-sized factories were included because they evolved from small beginnings.
5. The concept of technological capacity is somewhat broader than, but shows considerable overlap with, our concept of capability.
6. A few other interesting Zimbabwean cases are documented in Ndlela and Robinson (1995).
7. In addition, some studies report the *lack* of scientific methods. Hence, these studies also acknowledge the importance of this variable as a relevant measure of the degree of technological capability in small firms.
8. Jigs and fixtures are devices that can be clamped on machinery to help ensure standardization in the production of parts.
9. See Amsden (1977) on how lack of standardization held back the emergence of an efficient inter-firm division of labour in the machine-tools industry in Taiwan.
10. This seems to have much to do with the time-period of study. The Zimbabwean, Chinese, Argentinean and Brazilian studies cover half a century or more.
11. The term 'stimulus' is preferred to the term 'demand', since not all effort stimuli are demand driven. For example, in some of the studies competition from large firms or from imported products was also found to have a technological effort-inducing effect (Sethuraman, 1989; Nurul Amin, 1989; Khundker, 1989).
12. Other studies in the survey that have drawn attention to the importance of technological learning for the rising demand for farm equipment due to the adoption of new agricultural practices are Basant and Subrahmamian (1990), Nabi (1988), Child and Kaneda (1975), Mishra (1985), and Johnston and Kilby (1975).
13. For details about the influences exerted by these factors, see Romijn (1996).
14. An initial attempt to investigate capability building among smalll capital goods producers, involving more rigorous measurement of variables and testing of the alleged relationships between them, can be found in Romijn (1997).
15. An early exponent of this view is Hirschman, who argued that a certain degree of unfitness of a development project would be a strong argument for undertaking it in view of the possibilities for 'trait making' (i.e. development of desirable characteristics) that it affords.

In contrast, a project is 'trait taking' if the traits in the local situation are perfectly suited to its construction and operation. Such a project leaves the environment untouched except for the additional output (Hirschman, 1967, pp 131–2).

REFERENCES

Aftab, K. and E. Rahim (1986), 'The emergence of a small-scale engineering sector: the case of Tubewell Production in the Pakistan Punjab', *The Journal of Development Studies*, **23** (1), pp. 60–76.

Aftab, K. and E. Rahim (1989), '"Barriers" to the growth of informal sector firms: a case study', *The Journal of Development Studies*, **25** (4), pp. 490–507.

Ahmad, Q.K., K.M. Rahman, K.M.N. Islam and M.E. Ali (1984), 'Technology adaptation and employment in the agricultural tools and equipment industry of Bangladesh', World Employment Programme Working Papers 2-22/WP 134, International Labour Organisation, Geneva.

Alänge, S. (1987), *Acquisition of Capabilities through International Technology Transfer. The Case of Small Scale Industrialization in Tanzania*, Gothenburg: Chalmers University of Technology.

Amsden, A.H. (1977), 'The division of labour is limited by the type of the market: the case of the Taiwanese machine tool industry', *World Development*, **5** (3), pp. 217–33.

Amsden, A. (1989), *Asia's Next Giant. South Korea and Late Industrialization*, Oxford: Oxford University Press.

Arrow, K.J. (1962), 'The economic implications of learning by doing', *Review of Economic Studies*, **29**, pp. 166–70.

Barampara, A. (1987), 'Enquête sûr le profil technologique des micro-entreprises du secteur métallique de Kigali et Butare (Rwanda)', World Employment Programme Working Paper 2-19/WP 40, International Labour Organisation, Geneva.

Basant, R. (1990), 'Farmers, fabricators and formal R&D – the pipe frame multi-purpose tool bar in Gujarat, India', in M.S. Gamser, H. Appleton and N. Carter (eds), *Tinker, Tiller, Technical Change*, London: Intermediate Technology Publications.

Basant, R. and K.K. Subrahmamian (1990), *Agro-mechanical Diffusion in a Backward Region*, London: Intermediate Technology Publications.

Biggs, T., M. Shah and P. Srivastava (1995), 'Technological capability and learning in African enterprises', Technical Paper No. 288, The World Bank, Washington, DC.

Bouchrara, M. (1985), 'Industrialisation rampante et innovation clandestine en Tunesie', in Institut de Recherche Economique et de Planification du Développement (IREP) *Secteur Informel et Industrialisation Diffuse dans les Nouveaux Pays Industriels*, Cahiers IREP/développement, Université des Sciences Sociales de Grenoble.

Capt, J. (1987), 'Capacité et maîtrise technologique des micro-entreprises métalliques à Bamako et à Segou (Mali)', World Employment Programme Working Paper 2-19/WP 41, International Labour Organisation, Geneva.

Chávez, E. (1989), 'Options technologiques dans la branche des fabrications métalliques du secteur informel à Lima (Perou)', World Employment Programme Working Paper 2-22/WP 197, International Labour Organisation, Geneva.

Child, F.C. and H. Kaneda (1975), 'Links to the green revolution: a study of small-scale, agriculturally related industry in the Pakistan Punjab', *Economic Development and Cultural Change*, **23** (2), pp. 249–77.

Chudnovsky, D. and M. Nagao (1983), *Capital Goods Production in the Third World*, London: Frances Pinter.

Cortes, M. (1979), 'Technical development and technology exports to other LDCs', Annex I in *Argentina – Structural Change in the Industrial Sector*, Washington, DC: Development Economics Department, The World Bank.

Cortes, M., A. Berry and A. Ishaq (1987), *Success in Small and Medium-scale Enterprises. The Evidence from Colombia*, New York: Oxford University Press (for the World Bank).

Dahlman, C.J. and L.E. Westphal (1981), 'The meaning of technological mastery in relation to transfer of technology', *The Annals*, **458**, pp. 12–26.

Dawson, J. (1988), 'Small-scale industry development in Ghana: a case study of Kumasi', report for ESCOR, Overseas Development Administration, London.

Dijk, M.P. van and R. Rabellotti (1997), 'Clusters and networks as sources of co-operation and technology diffusion for small enterprises in developing countries', in M.P. van Dijk and R. Rabellotti (eds), *Enterprise Clusters and Networks in Developing Countries*. London: Frank Cass; in association with the European Association of Development Research and Training Institutes (EADI), Geneva, Chapter 1, pp. 1–10.

Evenson, R.E. and L.E. Westphal (1994), 'Technological change and technology strategy', Working Paper No. 12, The United Nations University Institute for New Technologies, Maastricht.

Farrell, G. (1989), 'Absorption des technologies et organisation de la production dans le secteur informel des fabrications métalliques à Quito (Equateur)', World Employment Programme Working Paper 2-22/WP 196, International Labour Organisation, Geneva.

Fransman, M. (1982), 'Learning and the capital goods sector under free trade: the case of Hong Kong', *World Development*, **10** (11), pp. 991–1014.

Fransman, M. and K. King (eds) (1984), *Technological Capability in the Third World*, London: Macmillan.

Gillis, M., D.H. Perkins, M. Roemer and D. R. Snodgrass (1996), *Economics of Development*, Fourth Edition, New York: W.W. Norton & Co.

Girvan, N.P. and G. Marcelle (1990), 'Overcoming technological dependency: the case of Electric Arc (Jamaica) Ltd., a small firm in a small developing country', *World Development*, **18** (1), pp. 91–107.

Gupta, B. (1994), 'Evolutionary development of technological skills: some case studies from Brazil' (Draft), Center for Economic Research, Tilburg University, Tilburg, mimeo.

Hirschman, A.O. (1967), *Development Projects Observed*, Washington, DC: The Brookings Institution.

Hobday, M. (1995), *Innovation in East Asia. The Challenge to Japan*, Cheltenham, Edward Elgar.

Ishikawa, S. (1981), *Essays on Technology, Employment and Institutions in Economic Development*, Economic Research Series, Hitotsubashi University, Tokyo.

Ishikawa, S. (1985), 'The development of capital-goods sector: the experience of pre-PRC China', World Employment Programme Working Paper 2-22/WP 139, International Labour Organisation, Geneva.

Johnston, B.F. and P. Kilby (1975), *Agriculture and Structural Transformation. Economic Strategies in Late-Developing Countries*, New York: Oxford University Press.

Juma, C. (1989), 'Intellectual property rights for "Jua Kali" innovations', in C. Juma and J.B. Ojwang (eds), *Innovation and Sovereignty: The Patent Debate in African Development*, Nairobi: African Centre for Technology Studies, pp. 123–44.

Katz, J.M. (ed.) (1987), *Technology Generation in Latin American Manufacturing Industries*, London: Macmillan.

Khundker, N. (1989), 'Technology adaptation and innovations in the informal sector of Dhaka (Bangladesh)', World Employment Programme Working Paper 2-22/WP 198, International Labour Organisation, Geneva.

King, K.J. (1974), 'Kenya's informal machine-makers: a study of small-scale industry in Kenya's emergent artisan society', *World Development*, **2** (4 & 5), April/May, pp. 9–28.

King, K.J. (1976), 'Improvisation and machine-making', *Appropriate Technology*, **2** (4), pp. 19–20.

King, K.J. (1984), 'Science, technology and education in the development of indigenous technological capability', in M. Fransman and K. King (eds), *Technological Capability in the Third World*, London: Macmillan, pp. 31–63.

King, K. (1996), *Jua Kali Kenya. Change and Development in an Informal Economy 1970–95*, London: James Curry.

King, K. (1997), 'Growing up, but will the informal sector mature?', *Appropriate Technology*, **24** (1), pp. 22–4.

Kirloskar Consultants (1985), 'Technology adaptation in plastic processing industry in the informal sector: a case study in India', World Employment Programme Working Paper 2-19/WP 36, International Labour Organisation, Geneva.

Lall, S. (1987), *Learning to Industrialize. The Acquisition of Technological Capability by India*, London: Macmillan.

Lall, S. (1992), 'Technological capabilities and industrialisation', *World Development*, **20** (2), pp. 165–86.

Lall, S., G.B. Navaretti, S. Teitel and G. Wignaraja (1994), *Technology and Enterprise Development. Ghana Under Structural Adjustment*, London: Macmillan.

Mahjoub, A. (1985), 'Processus d'adaptation, d'innovation et de diffusion des techniques dans le secteur informel de Tunis', in Institut de Recherche Economique et de Planification du Développement (IREP), *Secteur Informel et Industrialisation Diffuse dans les Nouveaux Pays Industriels*, Cahiers IREP/développement, Université des Sciences Sociales de Grenoble.

Maldonado, C. and S.V. Sethuraman (1992), *Technological Capability in the Informal Sector*, Geneva: International Labour Organisation.

Malgavkar, P.D. (1976), 'The role of techno-entrepreneurs in the adoption of new technology', in N. Jéquier (ed.), *Appropriate Technology. Problems and Promises*, Paris: OECD Development Centre.

Massaquoi, J.G.M. (1995), 'The effect of some sectoral development policies on technology – the case of the informal sector', in R. Heeks, P. Bhatt, M. Huq, C. Lewis and A. Shibli (eds), *Technology and Developing Countries. Practical Applications, Theoretical Issues*, London, Frank Cass, pp. 172–80.

Mingsarn S.K. (1986), 'Technological acquisition in the Thai rice milling and related capital goods industries', World Employment Programme Working Paper 2-22/WP 162, International Labour Organisation, Geneva.

Mishra, S.C. (1985), 'Technological adaptation and employment in the small-scale farm machinery industry: Uttar Pradesh, India', World Employment Programme Working Paper 2-22/WP 156, International Labour Organisation, Geneva.

Moulik, T.K. and P. Purushotham (1986), *Technology Transfer in Rural Industries. Cases and Analysis*, Bombay: Popular Prakashan.

Nabi, I. (1988), *Entrepreneurs and Markets in Early Industrialization. A Case Study from Pakistan*, San Francisco: ICS Press.

Ndlela, D. and P. Robinson (1995), 'Zimbabwe', in S.M. Wangwe (ed.), *Exporting Africa. Technology, Trade and Industrialization in Sub-Saharan Africa*, London and New York: Routledge, in association with the UNU Press, Chapter 7, pp. 143–98.

Nowshirwani, V.F. (1977), 'Employment, technology transfer and adaptation: the case of the agricultural machinery industry in Iran', World Employment Programme Working Paper 2-22/WP 31, International Labour Organisation, Geneva.

Nurul Amin, A.T.M. (1989), 'Technology adaptation in Bangkok's informal sector', World Employment Programme Working Paper 2-22/WP 203, Geneva: International Labour Organisation.

Powell, J. (1991), 'Kumasi University's involvement in grassroots industrial development', *Small Enterprise Development*, **2** (2), pp. 35–43.

Powell, J. (1995), *The Survival of the Fitter. Lives of Some African Engineers*, London: Intermediate Technology Publications.

de la Puente, F.V. (1989), *Innovaciones Tecnologicas en la Pequeña Industria. Casos del Sector Metal-mecánico*, Lima: Fundación Friedrich Ebert.

Rogers, E.M. (1983), *The Diffusion of Innovations*, third edn, London: Macmillan.

Romijn, H.A. (1996), 'Acquisition of technological capability in small firms in developing countries', PhD thesis, Tilburg University.

Romijn, H.A. (1997), 'Acquisition of technological capability in development: a quantitative case study of Pakistan's capital goods sector', *World Development*, **25** (3), pp. 359–77.

Romijn, H.A. (1999), *Acquisition of Technological Capability in Small Firms in Developing Countries*, London: Macmillan, and New York: St Martin's Press.

Sandee, H. (1994), 'The impact of technological change on inter-firm linkages: a case-study of clustered rural small-scale roof tile enterprises in central Java', in P.O. Pedersen, A. Sverrisson and M.P. van Dijk (eds), *Flexible Specialisation. The Dynamics of Small-scale Industries in the South*. London: Intermediate Technology Publications.

Sansom, R.L. (1969), 'The motor pump: a case study of innovation and development', *Oxford Economic Papers*, **21** (1), March, pp. 109–21.

Sen, A. (1985), *Commodities and Capabilities*, Amsterdam: North-Holland.

Sethuraman, S.V. (1989), 'Technology adaptation in micro-enterprises: the case of Bangalore (India)', World Employment Programme Working Paper 2-22/WP 205, International Labour Organisation, Geneva.

Smillie, I. (1991), 'Light engineering and the very late starters', in I. Smillie (ed.), *Mastering the Machine. Poverty, Aid and Technology*, London: Intermediate Technology Publications.

Stewart, F. (1978), *Technology and Underdevelopment*, London: Macmillan.

Stewart, F. (1981), 'International technology transfer: issues and policy options', in P. Streeten and R. Jolly (eds), *Recent Issues in World Development*, Oxford: Pergamon Press, pp. 67–110.

Stewart, F. and E. Ghani (1991), 'How significant are externalities for development?', *World Development*, **19** (6), pp. 569–94.

Stewart, F., S. Lall and S. Wangwe (ed.) (1992), *Alternative Development Strategies in Sub-Saharan Africa*, London: Macmillan.

Sverrisson, P.O. (1997), 'Enterprise networks and technological change: aspects of light engineering and metal working in Accra', in M.P. van Dijk and R. Rabellotti (eds) (1997).

Tanburn, J. (1996), 'Towards success: impact and sustainability in the FIT programme', *Small Enterprise Development*, **7** (1), pp. 42–51.

Tendler, J. and M. Amorim (1996), 'Small firms and their helpers: lessons in demand', *World Development*, **24** (3), pp. 407–26.

Watanabe, S. (1987), 'Technological capability and industrialisation. Effects of aid and sanctions in the United Republic of Tanzania and Zimbabwe', *International Labour Review*, **126** (5), Sept/Oct., pp. 525–41.

Westphal, L.E., L. Kim and C. Dahlman (1984), 'Reflections on Korea's acquisition of technological capability', Discussion Paper No. DRD 77, Development Research Department, The World Bank, Washington, DC.

3. Cluster trajectories and the likelihood of endogenous upgrading[1]

Peter Knorringa

This chapter identifies in which types of clusters one is more likely to find endogenous upgrading capabilities. While clusters in developing countries as a rule do not initiate radical innovations, they appear to differ significantly in the extent to which they depend on outside actors for implementing incremental (process) innovations. The capability of constellations of local actors in specific clusters to implement and build on incremental innovations – leaving aside where these innovations originate from – in this chapter denotes their potential for endogenous technological and organizational upgrading. For the more mature and export-oriented clusters operating in buyer-driven commodity chains, such endogenous upgrading capability is important because it makes them more attractive to the more demanding but also better paying global buyers in the more quality-driven market segments (Gereffi, 1999; Schmitz and Knorringa, 1999).

For this, the industrial-district literature offers the most obvious point of departure (Brusco, 1982; Pyke *et al.*, 1990). After all, this literature posits the most attractive end of the continuum: clusters of locally owned firms who, jointly with local institutions, compete successfully in international markets on the basis of their endogenous upgrading capabilities.

At first sight the recent European industrial district success stories, especially from the Third Italy, seem very relevant as an example for clusters in developing countries. These European industrial districts by and large share the following characteristics (Asheim, 1994; Schmitz and Musyck, 1994; Rabellotti, 1995). First, they tend to specialize in labour-intensive artisanal sectors, such as footwear or garments, in which less-developed countries are often thought to enjoy a comparative advantage. Secondly, the Italianate industrial districts are built on local firms, mainly of small and medium size. Most clusters in developing countries also consist overwhelmingly of small and very small firms. Moreover, local and regional policy makers in developing countries are desperately looking for ways to stimulate a more endogenous industrialization process. Thirdly, the Italian industrial districts are situated in regions that were rooted in small-scale agriculture and industrialized relatively late. This means these success stories were part of an industrial 'periphery'. Similarly, most clusters in developing countries are also located in the peripheral areas of their respective countries. In short, at a first glance the Italianate industrial district experience appears to show that a successful industrialization process built on locally owned firms is indeed possible after all, even in peripheral areas.

However, a fundamentally different institutional setting, with widespread poverty, a labour surplus and more extreme differences in bargaining power between cluster actors, may well lead to very different outcomes in developing countries. Besides, apart from being different from the Italian setting, the diversity of institutional settings within the developing world is also mind-boggling. Nevertheless, even though each cluster may have a unique story to tell and direct transferability of experiences may be absurd, it is also important not to become mentally imprisoned by history (Schmitz and Musyck, 1994). Therefore, without glossing over the fundamental differences in institutional settings, I feel it is useful to take the industrial-district literature as a frame of reference for an analysis of cluster trajectories in developing countries. Moreover, the extent of transferability of experiences appears to be much higher within a framework that focuses on trajectories instead of static models (Humphrey, 1995).[2]

This chapter first briefly looks at the large group of survival clusters for which the industrial-district model is not a suitable frame of reference. The third section positions a wide variety of case studies on three different stylized cluster trajectories and discusses the extent to which examples of endogenous upgrading were found. The next section aims to identify to what extent policy lessons from the Third Italy may be useful to local and regional policy makers in developing countries. The last section contains the conclusion.

SURVIVAL CLUSTERS AND BARRIERS TO UPGRADING

Probably the most common type of manufacturing clusters to be found in developing countries are survival clusters (on Indonesia, see for example Weijland, 1994; Klapwijk, 1997; on Africa, see for example Pedersen, 1997). In such clusters technology is limited to rudimentary equipment, and entrepreneurs and workers may not find any technical reason for collaboration, and so keep operating independently, without sharing labour, housing, or equipment. There is no evidence of interfirm division of labour within the commodity chain which is a prominent feature of mature clusters discussed below. Still, relatively lower transaction costs may be achieved because of lower search costs for potential customers (consumers as well as traders) and the presence of a local specialized labour pool. Because such transaction costs are often extremely high, especially in the least developed areas of the developing world, they often provide clustered enterprises with a crucial competitive edge to isolated firms. In comparison to other clusters perhaps the main feature of survival clusters is that they face very unstable conditions and are usually not the only and sometimes not even the main activity of participating actors. Heinen and Weijland (1989) raised the question of whether such clusters should be interpreted as a sign of poverty or progress. Micro-level studies reveal that rising incomes in some cases led to the collapse of such clusters, while in other cases it has led to a consolidation of the participants' commitments towards cluster activities. However, without wanting to be deterministic, consolidated survival clusters also face daunting barriers to develop into more mature clusters with, for example, increasing interfirm division of labour and building up of upgrading capabilities. A parallel with the informal sector and small enterprise literature may be useful here. The common understanding in much of this literature appears to be that in enterprise development 'little acorns do not as a rule grow into mighty oaks' (Grosh and Somolekae, 1996), or in order words, 'graduation' from survival to micro to small-scale is the exception rather than the rule (Farbmann and Lessik, 1989). A similar caution in assessing the opportunities of survival clusters to grow into more mature clusters seems justified.

Even though probably most of these survival clusters are found in rural areas, they are also found in metropolitan areas. The main difference is that most metropolitan clusters are built on survival-oriented self-employment, have fewer local roots and operate more in modern sectors (Alam, 1994; Benjamin, 1991), while the rural clusters tend to be concentrated in traditional sectors, often with artisanal roots (Klapwijk, 1997).[3] These sectoral specializations largely correspond with the well known European clusters: fashion-sensitive and labour-intensive sectors with significant market niches which attach surplus value to quality-competitive artisanal products, such as footwear, other leather products, clothing, (wooden) furniture, jewellery, glassware, some metal products and types of toys and handicrafts. Most of the more promising clusters are also found in these sectors, but are located in medium-sized towns, especially in Asia and Latin America.

In the literature so far it appears that Africa does not possess such more promising clusters (for a recent overview of African case studies, see McCormick, 1999). However, this observation should not be taken at face value. First, researchers on clusters in Africa have tended to focus on the informal (*jua kali*) segment of a particular subsector. Second, and related to the first point, the operationalization of the cluster concept has been much stricter in terms of geography.[4] Most cluster studies deal with, for example, an area on the outskirts of a bigger town where all vehicle repair shops/garages have concentrated (see, for example, Kinyanjui, 1997). To put it bluntly, as soon as one comes across a few printing workshops next to those garages, the cluster ends. In contrast, the Agra footwear cluster, notwithstanding concentrations in specific neighbourhoods, is spread out over a city of almost two million inhabitants, and encompasses large, modern factories up to informal home-based units (Knorringa, 1996). In the African context such variety within a subsector in one big city may well exist, but it would not be discussed as one cluster. For example, the garment subsector in Nairobi appears to encompass large, modern factories (often export oriented and often owned by white entrepreneurs), as well as a hidden medium-sized segment of workshops predominantly run by Asian entrepreneurs, and an informal survival segment run by indigenous black artisans (McCormick, 1999).

Notwithstanding such differences in approach, it seems safe to say that most clusters in developing countries are survival clusters with limited potential for endogenous technological and organizational upgrading of the kind that would make them more attractive to better paying buyers. Still, in terms of total employment and in terms of likely policy priorities for poverty alleviation, this large group of survival clusters may well be more important and more in need of support as compared to the more mature clusters. However, the industrial-district model and policies to strengthen endogenous upgrading do not offer a particularly useful angle to approach the problematic of these survival clusters. Therefore, in the remainder of this chapter I focus on the smaller group of relatively more mature clusters in developing countries.

Cluster Trajectories

Any typology of cluster trajectories inevitably simplifies. Moreover, such a typology may instil the wrong impression that clusters are homogeneous at the point of entering a particular trajectory. Clearly this is not the case. Clusters possess unique characteristics shaped by their respective social, cultural, political and economic environments. Notwithstanding this path-dependent uniqueness of clusters, many of the more mature clusters appear to evolve along three distinguishable trajectories. These three trajectories are derived from Markussen (1996),[5] who came up with the labels as part of a typology of industrial districts and their description for industrial economies, and from Humphrey (1995: 159), who described possible cluster trajectories in developing countries without providing labels. Remarkable enough, the trajectories sketched by Humphrey can be seen as running from a 'basic' agglomeration to one of the types of industrial districts that Markussen distinguishes. But, to start with, the first option of course is a stagnating cluster that does not evolve along any of the possible trajectories. Such clusters:

'...will continue to be agglomerations of firms enjoying the external economies of agglomeration but without the inter-firm linkages which are at the heart of the industrial district model' (Humphrey, 1995: 159). To be able to enter one of these relatively more successful trajectories requires a shift from 'static gains' to 'dynamic gains' (Rabellotti, 1995), or from competitive advantages 'just' derived from external economies to include processes of consciously pursued joint action by cluster participants (Schmitz, 1995).

In the first trajectory, a cluster evolves into the set of stylized facts that represent the Italianate industrial district. In Italy, it now appears as if at least some of its clusters are evolving into hub-and-spoke districts with a limited number of larger leading firms and many subcontractors. A second trajectory, more common in developing countries, concerns clusters that evolve from a 'basic' agglomeration to a hub-and-spoke district without an intermediate stage in which they have resembled the main features of the Italianate model. A third trajectory runs from a 'basic' agglomeration to a satellite district, in which most small and medium firms manufacture for leading firms located outside the cluster. There are indications that some satellite districts may subsequently evolve into hub-and-spoke districts. In the remainder of this section I take a selection of case studies from developing and developed countries on one of these trajectories and elaborate on their potential for endogenous upgrading. Given the scarcity of longitudinal case studies, this review necessarily predominantly relies on comparative statics.

Italianate Trajectory

The first trajectory, towards an Italianate type of industrial district, is also the most difficult to find in developing countries. In fact, only two such cases were found in the literature, the surgical instruments cluster in Sialkot (Pakistan) and the ceramic tile cluster in Cricuma (Brazil). The surgical instruments cluster in Sialkot appears, in particular, to have displayed a significant number of the Italianate features, at least in the beginning of the 1990s (Nadvi, 1996). As Humphrey wrote in his overview, the Sialkot cluster consisted of 'large numbers of small firms engaged in extensive inter-firm exchanges of service, horizontally and vertically, active producer associations, supportive local and regional governments, and the clusters' powerful position in the world market for basic surgical instruments.' (Humphrey, 1995: 159). However, a few years later this cluster appears to be on a trajectory towards a hub-and-spoke district. Nadvi (1999) reports on the consequences of the crisis for Sialkot's manufacturers. In May 1994 the Food and Drug Administration of the United States, the most important export market for Sialkot, embargoed the import of Pakistani-made surgical instruments (that is Sialkot) for failing to meet international quality standards. By 1996 Sialkot appears to have come out of this crisis even stronger than it was before. Sales are above the 1993 level, and overall quality has improved. At the same time, while a substantial number of manufacturers are nowadays certified as conforming with international Good Manufacturing Practices (GMP) standards, only a few manufacturers are now ISO 9002 certified. In order to establish or maintain contacts abroad, such certification becomes more and more a necessary but not sufficient condition. Therefore, doing direct business with quality conscious importers becomes the exclusive domain of those larger entrepreneurs with the proper certifications. Moreover, also within the associations and institutions of the Sialkot cluster a relatively small group of entrepreneurs appears to become more dominant.

In the case of the Criciúma cluster, local actors from firms and business associations deliberately try to build Italianate structures (Meyer-Stamer, 1997). The cluster consists of several medium- and two large-sized manufacturers of floor and wall tiles (all nationally owned) and a substantial number of suppliers (some nationally owned, some subsidiaries of leading firms from Italy and Spain). Unlike the case of Sassuolo, the world-wide leading tile cluster in Italy (Porter, 1990), there are no local equipment manufacturers in Criciúma. In the past there was fierce rivalry and little co-operation between the firms. This changed after the industry entered into a deep crisis around 1990. Two presidents of local business associations succeeded in establishing co-operation; one of the important outcomes was the creation of a local technology centre. It is important to understand two further aspects of why co-operation started. First, there was the observation that firms in Italy and Spain were mostly located in industrial districts and did actually co-operate; this helped in overcoming business–cultural obstacles. Second, firms can co-operate in fields like technology because they do not establish a competitive advantage; heavy investment in new equipment and a strong effort to establish quality management concepts like Kaizen and 5S are no more than a precondition for survival in an increasingly sophisticated industry. Competitive advantages are established through innovative design, logistics, and marketing concepts, and firms are keen not to reveal their tricks in these fields.

In a way these examples already put forward what may well be two of the more general reasons why the Italianate trajectory is hardly to be found in developing countries. First, for small firms in developing countries it is even harder to be able to afford the investments in technology to keep up with rising quality standards. While Italianate industrial districts have been very successful in implementing incremental innovations, a big question is whether they can cope with more radical changes in technology requirements. Therefore, it seems pretty unrealistic to expect from small firm clusters in developing countries that they would be able to conquer a part of the market niche now held by their more mechanized and computerized Italian counterparts who also possess much more experience with fashion-oriented high-street manufacturing. Nevertheless, the Italianate trajectory has the highest potential for creating endogenous upgrading capabilities, precisely because of its main strength: implementing incremental process (and product) innovations.

Moreover, the second more general reason to explain the absence of an Italianate trajectory in developing countries has to do with the social structure. To put it simply, I have not come across one developing-country case study that resembles the social boundary conditions for the Italianate trajectory. Clusters in developing countries are embedded in a fundamentally different setting from the Italian case studies (Amin, 1994). For example, social cohesion and the integrating role of local institutions, the pet themes in the industrial district literature, appear to be less prominent in clusters in developing countries. Instead, internal segmentation appears to reproduce and even strengthen inequalities. Because of extreme differences in bargaining power between actors in the cluster, possible benefits from collective efficiency are skewed in favour of leading actors and market agents (Smyth, 1992).

Perhaps there is one more reason not to be surprised to find so few clusters in developing countries on an Italianate trajectory. Also in the European and Italian debate it seems as if the Italianate features are now more and more seen as a phase in a broader restructuring process. Without suggesting that the Italianate model would be inherently unsustainable, it may well be less suitable to the situation of the 1990s in the world market for many of the relevant subsectors. Even in Italy, it now appears as if at least some of its clusters are evolving into hub-and-spoke districts with a limited number of larger leading firms and many subcontractors.[6]

Satellite Trajectory

A second trajectory runs towards a satellite district, in which most small and medium firms manufacture for leading firms located outside the cluster. Such leading firms need not necessarily be large manufacturers themselves, although they often were large manufacturers a few decades ago. In many of the relevant subsectors, the labour-intensive manufacturing process has – in steps – been transferred to manufacturers in developing countries. In many cases, the leading firms of such commodity chains in European countries have transformed themselves into trading houses, keeping a firm grip on design and marketing.

Most observers consider the satellite trajectory to be the least attractive, as it offers the fewest possibilities for building endogenous upgrading capabili-ties. Manufacturers who are attractive to leading international corporations for only one reason – cheap labour – are very vulnerable, as relative labour costs tend to keep changing between countries. Moreover, to be considered by global buyers for only a particular job is fatal, since jobs are constantly changing. By contrast, in resilient and interdependent interfirm relations, leading firms are more inclined to deal with a changing situation together with known partners. A leading firm must feel confident enough to rely on the specialized capabilities of their suppliers. Especially in fashion-sensitive industries, it is, nowadays, 'too costly and time consuming to perfect the design of new products and translate those designs into simply executed steps. Those formerly charged with the execution of plans – technicians, blue collar workers, outside suppliers – must now elaborate indicative instructions, transforming the final design in the very act of executing it' (Lazerson, 1993: 215). Evidently, this is a far cry from the Export Processing Zones' type of assembly line work where predominantly young women without previous artisanal experience work long hours for low wages.

However, being incorporated into a commodity chain controlled by a buyer outside the cluster is not necessarily all bad. Especially in the short run important benefits may accrue to local workers. To start with, the workers involved (usually women) may be able to learn industrial manufacturing skills, earn their own income, and as a result possibly strengthen their bargaining position at home. At a macro level, these increasing income opportunities for women may well contribute to a more equal income distribution. Secondly, it can, for a certain period, achieve a substantial production volume for both the domestic and export markets, and thus diversify the industrial structure. Moreover, although the conditions of this type of employment are not very promising, they are in many ways already an improvement over alternative job opportunities.

Moreover, entrepreneurs may also benefit from being part of such international commodity chains. Apart from earning large sums of money as intermediaries, they gain access to all sorts of relevant information on the international market in their specific subsector. In many cases local manufacturers may acquire endogenous upgrading capabilities within manufacturing. Moreover, in some cases entrepreneurs may in a next stage even try to venture out on their own by capturing the higher value-added stages in the commodity chain. This may start a process towards a hub-and-spoke trajectory, in which the leading actors in particular commodity chains are leading *local* entrepreneurs.

The footwear industry in and around Madras offers a successful example where a few local industrialists are slowly capturing higher-value added stages in the commodity chain (Rao, 1993). Nowadays most of the renowned firms have entered the footwear industry from a leather tanning background. These firms are long-standing suppliers of main European footwear firms. While the

Indian firms previously supplied finished leathers (1970s), and before that semi-finished leathers (1960s), they now also prepare uppers (1980s) and increasingly full shoes (1990s) for these leading actors. In turn, these foreign firms assist in setting up modern factories where badly paid and unorganized women work with modern, imported machines. One of these local hub-firms was the only company from India that had its own stall in one of the upper-market exhibition halls at the main European shoe fair in Dusseldorf (March 1997).

However, such examples are rare. On the whole, it seems that, while most groups of exporters can be positioned on a satellite trajectory, this trajectory also provides the least-likely environment for significant endogenous upgrading.

Hub-and-Spoke Trajectory

The last trajectory to be discussed is a hub-and-spoke trajectory, which appears to be the most common trajectory for clusters in developing countries. According to Schmitz and Nadvi (1994: 12): 'most LDC clusters tend to be distinguished by internal hierarchies'. The most typical example is no doubt the case of the Korean *chaebol,* where small firms orbit around large industrial complexes (Cho, 1992). In the Brazilian Sinos valley (a shoe cluster) small firms tend to operate rather separately from a few Fordist giants (Schmitz, 1995). In many of the south Asian clusters one tends to find a combination of the above two trends. A few leading families, who own the largest and more modern factories in the cluster (which are by international standards usually semi-mechanized medium-scale units), dominate the local industry through the local business associations and mould the cluster image as it is perceived by outsiders. Other smaller units either supply them as subcontractors or supply to other, usually less attractive, market channels. Examples include garments in Tirrupur (Cawthorne, 1995; Swaminathan and Jeyaranjan, 1994) and Ahmedabad (Das, 1996a); flooring tiles in Gujarat (Das, 1996b); textile printing in Jetpur (Dupont, 1994); bicycles in Ludhiana (Kattuman, 1994); and footwear in Agra (Knorringa, 1996, 1999). Moreover, this characterization also applies to for example the Tegalwangi rattan furniture cluster in Indonesia (Smyth, 1992), and the footwear clusters, and Mexico's Leon and Guadelajara (Rabellotti, 1993).

In most of these clusters one finds at least three tiers of firms:

> At the lowest tier of the hierarchy are households and small workshops which have limited resources, produce for local consumption and seek to survive. The medium tier is occupied by firms who are better endowed (in capital and skills), are able to generate an investable surplus and produce, either directly or on (sub)contract, for the domestic and often export markets. The third tier includes firms which maintain

high levels of quality, are technically innovative, capable of entering export markets, and have growth aspirations. (Nadvi and Schmitz, 1994: 12)

Perhaps the main risk in a hub-and-spoke trajectory, in terms of acquiring capabilities for endogenous upgrading, is that often a few leading families try to monopolize benefits and become a source of conservatism instead of innovation, even though they have the financial capacity to invest in upgrading. Many of the south Asian case studies in particular tend to indicate how such 'fat cats' are often a drag on innovative behaviour or at least prevent cluster-wide diffusion of the acquisition of upgrading capabilities (Cawthorne, 1995; Das, 1996a; Knorringa, 1996).

Clusters do not only need to acquire capabilities to implement incremental innovations. Not exclusively, but perhaps especially clusters in developing countries also need to be able to deal with radical changes in their environment. A main threat-cum-challenge for the manufacturing of tradables in many developing countries is the onslaught of the New Competition (Best 1990) in export markets, combined with a general trend of economic liberalization in developing countries. The few available case studies on the impact of the New Competition and economic liberalization on the performance of clusters appear to show that they are resilient and they do upgrade but that, as a response, the internal structure of clusters also changes.[7] Some actors lose out, power becomes more concentrated, and the hub-and-spoke trajectory appears to become more pronounced.

To summarize, the potential for endogenous upgrading is highest in the least-found Italianate trajectory, while it is lowest in the most frequently found satellite trajectory. The hub-and-spoke trajectory forms the intermediate case: it is increasingly found and it possesses a potential for endogenous upgrading. The next section on policy aims to discuss how policy makers may contribute to realizing more of the potential for endogenous upgrading in hub-and-spoke trajectories.

POLICY OPTIONS

The clearest and hardest message emerging from the European industrial district literature is that: 'none of the industrial districts are the result of planned action, of a local or regional industrial strategy. They all developed spontaneously' (Schmitz and Musyck, 1994: 902). Even up to what Brusco (1990) has coined as the Mark I stage, growth is largely spontaneous, and it is only in the Mark II stage that: 'industry requires support from local and regional institutions in order to speed up innovation, expand into new markets and thus consolidate growth' (Schmitz and Musyck, 1994: 902).

Thus, to state the obvious, industrial districts were not created from scratch. Therefore, the remainder of this section again focuses on the more mature clusters because the European experience may be of greater relevance to them.

Despite the enormous attention given to the Third Italy success story there is relatively little concrete empirical evidence of a direct causal link between the acquisition of endogenous upgrading capabilities and specific policies (Schmitz and Musyck, 1994). Nevertheless, a few lessons may be distilled. What does not work, according to Zeitlin (1990: 10) is centralized planning or *laissez faire* liberalization. One needs to define a policy in between these two extremes, that builds on an already existing local and/or regional specialization and is carried out through local and regional institutions that take their cue from local business associations, local labour unions and other embedded local collective actors. Such institutions can be particularly useful to the upgrading of local industry when providing a range of 'real services' (Brusco, 1992). A serious problem in transferring such experiences to developing countries is again related to the different institutional settings. In many of the developing-country case studies, local and regional associations and institutions are monopolized by a few leading families or clans, which often blocks rather than enhances the diffusion of upgrading capabilities that typifies the Italianate districts. This is not to say that successful European clusters have not experienced any internal power struggles. History shows that the very successful clusters of today often also experienced bitter internal struggles before becoming prosperous, notwithstanding the collective amnesia once success came their way (Sabel, 1992: 225–9). The point is that the social structure has allowed the distinct actors in the cluster to fight it out among themselves and to work out solutions that have led to increased overall performance instead of a solution in which a small elite is able to stay in full control. Such countervailing power appears to be much less present in most clusters in developing countries. Therefore, local and regional policy makers should contribute to building such countervailing power. Not siding automatically with the local leaders may provide an important signal to other collective actors, and may lead to a more balanced conflict resolution.

At least equally difficult to achieve is another main challenge facing clusters in developing countries: how to capture more of the higher value-added stages in the commodity chain. Here, policy makers should take their cue from the needs felt by local entrepreneurs and business associations, and especially support locally embedded attempts to strengthen non-manufacturing capabilities. More locally embedded capabilities in, for example, design, marketing and distribution, can significantly strengthen the cluster's potential for endogenous upgrading.

CONCLUSION

Clusters in developing countries can be situated on at least three different trajectories that possess distinct potentials for endogenous upgrading. In this chapter I have used the industrial-district model as a frame of reference. However, for the large group of survival clusters this model is not particularly useful. Therefore, the discussion is limited to the smaller group of relatively more mature clusters.

The Italianate trajectory, which offers most potential for endogenous upgrading, is very rare in developing countries. Reasons include the lack of technological innovative capabilities and resources in most clusters in developing countries, and the fundamentally different institutional setting in which social inequalities are often strengthened because of extreme differences in bargaining power between actors in the cluster. In contrast, the satellite trajectory, which appears to offer the least potential for endogenous upgrading, is the most commonly found among clusters in developing countries.

Alternatively, a hub-and-spoke trajectory offers an intermediate situation: it provides more potential for endogenous upgrading than the satellite trajectory, and an increasing number of clusters in developing countries seem to portray hub-and-spoke features. Of the three stylized trajectories I have argued that for policy makers a trajectory towards a hub-and-spoke district is the most feasible and potentially most useful metaphor to keep in mind, with the following qualifications. Policy makers should aim to facilitate capturing higher-value-added stages in the commodity chain, support attempts to acquire (innovative) technological capabilities, and especially facilitate platforms to enable internal conflicts to be resolved. It would be a primary task of policy implementers to contribute to internal conflict resolution by not siding automatically with the leading entrepreneurs but to try to operate as a mediator in local power struggles through supporting the build-up of countervailing power. It is of crucial importance that local conflicts are addressed, and not neglected or hidden, because the Italian experience appears to indicate that periods of innovative growth tend to be preceded by such struggles.

Clearly, this is a paradoxical conclusion as it advises policy makers to aim for a hub-and-spoke trajectory and at the same time it stresses the need, particularly in developing countries, to curb the power of local leading entrepreneurs to such an extent that other cluster actors may also benefit. Moreover, even when policy implementers would be able to live up to such a tall order, success is far from secured. Most of the more mature clusters in developing countries appear to depend on rather volatile markets. Notwithstanding the importance of all sorts of external conditions, it seems plausible to assume that clusters with more endogenous upgrading capabilities would be better equipped to face such volatile markets. Therefore, an important issue for new research would be to identify more systematically factors and processes that enhance or inhibit the acquisition of endogenous upgrading capabilities in clusters.

NOTES

1. Earlier versions of this chapter were presented at a European Management and Organisation in Transition (EMOT) workshop, at the ISTUD, in Stresa, Italy, 11–14 September 1997 and an EADI workshop on the importance of innovation for small enterprise development in the Third World at the Institute of Social Studies (ISS), The Hague, 18–19 September 1998. I thank participants in these workshops for their constructive comments.
2. While it is now commonplace in cluster studies from developing countries to refer to the Third Italy, only few studies have so far tried to incorporate the idea of growth stages. A notable early exception is Swaminathan and Jeyaranjan (1994) who have tried to analyse the Tiruppur knitwear cluster through a trajectory from artisan to dependent subcontractor to Mark I and to Mark II stages, as coined by Brusco (1990).
3. For an in-depth longitudinal case study on the impact of technological change on cluster formation in rural Java, see Sandee (1995).
4. From a discussion with D. McCormick, W. Mitullah and M. Kinyanjui at the IDS, Sussex University, April 1997.
5. The fourth type of industrial district identified by Markussen, the State Anchored District, is not dealt with in this chapter. However, it could be a useful metaphor in a discussion on the role of the state in trying to create industrial districts from scratch. However, among researchers in the area of small enterprise development in developing countries there exists a consensus that this is impossible (Humphrey and Schmitz, 1996).
6. On Italy see, for example, Lazerson and Lorenzoni (1996); Albino *et al.* (1996); for an analogy with one of the oldest industrial districts, Rochdale (Manchester), see Penn (1994).
7. Most of these case studies are brought together in a Special Issue of World Development from September 1999.

BIBLIOGRAPHY

Alam, G. (1994), 'Industrial districts and technological change: a study of the garment industry in Delhi', UNCTAD – *Technological Dynamism in Industrial Districts: An Alternative Approach to Industrialization in Developing Countries?*, New York and Geneva: UNCTAD, pp. 257–66.

Albino, V., A.C. Garavelli and P. Pontrandolfo (1996), 'Local factors and global strategies of the leader firm of an industrial district', Paper presented at EurOMA Conference on Manufacturing Strategy, London, June.

Amin, A. (1989), 'Specialization without growth: small footwear firms in Naples', in E. Goodman, J. Bamford and P. Saynor (eds), *Small Firms and Industrial Districts in Italy*, London: Routledge, pp. 239–58.

Amin, A. (1994), 'The potential for turning informal economies into Marshallian industrial districts', *Technological Dynamism in Industrial Districts: An Alternative Approach to Industrialization in Developing Countries?*, New York and Geneva: UNCTAD, pp. 51–72.

Amin, A. and K. Robbins (1990a), 'The re-emergence of regional economies? The mythical geography of flexible accumulation', *Environment and Planning D: Society and Space*, **8**, pp. 7-34.

Amin, A. and K. Robbins (1990b), 'Industrial districts and regional development: limits and possibilities', in F. Pyke, G. Becattini and W. Sengenberger (eds), *Industrial Districts and Inter-Firm Co-operation in Italy*, Geneva: International Institute for Labour Studies, pp. 185-219.

Asheim, B.T. (1992), 'Flexible specialisation, industrial districts and small firms: a critical appraisal', in H. Ernste and V. Meier (eds), *Regional Development and Contemporary Industrial Response. Extending Flexible Specialisation*, London: Belhaven Press, pp. 45-63.

Asheim, B.T. (1994), 'Industrial districts, inter-firm co-operation and endogenous technological development: the experience of developed countries', *Technological Dynamism in Industrial Districts: An Alternative Approach to Industrialization in Developing Countries?*, New York and Geneva: UNCTAD, pp. 91-142.

Asheim, B.T. (1996), 'Industrial districts as "learning regions": a condition for prosperity', *European Planning Studies*, **4** (4), pp. 379-400.

Becattini, G. (1990), 'The Marshallian industrial district as a socio-economic notion', in F. Pyke, G. Becattini and W. Sengenberger (eds), *Industrial Districts and Inter-Firm Co-operation in Italy*, Geneva: International Institute for Labour Studies, pp. 37-51.

Benjamin, S.J. (1991), *Jobs, Land and Urban Development. The Economic Success of Small Manufacturers in East Delhi, India*, Cambridge, Massachussets: Lincoln Institute of Land Policy.

Benton, L.A. (1989), 'Homework and industrial development: gender roles and restructuring in the Spanish shoe industry', *World Development*, **17** (2), pp. 255-66.

Benton, L.A. (1990), 'The emergence of industrial districts in Spain: industrial restructuring and diverging regional responses', Paper presented at a conference on Industrial Districts and Local Economic Regeneration, Geneva, October.

Best, M.H. (1990), *The New Competition. Institutions of Industrial Restructuring*, Cambridge: Polity Press.

Brusco, S. (1982), 'The Emilian model: productive decentralisation and social integration', *Cambridge Journal of Economics*, **6**, pp. 167-84.

Brusco, S. (1990), 'The idea of the industrial district: its genesis', in F. Pyke, G. Becattini and W. Sengenberger (eds), *Industrial Districts and Inter-Firm Co-operation in Italy*, Geneva: International Institute for Labour Studies, pp. 10-19.

Brusco, S. (1992), 'Small firms and the provision of real services', in F. Pyke and W. Sengenberger (eds), *Industrial Districts and Local Economic Regeneration*, Geneva: International Institute for Labour Studies, pp. 177-96.

Cawthorne, P.M. (1995), 'Of networks and markets: the rise and rise of a south Indian town, the example of Tiruppur's cotton knitwear industry', *World Development*, **23** (1), pp. 43-56.

Chaudhuri, B. (1994), 'Entrepreneur-government relationship in small and medium industries: a case study of the textile industry in Bhilwara, Rajasthan', Paper presented at an EADI workshop in Vienna, November.

Das, K. (1996a), 'Flexibly together: surviving and growing in a garment cluster, Ahmedabad, India', *Journal of Entrepreneurship*, **2**, pp. 47-68.

Das, K. (1996b), 'Collective dynamism and firm strategy: the flooring tile cluster in Gujarat, India', Gujarat Institute of Development Research, Working Paper no. 76.

Dei Ottati, G. (1994), 'Trust, interlinking transactions and credit in the industrial district', *Cambridge Journal of Economics*, **18** (6), pp. 529–46.

Dupont, V. (1994), 'Facets of industrial clustering and flexibility in the textile-printing industry of Jetpur (West India)', Paper presented to a workshop on Flexible Specialization in Pondicherry, India, 25–26 March.

Farbman, M. and A. Lessik (1989), 'The impact of classification on policy', in A. Gosses *et al.* (eds), *Small Enterprises, New Approaches, Proceedings of the Workshop Small Scale Enterprise Development, In Search of New Dutch Approaches, March 6 and 7*, The Hague: Ministry of Foreign Affairs, Directorate General International Cooperation, pp. 105–22.

Gereffi, G. (1999), 'International trade and industrial upgrading in the apparel commodity chain', *Journal of International Economics*, **48** (1), pp. 37–70.

Goodman, E., J. Bamford and P. Saynor (eds) (1989), *Small Firms and Industrial Districts in Italy*, London: Routledge.

Granovetter, M. (1985), 'Economic action and social structure: the problem of embeddedness', *American Journal of Sociology*, **91** (3), pp. 481–510.

Granovetter, M. (1992), 'Economic institutions as social constructions: a framework for analysis', *Acta Sociologica*, **35**, pp. 3–11.

Granovetter, M. and R. Swedberg (1992), *The Sociology of Economic Life*, Boulder, Colorado: Westview Press.

Grosh, B. and G. Somolekae (1996), 'Mighty oaks from little acorns: can microenterprise serve as the seedbed of industrialization?', *World Development*, **24** (12), pp. 1879–90.

Harrison, B. (1992), 'Industrial districts: old wine in new bottles?', *Regional Studies*, **25** (5), 469–83.

Heinen, E. and H. Weijland (1989), 'Rural industry in progress and decline', in P. van Gelder and J. Bijlmer (eds), *About Fringes, Margins and Lucky Dips. The Informal Sector in Third World Countries. Research Developments in Research and Policy*, Amsterdam: Free University Press, pp. 13–34.

Holmström, M. (1993), 'Flexible specialization in India?', *Economic and Political Weekly*, 28 August, pp. M82–M86.

Holmström, M. (1994), 'Bangalore as an industrial district: flexible specialization in a labour surplus economy?', Paper presented to a workshop on Flexible Specialization in Pondicherry, India, 25–6 March.

Humphrey, J. (1995), 'Industrial reorganization in developing countries: from models to trajectories', *World Development*, **23** (1), pp. 149–62.

Humphrey, J. and H. Schmitz (1996), 'The triple C approach to local industrial policy', *World Development*, **24** (12), pp. 1859–77.

Kattuman, P.A. (1994), 'The role of history in the transition to an industrial district: the case of the Indian bicycle industry', Paper prepared for a workshop on Flexible Specialization in Pondicherry, India, 25–6 March.

Kinyanjui, M.N. (1997), 'Tapping opportunities in enterprise clusters in Kenya: the case of enterprises in Ziwani and Kigandaini', Paper presented at a workshop on Collective Efficiency at the Institute of Development Studies, Sussex University, April.

Klapwijk, M. (1997), 'Rural industry clusters in central Java, Indonesia. An empirical assessment of their role in rural industrialisation', Tinbergen Institute Research Series No. 153, Vrije Universiteit, Amsterdam.

Knorringa, P. (1994), 'Lack of interaction between traders and producers in the Agra footwear cluster', in Pedersen *et al.* (eds).

Knorringa, P. (1996), *Economics of Collaboration; Indian Shoemakers Between Market and Hierarchy*, New Delhi and London: Sage Publications.

Knorringa, P. (1999), 'Agra: an old cluster facing the new competition', *World Development*, **27** (9), pp. 1587–604.

Knorringa, P. and H.J.W. Weijland (1993), 'Subcontracting: the incorporation of small producers in dynamic industrial networks', in I.S.A. Baud and G.A. de Bruijne (eds), *Gender, Small-Scale Industry and Development Policy*, London: Intermediate Technology Publications, pp. 35–46.

Lazerson, M. (1993), 'Factory or putting-out? Knitting networks in Modena', in G. Grabher (ed.), *The Embedded Firm. On the Socioeconomics of Industrial Networks*, London: Routledge, pp. 203–26.

Lazerson, M. and G. Lorenzoni (1996), 'A return to the Italian source: the networks that feed industrial districts'. Mimeo.

Lipparini, A. and M. Sobrero (1994), 'The glue and the pieces: entrepreneurship and innovation in small-firm networks', *Journal of Business Venturing*, **9**, pp. 125–40.

Lorenz, E.H. (1990), 'Trust, community and flexibility: toward a theory of industrial districts', Paper presented at a conference on 'Pathways to Industrialization and Regional Development in the 1990s', Lake Arrowhead, March.

Maillat, D. (1995), 'Territorial dynamic, innovative milieus and regional policy', *Entrepreneurship and Regional Development*, **7**, pp. 157–65.

Markussen, A. (1996), 'Sticky places in slippery space: a typology of industrial districts', *Economic Geography*, pp. 293–313.

Masinde, C.K.M. (1994), 'Small enterprise development through outsourcing activities of large firms in Kenya's motor industry', Paper presented at an EADI workshop in Vienna, November.

McCormick, D. (1994), *Industrial District or Garment Ghetto? The Case of Nairobi's Mini-Manaufacturers*, paper presented at an EADI workshop in Vienna, November 1994.

McCormick, D. (1999), 'African enterprise clusters and industrialisation: theory and reality', *World Development*, **27** (9), pp. 1531–52.

Meyer-Stamer, J. (1997), 'Path dependence in regional development: persistence and change in three industrial clusters in Santa Catarina, Brazil', Paper presented at a workshop on Collective Efficiency at the Institute of Development Studies, Sussex University, April.

Mitullah, W.V. (1997), 'Firm interactions in Uhanya cluster: the dynamics of small scale fish processing', Paper presented at a workshop on Collective Efficiency at the Institute of Development Studies, Sussex University, April.

Nadvi, K. (1996), 'Small firm industrial districts in Pakistan', Doctoral thesis Institute of Development Studies, Sussex University.

Nadvi, K. (1999), 'Collective efficiency and collective failure', *World Development*, **27** (9), 1605–26.

Nadvi, K. and H. Schmitz (1994), 'Industrial clusters in less developed countries: review of experiences and research agenda', Discussion Paper, Nr. 339. Institute of Development Studies, Sussex University.

Pedersen, P.O., A. Sverrisson and M.P. van Dijk (eds) (1994), *Flexible Specialization. The Dynamics of Small-Scale Industries in the South*, London: Intermediate Technology Publications.

Pedersen, P.O. (1997), 'Clusters of enterprises within systems of production and distribution: collective efficiency and transaction costs', in M.P. van Dijk and

R. Rabellotti (eds), *Enterprise Clusters and Networks in Developing Countries*, London: Frank Cass, pp. 11-29.

Penn, R. (1994), 'Contemporary relationships between firms in a classic industrial locality', in J. Rubey and F. Wilkinson (eds), *Employment Strategy and the Labour Market*, Oxford: Oxford University Press.

Piore, M.J. and C.F. Sabel (1984), *The Second Industrial Divide*, New York: Basic Books.

Pollert, A. (1988), 'Dismantling flexibility', *Capital and Class*, **34**, pp. 42-75.

Porter, M.E. (1990), *The Competitive Advantage of Nations*, Hong Kong: Macmillan Press,

Pyke, F. and W. Sengenberger (eds) (1992), *Industrial Districts and Local Economic Regeneration*, Geneva: International Institute for Labour Studies.

Pyke, F., G. Becattini and W. Sengenberger (eds) (1990), *Industrial Districts and Inter-Firm Co-operation in Italy*, Geneva: International Institute for Labour Studies.

Rabellotti, R. (1993), 'Is there an industrial district model? A comparison of footwear districts in Italy and Mexico', Paper presented at a workshop on Intra-firm Reorganization in Third World Manufacturing Industry, Brighton, 14-16 April.

Rabellotti, R. (1994), 'Industrial districts in Mexico: the case of the footwear industry in Guadalajara and Leon', in Pedersen *et al.* (eds).

Rabellotti, R. (1995), 'Is there an "industrial district" model? Footwear districts in Italy and Mexico compared', *World Development*, **23** (1), pp. 29-41.

Rabellotti, R. (1997), 'Devaluation bonanza or something more? Increasing collective efficiency behind the recovery of the Mexican footwear clusters', Paper presented at a workshop on Collective Efficiency at the Institute of Development Studies, Sussex University, April.

Rao, K.V. (1993), 'Development in the Indian leather and leather-products industry', in I. Baud and G.A. de Bruije (eds), *Gender, Small-scale Industry and Development Policy*, London: Intermediate Technology Publications, pp. 151-69.

Rasmussen, J., H. Schmitz and M.P. van Dijk (eds) (1992), 'Flexible specialisation: a new view on small industry?', *IDS Bulletin*, **23** (3).

Sabel, C.F. (1992), 'Studied trust: building new forms of co-operation in a volatile economy', in F. Pyke and W. Sengenberger (eds), *Industrial Districts and Local Economic Regeneration*, Geneva: International Institute for Labour Studies, pp. 215-50.

Sabel, C. and J. Zeitlin (1985), 'Historical alternatives to mass production: politics, markets and technology in nineteenth-century industrialization', *Past and Present*, **108**, pp. 133-76.

Sandee, H. (1995), *Innovation Adoption in Rural Industry. Technological Change in Roof Tile Clusters in Central Java, Indonesia*, Amsterdam: Vrije Universiteit.

Schmitz, H. (1990), *Flexible Specialisation in Third World Industry: Prospects and Research Requirements*, Industrialization Seminar, No. 5, The Hague: Institute of Social Studies.

Schmitz, H. (1992), 'On the clustering of small firms', in Rasmussen *et al.* (eds).

Schmitz, H. (1993), 'Small shoemakers and Fordist giants: tale of a supercluster', *Discussion Paper*, No. 331, Institute of Development Studies, Sussex University.

Schmitz, H. (1995), 'Collective efficiency: growth path for small-scale industry', *Journal of Development Studies*, **31** (4), pp. 529-66.

Schmitz, H. (1997), 'Progress and failure in responding strategically to the new competition: cooperation and conflict in the Sinos Valley', Paper presented at a workshop on Collective Efficiency at the Institute of Development Studies, Sussex University, April.

Schmitz, H. and P. Knorringa (1999), 'Learning from global buyers', IDS Working Paper, No. 100. Institute of Development Studies, Sussex University.

Schmitz, H. and B. Musyck (1994), 'Industrial districts in Europe: policy lessons for developing countries?', *World Development*, **22** (6), pp. 889–910.

Sengenberger, W. and F. Pyke (1992), 'Small firm industrial districts and local economic regeneration: research and policy issues', in F. Pyke and W. Sengenberger (eds), *Industrial Districts and Local Economic Regeneration*, Geneva: International Institute for Labour Studies, pp. 3–30.

Smyth, I. (1992), 'Collective efficiency and selective benefits: the growth of the rattan industry of Tegalwangi (Indonesia)', in J. Rasmussen, H. Schmitz and M.P. van Dijk (eds), *Flexible Specialisation: A New View on Small Industry?*, IDS Bulletin, **23** (3), pp. 51–6.

Solinas, G. (1988), 'Productive structure and competitiveness in the Italian footwear industry', Paper presented at the 10th Conference of the International Working Party on Labour Market Segmentation, Porto: University of Porto.

Storper, M. (1993), 'Regional "worlds" of production: learning and innovation in the technology districts of France, Italy and the USA', *Regional Studies*, **27** (5), pp. 433–55.

Storper, M. and R. Walker (1989), *The Capitalist Imperative: Territory, Technology and Industrial Growth*, Oxford: Blackwell.

Swaminathan, P. and J. Jeyaranjan (1994), 'The knitwear cluster in Tiruppur: an Indian industrial district in the making?', Working Paper No. 126, Madras Institute of Development Studies.

Tavara, J.I. (1993), 'From survival activities to industrial strategies: local systems of interfirm cooperation in Peru', unpublished Ph.D., Massachusetts: Department of Economics, University of Massachusetts.

UNCTAD (1994), *Technological Dynamism in Industrial Districts: An Alternative Approach to Industrialization in Developing Countries?*, New York and Geneva: UNCTAD.

Weijland, H. (1994), 'Trade networks for flexible rural industry', in P.O. Pedersen, A. Sverrisson and M.P. van Dijk (eds), *Flexible Specialisation, The Dynamics of Small-scale Industries in the South*, London: Intermediate Technology Publications, pp. 97–110.

Zeitlin, J. (1990), 'Industrial districts and local economic regeneration: models, institutions and policies', Paper presented at a conference on Industrial Districts and Local Economic Regeneration, Geneva, October 1990.

PART II

Cases of SMEs and Innovation

4. Trying to innovate far from international frontiers: case study from the small-scale briquetting industry in India

Joy Clancy

Briquetting is the compression of loose organic waste materials, such as sawdust or rice husk, to a more compact form (*briquette*) that makes the waste into a marketable product as a substitute for fuelwood or coal. The technology for briquetting is not complex in the sense that it does not use microelectronics for its operation nor does it demand highly sophisticated operating conditions or techniques, such as a clean room or genetic engineering. It uses local materials as part of the process inputs. The equipment can be made in standard engineering workshops. Briquetting therefore can be considered as a particularly appropriate technology for indigenous production and use in rural areas of a developing country such as India. It is appropriate in the sense that mastery of the technology requires the type of skills that would be expected in a country with an existing metal working and mechanical engineering industry.

The briquettes are only intended for the internal (domestic) market. Industries which serve the indigenous market fall outside the mainstream of the literature on innovation which emphasizes that the competition arising from international trade is one of the most important stimulants to innovation (Lall, 1992). The focus has been on the science-based sectors such as electronic capital goods and biotechnology, and innovation has been considered only to take place at international frontiers. Cooper (1991) has pointed out that innovation also occurs in the 'traditional' sectors through using new technology rather than producing it. The briquetting industry can be allocated to this sector.

It can also be argued that competition to stimulate innovation potentially exists in the domestic fuel market in India. The market is sufficiently large to permit scales of production one would normally associate with an international market and therefore it is capable of stimulating efficiencies of production. Competition exists not only from other potential briquetting firms but also from a number of *well-established* alternative products (coal and fuelwood) as well as new options (liquefied petroleum gas (LPG) and natural gas)[1] that are more attractive to the consumer.[2] The consumer has already well-developed criteria concerning the requirements of the product to meet his or her needs and the entrepreneur has to meet those criteria to succeed. The consumer also already owns the equipment for burning a (usually solid) fuel and since this represents a major investment he or she will be reluctant to buy new equipment. The briquetting entrepreneur can therefore aim to offer a price (and supply availability) advantage over other solid fuels, and has an advantage over gaseous fuels as there is no requirement to invest in new conversion equipment. It is the former which is likely to produce the external stimulus for innovation.

Innovation in the type of industry that is both infant and orientated to the internal market, is one of a broad definition of creating adjustments to produce efficiency improvements. This encompasses not only improvements in hardware but also in organizational aspects, which are often ignored. Lall (1992) has proposed that innovation can then be taken to include all efforts towards technological mastery, adaptation of the technology to new conditions and improvements in the technology (either slight or significant). These require the development of appropriate technological capabilities at the firm level as well as at the national level. The stimulus for the development of technological capabilities comes from international trade. However, do these capabilities automatically transfer to those companies which are not operating at international frontiers? This chapter explores the level of the capabilities for innovation as they relate to the briquetting industry in India and attempts to gain an insight into whether or not technological capabilities are appearing in small-scale industries in India. At the time of the survey, briquetting technology was going through a second cycle of improving technological capabilities. Attempts at the beginning of the 1980s had failed. Indications are that weaknesses in technological capabilities at the firm level and in the external environment were contributing factors (Technology and Development Group, 1990).

APPROACH

This chapter focuses on the innovative capabilities of briquette producers rather than the equipment producers and is based on two surveys (Noordman, 1992; and Post, 1995) within the briquetting industry as well as supporting data from a later fieldwork in the small-scale dyestuffs industry in India (Lakmaaker, 1998). The objectives are to explore the level of capabilities at the firm level and to identify if there are constraints to innovation within the briquetting industry, either intrafirm and/or in the external environment. In the first survey open-ended interviews were carried out with key informants from the different stakeholder groups: governmental agencies, non-governmental agencies, research institutes, financial institutes and manufacturers of briquetting plants. These data, plus additional material from secondary sources, have been used to assess the national level of technological capability (Noordman, 1992). The interviews were complemented by visits to seven briquetting plants in different parts of the country for more detailed data collection to assess the technological capabilities. Structured questionnaires were used to interview the managing directors (who were also generally the owners) of each plant. Each plant was visited twice. A year later a follow-up survey was made of 20 additional plants (Post, 1995). In both surveys it often proved difficult to interview more junior staff due to reluctance by the management. Where it was possible, the manager would sometimes insist on being present which may have influenced the responses. Similar problems were encountered by Lakmaaker (1998) in his surveys in the dyestuffs industry. The interviewer therefore had to use visual observation to try to verify some of the statements.

Firms were usually operating with only one press and so there was generally no differentiation into different departments. More than half of the sample were using presses from the same manufacturer. No plants were annexed to major agro-processing industries. Six plants were operating only on sawdust, while four plants were not using sawdust as a feedstock. The rest were using a mixture. The briquetting plants surveyed were selected on the basis that they had been operating for more than a year. This was to ensure that any problems associated with initial start-up had been overcome and that the operators should have mastered the technology. They should be at the stage where they are making innovations to improve efficiency and improve product quality.

The chapter begins with a short description of the fuel market in India where briquetting entrepreneurs wish to enter. This is followed by a description of the technology characteristics since these have implications for technology selection, the process parameters that need to be understood (in order to pass beyond the black box operation phase) and the organizational aspects of the process engineering. A brief history of briquetting in India is given to provide some insight into weaknesses within firms for absorbing new technologies to which the external environment should have reacted. The briquetting firms are then analysed in terms of their technological capabilities using a framework suggested by Lall (1992). This is followed by an analysis of the external environment in India.

THE MARKET BRIQUETTING ENTREPRENEURS ARE TRYING TO ENTER

Entrepreneurs in India see a potentially lucrative product in briquettes. Briquetting uses as an input material (agricultural residues) that is available in enormous quantities in India and in many cases is a nuisance to the owner since its disposal is an added cost. Therefore the input material is perceived as being available at low cost. Everyone needs energy, therefore the size of the potential market in India is huge, and energy is in short supply. Both households and industry use solid fuels for their process heat requirements. The choice is influenced very much by location. Industry close to the coalfields in Bihar tends to use coal, as do many households. The further from the coalfields, the greater is the disruption in supply and the more wood is used by industries, particularly small- and medium-scale industries. Households use a variety of biomass fuels (wood, agricultural residues, cow dung) with a distinct difference between rural and urban households, with the former still operating predominantly in a non-monetary market, while the latter has a predominantly commercial market, with a distinct class structure to the selection. It is important to note that the coal is generally of low quality and supply is subject to disruption (the more pronounced, the further from Bihar) which creates difficulties for industry. There is evidence to suggest that industries in India would be prepared to pay a premium for an alternative fuel which is of good quality and of regular supply. The solid fuel market in India is not homogeneous. Different categories of customers will have different requirements for their fuels. An entrepreneur attempting to enter this market should have an understanding of the market structure to ensure that the correct technology capable of supplying the product to meet customers' requirements is selected.

CHARACTERISTICS OF THE TECHNOLOGY THAT ENTREPRENEURS HAVE TO MASTER

The properties of a fuel depend upon its physical and chemical properties. Fuels are generally selected on their combustion and ignition characteristics and their suitability for handling. The former depend upon the type and moisture content of the raw material while the latter depends upon mechanical properties due to the pressure and temperature during compression and the moisture content of the raw material.

There are a number of different technologies available which can compress biomass into briquettes. Each technology produces products with specific characteristics. The technology can be divided into low- and high-pressure briquetting which produce briquettes with different densities and hence different properties. Low-pressure briquetting requires a binder to be added to the biomass material before compression to give a stable form to the briquette. Binders can improve the combustion properties although household users have complained about the smell when molasses (the most common binder) has been used, which has led to their rejection by some users. If the user requires a smokeless fuel the biomass needs to be carbonized. With a low-pressure technology, the material needs to be carbonized before compression.

High-pressure briquetting uses no external binder but uses one to the constituents of biomass to function as a binder. There are a number of technical options, producing briquettes with different properties:

- piston press
- screw extruder
- pellet press
- roller press

The piston press produces briquettes that are prone to breaking and they cannot be carbonized (the lack of added binder also means that pre-carbonized material cannot be used). The screw press produces briquettes that are stronger[3] and have better combustion characteristics than the piston press. Both technologies are usually dimensioned to produce briquettes with a diameter in the region of 50mm. The pellet press produces much smaller briquettes and is based on the technology for producing cattle fodder. The roller press uses a binder and has been extensively used for coal and charcoal fines.

The raw material often has to undergo some form of pre-treatment before it can be compressed. The preparation can involve a number of different stages, for example:

- shredding and grinding to reduce the particle size of the biomass
- drying of the biomass to reduce its moisture content
- screening the raw material to remove impurities such as stones and small pieces of metal.

Low-density briquettes have to be dried after compression, while high-density briquettes have to be cooled.

The scale of briquetting is flexible. Presses have throughputs of a few hundred kilograms to a tonne per hour. It is possible to operate commercially with one machine. The maximum number of machines is strongly dependent on the flow of raw material to the plant. Commercial briquetting requires energy inputs in the form of mechanical energy and process heat. It is common to use electricity to provide the mechanical drive. In India, grid electricity is subject to disruption and this can cause variable amounts of down-time (depending upon the technology) since the biomass jams in the press and has to be removed before operation can begin again.

Both the piston and screw presses were designed and optimized for operation on sawdust, which has a particular particle size and moisture content. Both these parameters are important for producing good briquettes. Any biomass material can be used for briquettes. However, biomass comes in different physical forms (compare, for example, rice husk and maize cob) and varies in its moisture content and to some extent in its chemical composition (most notably silica and ash). This means that there are different requirements for pre-treatment and that the material can cause different amounts of wear within the press. The production output is lower with other residues compared to sawdust, which influences profitability.

Residues are also seasonal which can influence the need for storage and therefore affects profitability. Collection of residues and ensuring sufficient supply are also important in influencing profitability. Many residues generated on the fields are already part of the agricultural system and those that are not utilized have no mechanized means of collection. Annexation to agro-processing industries such as rice mills and wood sawmills would be a lower risk venture. The market for residues is not static and new competitors can enter the market due to resource constraints or environmental pressures. For example, rice husk has been one of the most popular alternatives to sawdust as a briquetting feed stock; however, in India there is a lucrative market for rice husk as a feedstock for the production of the chemical intermediate furfural.

BRIEF HISTORY OF BRIQUETTING IN INDIA

Since the beginning of the 1980s there have been three different types of briquetting technologies introduced into India: PARU, screw extruder and piston press. PARU technology uses a binder with carbonized biomass to produce charcoal briquettes. The technology was developed by the Indian Institute of Technology (IIT) in Delhi and is therefore an indigenously developed technology. A number of companies were licensed to produce the equipment. Between 1982 and 1986, 70 entrepreneurs bought the technology. All but six or seven of these plants became non-functional within three months to two years of start-up, and there are none now in operation. This high failure rate was attributed to the licensees using inferior materials in the construction of the equipment (to increase their profit margins) and altering the design without consultation with IIT (Reines, 1986). Lack of operating instructions, insufficient training of operators and inadequate maintenance and management were also contributing factors. The process seems to have been brought to market as a commercial product when it should have been classified as a pilot project.

Entrepreneurs in South India imported twenty screw extruders from Taiwan. Although the briquettes were well accepted by the customers, there was excessive wear in the press due to the use of rice husk (a particularly abrasive material) as the feedstock. Only one functioning plant using this technology was found during the survey work. There was one manufacturer of screw extrusion briquetting presses at the time of the survey that had supplied equipment to 12 companies. The screw extruder is considered to be more appropriate to the Indian electricity supply situation since the down-time associated with power disruption is significantly less than that for a piston press (half an hour compared to four hours). The disadvantages of this type of press are the higher investment costs compared to the piston press and the need for skilled welding to repair the screw.

The piston press is the technology that has been most widely used on a commercial basis in India with any degree of success. The technology was first introduced in India in 1981 with the importation of a piston press produced by a Swiss company, Fred Hausmann Corporation. Although a few more Hausmann presses were imported, there was no major importation since the costs proved prohibitive. However, a number of manufacturers saw an opportunity for producing a product with a good potential market. At the time of the survey, there were four manufacturers of piston presses, with one company having a market domination. In 1993, 35 plants were identified using these indigenously produced plants. Plant owners had reported a range of operating experiences and not all plants were functioning profitably.

TECHNOLOGICAL CAPABILITIES WITHIN BRIQUETTING FIRMS

All firms in the surveys had had difficulties in assimilating the equipment. Many of these difficulties amounted to more than trouble-shooting due to the non-optimal state of the equipment rather than planned technological effort. All firms therefore had to undertake considerable technological effort to improve their efficiencies. Some were more successful than others. Two had ceased operation but were willing to continue if solutions could be found to their technical problems.[4] One entrepreneur felt that he had mastered the technology and was beginning production of his own presses.

Mastery of the technology as an indicator of technical capabilities appears to be poor when measured using the capacity utilization factor. The average value was 45 per cent (the best plant was operating at 67 per cent) which is considerably less than the 75 per cent considered feasible by expert opinion. Low capacity utilization is not uncommon in developing countries, the reasons lying both exogenous to the firm and in-house (Katrak, 1997). The reasons for the low capacity utilization in the briquetting industry in India were identified as (Noordman, 1992; Post, 1995):

- Poor availability (seasonality)
- Cost
- Vulnerability of stored material
- High moisture content of biomass

Technology

- Jamming of ram in die-holder
- Wear in press
- Space required for drying and storage
- High maintenance costs
- Non-standard parts

Markets

- Stimulating the market
- Dependency on one client
- Cost of briquettes compared to other solid fuels
- Intermittent production causing marketing problems
- Clients with different specifications

Other problems

- Poor communications between stakeholders
- Poor aftersales service of equipment manufacturers
- Electricity supply disruption
- High electricity costs
- Distance to repair facility
- Spare part availability
- Poor product quality
- Mismatch between press and auxiliary equipment
- Seasonal labour shortages

Exogenous problems: power shortages, monsoon, non-availability of spare parts locally, *in-house problems*: lack of working capital, lack of customers, mismatch of auxiliary equipment, lack of preventative maintenance, organizational inefficiency.

Each firm displayed at least two of these factors. The innovations to solve the problems can either be technical or organizational and usually there exists a choice of solutions. Figure 4.1 illustrates the range of options for one of these problems, the jamming of the ram in the piston press die holder. Which solutions an entrepreneur will select depends upon the capabilities inhouse or that are available through the external environment. Even for some of the problems classified as exogenous there are possible inhouse solutions if the capabilities exist. For example, the monsoon was a problem for an entrepreneur who used solar drying. Investment in a drying system would have resulted in a much better capacity utilization factor and the return on the investment in the additional equipment would have been repaid.[5] In this case there is a weakness in the organizational/management skills. If sensible interventions are to be designed then it is important to disaggregate the inhouse skills in order to identify the nature of the weaknesses. Entrepreneurs tended to concentrate on technical solutions, whereas many organizational solutions could have been implemented at lower cost.

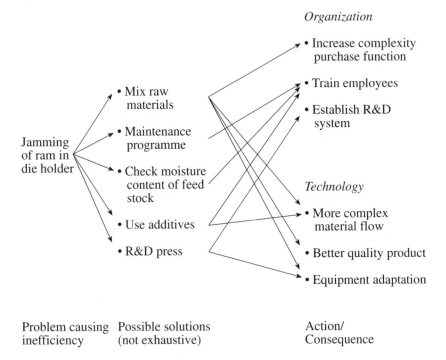

Figure 4.1   Possible solutions for the problem of a piston press die holder

In order for a firm to function as an organization it has to integrate the various components of its technological capabilities successfully: technical skills, knowledge and management/organizational skills. For a briquetting firm the feedstock inputs have to conform to technical specifications to produce good quality briquettes.[6] Presses have been optimized around sawdust and the use of different raw materials alters process parameters and influences product quality. The most important parameters of the raw material are the moisture content (a key parameter influencing briquette quality and functioning of the press, and hence company profitability), particle size and contamination by extraneous material (for example with stones). These requirements vary with the technology form. To enable the feedstock to meet the press specifications requires good performance from the auxiliary equipment (dryer, grinder and sieve) and that their capacities match those of the press. The raw materials have to reach the plant at an appropriate rate to keep storage costs down but they should not create a bottleneck and reduce capacity utilization. This is a more difficult problem for firms that are not annexed to a major producer of residues, such as a sawmill. The organizational complexity increases with the different number of residues used as feedstock. The briquettes have to meet users' requirements based on which market for briquettes has to be developed.

Lall (1992) analysed the intrafirm technological capabilities in terms of *investment*, *production* and *linkage* capabilities. *Investment* capabilities are those skills which lead to the establishment of the enterprise rather than a narrow definition of access to financial resources. While it might be tempting to think that these are purely management skills in terms of ability to carry out, for example, feasibility studies and negotiate contracts, there is also a requirement for technical knowledge. The feasibility study is important in determining the market characteristics including the potential clients' product requirements. These specifications then need to be translated into technical requirements. This needs some prior knowledge of both the process and product, for example, the influence of raw material characteristics on the product quality and process. The choice of raw material has a significant influence on the financial viability of the plant. Therefore, general engineering knowledge would not be sufficient, but some more specific knowledge related to densification of materials would enable a better evaluation of the viability of a plant.[7]

The investment capabilities amongst briquetting entrepreneurs appear to be weak. Noordman (1992) found evidence of only one feasibility study, which led to the rejection of the project by the potential entrepreneur. Although the more extensive second survey did not deal specifically with this issue, it can be deduced *a priori* that if such studies exist, they were not well done. Either situation exhibits a weakness in investment capabilities. At least four of the plants reported labour supply problems during the harvest periods. Since briquetting plants are generally located in rural areas, fluctuations in labour availability should hardly have come as a surprise. Another plant was not operating due to a lack of customers for briquettes. Leffers (1993) found in a feasibility study of six briquetting plants that four were operating with a negative net present value (NPV), one marginally and only one with a positive NPV. The need for good feasibility studies in the context of this technology would therefore be self-evident. In addition, any technological search should have produced evidence based on the indigenous experience with the PARU technology that problems were likely to be encountered. This poor attention to basic sound business planning is of particular concern, since three owners had a Bachelor's Degree in Commerce and two had a Master's Degree.

Production capabilities are the skills to assimilate the product and process, followed at a later stage by adaptation and R&D. General engineering knowledge is needed to operate the press and its auxiliary equipment, of when to replace parts, on how to re-weld parts and to undertake a maintenance programme. Knowledge specific to briquetting is the optimization of a material mix. For example, mixing with other residues can reduce wear in the press from using rice husk, although this also alters other parameters, both technical and organizational. A briquetting plant can be operated successfully with only formalized knowledge, that is knowledge which is either experienced based or externally formulated (for example, from the equipment producer or consultants). It is the know-how of the input requirements and an ability to follow a detailed prescription of the process operations. The firm should have the capabilities to identify differences in product quality to assess the commercial value of the product. This is possible if the process technology has been well developed and is a commercially mature technology. This is indeed what many of the entrepreneurs who have taken up briquetting had thought that they were acquiring. However, this was far from the case. Most of the available presses were based on reverse engineering (copies of imported technology) and which had not been fully optimized. This meant that if the entrepreneurs were to improve their efficiency they would actively have to undertake technological effort, in other words innovate. All firms reported that they had to undertake R&D, however this was more at the level of de-bugging. To succeed, they would need more specialized knowledge which can either be inhouse or exogenous to the firm. The specialized knowledge can be considered *partially derived*[8] in the sense that it does not require an understanding of the fundamentals of science or engineering (*derived* knowledge), in this case of mechanical engineering and materials. Partially derived knowledge is an ability to understand the relationships between cause and effect of operations, for example, the influence of moisture content of briquette quality. This type of knowledge can be considered weak within the firms surveyed. For example, at least five of the firms did not posses a moisture meter and did not consider it important to monitor moisture content, a property which has a significant influence on product quality.

Possession of derived knowledge (*know-why*) allows a scientific determination and adaptation of the operational requirements to enable the development of new products or improvements in the technology. For example, in the case of briquetting, an understanding of the causes of wear could be used to develop new surface facings in the press to reduce wear. It would be surprising to find this type of knowledge within briquette producing firms, given their size, although one might expect it in the press manufacturers. Indeed, the machine supplier is an important source of knowledge for the briquetting entrepreneur and it is in the press manufacturers' own interests to interact with their customers in the innovation process as part of their own efforts. However, contact with manufacturers was poor. Entrepreneurs also searched outside the firm for assistance, although they were hampered by the lack of specialized knowledge on briquetting within India and could not afford international expert assistance. One owner did manage to buy in expertise from a competitor by offering a financial inducement to an experienced technical employee.

Linkage capabilities are the skills needed to transmit information, skills and technology to, and receive from, all external parties the firm interacts with, for example suppliers, contractors, consultants and technology institutes. These were variable but overall could be regarded as weak. Entrepreneurs seemed well bedded into their local communities, which is hardly surprising since they were mainly family-run firms in rural areas. They were able to identify and select good quality welding and repair workshops. However, they were not effective at searching outside this community. There was a tendency to rely on family and friends to provide technical support, although this may be as a result of the negative image of R&D institutions rather than the absence of a particular skill within the firms. Poor matching of equipment indicated not only a lack of process skills but also an inability to discuss requirements with suppliers. Negotiation skills with the manufacturers of the presses also failed to reveal the level of development of the technology and to extract conditions for technological support.

The organization of an enterprise combines knowledge and techniques to yield a product of commercial value. The form of organization has an influence on the operational capabilities. The briquetting industry in India is solely in the small-scale sector. Firms are predominantly family-run enterprises.[9] The organization is generally characterized as hierarchical, with a minimum of explicit organizational procedures and centralized decision making by the managing director who is usually the owner (Noordman, 1992).

The lower levels in the hierarchy are not expected to deploy initiatives outside of their job description. Although the level of knowledge of people lower down the hierarchy is often greater than that of the owner, they are not consulted in the decision making.[10] This is unfortunate since it stifles one of the factors in innovation: human nature. The particular characteristics of curiosity (*what happens if I do this?*) and laziness (*there must be an easier way to do this!*) are driving forces in innovation (Cooke and Mayes, 1996). It also seems that the lessons from the failure of firms using the PARU technology have not been learnt (Reines, 1986).

EXTERNAL ENVIRONMENT

Government Policies and Incentives

The briquetting industry falls under two priority sectors within government policy: energy and small-scale industries. The main support to the briquetting industry at the government level has been through the Department of Non-Conventional Energy Sources (DNES) which is part of the Ministry of Power and Non-Conventional Energy Sources. This department is responsible for the implementation of the policies and programmes which fall under its remit. Biomass is one of the renewable energies which have received support and in this regard DNES has funded a number of studies and supported R&D on briquetting. DNES considers that there is a good potential for briquetting and has been keen to identify a good technology suitable for any material other than sawdust. The Department took steps to try to ensure that briquetting retained a good name after the problems with the PARU technology in the early 1980s. It commissioned a study to see if it was possible to rehabilitate the equipment; however, this turned out to be too costly and no further action was taken.

The Ministry of Industry was also active in its support to briquetting entrepreneurs through the National Small Industries Corporation Ltd based in New Delhi which developed a piston press. Entrepreneurs who bought the press expressed dissatisfaction due to jamming of the die, linked to frequent power disruption, and most were abandoned.

A number of financial incentives both at national and state level were available to entrepreneurs wishing to take up briquetting. One hundred per cent depreciation of the total value of the plant and machinery is allowed in the first year after start-up. Briquettes were exempted from excise duty and a number of states exempted them from sales tax. Financial institutions were allowed to offer loans at low rates of interest for capital goods and working capital (see below). DNES established a national level financial institution specifically to administer loans for all projects in the renewable energy sector. No licence was required to establish a briquetting plant.

At the time of the survey, equipment and machinery for briquetting were not treated so favourably. There were no tax exemptions. Indeed the import taxes on briquetting presses proved prohibitive to their importation. Indigenous manufacturers therefore responded to the policy of import substitution and by the process of reverse engineering began to produce piston presses. Even though this form of the technology requires no highly specialized engineering skills or advanced equipment, there have been complaints from all entrepreneurs about the quality of the presses (for example, Grover, 1990; and Post, 1995). Parts were often non-standard and there were long delays in the supply of parts by manufacturers. One entrepreneur in our survey owned an imported Hausmann machine and two other types of presses indigenously produced. He reported that the indigenous products could not match the imported product.[11]

Finance

DNES established the Indian Renewable Development Energy Agency (IREDA) in 1987 with the remit to provide soft loans to (co-)finance renewable energy projects. Briquetting is one of the technologies qualifying. At the time of the survey, IREDA had sanctioned around 28 projects, with financing for capital equipment costs. However, many of these plants faced a number of problems including poor operation, high conversion costs, frequent breakdowns and poor capacity utilization (Naidu, 1996). In response, IREDA decided to establish a facility to provide back-up technical support to the briquette manufacturers it financed. In 1994, the School of Energy, Bharathidasan University, Tiruchirapalli in Tamil asked Nadu to establish a 'Technical Back up Cell' which identified what modifications to the technology were required to overcome these problems. In addition, a consultancy firm was hired to conduct a diagnostic study on non-IREDA assisted briquetting projects.

There are a number of other financial institutions, both private and government, for investment in briquetting. There is however a constantly heard complaint from entrepreneurs that loan applications to these institutions (including IREDA) take a long time and the procedures are cumbersome.[12] This means that entrepreneurs use other sources of finance, including their own resources. The disadvantage is that there is frequently no requirement to produce a business plan/feasibility study which is required for an IREDA loan. Briquetting plants have experienced severe unforeseen problems after starting up. A number experienced problems with working capital. The price of the inputs did not develop as expected or the market did not react to the product as expected. These are the factors which would be assessed as part of a business plan and could have done much either to prevent wasted investment or allow corrective measures to be taken in advance. In the surveys carried out for the Technology and Development Group, entrepreneurs in five of the twenty-four companies[13] reported poor availability and/or cost of the raw material as a problem. Biomass raw material cost has been identified as one of the most significant factors influencing the profitability of briquetting plants (Leffers, 1993; Technology and Development Group, University of Twente, 1995). Entrepreneurs did not seem to see the need for business plans or feasibility studies (see below). Cooke and Mayes (1996) have identified the business plan as one of the key tools of the innovation process.

Skills

The skills level can be considered from three perspectives, within the firm, manufacturers of presses and workshops for repair and spare parts provision. Within the firms surveyed the owners had mixed educational backgrounds, including degrees in commerce and engineering. Two owners were retired military officers. In small firms the background of the owner is considered significant since this is where decision making resides within the firm. In our survey there appeared to be no distinct correlation. Owners of one plant whose education level classified them as semi-skilled (knowledge gained through experience) had managed to reverse-engineer a press and had gone into production.[14] Another owner with a Bachelor's degree in commerce had made a technical modification to his press and had succeeded in improving the efficiency as well as reducing maintenance costs. However, another owner with a similar degree had problems in reading technical drawings.

Technical support came from a number of sources. Some owners were able to solve problems themselves and several were interested in the process and engaged in technological efforts to master the technology. Only three firms in the sample appeared to have in-house technical support. Other sources were also consulted including relatives, friends and universities. One press manufacturer appeared to be very active in providing support. The major supplier was variable in its response to requests for help. One firm had no inhouse technical support and, having failed to locate exogenous support, was not operating.

All of the factories in the sample employed either skilled or semi-skilled labour[15] to operate and maintain the press. In this case a skilled employee has, after the basic primary education, either followed a course at an Industrial Training Institute (ITI) for two years or has a Diploma in Engineering after three years of study at an Engineering School. Unskilled labour were generally illiterate or had had only very basic schooling. Unskilled labour carried out menial tasks such as handling the raw material. Firms provided on-the-job training for their employees. Training outside the firm was not considered appropriate or beneficial. Engineers with degrees were regarded as too expensive and not practical enough.[16]

The skills in the manufacturing companies supplying the presses were clearly not up to international competitive standards since they were not able to reverse-engineer equipment which consists solely of mechanical moving parts and which requires no special materials. The presses they produced were more at the level of pilot projects. There is nothing wrong with a manufacturer building up their own technological capabilities through this route, however it requires good interaction with the entrepreneurs who have bought the equipment and it needs to be made clear from the start that what has been acquired is not off-the-shelf technology. This type of communication was lacking, although one of the smaller press manufacturers was reported to give good support. Perhaps a form of operating the equipment under licence at this stage would have been more effective.

Workshops are available throughout India, from small villages to large metropolitan centres. However, there are differences in the level and range of their work, its quality, as well as the equipment at their disposal. Larger centres have specialized workshops. Workshops with links to agriculture demonstrate a technical capability to adapt to the properties of crops grown in the region, for example cottonseed will require a different type of oil press to groundnuts. Entrepreneurs were able to differentiate between and identify those workshops of sufficient quality to manufacture their spare parts. The search process could be quite time-consuming. Location of workshops capable of carrying out the specialized tungsten carbide welding, which is required for repairing the screw in the screw press, to a high standard were also found to be readily available in larger towns (Technology and Development Group, 1995).

Institutional Support

Since briquetting firms are small-scale enterprises their in-house capabilities for problem solving will be resource limited (both capital and labour). Therefore, in order to develop technological capabilities, briquetting entrepreneurs need some form of institutional support.

A number of actors have been involved in R&D related to briquetting. There appears to have been little attempt to co-ordinate these activities. IREDA only established the Technical Back-up Cell after the firms with which they had loans got into difficulties. The Back-Up Cell is based in Tamil Nadu whereas entrepreneurs are dispersed across India, which would require concerted efforts to communicate with them.

Noordman (1992) found a gap between the research carried out by research institutions and the type of research needed to improve the performance of briquetting plants. The research was felt to focus more on the long-term development of the industry than on meeting the current needs of the briquetting entrepreneurs. This type of criticism of the relationship between R&D institutes is common (see Katrak, 1997).

The communication between the different actors involved in briquetting was found to be minimal. Exchange of information and experience between entrepreneurs, equipment manufacturers, research institutes and government agencies was done on an *ad hoc* basis. Since briquetting is a new industry and the numbers of firms established is less than 100, a critical mass has not been reached for the establishment of a branch organization. The wide distribution of entrepreneurs in a country the size of India with poor telecommunications makes contact difficult.

Infrastructure

Energy resources in India are subject to disruption. This provides, on the one hand, an opportunity for briquetting entrepreneurs by allowing them to offer a continuous supply of a good quality fuel as an alternative to coal. On the other hand, frequent disruptions to power supplies create problems for users of piston presses leading to low capacity utilization factors due to the time taken to dismantle the press to un-jam it.

The raw materials are indigenous and sustainable. Variations in supply are predictable in terms of annual flows, although there may be variations in crop yield from year to year due to the weather. Communications are poor and the distances large, which hinders contact between the briquetting entrepreneur and press manufacturers, as well as other institutional support.

DISCUSSION AND CONCLUSIONS

From the survey results presented here it is too early to distinguish truly entrepreneurial firms since most were still trouble-shooting and probably were not past the start-up phase, despite having been in operation for more than a year. This supports the idea that acquisition of technological capabilities is a slow process, even those skills required for the broader definition of innovation used here as 'adjustments to create efficiency improvements'. The spread of capacity utilization factors indicates that technological efficiency varies from firm to firm. These variations are due to the lack of technological capabilities within the firms and weaknesses in the external environment, as well as being policy induced.

Technological capabilities can be divided into investment, process and linkage capabilities. The firms themselves had weaknesses in all three areas. The most serious were:

- Lack of basic business skills (for example failure to carry out feasibility studies)
- Lack of partially derived knowledge (for example failure to understand key parameters that affected product quality)
- Lack of organizational skills (for example failure to ensure sufficient supply of raw materials)
- Poor communication with suppliers and customers (for example failure to size and match equipment components)

These weaknesses reinforce each other to inhibit innovation. Among the causes or barriers to innovation identified by Cooke and Mayes (1996) are:

- Management attitudes
- Poor information flows
- Weak links with customers and suppliers

These have all been identified in the firms surveyed.

The influence of management attitude on the creation of efficiency improvements appears in a number of ways. All but one of the firms was owner-managed. Lecraw (1978) states that an advantage of an owner-managed firm is that they should have good organization efficiency because the owner has direct access to the firms' information flows and is in a position to make decisions. However, this presupposes that the owner-manager also has the appropriate skills to assess the options and take decisions or is open to suggestions from subordinates. The findings in these surveys and in other work carried out by the Technology and Development Group are that organizational aspects, such as procedures for the procurement of raw materials, establishment of monitoring systems, inventory management, and maintenance schedules, were missing. Poor record-keeping can of course be a deliberate management strategy to frustrate authorities.

It is well known that most enterprises in developing countries invest little in upgrading the skills of their employees (Lall, 1993), yet training is one of the mechanisms of acquiring technical and managerial skills. The attitude of managers in our surveys was negative to training outside the firm. Most of the training was given on the job which was basically operation of the press as a black-box. Skills could be bought in as and when required to cover deficiencies. This was a short-sighted approach given the lack of general experience with briquetting in India. The reason given for not providing employees with the opportunity to upgrade skills is that trained employees may leave the firm. Given the weaknesses identified in the technological capabilities which were linked to lack of technical knowledge, the reluctance to upgrade skills may be due to managers not being aware of the levels of skills needed. Reines (1986) had clearly identified a lack of understanding of the requirements for operating a briquetting plant as a contributing factor in the failure to assimilate the PARU technology.

Learning-by-doing has often been cited as a mechanism that can lead to technological learning and the development of technological capabilities. However, an important aspect of this mechanism is: who is doing the 'doing' and 'learning'? Are they in a position to influence the innovation process? Operation of the equipment was under the supervision of operators who were classified as skilled or semi-skilled and certainly capable of learning by doing. Those who were interviewed had ideas for improvements in the operation of the plant (and not only in terms of the hardware), that is they knew how to innovate. However, the culture inside the firms did not lend itself to junior staff members contributing ideas or suggestions, particularly if they lay outside areas of their direct responsibility.

Romijn (1997) has pointed out that only a small part of technological effort takes the form of formal R&D by specialized engineers. The effort predominantly consists of practical shop-floor-based problem solving involved in setting, running, maintaining, repairing and making minor changes to technology in response to local conditions. This means that small-scale industries should be able to engage in technological effort which will lead to innovation. Romijn appears to imply a rather hardware-orientated approach to technological effort which neglects the need to upgrade organization and management skills.

The linkages with customers and suppliers were weak. There was no attempt to understand the market fully as can be seen by the lack of business plans and feasibility studies. Entrepreneurs took an opportunistic approach when they perceived a need created by disruptions in energy supply and the availability of loans below market rates to take up briquetting. Feedback from customers was regarded as irrelevant since as the market was so huge, it was assumed that there would be plenty of people who would be prepared to buy their product. However, the market turned out to be more sophisticated than had been realized and not a straightforward matter of price competition. It came as a surprise to entrepreneurs when customers cared about product quality and how it performed in their conversion equipment, and not just about product availability at a cheap price. Technologies were acquired without fully understanding the parameter affecting the product quality and so entrepreneurs were in a weak position to respond. Entrepreneurs showed considerable deficiency in their investment capabilities when dealing with the equipment suppliers. Their lack of technical knowledge and negotiating skills contributed to them acquiring a technology that was not mature and for which there was no readily accessible support system in the external environment. Their own small size would make it difficult to find solutions to many of these problems alone since many required derived or partially derived knowledge.

Entrepreneurs were able to seek out workshops capable of producing good quality spares and carrying out repairs. However, these were usually in the local environment. When the need to search further afield for solutions to problems requiring derived or partially derived knowledge, they were not so successful.

In the external environment two major factors have been a barrier to innovation in the briquetting industry: the roles of the briquetting press manufacturers and R&D institutions. The indigenous technology presented to the Indian market was not mature, although on the world market there is a choice of technologies and suppliers being used by profitable companies. Local producers tried to copy imported technology. While this might be regarded as an effort towards developing technological capability and adapting the technology to local conditions, the results were below standard. Producers have been known to substitute raw materials when building the presses. Ishikawa (1985, quoted in Romijn, 1997) considers this to result from a lack of knowledge about the properties of different metals and the stresses they have to be able to withstand when the equipment is in use. This is certainly the case with the indigenously produced piston press, where the failure to calculate the stresses incurred during compression have been identified as a major cause of problems (Naidu, 1996).

The fact that the technology was not mature, means that the manufacturers will need to provide more support to the briquetting entrepreneurs, not only to satisfy the client but also to build their own technological capabilities and to innovate. General knowledge about briquetting was not readily available in India and a number of entrepreneurs had tried to search for help. This made the support by the manufacturer even more important. However, this support has in general been poor. Contacts between manufacturers and clients seems to have a correlation with distance. The shorter the physical distance between the entrepreneur and the manufacturer enterprises, the more likely the entrepreneur was to receive support. Some entrepreneurs were left to their own devices. Whilst this must have added considerably to their efforts to build their own technological capabilities, this cannot have been without cost to the individual firm. Some firms had had to cease operation because they had insufficient inhouse capabilities. Since some of the problems were due to factors which would require derived knowledge to solve, then, it was not surprising that firms have not been able to achieve acceptable levels of efficiency.

This institutional support has also been found to be weak. The Government was still interested in developing briquetting as an energy source, however it did not appear to take steps to learn the lessons from the evaluation of the failures of the PARU technology. It was left to IREDA to try to establish a back-up unit to try to assist entrepreneurs with their problems. However, this was not until after problems emerged which could have been predicted based on the experiences with the PARU technology. The unit was based in Tamil Nadu and, while there are a number of entrepreneurs in Tamil Nadu, many are located in states further away, for example, Punjab and Uttar Pradesh. It is rather symptomatic of the lack of co-ordination within the briquetting sector that the establishment of such a unit was left to a financing agency. Also IIT Delhi which had developed considerable expertise in briquetting was not asked to fulfil this function. The back-up units have taken the approach of tackling problems only from a hardware perspective. Communication between different actors in the briquetting industry was minimal. Exchange of information and experiences between all actors was on an *ad hoc* basis. The reasons for this are poor infrastructure (telecommunications and transport), the size of the country, lack of institutionalized lines of communication and the actors not knowing each other.

Three significant policy-induced constraints can be identified: import restrictions, fiscal incentives, and lack of early response to previous problems with briquetting technology. The import restrictions hindered optimal technological choices being made. The screw press is better suited than the piston press to the power conditions in India. However, the problems encountered with the piston press were not entirely related to the die jamming when the power failed, and higher capacity utilization factors could have been anticipated even under these circumstances. Whichever press was chosen it would have needed to be adapted to local conditions. For example, the screw press has given much higher wear rates with sawdust in India than in Europe. Indian sawdust shows much higher levels of contamination than that in Europe. Perhaps manufacturing the presses under licence, as initially had happened with the Hausmann machines and one manufacturer, would have allowed for a more systematic development of technological capabilities.

The fiscal incentives include low loan rates offered to entrepreneurs wishing to establish briquetting plants, and tax advantages to investors in this priority sector. These incentives have attracted a number of players who were purely opportunistic. Access to these loans did not seem to require comprehensive feasibility studies or business plans. In addition, the lending institutions' own capabilities for assessing a new technology were insufficient.

The government did not learn from the lessons with the PARU technology, particularly the need to address non-hardware aspects. It has continued to take a top–down approach to the development of the briquetting industry.

Availability of raw materials, technologies and potential markets are assessed at the national level. In a country the size and diversity of India this will lead to inaccuracies since its significant regional differences become blurred. Research has been controlled at a central level from Delhi. As a consequence it is remote from entrepreneurs and does not respond to local needs nor learn from local experiences. There is a particular need to co-ordinate information and experiences.

In conclusion, it can be said that all is not well far from international frontiers of trade. There seem to be problems with the diffusion of metalworking skills and mechanical engineering knowledge in smaller manufacturing units. Assimilation and adaptation of technology, even of not particularly complex technology, in order to meet local needs is still encountering difficulties. Technology still appears to be equated with hardware whereas many of the problems in the small-scale industry sector are linked to management and organizational problems. The government also appears only to consider the problem as one of improving the hardware.

At the level of the firm it is obvious that maturation is not achieved passively, effortlessly and automatically. It requires explicit technological effort to produce changes in processes, procedures and organizational arrangements. Small-scale enterprises find capability development very difficult, slow and expensive to undertake, because they are starting at a lower level of capability. Amongst the briquetting firms it has left some with poor abilities to operate efficiently and some have had to abandon their operations. This represents a waste of resources. Entrepreneurs should not be left in isolation to try to develop their technological capabilities. The creation of skills and diffusion of information do not function well in developing countries and India is no exception. It is important for the government to abandon its top–down approach to developing the briquetting industry and to allow for a more local-level approach, which will take into account local needs and conditions and also enable more effective communication between various actors.

Entrepreneurs must be encouraged to realize that investing in technological capabilities development is needed and can be profitable. It is also important that these capabilities are recognized as encompassing more than technical capabilities and that management and organizational skills also have to be upgraded.

NOTES

1. In the Indian context this competition is hindered by the existence of subsidies which produce distortions in the market.
2. In the sense of cleaner and more convenient to use.

3. In terms of mechanical strength and resistance to moisture absorption, which are important parameters for transport and handling and for storage.
4. One of the owners had made extensive searches outside the firm even travelling abroad at his own expense in an effort to find solutions to his problems.
5. This firm was in Gujarat where coal prices are much higher and the availability poorer in the monsoon. So the ability to produce an alternative fuel at a lower price creates a good potential market to offset increased investment costs. The maintenance record of this firm was excellent, so in all probability a high capacity utilization factor is a viable option.
6. Defined here as resistance to breakage in transport and handling, resistance to moisture absorption and good ignition properties.
7. This would appear to be in contradiction with Dahlman and Westphal (1982) who stated that only formal education is required to carry out pre-investment feasibility studies.
8. This term could be taken to equate with the 'active' component of know-how in Lall, 1987.
9. One of the plants in the survey had been set up by a father to give his son something to do!
10. Lakmaaker (1998) reports similar findings in the small-scale dye industry in India.
11. One might need to allow for bias in the form of foreign produced = good; local produced = bad.
12. This bottleneck is not confined to the briquetting sector (see, for example, Lall, 1987.)
13. It should be noted that these are the companies which were still in operation. It is not possible to assess what material availability or costs contributed to the failures of briquetting plants. However, Noordman (1992) was able to interview one owner of a failed plant who reported that high material cost was a contributing factor to the company failure.
14. It was not possible to assess the quality of the presses.
15. Skilled labour is defined as including all grades of labour that involve some degree of education or training above the minimum established in society. Unskilled labour has only the most basic education available in a specific society.
16. Lakmaaker (1998) found exactly the same attitudes in the small-scale dyestuffs industry in India and Romijn (1997) makes a similar observation based on work in Pakistan.

REFERENCES

Chantramonklasri, N. (1990), 'Acquisition of technological and managerial capability in the developing countries', in M. Chatterji, *Technology Transfer in the Developing Countries*, Basingstoke: MacMillan.

Cooke, I. and P. Mayes (1996), *Introduction to Innovation and Technology Transfer*, London and Boston: Artech House.

Cooper, C. (1991), 'Are innovation studies on industrialised economies relevant to technology policy in developing countries?', UNU/INTECH Working Paper No. 3.

Dahlman, C. and L. Westphal (1982), 'Technological effort in industrial development – an interpretative survey of recent research', in F. Stewart and J. James (eds), *The Economics of New Technology in Developing Countries*, London: Frances Pinter and Boulder, Colorado: Westview Press.

Grover, P.D. (1990), 'Status of biomass densification in India', Report as part of The Biomass Densification Research Project: Phase One. Technology and Development Group, University of Twente.

Katrak, H. (1997), 'The private use of publicly funded industrial technologies in developing countries: empirical tests for an industrial research institute in India', *World Development*, **25** (9), pp. 1541–50.

Lakmaaker, M. (1998), 'The small-scale Indian dye industry and the environment', M.Sc. thesis, Department of Chemical Engineering/Technology and Development Group, University of Twente.

Lall, S. (1987), *Learning to Industrialise: The Acquisition of Technological Capability by India*, Basingstoke and London: Macmillan.

Lall, S. (1992), 'Technological capabilities and industrialisation', *World Development*, **20** (2), pp. 165–86.

Lall, S. (1993), 'Understanding technology development', *Development and Change*, **24**, pp. 719–53.

Lecraw, D.J. (1978), 'Determinants of capacity utilisation by firms in less developed countries', *Journal of Development Economics*, **5**, pp. 139–53.

Leffers, B.F. (1993), 'High-density briquetting industry in India: a feasibility study', M.Sc. thesis, Department of Economics, University of Groningen.

Naidu, B.S.K (1996), 'Biomass briquetting – an Indian perspective', International Workshop on Biomass Briquetting, 3–6 April 1995, New Delhi, India. RWEDP Report No. 23, Bangkok, Thailand: FAO.

Noordman, M. (1992), 'Briquetting in India: solving problems – an evaluation of the role of technology, organisation and institutions', M.Sc. thesis, Technology and Development Group, University of Twente.

Post, A. (1995), 'Technical feasibility of the high densification screw extrusion press using biomass residues in India', M.Sc. thesis, Technology and Development Group, University of Twente.

Reines, R.G. (1986), *Technical and Economical Appraisal of Biocoal Plants Manufactured by Biomass Energy Systems (P) Ltd, Madras, India*, M.Sc. thesis, Technology and Development Group, University of Twente.

Romijn, H. (1997), 'Acquisition of technological capability in development: a quantitative case study of Pakistan's capital goods sector', *World Development*, **25** (3), pp. 359–77.

Technology and Development Group, University of Twente (1990), 'Report of the Biomass Densification Research Project: Phase One, Volume B'.

Technology and Development Group, University of Twente (1995), 'Report of the Biomass Densification Research Project: Phase Two, Final Report'.

5. Competitive response, innovation and creating an innovative milieu in the manufacturing industry in Bulawayo, Zimbabwe

A.H.J. (Bert) Helmsing

Innovation is increasingly recognized as a key variable in explaining local industrial growth. On the one hand, innovation has become a critical element in maintaining competitiveness. On the other hand, the capacity of firms to innovate depends not only on firm-level characteristics but also on 'structure' and 'local conditions'.

Best (1990) has given a powerful interpretation of the changing nature of competition, with his theory of 'new competition'. New competition distinguishes itself from 'old' competition in four dimensions. First, and at the centre of his theory is the entrepreneurial firm, which is 'an enterprise that is organised, from top to bottom to pursue continuous improvement in methods, products and processes'. The latter constitutes the basis of strategic advantage, rather than lower production costs *per se*. Best rejects the notion of the product cycle, according to which technological innovation passes through a sequential process, ultimately leading to a low-cost mass production technology. Instead, a firm would have to pursue continuous improvements, something that has organizational requirements and demands attention to detail. The second dimension is the importance of the production or commodity chain. Competitiveness depends as much on the firm itself as on that of its suppliers. Suppliers are an important source of innovation and improvement. Under new competition conditions, supplier and buyer invest in long-term relationships, consult and jointly establish quality norms and standards. The third dimension concerns the importance of so-called 'sector institutions': 'A sector can include a variety of inter-firm practices and extra-firm agencies such as trade associations, apprenticeship programmes, labour education facilities, joint marketing arrangements and regulatory commissions, each of which facilitates inter-firm co-operation' (ibid: 17). In other words, 'firms not only compete, but they can also co-operate to provide common services, to shape "the rules of the game" and to shape complementary investment strategies' (ibid). The fourth aspect is a strategic industrial policy on the part of government which would need to have a production rather than a distribution focus, seeking to shape markets, stimulating and undertaking complementary investments in support systems, and encouraging firms to develop strategic alliances.

Is the local 'structure' conducive to co-operation between firms? Local 'conditions' refer, amongst others, to basic infrastructure and to the existence of institutions, such as science and technology centres, intermediary support organizations and so on. Are local conditions conducive to innovation by firms? (Helmsing, 1998a). Indeed in developed countries, technology gaps help to explain (inter-)regional growth differentials (for example Landabaso, 1997). Technology gaps refer to the lack of innovation effort by public and private sectors and the poor adaptation of R&D efforts to the specific needs of firms in the region concerned. The EU has launched an ambitious programme for the promotion of innovation in the less-favoured regions of the EU (the STRIDE programme) which is seen by several commentators as an answer to the real causes rather than only dealing with symptoms of high unemployment. Morgan (1997) proposed the notion of the learning region and emphasized that innovation is an interactive process between a firm and its environment. In the latter, clients, other firms and science and technology and regulatory institutions play key roles. Storper and Scott (1992) argued that innovation requires both technological and organizational learning. Industrial agglomerations provide the basis for both, not only in terms of localized input–output relations between firms, but also in terms of so-called *untraded* interdependencies. These include labour markets, local regional industrial practices, 'rules of the games', and public and collective institutions. Maillat (1997) formulated the notion of innovative milieu and argued that the (economic) attractiveness of a city or 'territory' is 'no longer a function of the locational factor it offers but of its production system's ability to create specific resources and to generate innovation processes' (1998: 9). The innovative milieu consists of patterns of interaction between firms and science and technology and regulatory institutions to enhance the innovative capacity of firms. Most of this theoretical discussion takes place on and in OECD countries. Do these propositions apply to middle-income countries that have been going through processes of structural adjustment and liberalization? There is relatively little research on this and this chapter is only a partial contribution.

This chapter is based on a research project, entitled 'Urban economic restructuring and local institutional response'.[1] We seek to address the following questions: To what extent have firms followed innovative responses? Are there any differences between innovative and non-innovative firms in terms of their concrete actions, and in terms of the role played by support services? Do innovative firms differ in terms of their demand for business or producer services? By dealing with these issues, we seek to answer the question: is there a basis for creating an innovative milieu in Bulawayo? The second section is devoted to a background review of recent changes in the Zimbabwean economy and of Bulawayo, where the research has been conducted. The third section introduces the research and describes threats, strategic responses and actions of all firms and examines differences between 'innovative' and 'defensive' firms. The fourth section examines the role of enterprise support services and institutional preferences of firms. The fifth section looks at business or producer services. The final section makes some concluding observations in terms of the basis for creating an innovative milieu in Bulawayo.

ZIMBABWEAN ECONOMY BEFORE AND SINCE STRUCTURAL ADJUSTMENT

Prior to ESAP

The immediate post-independence boom was cut short by a severe drought, poor world economic performance as well as acts of South African destabilization. The average economic growth was not more than 1.6 per cent per annum over the first five years after 1980. The second half of the 1980s gave a more favourable picture. For the decade as a whole an average of 3.4 per cent real growth per annum was achieved. Given the high population growth (of nearly 3 per cent), per capita income declined in the first half, and slightly improved during the second half of the 1980s.

The industrial sector with all its diversity is relatively small. According to the Census of Manufacturing, there are less than 1100 units. They produce as many as 6000 products but markets are small, and competitors few. The domestic market had been almost completely shielded from competing imports since the early sixties and this generated monopolistic and heavily oligopolistic enterprises, which over time diversified into other existing or new product market areas. Many of these economic activities are controlled by a small number of economic conglomerates such as the Delta Corporation and the TM group, in which the foreign investment component was and still is very high.

There was notably little 'structural change' in industry after Independence. The most noteworthy is the relative decline of metal and metal products, and the relative increase in drinks and tobacco and chemical and petroleum products subsectors. On balance the 1980s resulted in a 3.6 per cent increase in real output per annum and a 2.1 per cent annual increase in employment.

Apart from the low employment growth, the most important disturbing post-independence feature has been the lack of industrial investment. It is difficult to get a reasonably balanced picture of the major constraints on investment. A survey in the late 1980s reported the following factors influencing new investment (in order of importance): expected return on investment; forex availability; insufficient local demand; business confidence (Hawkins *et al.*, 1988). Whatever the 'success' in Zimbabwe's industrial sector, the fact is that the investment rate dramatically declined in the 1980s. The relative stagnation and the failure to generate employment and income generating opportunities for a fast-growing labour force, is generally seen as the principal driving force that pushed the Government to adopt a package of economic reform measures, which became known as the Economic Structural Adjustment Programme (ESAP).

Economic Structural Adjustment Programme

The ESAP was launched in 1991 in order to revitalize the private sector through deregulation and reduced government intervention and by decreasing the latter's absorption of resources (GoZ, 1991). The programme had a number of specific objectives of trade and exchange rate liberalization by creating a market-based foreign exchange system and by gradually replacing the administrative import restrictions by (reduced) tariff-based protection. In addition, the programme aimed at commercialization of public enterprises so as to reduce their operational losses, which were constituting a heavy burden on the national budget. Furthermore, a civil service reform was meant to reduce the public sector wage bill by substantial reduction in the number of public sector employees. The last two mentioned policies would contribute to a substantial reduction of the central government budget deficit. A liberalization of the financial sector was announced. The programme aimed at a domestic deregulation of product and labour markets and announced measures to promote foreign investment.

The reform measures, partially or wholly implemented, had direct impacts on the operations of manufacturing industry. In their detailed review of manufacturing industry trends, Braunerhjelm and Fors (1996) estimated that in the first two years of ESAP manufacturing employment shrank by some 20 000 jobs. The sectors that lost heavily were metal and metal products (5300), textiles (2600), clothing and footwear (2100) and the paper industry (2600). The relative decline in employment is, however, somewhat less than the decline in output in the same period. ESAP and drought exerted their toll. Exports did not grow as had been expected on the basis of the large initial devaluation of the local currency (in the early 1990s). When the exchange rate later stabilized, in spite of high levels of inflation, it became even less attractive for industries to export. In this chapter we aim to shed more light on firm-level adjustments.

City of Bulawayo

Bulawayo is the second largest city of the country. It is located in the southern region and represents an important international transportation node for traffic flows between South Africa and countries north of the Limpopo river. During the early period of white settlement of what became known as Rhodesia, Bulawayo was the largest and most important urban centre, only to be surpassed by Harare (formerly known as Salisbury), when that city became the administrative centre of the then 'self governing colony' and later became the capital of the country. Generally the pace of life in Bulawayo is slower than Harare, and the mood is more provincial.

Bulawayo is also the second largest industrial centre. Notwithstanding, the industrial community is fairly small and well established. Most sectors are dominated by family-owned businesses. Their owner/managers have often technical rather than financial orientation. Its manufacturing industry represented, according to CSO figures of 1994, 30 per cent of total manufacturing employment in the country. The city didn't participate much in the early post-Independence boom. The Matabeleland region as a whole suffered from domestic political troubles which negatively influenced economic performance. Only in the second half of the 1980s and after the domestic political settlement in 1987, did Bulawayo employment grow.

The manufacturing sector is the most important source of formal sector employment in the city. It represents 38 per cent of the total, a share that has been rising somewhat. Immediately after Independence in 1980 employment growth stagnated and declined marginally, but both in the remaining pre-ESAP period and in the 1990s employment growth of Bulawayo exceeded the national average. For Bulawayo the manufacturing sector remains a key provider of formal sector employment, alongside construction and education (the latter thanks to the extension of primary education and the establishment of a new National University of Science and Technology).

There is little concrete evidence on the impact of adjustment on sectors and firms in Bulawayo. In 1991, the signs of ESAP were positive: low interest rates, ample savings, export incentive scheme to import inputs and government programme to finance the import of machinery and equipment to enable the manufacturing firms to modernize their equipment. Firms began to invest using bank borrowing as finance. However, in 1992/3 the picture changed radically. Real interest rates rose rapidly, as did inflation. Import liberalization opened markets to competing imports, drought reduced domestic demand further, and as the Zimbabwe dollar depreciated imported inputs and equipment became more expensive. Firms were unprepared, and were hit while being in the middle of their modernization programmes. Some of them got caught in a debt trap and ran into liquidity problems. Assets that served as security became overvalued, and were insufficient to cover debts.

A number of firms actually collapsed in 1992/3, such as G&D shoes, ZECO Engineering Ltd, two textile mills, an electrical consumer goods manufacturer and smaller clothing companies.[2] Others survived by down-sizing, retrenching workers and by economizing. Again others sought to return to their core business but found it difficult to find buyers for their non-core operations. Some others managed to penetrate export markets but did not diversify their export clients and markets, being at risk. Again others sought (links with) foreign buyers or franchising. Micro-level adjustment strategies varied across sectors and firms and it is to that issue that we will now turn.

FIRM-LEVEL RESTRUCTURING: THREATS, STRATEGIC RESPONSES AND ACTIONS

Introduction to the Research

In 1996 researchers of the Institute of Social Studies (ISS), and the Institute of Housing and Urban Development Studies (IHS) launched a collaborative research effort on urban economic restructuring and local institutional responses. The joint research effort consisted of several research projects on economic and urban management aspects of restructuring and was implemented with research partners in Colombia, India and Zimbabwe. One of these project focused on examining processes of economic restructuring in Bulawayo, Zimbabwe, the strategic responses and concrete actions that were adopted by local firms, business interest associations, government agencies and by the Bulawayo City Council to improve the capacity of local firms to respond to competitive challenges and to strengthen the capacity of local institutions to cope with future economic challenges. The data presented and analysed in this chapter is generated by this research project.

The research concentrated on a limited number of sectors that make up an important part of the economy of Bulawayo. On the basis of interviews with local business and government leaders, and unpublished data of the national Central Statistics Office (CSO), it appeared that wearing apparel (3220), furniture (3320) and metal fabrication (3810) were the three largest sectors in terms of the number of manufacturing firms. The inclusion of the fourth sector, non-electrical machinery and equipment (3820), has been motivated by its importance as a capital goods producing sector. Together these sectors provide 33 per cent of manufacturing employment in Bulawayo in 1992/3. An attempt was made to obtain data from the CSO concerning the enterprise sector and size structure for Bulawayo. Unfortunately, it was not possible to obtain the CSO listing of the firms and their basic characteristics, on the basis of which a sample might be drawn. It was therefore necessary to construct a basic listing and it was decided to begin with the membership lists of the Matabeleland Chamber of Industries. The Chamber represents only a part of all manufacturing firms, therefore the list had to be complemented by other means.[3] Additional sources used were the Directory of Brand Names and Products, published by the Zimbabwe National Chamber of Commerce and the Bulawayo Yellow Pages. A United States Agency for International Development (USAID) sponsored local projects to identify opportunities for subcontracting, provided additional data to complement the basic list of names of firms. According to local informants this generated a fairly complete list of all manufacturing firms in the selected sectors in Bulawayo. Subsequently, the firms in the sample were selected in a systematic random manner from this basic list. The operational target was 30 interviews per sector in order to facilitate comparisons. In total 121 firms took part in the survey. A first round of results has been presented separately (Helmsing, 1988b). In this chapter the focus is on the threats that firms perceived, the nature of their responses and the concrete actions they have undertaken.

Threats

Competitive threats in the period 1993–6 have arisen in the domestic market as well as in export markets. Firms found it more difficult to maintain their position and profitability. In the domestic market, the main force of competitive threats emanated from existing rival firms and from newly entered firms. Competitive threats emanating from clients and from competing imports were of secondary importance. Finally, suppliers and substitutes were not considered to be important new sources of competition. ESAP has no doubt contributed to the emergence of these competitive threats, directly via its liberalization of imports (raw materials, intermediate and capital goods) and by allowing the emergence of competing imports (hitherto a negligible issue, except for 'popular' smuggling) and indirectly by reducing impediments to private sector development. In export markets firms reported increased competitive threats, which, as in the domestic market, were primarily caused by existing rival firms and newly entered firms and by the more price sensitive clients.

The second most important threat in the period has been unrelated to ESAP, namely the 1994/5 drought. In the case of Bulawayo the drought had not only demand-side but also supply-side consequences. The first consisted of a severe cut in consumer demand of the drought-affected rural population, and the reduction in general demand because of declining purchasing power as a result of high inflation caused by government spending on drought relief. Supply-side problems emanated from shortages in water supply and water rationing in the second year of the drought, affecting the operations of industry.

Macroeconomic issues have preoccupied the firms but these preoccupations centred on inflation affecting purchasing power and threats emanating from trade liberalization. Financial variables such as interest rate and exchange rate were less of a concern. In input markets two issues played a role. The one was the rising price levels of (imported) inputs. The other refers to the increased availability of inputs. In the past pre-ESAP period, access to inputs was controlled by firms existing in the market through their (near preferential) allocation of foreign exchange. With liberalization existing, firms lost that advantage and potential rival firms obtained easier access to needed inputs, raising competition.

Strategic Responses

How have firms responded to these threats? The survey instrument identified 16 different responses (and one open option) and respondents were asked to indicate one or more of these responses that they considered best described the course(s) of action formulated and actually followed by them in the past three years. These strategic responses are grouped into five categories: i) exit responses; ii) client oriented defensive responses; iii) belt tightening defensive responses; iv) rationalization of productive processes, and v) development of new markets and products. Below we discuss each in more detail.

One of the passive exit responses is that a firm decides to adjust to lower sales volumes, leading to a downsizing of operations and possibly to retrenchments of staff and workers. A firm responding in this way would accept that the terms and conditions of competition in the market have changed, and that it would be beyond the control of the firm itself to regain market share and/or sales volume to restore profitability. In the case of Zimbabwe, the protection of the domestic market was lifted by the change in policy regime. Another response is that firms that have been active in the end assembly of imported components and parts, exit wholly or partially from manufacturing and switch to (import) trade. They recognize the difficulty of competing with superior or better priced imports but consider their own distribution networks as an important asset. Obtaining exclusive distribution rights of major international brands is in such a case often a complementary strategic action.

Client oriented defensive responses refer to those where firms step up sales efforts in order to maintain a market position, increase efforts to acquire new clients and/or try to retain customers by improving client services. These are typically immediate responses to declining sales, that is, responses that they may be undertaking without radically altering firm practices.

'Belt tightening' responses are also immediate ones. One is simply economizing. That is to say to reduce costs either by not doing or by postponing cash outlays (skimming). A stepped up version of cost reduction would be the adoption of efficiency measures, whereby the firm critically reviews inputs in relation to outputs. A third belt tightening response would be to accept lower profit margins in an attempt to 'ride out the storm, hoping for better times'. These three responses are primarily responses of a 'status quo' nature. Firms do not change radically what they do and how they do it.

A more radical set of responses concerns rationalization of the productive processes of the firm. Firms often begin with improving the existing production processes, investing in new equipment so as to improve quality and raise efficiency. Firms that have established themselves in the context of import substitution in small domestic markets, often have taken on the production of parts and components in the absence of domestic suppliers but also in their attempt to expand their share in the value chain. Foreign exchange scarcities provided an additional stimulus to manufacture these components internally despite the small demand and problems of quality. Lifting domestic trade protection and financial liberalization therefore often leads to a rationalization of production processes. Several aspects have been identified. One response may be to subcontract the manufacture of parts and components, or to out-contract producer services or may even involve development of networks and alliances with other firms. Thus, while downsizing is a passive and negative response, rationalization is an active and innovative response. It is recognized that old production processes and arrangements (including vertical integration) cannot be sustained any more in the face of changing market conditions, and new production arrangements are introduced.

The fifth set of responses concern the development of new markets and of improved and new products. Five specific responses have been identified. A firm may change market orientation by developing new market segments in existing product markets; export markets may be another option; improvement of product quality may take place by improving the design of the product. Lastly, the firm may opt to develop entirely new products.

The working hypothesis is that firms have adopted any one type of response. However, one should take into account the possibility that firms have not developed any explicit response. Several reasons may be forwarded. A firm may be part of a large group of firms or be a subsidiary with no autonomy in these matters. Furthermore, it is conceivable that the management of firms may simply not have responded in an alert or explicit manner or may have discussed the strategic choices but were unable to choose any concrete response. Lastly, some firms were very recently established and hence no change in behaviour may be noticeable. In order to separate these situations, a filter was applied. It turned out that of the 121 firms interviewed, 106 (88 per cent) have discussed external threats, and their implications for their competitiveness, and have set out concrete line(s) of action. The findings presented below are restricted to these 106 firms. Table 5.1 gives an overview of the specific types of strategic response.

The six most frequently cited responses were all in the market oriented and belt tightening categories. Improving process design and improving product design were specific responses of secondary importance (reported by more than 20 firms). Differences between sectors are not very pronounced except in some instances. Downsizing is typically a response practised in the clothing sector, while switching to trade is an exit response of non-electrical machinery

Table 5.1   Type of strategic response, by firm-selected sectors, Bulawayo

Type of response	Total (#)	Total (%)	Clothing (%)	Furniture (%)	Metal fabr. (%)	Non-elec mach. (%)
Exit responses						
downsize	17	3.3	5.1	3.8	2.2	1.8
switch to trade	7	1.4	0.0	0.0	1.4	4.5
Market oriented response						
increase sales effort	79	15.5	14.1	15.1	15.9	17.3
seek new clients	44	8.6	10.9	5.7	9.4	7.3
improve client service	44	8.6	10.3	7.5	8.7	7.3
Belt tightening response						
economize	50	9.8	9.0	9.4	10.9	10.0
efficiency measures	64	12.5	12.8	11.3	13.8	11.8
lower profit margins	52	10.2	6.4	11.3	11.6	12.7
Rationalization of product						
subcontract manufacture	9	1.8	1.3	3.8	1.4	0.9
outcontract service	3	0.6	0.0	0.9	0.7	0.9
improve process design	34	6.7	7.1	7.5	7.2	4.5
networking and alliance	9	1.8	1.3	1.9	1.4	2.7
New markets and product						
improve product design	42	8.2	9.6	10.4	5.8	7.3
new products	23	4.5	4.5	5.7	3.6	4.5
new market segment	18	3.5	3.8	2.8	3.6	3.6
new export markets	15	2.9	3.8	2.8	2.2	2.7

Source: Survey.

firms. The latter are also more active in increasing sales efforts among existing clients, while the clothing sector puts more emphasis on seeking new clients in existing markets and on improving client services.

Belt tightening responses are practised across the board with little sectoral variation, except that the clothing sector is notably more reluctant to accept lower profit margins. Subcontracting appears to make more sense in the furniture industry than in the other sectors, like non-electrical machinery. This sector has a wide range of products, which are often made in small batches, hence, subcontracting is more difficult to organize here than in furniture making. Improvement of product design is a more frequent response in the consumer goods industries than in the capital goods producing sectors. Clothing firms have been relatively speaking more active in developing new markets, including abroad.

Defensive strategies have been most prevalent. Undertaking efforts in existing markets and belt tightening have been the predominant responses of the Bulawayo firms. New markets and new products and rationalization of production have received much less attention. Exit responses are surprisingly unimportant. It should be added though that the survey was only applied to firms still in operation at the time of the survey. Firms that had exited altogether have not been covered, leading to an underestimation of responses in this category. Looking at differences by sectors, it may be observed that the clothing and metal fabrication sectors have had a greater preference for market oriented responses than the other sectors. The belt tightening has also been a more preferred option in the engineering sectors. On the other hand, clothing and furniture have developed more responses aiming at new markets and new products. Rationalization of productive processes is more predominant in furniture.

If one were to qualify the exit, market oriented and belt tightening as defensive responses and the rationalization of production and new products and markets as the innovative responses, then we may conclude that the defensive responses of the firms have predominated. Innovative responses constitute only 30 per cent of all strategic responses. From a sectoral point of view it may be concluded that the furniture sector has the highest proportion of innovative responses, while metal fabrication and non-electrical machinery have the least proportion of innovative responses. The clothing sector finds itself in an intermediate position.

From Strategies to Firms

The table presented an aggregate picture of the frequency and relative importance of the different strategic responses. The next step is to examine patterns of response at the level of firms. It is important to note here that respondents could indicate more than one response. Examining patterns at the level of each firm, several interesting findings emerged. First of all, there are firms that had chosen exclusively defensive responses, but there are no firms that had adopted exclusively innovative responses. In other words, innovation takes place in the context of defensive measures.

Some firms are more focused than others in their response (as indicated by the number of responses that were marked by them). For the purpose of the analysis below, firms have been categorized into three groups. First, firms that have adopted only defensive responses; second firms that combined defensive with innovative responses. The final group consists of 'indecisive' firms that have either not made any strategic choice (that is, firms that did not pass the filter mentioned above) or their responses had been so broad and multiple and were seen as lacking any real choice.[4] Table 5.2 below presents the overall and sectoral pattern. There is no clear tendency towards any category of response and it would appear that strategic responses and sector are unrelated to each other.[5] The latter confirms the hypothesis expressed by Braunerhjelm and Fors (1996), and referred to above, that restructuring depends on firm behaviour that is largely independent of the sector to which the firm belongs.

Table 5.2   Strategic behaviour of firms: selected manufacturing sectors, Bulawayo

Strategy	Total	Clothing	Furniture	Metal fabrication	Non-elec. machinery
Indecisive	38	13	7	13	5
	(31.4%)	(38.2%)	(25.0%)	(40.6%)	(18.5%)
Defensive only	40	10	11	11	8
	(33.1%)	(29.4%)	(39.3%)	(34.4%)	(29.6%)
Defensive and	43	11	10	8	14
Innovative	(35.5%)	(32.4%)	(35.7%)	(25.1%)	(51.8%)
Total	121	34	28	32	27
	(100%)	(28.1%)	(23.1%)	(26.4%)	(22.3%)

Table 5.3 examines strategic behaviour by firm size. Smaller firms are somewhat more prone to adopt an innovative strategy than larger firms. Small firms and even more so medium-sized firms are also more indecisive in comparison to large and very large firms. Large and very large firms have a more than proportional representation in the defensive and combination strategies. Differences are, however, small. When looked at in terms of size, it would seem that strategy and size are unrelated to each other.[6]

Table 5.3   *Strategic behaviour of firms and firm size: selected sectors,*
            Bulawayo

Strategy	Total	<25	26–100	101–250	> 250
Indecisive firms	38	12	16	3	7
	(31.4%)	(34.3%)	(42.1%)	(15.0%)	(25.9%)
Defensive only	40	10	12	7	10
	(33.1%)	(28.6%)	(31.6%)	(35.0%)	(37.0%)
Defensive and	43	13	10	10	10
Innovative	(35.5%)	(37.1%)	(26.3%)	(50.0%)	(44.4%)
Total	121	35	38	20	27
	(100%)	(100%)	(100%)	(100%)	(100%)

Concrete Actions Taken by Firms

The strategies that firms formulate in response to perceived threats are
statements of overall goals and of broad indications as to how these may be
achieved. These strategies guide subsequent action in the main functional
areas of the firm, such as the physical process of manufacturing, physical
aspects of the products, management, finance, labour relations and human
resource development, marketing, networking and interfirm relations. The
second part of the research consists of examining how overall strategies are
translated into concrete actions in each of these functional areas of the firm.
By analysing concrete actions a more detailed picture is generated of firm
level restructuring patterns. The field instrument identified a series of possible
courses of action. These concrete actions were grouped under nine categories
as shown in Table 5.4.[7] It gives an overview of the categories and of the most
important actions within each category. This table is based on the indicated
'dominant action' within each category.[8] It may be concluded that five types
of concrete actions have predominated. First of all, more that 90 per cent of
the firms have undertaken concrete actions to change the physical process of
manufacturing and physical aspects of the products. Thus, product and process
innovations of different types and intensity have been adopted by a large
majority of the firms. The most prevalent type of action is of an engineering
type. The other three important categories of action were marketing, human
resource development and management. Areas of action, such as networking,
interfirm co-operation, finance and downsizing, have only been adopted by a
small proportion of firms.

In terms of product innovations the emphasis has been on improving the
technical specifications and change in physical characteristics of *existing*

*Table 5.4   Actions undertaken by firms in last three years: selected sectors,
Bulawayo, 1996*

Dominant action	Total	Clothing	Furniture	Metal fabrication	Machinery
Downsizing	18.2	32.4	32.1	3.1	3.7
discontinue least profitable	14.0	23.5	28.6	0.0	3.7
Product innovations	92.6	97.1	89.3	90.6	96.3
improve technical specifications	29.8	14.7	46.4	28.1	33.3
change physical character	13.2	23.5	14.3	6.3	7.4
new products	16.5	17.6	10.7	18.8	18.5
new product groups	14.9	26.5	3.6	15.6	11.1
Process innovations	90.9	85.3	96.4	96.9	85.2
quality control	24.8	20.6	17.9	28.1	33.3
upgrading plant & equipment	19.0	14.7	17.9	18.8	25.9
acquisition new plant & equipment	15.7	20.6	21.4	12.5	7.4
improving inputs	11.6	17.6	10.7	12.5	3.7
re-design plant/process	11.6	8.8	21.4	9.4	7.4
Management	83.5	85.3	75.0	87.5	85.2
financial management	20.7	17.6	17.9	31.3	14.8
internal control	15.7	11.8	25.0	12.5	14.8
quality management	12.4	5.9	7.1	18.8	22.2
integration prod/sales management	11.6	11.8	3.6	9.4	22.2
Financial restructuring	23.1	29.4	17.9	18.8	25.9
rescheduling of debts	8.3	8.8	7.1	9.4	7.4
HRD	86.0	73.5	85.7	93.8	92.6
skill upgrading	31.4	32.4	28.6	40.6	22.2
delegation responsibilities	19.8	17.6	25.0	25.0	11.1
personal career development	11.6	2.9	7.1	9.4	29.6
Marketing	86.8	88.2	85.7	84.4	88.9
existing markets	28.1	38.2	21.4	21.9	29.6
existing products	19.0	17.6	10.7	21.9	25.9
new products	12.4	11.8	17.9	9.4	11.1
specific advertising	9.9	5.9	14.3	12.5	7.4
Networking	27.3	23.5	25.0	34.4	25.9
subcontract subprocess	9.9	8.8	14.3	3.1	7.4
subcontract local competence	9.1	2.9	3.6	21.9	11.1
IF co-operation	28.9	41.2	14.3	31.3	25.9
joint marketing	9.9	14.7	3.6	15.6	3.7

Source: Survey.

products, and for a minority of firms it consisted of introducing *new* products and *new* product groups. Two sectors show some variation. One is the furniture making industry which has put far greater effort into improving the technical characteristics of existing products and proportionally far less effort into new products and new product groups. The other is the clothing industry which has shown a much greater propensity to develop new product groups and towards changing physical appearance.

As regards process innovations, the emphasis has been generally on improving quality control and on upgrading existing plant and equipment and acquiring new plant and equipment. A physical re-design of the organization of production processes, so as to improve workflow, has been much less practised, except in the furniture making industry. An organizational re-design of operations, including decentralization of production decisions involving workers in quality control, have not been important actions among the firms.

The concrete actions in the area of marketing have the same order of priority, namely first and foremost clients and products in existing markets and market development for existing products (notably in the clothing industry) and much less in relation to market development for new products. Again the furniture making industry is, in relative terms, a favourable exception.

The concrete actions in the area of human resource development (HRD) have been fairly conventional. That is to say, skill upgrading in areas of immediate need has been, by far, the most important (but narrow) concern of the firms, while only a small minority has given more attention to delegation of responsibilities and to personnel development programmes. Other areas of action, such as worker involvement in decision making, and change in reward systems have hardly figured among the dominant actions taken by the firms in the past three years. It is interesting to note differences between sectors which relate to skill content of production processes. The clothing industry has been notably less active in the area of human resource development, but on the other hand, metal fabrication and machinery sectors have paid far more attention to these issues.

Strengthening of management capacity is the fifth area of concrete actions undertaken by the firms. Most attention has been given to increasing financial and cost control and control of internal operations by management and to a lesser extent on management of quality control. The integration of production and sales/marketing management so as to be able to translate changes in markets more swiftly into products and production has only been adopted by a small minority of firms. Other important areas, such as human resource management, sourcing of inputs, research and development and strategic management, have received very little attention.

The four areas in which firms have been least active in the period analysed were networking, interfirm co-operation, financial restructuring and downsizing. Starting with the latter, it is important to note that downsizing has been restricted primarily to the clothing and furniture making industries. In the other two sectors downsizing (other than a complete closure of the company) has been negligible. In almost all instances, downsizing focused on closing down the least profitable product groups, without switching to trading. Other alternatives, such as closing down subprocesses or manufacture of components and parts, with or without subcontracting, have not been contemplated on any scale by the respondents. This is a somewhat surprising result because firms that have established themselves in a long period of (forced) import substitution would have, in all likelihood, engaged themselves in the (sub-optimal) manufacture of components and parts in order to save the very scarce foreign exchange. One would expect trade liberalization to trigger micro-level adjustment in the composition of production processes.

Surprisingly few firms engaged in financial restructuring. Most actions concentrated on debt rescheduling and debt conversion. Other actions such as expanding equity and acquiring new domestic or foreign partners were hardly registered. Zimbabwean industry has traditionally been self financing. The debt problem that emerged in the early to mid 1990s had several causes. One is the substantial investments made by firms in plant and equipment which was partly financed with bank loans; the second is the unexpected high level of interest rates which followed the financial liberalization; and the third was the rapid decline in sales as a result of recession and drought.

Networking and interfirm co-operation have been relatively unimportant areas of action undertaken by the firms in the past three years. Networking has primarily focused on subcontracting of subprocesses and the manufacture of components by local firms. Its relatively minor importance (less than 10 per cent of the firms undertook some action) is consistent with the observations made earlier in relation to process innovations, where subcontracting was found to be adopted by only a small proportion of the firms. International networking, either through subcontracting components or parts or through manufacture under licence, has not played any significant role. Interfirm co-operation focused on joint marketing efforts in export markets. Other forms of co-operation, such as sharing or pooling facilities, jointly purchasing or contracting inputs and services or co-manufacturing and joint tendering have not been practised.

Surveying these responses, one is tempted to conclude that the firms in Bulawayo are as yet adopting fairly conventional actions, in areas of product and process innovations, in marketing, in HRD and in management. 'New' competition and micro-level transition towards an 'entrepreneurial firm', as defined by Best above, would however require more actions in the areas of product and product group development not necessarily via more hardware but via reorganization of production processes within the firm, changing management of internal processes as well as more actions in the areas of networking and interfirm co-operation.

Actions by Defensive versus Actions by Innovative Firms

Do innovative firms adopt similar actions to defensively responding firms? Below we have examined this issue with respect to the actions undertaken by the firms in the 1992–95 period as well as to the actions that were identified, by the respondents, to be undertaken in the next three years.[9] In the table below we have summarized those instances where differences in the distribution are significant, using the chi square test. In all instances, innovative firms are more prone to adopt these actions than defensive firms.

With regard to actions in the past three years, the differences between the two types of firms have not been very strong and are restricted to only four issues, namely, diversification into new product groups, integrating management of production, sales and marketing, research on existing markets and individual advertising. Nevertheless, these are relevant ones in terms of innovation and 'new competition'. One possible explanation for the lack of differentiated responses between predominantly innovative and defensive firms is that the two groups partially overlap (there are no exclusively innovative firms). That is to say, *all* firms undertake certain immediate defensive responses. A second factor could be the time lag in developing actions addressing the longer term. In other words it would take time for differences in strategies to manifest themselves in actions.

With regard to areas of future action, there are more differences between the two types of firms. In comparison to defensive firms, a greater proportion of innovative firms seek to be active in product innovations (of both existing and new products), and pay more attention to process innovation in terms of upgrading of equipment, improving quality of inputs and improving quality control. Also in the area of management, innovative firms orient themselves more towards strengthening of control of operations, integrating production, sales and marketing, and put more emphasis on sourcing of inputs and management of R&D processes. More attention to management is also reflected in future training efforts. Lastly, innovative firms are more prone to engage in component subcontracting than defensive firms. One is tempted to conclude that although overall the actions of the Bulawayo firms have followed existing paths, at least among the innovative firms, some elements of 'new' competition become visible.

Table 5.5 Past and future actions: defensive only and innovative firms

Type of action		Chi Square	Significance
Actions in past 3 years			
Diversifying into new product groups	I>D	2.726	.09867
Integrating production, sales and			
marketing management	I>D	3.201	.07360
Research on existing markets	I>D	4.372	.03653
Individual advertising	I>D	2.986	.08399
Desirable future actions			
Downsize switching to trading	I>D	8.236	.00411
Improve technical characteristics of			
existing product	I>D	2.960	.08536
Change physical appearance	I>D	4.723	.02975
New product development	I>D	3.616	.05720
Diversify into new product group	I>D	3.020	.08223
Upgrade plant & equipment	I>D	7.432	.00641
Improve inputs	I>D	4.155	.04152
Improve quality control	I>D	5.382	.02034
Strengthen internal control of operations	I>D	9.103	.00255
Integrate production, sales and			
marketing management	I>D	4.359	.03680
Procurement/Sourcing of inputs	I>D	7.274	.00700
Management of research & development	I>D	2.795	.09454
Skill upgrading	I>D	3.394	.06542
Management training	I>D	5.032	.02488
Component subcontracting	I>D	8.236	.00411

Source: Computed from survey.

ENTERPRISE SUPPORT SERVICES

The research has made an inventory of enterprise support services and has established which of these have played a key role in the firms in the implementation of their strategic actions. In addition, respondents to the survey have been asked to indicate which support services are important for their planned future actions. The comparison of the two gives some indication of the trends in demand for support services. In addition respondents were asked to indicate their institutional preferences. That is to say they were asked to identify which would be the most desirable institutional forms through which particular support services ought to be delivered in the future. Table 5.6 presents an overview of the different types of support services, which according to the respondents have been instrumental in the success of the firm in the past.

Table 5.6   Relative importance of enterprise support services

Category – type of support service	Frequency
General information and enterprise assistance	
● general information & promotion	33 (27%)
● local/regional promotion	25 (21%)
● information regulatory policies	19 (16%)
● small enterprise promotion	12 (10%)
Technological support services	
● product design services	57 (47%)
● quality control and standards	39 (32%)
● R&D on manufacturing technologies	26 (21%)
● technical assistance and industrial extension	12 (10%)
● databases/technological information services	5 (4%)
Marketing support services	
● organization of domestic fairs	47 (39%)
● general market & export information services	25 (21%)
● identification of export opportunities	20 (16%)
● representation in international fairs	15 (12%)
● identification of buyers abroad	11 (9%)
● identification of international trading firms	10 (8%)
● information on design & standards for exports	10 (8%)
● distribution of publicity material abroad	6 (5%)
● representation in international tenders etc.	1 (1%)
Financial support services	
● investment loans	58 (48%)
● venture capital	11 (9%)
● *leasing*	7 (6%)
● loan guarantees	7 (6%)
● credit insurance	6 (5%)
● reprogramming of debts	6 (5%)
● cofinancing of training projects	1 (1%)
● cofinancing of technology updating projects	–
● cofinancing of marketing projects	2 (2%)
● cofinance management improvement programme	1 (1%)

Category – type of support service	Frequency
Training services	
• vocational training	50 (41%)
• technological updating	29 (24%)
• management training	28 (23%)
• training supervisory management	38 (31%)
• financial management training	40 (33%)
• training in marketing & exports	24 (20%)

Several conclusions may be drawn. First of all, enterprise support in the past few years has been oriented primarily towards training services. Of the ten most frequently cited support services, firms list five training services. This is somewhat unexpected as Zimbabwe doesn't have a specialized training service for industry nor a particular performance record in this area. Bulawayo, however, has an important Polytechnic College specialized in trades for industry and the National University of Science & Technology which was established in Bulawayo in the late 1980s to respond to demands for high-level technical training.

A large number of firms mention investment loans as a key support service. This may be explained by the World Bank-financed, loan facility that was made available to manufacturing industry under the Economic Structural Adjustment Programme. Marketing support services have been of a relatively limited importance, in spite of the increasing attention firms have begun to pay to maintaining existing markets and to entering new ones. The Bulawayo Industry Fair is the country's second largest domestic fair (after Harare's Agricultural Show) and is the most important one to the local industry. With regard to technological support services, firms list quality control and standards (Southern African Institute of Standards) and product design as key areas where they used support services.

Differences between Defensive and Innovative Firms

Do innovative firms demand different support services than defensive firms? Table 5.7 gives the results of the comparisons. Differences are found in marketing and general promotion and information and reprogramming of debts. On the whole, however, the evidence is not very strong and at this moment would not warrant a plea to steer the development of the support system in any special direction.

Table 5.7   Use of support services in past three years: defensive and innovative firms

Support services used in past three years		Chi Square	Significance
General enterprise promotion and information with local orientation	I>D	5.8286	.01577
Technological support: technological databases	I>D	2.895	.08884
Marketing support: information on product standards, design & packaging	I>D	2.895	.08884
Marketing support: distribution promotion materials abroad	I>D	2.895	.08884
Marketing support: introduction of foreign buyers	I>D	3.909	.04802
Financial support services: reprogramming of debt	I>D	2.895	.08884

Source: Survey.

Institutional Preferences for Service Delivery

In the past decade or so, enterprise support systems underwent considerable changes in many countries. State or public sector services lost their dominant position due to their performance and to changes in the demand for services. On the whole, a greater institutional diversity emerged. Public or parastatal services exist alongside the private sector and there is a great variety of mixed public–private modalities. One would readily accept a certain degree of 'path dependency' as regards the evolution of institutional support services, that is that the historical institutional context in a particular country or region would have a considerable influence as to which kinds of institutional modality form would have greater acceptance than others. There is however relatively little theory to explain what is the most appropriate institutional form in which particular support services can be organized and delivered.

Taking this into account, the research approached the matter in an empirical manner and focused on identifying the institutional preferences of the users of these services, the firms in our survey. The following procedure was adopted. First a list of specialist support services was given and respondents were asked to identify which they considered important, taking into account the actions they had in mind to strengthen their competitive capacity in the near future. Subsequently, and based on international literature, various institutional delivery options were listed out of which the respondent could make a choice

(Levy, 1994). The answer to our questions varied by type of service. Table 5.8 presents an overall view of the findings.

Table 5.8   Support services and institutional preferences

Type of service	Frequency	Preferred institutional modality
General enterprise support services		
• general business advice	56 (46%)	industry or sector association
• local economic development promotion	52 (43%)	local government
• business information centres	48 (40%)	industry association
Technological support services		
• quality control and standards	68 (56%)	government agency
• R&D on manufacturing technology	56 (46%)	sector association
• product design services	54 (45%)	commercial firms; sector association
• technical assistance & industrial extension	34 (28%)	sector association; equipment suppliers
• data bases and technological information services	32 (26%)	sector association
Marketing support services		
• organization of domestic fairs	66 (55%)	government agency
• information services on export markets	41 (34%)	sector associations; government agency
• representation in international fairs	26 (22%)	government agency; international trading firms
• identification of export opportunities	22 (19%)	government agency; sector association
• export insurance association	7 (6%)	government agency; sector
Financial services		
• investment finance	61 (50%)	commercial banks
• venture capital	26 (22%)	central government
• loan guarantees	19 (16%)	commercial banks
• rescheduling of debt	11 (9%)	commercial banks
• credit insurance	10 (8%)	central government agency; banks
• cofinancing of technical projects	8 (7%)	government agency

Type of service	Frequency	Preferred institutional modality
● cofinancing management improvement programme	5 (4%)	sector association
● cofinancing of marketing projects	3 (3%)	government agency
Training services		
● vocational training	81 (67%)	academic centre
● training of supervisory staff	52 (43%)	sector association; academic centre
● management training	52 (43%)	sector association; academic centre
● financial management training	50 (41%)	academic centre
● technological updating	45 (37%)	sector association; private consultants
● training in marketing and export	38 (31%)	private consultants; sector associations

Source: Survey.

As regards general assistance services there is a clear preference for general or sector-specific business associations and for local government. Private and non-profit foundations, which do exist for the purpose of enterprise development play little or no role in the institutional preferences of the respondents.

The firms have a clear preference for sector associations as providers of technological support services. Government is only seen to play a role in the specification and testing of quality control and standards. Equipment suppliers are often seen as important sources of technological information to firms. For product design private or commercial providers are seen as an important source. Academic centres play a relatively minor role as regards technological support services, in spite of the establishment of the National University of Science & Technology in Bulawayo (with specialization in engineering).

The interviewed firms continue to see a considerable role for central government in the provision of marketing services, especially in relation to export markets (roles currently performed by ZIMTRADE) and in the organization of domestic trade and industry fairs. Interfirm organization at the sector level is, once more, considered an important secondary option in organizing marketing support services. Private sector based specialist marketing consultants are not considered to be a viable alternative.

As regards financial services, the dominant role of commercial banks is re-affirmed though there remains a role seen for government, especially as regards venture capital (Zimbabwe Venture Capital Company). The latter is somewhat unexpected given the rapid expansion and diversification of Zimbabwe's financial sector since financial liberalization in the early 1990s. Partnerships between the public and private sector for industrial restructuring and innovation have not gained much credibility. Only a small minority of firms consider these as relevant options. Last but not least, training services remain firmly in the realm of academic centres, but there is a clear shift towards sector associations and private commercial providers.

Do defensive firms have different institutional preferences than innovative firms? Are the latter 'loners' and the defensive firms more dependent on government? These issues have not yet been researched.

PRODUCER SERVICES

Under 'new competition', producer services (such as accounting, publicity, finance, computer, design, transport and distribution, engineering, procurement, marketing etc.) play an important role. The reason for this is that determinants of competitive capacity of enterprises have become manifold and are extended into all major functional areas of the enterprise (Goe, 1991). In the majority of cases these services, if provided internally from within the firms, represent high fixed costs and often have a high cost risk. Often a firm may not have sufficient internal demand or the services have a high level of complexity which makes it difficult for a company to internalize them. In these cases it would be advantageous for the firm to draw on external expertise. It is often also argued that firms that grew up under protected markets of the import substitution era have either incorporated certain functions for control purposes (for example, transport) or have not developed certain functions, such as marketing (Helmsing, 1993). The existence of a seller's market gave the firms little incentive to do so. Alternatively, functions may not have been available in the market and firms therefore have to internalize them (for example, computer hardware and software). Thus, there are several factors that may lead to the hypothesis that firms would increasingly rely on external expert services as competition heightens (due to liberalization) and the terms of competition change (due to 'new competition').

The research has sought to establish the status of producer services, their recent evolution and the factors that have caused any changes in the manner in which a firm caters for them. Table 5.9 gives a panoramic overview of these issues for each of the 20 producer services.

It is worth noting that certain services are not readily used by all firms, for example, catering services, advertising and publicity, computers. For these services, these firms don't make a choice for either 'make' or 'buy'.[10] The

Table 5.9 Producer services: internalized and contracted and frequency of change

Producer service	Key service in past 3 years*	Desirable service in future**	Internal service	Fully external contracted service	Partially contracted	Proportion contracted (n)	Frequency of change in past 3 years***
Accounting	20.5	46%	48%	31%	23%	46% (27)	2%
Advertising & Publicity	26.8	55%	58%	16%	9%	69% (14)	2%
Banking & Financial Services	11.1	31%	92%	6%	2%	35% (7)	2%
Catering	0.8	7%	40%	5%	5%	26%(10)	2%
Cleaning	19.5	7%	77%	7%	14%	33%(20)	0%
Computer hardware	14.7	37%	53%	7%	6%	29% (7)	1%
Computer software	12.9	35%	35%	16%	7%	30%(10)	2%
Design service	20.0	50%	86%	5%	3%	24% (9)	0%
Employment agency	2.6	12%	67%	14%	13%	29%(20)	1%
Labour recruitment	2.9	19%	75%	9%	10%	27%(16)	0%
Engineering & repair	9.9	24%	34%	24%	40%	24%(55)	0%
Legal services	2.3	11%	2%	85%	1%	90% (5)	0%
Grounds & buildings maintenance	19.3	5%	67%	11%	5%	71% (11)	0%
Management services	10.7	29%	69%	12%	13%	46% (22)	0%
Marketing	21.5	45%	86%	5%	5%	70% (9)	0%
Procurement	7.3	16%	88%	2%	8%	61% (15)	0%
Security	7.8	14%	42%	19%	37%	55% (50)	0%
Training	31.1	69%	6%	1%	2%	25% (2)	0%
Transport & distribution	9.0	19%	59%	4%	2%	73% (7)	0%

Producer service	Key service in past 3 years*	Desirable service in future**	Internal service	Fully external contracted service	Partially contracted	Proportion contracted (n)	Frequency of change in past 3 years***
Transport of staff	3.5	14%	78%	2%	4%	56% (10)	0%

Notes

* respondents were asked to assess on a scale of 1 to 5 the role the service played in raising competitiveness of the firm; these assessment were summed and divided by the sum total maximum score for each service.

** percentage of firms responding.

*** number of firms that has changed the provision of the service in the past three years increasing contracting.

Source: Survey.

services that are most frequently contracted externally are legal services, accounting services, engineering and repairs, security, advertising and publicity, and computer software. It is worth noting that most of these contracted-out services are not considered critical to raising competitiveness, for example legal services, engineering and repairs, and security, and possibly with the exception of accounting services and advertising.

The services in which one would expect more external (specialist) contracting for the purposes of strengthening 'new' competition capacity, such as design services, financial services, marketing and procurement (global sourcing), show that externalization is not taking place. Indeed in three of the five services that are considered, by the firms, as being a key to raising competitiveness, there is little contracting-out (notably design, training and marketing). The only positive sign is the fact that these services are considered to be ones that the respondents would wish to have locally available in the future. Even in traditional services such as industry and office cleaning, logistics and distribution, and transport of staff, external contracting of services is relatively low.

Finally, it is important to stress the lack of change with respect to the contracting-out and externalization of producer services. In this respect the situation is not much different from the one concerning industrial subcontracting. In both instances there is, on the whole, a relatively low degree of externalization.

In view of this evidence, the hypothesis formulated above needs to be rejected: Zimbabwen firms are not 'vertically disintegrating' in as far as producer services are concerned. Externalization is generally at low levels and no significant increase can be detected.

Are there differences in the pattern of externalization and contracting-out of producer services between defensive and innovative firms? As we saw above, there is generally little externalization and contracting-out and few changes were observed in the period 1992–5. The numbers are small and the differences between innovative and defensive firms are too small to be significant.

CONCLUDING OBSERVATIONS

With the implementation of the structural adjustment programme 'old' institutions have fallen away (for example forex allocation, import controls, seller's markets) and firms have been exposed to a greater variety of external and competitive threats. Not all firms responded to these external changes in innovative ways. A large number are 'indecisive' and made no explicit real choices. Others reacted defensively, and these firms may indeed take the 'low road' of (de-)industrialization. The strong impression the research (survey and interviews) has generated is that these defensive responses are born out of necessity and lack of knowledge as to possible avenues and options of change, while keeping the business running 'as usual' but under increasing stresses and strains.

In adjusting to liberalized markets, firms have to redefine their routines and practices on many fronts, that is not only in terms of technology. Product and process innovations are needed, but also strengthening of management, developing of marketing functions and engaging in HRD. In this context, we do observe some differences between defensive and innovative firms. The latter pay more attention to areas that are listed as critical to 'new competition' (product and product group development, better integration of production, marketing and sales and other management improvements, and those in the area of marketing).

The competitive capacity of a firm depends not only on its internal capacity, but also on the efficiency and capacity of its suppliers and on the environment in which they operate. Support institutions are part of this environment. One of the 'blind spots' in structural adjustment policies has been the creation of new institutions that enable firms to compete effectively. Enterprise support services for industry continue to play a role, but there is little theory that guides its institutionalization. This study has shown that there continues to be use of and demand for enterprise support services.

As for the institutional modalities of services delivery and the preferences of firms, it may be concluded that firms in Bulawayo have not *en masse* turned away from public agencies, though the functions these agencies play are more narrowly defined than in the past. Private sector firms perform only particular roles (notably product design, training and international trade). Sector associations have become one of the key intermediaries through which firms acquire information and support.[11]

The notion of 'innovative milieu' centres around public, collective and private institutions involved in R&D, generating and transmitting technological innovations. In an innovative milieu there is interaction between firms and the institutions concerned in order to co-ordinate the direction of information gathering and R&D efforts. Perhaps the most sobering point in the case of Bulawayo is the notable absence of academic institutions among the agencies most preferred to deliver technological support services. This would seem to be indicative of an absence of concrete interactions. Sector associations are the key intermediary with respect to technological support services, with commercial firms and government agencies performing particular roles. The role of these sector associations, their strengths and weaknesses, are as yet not well understood.

Producer or business services refer to functions that support internal co-ordination and external transactions as well as direct services that support manufacturing operations. There is some overlap between these producer services and the enterprise support services examined above. Both types of services contribute to the creation of an innovative milieu. Specialist producer service firms that establish themselves in response to externalization of these services by established manufacturing firms create agglomeration advantages for other (and smaller) firms that hitherto had not internalized these services nor had any access to them. The research found that relatively little externalization of these producer services had actually taken place among established manufacturing firms since adjustment began. The ones that have been externalized refer to 'conventional' producer services, but not to those that play a role in 'new' competition. Very few firms shifted towards contracting-out of producer services during the period analysed, and no differences could be detected between innovative and defensive firms. It would therefore seem reasonable to conclude that, in the case of Bulawayo, producer services do not as yet contribute to creating an innovative milieu.

For the creation of a local innovative milieu 'it takes two to tango'. Both firms and support systems have to come into tune with each other. However, both have been subjected to adjustment. There is a tendency towards 'vertical link up' via the sector associations. There would seem to be however, as yet, insufficient interaction between the firms themselves and between firms and the support institutions to co-ordinate actions to strengthen local competitive capacity.

NOTES

1. This research project has the following aims: i) to examine the competitive responses of manufacturing firms in the city of Bulawayo, to liberalization and opening up of the Zimbabwean economy; ii) to examine the use of support services, and iii) to examine the role of business or producer services.
2. Chronicle, 6/10/94. The Chronicle of 27/6/95 reported that in the first half of 1995, 22 firms had been liquidated. Since 1991 a total of 130 manufacturing companies had gone into liquidation, another 82 were declared insolvent and at least ten others were placed under judicial management. These are nationwide figures.
3. On the basis of our estimates, the membership of the local chamber currently covers approximately 40 per cent of all registered firms.
4. Selection of firms was done with the following criteria. Firms that had not explicitly taken measures to implement their adopted strategies were excluded. Furthermore, firms that adopted more than six responses were excluded from the analysis. The cut-off criterion is somewhat arbitrary and intuitive. It is motivated by the need to screen out undeciding entrepreneurs and non-revealers. The defensive and innovative category is defined as firms having responses in both categories. The overall percentage of firms retained in the sample is 68 per cent and varies somewhat by sector. Clothing and metal fabrication have the highest proportion of firms screen-out (62 and 59 per cent respectively), while three-quarters of the furniture firms and 81.5 per cent of the engineering firms were retained.
5. The cross-tabulation yielded a chi square (6.862), significance (0.334).

6. The cross-tabulation gave a chi square of (5.91), significance (0.433).
7. A detailed enumeration of actions identified under each of the areas can be seen in appendix 1 of Helmsing (1998b).
8. Respondents could give multiple answers in each category as well as add their own actions, in addition to the ones listed. In order to reduce the range to be analysed, firms were asked to indicate which of the selected actions had been the dominant one.
9. For each action the respondent could respond 'yes' or 'no'. Cross tabulating for two subgroups of firms generated 2*2 tables for which chi squares were computed. These are reproduced in table 5.6 in the main text.
10. This explains why the percentages of columns 4, 5 and 6 do not add up to 100.
11. This may be partly explained by having lost its function in the (pre-ESAP) forex allocation system.

REFERENCES

Best, M.H. (1990), *The New Competition. Institutions of Industrial Restructuring*, Cambridge, Mass.: Harvard University Press.
Braunerhjelm, P. and G. Fors (1996), 'The Zimbabwean manufacturing sector. Current status and future development', Stockholm, Industrial Institute for Economic and Social Research.
Central Statistics Office, various years, Quarterly Digest of Statistics, Harare: CSO.
Central Statistics Office, various years, Census of Manufacturing Industry, Harare: CSO.
Goe, W.R. (1991), 'The growth of producer service industries: sorting out the externalization debate', *Growth and Change*, Fall, pp. 118–41.
GoZ (1991), *Zimbabwe. A Framework for Economic Reform (1991-95)*, Harare.
Hawkins, A. *et al.* (1998), 'Formal sector employment demand conditions in Zimbabwe', University of Zimbabwe, Harare.
Helmsing, A.H.J. (1993), 'Small enterprise and industrialization policies in Afrika: some notes', in Helmsing and Kolstee (eds).
Helmsing, A.H.J. (1998a), 'Theories of regional industrial development and "second" and "third" generation regional policies', Paper at Fourth International Seminar Iber-American Network of Researchers on Globalization and Territory, Bogota, 22-4 April 1998.
Helmsing, A.H.J. (1998b), *Survey of Economic Restructuring and Competitiveness of Manufacturing Industries, Bulawayo, Zimbabwe*, The Hague: Institute of Social Studies.
Helmsing, A.H.J. and Th. Kolstee (eds) (1993), *Small enterprises and changing policies*, London: IT Publications.
Landabaso, M. (1997), 'The promotion of innovation in regional policy: proposals for a regional innovation strategy', *Entrepreneurship and Regional Development*, **9**, 1–24
Levy, B. (1994), *Succesful Small and Medium Enterprises and their Support Systems: a Comparative Analysis of Four Countries*, Washington, DC: World Bank.
Maillat, D. (1997), 'Territorial dynamic, innovative milieus and regional policy', *Entrepreneurship and Regional Development*, **7**, pp. 157–65.
Morgan, K. (1997), 'The learning region: institutions, innovation and regional renewal', *Regional Studies*, **31** (5), pp. 491–503.
Storper, M. and A.J. Scott (eds) (1992), *Pathways to Industrialization and Regional Development*, London: Routledge.

6. Innovation and small enterprise development examples from Burkina Faso, Ghana and Zimbabwe

Meine Pieter van Dijk

Innovation is crucial for small enterprises to become and remain competitive. We would like to assess what experience has been gained with technological development, the promotion of innovation and its diffusion in a third world context and in particular in two West African countries and one southern African country. Three levels of analysis were distinguished in Chapter 1. First, the policy level promoting (or discouraging) innovation and innovation diffusion. Secondly, the level of the business support system and the importance that technological development and innovation play at that level and, finally, the level of the enterprise or a cluster of enterprises where the actual development and diffusion should take place. Our data for Burkina Faso, Ghana and Zimbabwe are at the latter level.

In the global economy a great deal of technology is available on the shelf and can be bought. Even poor countries like Bangladesh tend to buy modern technologies, fearing that their exports would otherwise not be able to compete on the world market (Van Dijk, 1995). In this contribution we will also look at the mechanisms of technology transfer, the local capacity to adapt and develop technologies and the degree to which government, private sector associations and donor organizations can influence the process.

Some examples will be given of enterprise co-operation stimulating innovation in Ghana. Subsequently different forms of interfirm relations will be discussed for small entrepreneurs in Burkina Faso to assess to what extent they stimulate innovation. Finally, the importance of clusters and networks for small enterprises, allowing them to co-operate, is illustrated together with data collected in Burkina Faso.

INNOVATION THEORY

Different theoretical perspectives can be pursued concerning innovation and

SMEs, but the emphasis is on what promotes innovation for small enterprise development. According to traditional neo-classical growth theory, the long-term rate of growth of an economy equals the rate of growth of the labour force. An increase in investments would only temporarily lead to a higher rate of growth (Kolnaar, 1999). The theory does not distinguish between the effects of these investments for small or large enterprises.

The more recent endogenous growth theory has pointed to the importance of supply-side oriented policies for economic growth. The endogenous growth theory stresses the importance of economies of scale and endogenous labour-saving developments. It brings in scale, and the theory emphasizes the importance of endogenous technological development. Such development is influenced by research and development activities but also by learning-by-doing. The later aspect makes it relevant for the small enterprise field and allows a link with the flexible specialization concept studied previously (Pedersen *et al.*, 1994). Is innovation a combination of an innovative mentality, skilled labour and multipurpose equipment? Does flexible specialization lead to innovation? It has been proven that industrial districts can contribute to the process of innovation and technological development (Pyke and Sengenberger, 1992). That leads to the question: can flexible specialization and industrial districts be promoted (Van Dijk, 2001)?

Solow (1957) was the first to recognize the importance of research and development (R&D) for economic development. The endogenization of innovation in the productive process has been one of the reasons why developed countries could continue growing, while wages in developing countries were sometimes ten times as low. If this is the case, what can governments do to intensify the R&D benefit to small enterprises and what can be done to ensure the quickest possible diffusion of innovative results to them?

Galbraith (1967) showed that innovations are not any more spontaneous, but the result of systematic R&D to manipulate consumer tastes to raise profits over time. New product innovations share common traits, and they often occur in production units located in, or near, affluent markets with strong science-based universities or other research institutions and enterpreneurially oriented financial institutions (Abarnathy and Utterback, 1978). Spillovers are facilitated by the geographic nearness of enterprises and research centres within a certain region. Systematic research benefiting small enterprises may be rare, but their tendency to be geographically concentrated may help them to absorb new ideas and ways of producing goods and services.

It is important to find out how R&D spills over from research centres and R&D departments of industrial corporations to third-party firms. It would be helpful in that case if the differences could be assessed between the ways in which large and small enterprises are taking advantage of such R&D

spillovers. Acs *et al.* (1992) found for example that corporate R&D is a relatively more important source for generating innovation in large firms, while spillovers from university research laboratories are more important in stimulating innovative activities in small firms.

Innovation at the level of the firm is in the first place the outcome of a cumulative process. It is cumulative in the sense that technologies of production used today influence learning processes and the nature of accumulated experience in the individual firm or the collectivity of firms in an industrial district. Calbrese and Rolfo (1992) made a study of the introduction of product and process innovations in small firms and conclude that the factors which have positively or negatively conditioned the firms in their innovative process change according to the technological level of the single innovation and to the organization and management implications connected.

Schumpeter (1942) pointed to the innovative entrepreneur creating and resolving various kinds of technological and organizational disequilibria. However, neo-classical theory uses a very narrow definition of technology and does not take continuous innovation into account. Defined in a broad way, technology is not just a question of machines or tools. Technology and innovation for small and medium enterprises are also related to the design and quality of the product, to the type and quality of raw materials used, to the organization of production and the packaging and selling of the final product. Given the broader definition of technology, it is not something fixed, but rather something changing constantly, resulting in different cost of production and increased productivity.

CHOICE OF TECHNOLOGY IN THE CASE OF SMALL ENTERPRISES

Trulsson (1997: 208) argues that economists tend to treat the choice of technology as an endogenous factor, determined primarily by economic considerations. Important variables would be scale of production, the necessary investments (determining the capital-intensity of the project) and the running cost (including repair and maintenance). This would lead to a perspective of technological determinism, or path dependence in technology development. Developing countries would have to follow the same technology development path as developed economies in order to succeed. This suggests an increasingly capital intensive way of production over time, when labour becomes more expensive in the course of the development process (Rostov, 1956).[1]

Technological determinism has been challenged from two directions. On the one hand, the appropriate technology movement has criticized it, arguing that given the availability of cheap and low-skilled labour in developing countries, other technologies may be more appropriate (Schutter and Bremer, eds, 1980). On the other hand, some studies of the Asian tiger economies have argued that these countries have managed to leapfrog in the case of technology (Van Hoesel, 1997: 171).

According to Trulsson's more sociological approach to the subject there are three approaches to choosing technology:

- product quality orientation (50 per cent of his entrepreneurs find the means to produce a particular product, often with certain quality characteristics),
- opportunity seizure (in particular the inexperienced entrepreneurs leave it to the organization willing to help them to choose the technology and sometimes even the product), and
- imitation (if no assistance is obtained you imitate the technology choices of others).

Trulsson stresses, however, that the choice of product comes first, suggesting that the entrepreneur limits his options because he has in mind a certain product of a certain quality. These considerations are linked to his/her knowledge of the potential market for that product of a certain quality and the potential competitors available. This approach is linked to what is called 'social constructivists'. The social constructivists argue that technological solutions are not the result of technological considerations alone, but of highly social considerations as well. This school of thought emphasizes the 'social embeddedness' of the choice of technology and goes as far as saying that it determines 'the efficiency or functionality of specific technologies' (Trulsson, 1997: 209).

INNOVATIONS

Schumpeter (1942) had already stressed the role of innovative entrepreneurs in economic development, while McClelland analysed entrepreneurship and argued that this characteristic can be developed in a systematic way. Their ideas combined with a third world context led to an interest in entrepreneurship development. Others argue that Western countries have made major innovations (in the capital goods sector), while developing countries have not had the opportunity to make capital-saving innovations and have usually imported capital goods. This implies that they have not developed the technological base skills: 'the knowledge, facilities and organizations upon which further technical progress so largely depends'. This is what we would call technological capacity (Van Dijk, 1995).

Relevant to the local innovation system are certainly the following: local development, adaptation and diffusion of technologies and the role of research and development institutes and institutions for higher education and training. Technology partnerships could be another example, but one can also think of a similar role played by clusters, networks, industrial districts, and so on. In the literature a distinction is made between inventions and innovations, between the core technology of an industrial enterprise and auxiliary technologies (concerning the organization, the marketing, financing, and the handling of inputs and the final product).[2] A distinction can also be made between best technology and appropriate technology. Barnett (1995) stresses the importance of technology sophisticated in design, but robust and simple in its use.

The choice of technology is not only a question of prices of capital and labour, it also has to do with the requirements on the world market, the possibility of maintaining and adapting the technology locally and the possibilities of delinking technologies, separating core production technologies, input treatment and output packaging. Technology transfer also takes place more or less spontaneously in the framework of globalization, subcontracting and innovation diffusion.

Introducing new technologies is a question of first making them known to potential users. Subsequently they need to be made available and finally their introduction can be facilitated through financial, technical or other incentives. On top of that the local capacity to maintain, adapt and develop these technologies is important. This local technological capacity needs to be developed. If such capacity is available, there is no longer a need to transfer technologies lock, stock and barrel, but local adaptation and development will take place. The science and technology policy of a country can help to develop such a capacity (see OECD, 1991).[3] Technology partnerships can also help to achieve this.

In the past, the factor scale has received too much attention in the literature on technology. Large scale was considered to be more competitive than small scale. We have learned that small scale can compete through clustering, networks, interfirm relations and flexible specialization. New technologies have become available which are profitable on a small scale. UNCTAD (1998) also stresses the importance of interfirm co-operation to enable firms to meet the challenges of the new international competitive environment.

Concepts like flexible specialization (Van Dijk, 1992) and industrial districts (Van Dijk, 1993) stress the importance of certain entrepreneurial characteristics, such as an innovative mentality. Flexible specialization strategies have enabled small entrepreneurs in different countries to survive, and have allowed their enterprises to become competitive with larger enterprises.[4] Dijkman and Van Dijk (1997) checked each enterprise in a sample of small entrepreneurs for market and product innovation. They noted down instances of market innovation using subcontracting, different forms of co-operation between small enterprises and links with other sectors (inputs from the informal or the formal sector). Process innovation is defined as changing the production of a product, by enhancing the efficiency or the effectiveness of the production process. Enterprises were often part of a cluster and the entrepreneur's function in networks.[5]

Van Dijk (1992) defines flexible specialization as a higher-order concept, which points to six important, and often interrelated, characteristics of the dynamic small enterprise sector:

1. an innovative mentality on the part of the entrepreneur;
2. the technology used by personnel trained on the job, which often has a multi-purpose character;
3. interfirm co-operation often in the form of subcontracting;
4. clustering of micro and small enterprises (cluster as a geographical grouping);
5. networking of micro and small entrepreneurs (networking defined as the set of relations in which an entrepreneur operates); and
6. specialization and proven flexibility.

The result of the interplay of these characteristics is often a collective efficiency for the units working in the cluster (Schmitz, 1992).

CO-OPERATION BETWEEN SMALL ENTERPRISES AND INNOVATION IN ACCRA

Research undertaken for the World Bank concerned the effects of structural adjustment for the working poor.[6] Constraints for small and medium enterprises in Accra, the capital of Ghana, were classified as related to the macroeconomic environment (the negative policy context, the discouraging impact of taxes and regulations), related to the entrepreneur (limited education, training, business skills), the enterprise (low initial investments, the chosen technology, location, etc.) and related to the market (the demand for these products and services). The resulting low productivity could be explained through a series of factors: small initial investments and no access to capital, low levels of technology and training, a poorly developed infrastructure and high production costs.

However, much differentiation between enterprises was found, ranging from very marginal to very promising cases. This phenomenon is related to the qualities of entrepreneurs, the technology used and the new opportunities provided in a liberalized market. Typically the more innovative entrepreneurs were found at the edge of the neighbourhood studied (Abeka), along the major roads. Some of these entrepreneurs were ready to move to a location identified by local government for the concentration of metal-related trades (Ofanko). They expected a number of advantages from being there, together with other entrepreneurs. Most of the enterprises at the edge of the neighbourhood studied were very specialized and used machines. They often developed new products and were competing with producers elsewhere in Accra.

Two very innovative entrepreneurs were interviewed at the edge of Abeka making moulds and parts. One has heavy machines to make aluminium moulds for local production of household utensils, while the other is a real innovator. The first one would like to design his own machines and to manufacture 'things that can move'. He complains that it is difficult to get the latest machines. He knows about the Intermediate Technology Transfer Unit (ITTU) which helps small and medium enterprises to buy second hand equipment. The other can make almost everything. He makes block making machines, car parts, gas cookers and gas containers for welders (carbide pots). He can also make tools for carpentry, spraying machines and nuts and bolts. He also wants to move to Ofanka, where he expects more space and a larger number of colleagues and customers. The higher turnover, the higher salaries and the innovative capacity of a number of these entrepreneurs at the edge of Abeka is striking.

Examples of co-operation between entrepreneurs' stimulating innovation were also found. Ethnic affiliations play quite an important role in labour networks and different forms of enterprise co-operation. Effectively exploring employment opportunities is hardly feasible without the assistance of tribesmen; masters usually hire apprentices of their own kin; subcontracting is delegated to tribe members; co-operation between different masters is quite often based on kinship. The access to jobs or apprenticeship training, and the participation in clusters are highly influenced by ethnic affiliations.

An interesting case can illustrate these mechanisms. The stand of a wheelcover and brake fluid seller is very well located in the curve of the Nima Highway, observable from far and everybody has to slow down to get through the curve. His proximity to the cluster of fitting shops gives him an additional locational advantage. An electrical mechanic is part of the same cluster and receives his comparative advantage from the fact that he is the only one within the cluster who owns a charging machine to test batteries. The enterprises located at the edge of Abeka, along the 'Motorway' and along the main road to Kumasi were generally more dynamic than the enterprises located in the interior of the neighbourhood. The success story of the wheelcover and brake fluid seller is again a good example of someone who is able to find a niche in the market. He anticipated new developments in the second-hand car market and could outwit his competition through diversification and location. Economies of scale and co-operation in clusters, leading to new ideas and new ways of doing things turned out to be important conditions to develop an enterprise's potential for growth.

INTERFIRM CO-OPERATION AND INNOVATION IN BURKINA FASO

Competition is fierce in Ouagadougou and some entrepreneurs have tried new ways to access clients, for example by moving their enterprises to a more favourable spot. These examples fit in the broad definition of innovation given in Chapter 1. Entrepreneurs have tried to make their products more attractive by improving the quality of the product or the way in which the product is presented, by offering clients credit or by adding something special to the product. Some entrepreneurs have tried to attract clients by selling their goods on credit. Beer brewers build improved stoves to reduce the wood needed to prepare beer. One entrepreneur was the first in Ouagadougou to start making spare parts for motorcycles. He has trained a number of apprentices since. These spare parts are now produced in considerable quantities in Ouagadougou.

Five forms of interfirm co-operation between small enterprises were distinguished and will be discussed. First, entrepreneurs in one activity work together to limit competition or to reduce costs. Secondly, entrepreneurs in different, but complementary activities work together to be more attractive to clients. Thirdly, entrepreneurs make use of other enterprises to obtain equipment and/or training and gradually develop their own business. Fourthly, people simply become co-entrepreneurs and, finally, entrepreneurs let their workshop to another entrepreneur, or they open a branch office. To reduce costs or to limit competition, some entrepreneurs in the same activity work together. For instance, electrical repairmen regularly provide spare parts to each other from broken down equipment. Women brewing beer in some neighbourhoods have agreed to take turns brewing, so that they do not have to face competition. A similar arrangement seems to have been made by mobile tailors. They have divided the city into areas and walk through their neighbourhoods with their machine on their head. Another example is a woman who sells fruit and vegetables. She often buys in bulk with other women; they share the products and sell independently. Some young women rent a space together for weaving cloth. They were trained at a centre for handicapped people and decided afterwards to stay together, but work individually. One woman, who grills groundnuts and makes groundnut oil, shares her equipment with several other women. The machines used to grill the groundnuts are owned by a group of nine women.

Entrepreneurs in different but complementary activities can work together to make their business more attractive for customers. This can either be done by a sharing arrangement, or by some form of subcontracting. For instance, one carpenter decided to associate with an entrepreneur in upholstery. A car repairman has established his workplace near the small workshops of electrical repairmen to whom he entrusts certain jobs. The same man asked a welder and a sheet metal worker to install themselves at the same location. The three types of enterprises remain independent but work together. Two brothers made similar arrangements: one of them fixes lorry engines, the other has a welding shop. The enterprises are separate but they complement each other. Some entrepreneurs locate complementary activities in one place increasing sales for all. One brewer sells beer alongside a woman (another wife of her husband) who sells rice. The two work together. One woman who sells rice asked another woman who sells 'bassi' (a product made of millet or red sorghum) and yoghurt to join her at the same spot.

Informal sector entrepreneurs have proved to be very good at creating an enterprise out of virtually nothing. Through other people, they are able to acquire skills, equipment, or a workplace and to develop their enterprise gradually. Entrepreneurs get their education in various ways. They sometimes go to other countries to learn new skills. A male metal furniture maker went to Ivory Coast to learn how to assure watertightness and airtightness, allowing him to make tanks. Examples of informal sector entrepreneurs who employ skilled labour are scarce. Skills are important, however. A male bricklayer, for example, says he works with precision to gain the trust of his clients and to get good references from them. Many skilled people start their own businesses and train the apprentices or labourers themselves.

Numerous other examples of co-operation were found. A female weaver worked with her mother, who does the same work. Now she is married and rents the loom from her mother. A female tailor started with a rented sewing machine. After a few years, she was able to buy two sewing machines. Similarly, a man making bricks rented his tools, but has gradually been able to buy his own. A young man transporting and selling water (using a cart, two barrels and a donkey) sometimes rents an extra cart and employs a boy in order to make extra profits. One of his colleagues uses two barrels, which he pulls himself. One barrel is his; the other one is rented. In the long queues for water he aligns one barrel under the tap, while he leaves to sell the contents of other one. The owner of the second barrel is paid at the end of the day with two full barrels of water.

In only six cases out of 350 did the interviewed entrepreneurs work together with somebody else, apparently sharing management and profits. Often, these were two wives of the same husband. They could either work together full-time, or take turns working at home and working for their enterprise. Men sometimes do the same. For instance, a construction worker is sometimes assisted by his older brother and a female tailor works with her brother.

Finally, the following are two examples of the fifth type of interfirm co-operation. One male tailor worked in Ivory Coast but returned because he preferred his own country. He left behind a workshop in Abidjan with an electric sewing machine, which is now rented to another tailor. A female entrepreneur in Ouagadougou sells meals and had two sisters working for her as family labour. She recently installed one sister at another spot, but continues to co-operate with her.

THE EFFECTS OF CLUSTERING IN BURKINA FASO

Both modern and traditional forms of clustering and networks exist in Ouagadougou. Entrepreneurs take advantage of those forms that are beneficial to them. Different forms of networks distinguished are large, formal groups; small informal groups such as the Rotating Savings and Credit Associations (RoSCAs or tontines in Burkina Faso); and small groups of mutual supporting entrepreneurs, based on family, tribe or regional relations. Traditional clusters can be clusters of entrepreneurs belonging to one tribal group or clusters of enterprises closely located on their own initiative and benefiting from being together. Industrial estates, handicraft zones and municipal markets are considered modern clusters. Family networks will be treated in the next section.

A large number of Burkinabè entrepreneurs are reluctant to work in groups. When asked if they would like to co-operate, almost a third answered that people were not to be trusted (*les gens ne sont pas honnêtes*). Others refused to co-operate unless they were forced to (*à moins que l'état me l'oblige!*), or stated that it is difficult to work with other women (*les femmes sont difficiles à comprendre*). A young man who transports water literally said that other people are not to be trusted (*les gens sont des faux types*). Another male entrepreneur sighed: 'can we work in a co-operative, given the mentality of the people'? (*on se demande si l'on pourra travailler en coopérative à cause de la mentalité des gens*).

Others are willing to work in a co-operative. Half of the entrepreneurs responded positively to this question, while about a sixth formulated some conditions. One tailor was very much interested in co-operation. He had previously been a representative for other tailors, when they were asked by the authorities to co-operate. By doing so, the tailors accessed new markets, for instance, for school uniforms. Similarly, a female tailor joined such a co-operative. A male artist was a member of two associations: the '*association des artistes plasticiens du Burkina*' and the '*association internationale des arts plastiques*'.

Women often form tontines or use their networks to generate money. For instance, a beer brewer participates in a tontine of ten women. Each contributes 3000 FCFA per month. Each month the total amount collected is given to one of the members. Another woman sells a local soft drink called *bisap* and runs a tontine of 12 women. Each pays 5000 FCFA per month. A woman selling fruit and vegetables participates in a tontine of 12 women, each of which puts aside 200 FCFA per day.

Sometimes the fact that other enterprises are located nearby becomes a decisive factor for an entrepreneur who wishes to locate his/her enterprise in a specific spot. For instance, an entrepreneur who sells corrugated iron chose a place near where a metal worker and a welder were already working. Caste or tribe can also influence the choice of a location. A Nigerian male hairdresser chose to settle in a particular place, where other Yorubas live.

NETWORKS OF ENTERPRISES, FAMILY AND FRIENDS IN OUAGADOUGOU

The subject of networks of family and friends was investigated in a number of different ways. Family and friends can be very helpful to entrepreneurs by providing them labour, work space or capital. Relatives can provide cheap family labour, and a workshop, a plot or shed can be provided at a reduced price. Finally, family or friends can provide the capital for initial or additional investments. Almost two thirds of the entrepreneurs make use of help from their family or friends. One fifth even use the help in more than one way. Women, more often than men, use their connections (72 versus 54 per cent, respectively).

In some activities entrepreneurs make more use of aid from family and friends than in other activities. This occurs in edible products (in 19 out of 25 cases); metal working (in 13 out of 22) and electrical repair (9 out of 17). These data are probably an underestimation, since other relations between the enterprise and the family (the use of family for channelling output or receiving training) were not recorded systematically.

Entrepreneurs can receive informal education through their family or friends, or they can be dependent on them for the purchase of inputs or the sales of outputs. Some entrepreneurs indicated that they lack these relations and, therefore, have problems in developing their enterprises. One entrepreneur reported having good relations with someone in the government through whom he received large government orders.

Household expenditures also interact with running the business. Entrepreneurs can provide their family or friends with money or gifts, but can also receive help from them. For instance, a woman selling meals gives money to a family member who lives in a village and to others who live in Ouagadougou. A female tailor specified that she spends about 20 000 FCFA per year for her mother and 5000 FCFA for her father.

Assistance can also be given the other way around. For instance, a male bicycle repairman cum farmer and his wife, who sells vegetables, cannot earn enough to support themselves and their five children. Often, they receive assistance from friends and family. A female entrepreneur whose husband is ill is sometimes supported by her son, who is a carpenter. Male entrepreneurs are also supported by their wife/wives and other relatives so they can satisfy the basic household needs. For instance, a male entrepreneur who makes metal furniture is unable to provide sufficient food for his eight children. His wife sells peanut butter and his daughter also works, to support the family.

ENTERPRISE CO-OPERATION AND INNOVATION IN ZIMBABWE

Two different types of enterprise co-operation can be distinguished. One is that between small and medium enterprises as the ones discussed, and the second is the co-operation between large international enterprises and local enterprises as in this case of Zimbabwe.

The *Business Herald* in Zimbabwe (9 July 1998) recently provided information on two partnerships between large international enterprises and local enterprises. A local mining company is seeking technical partners under a major restructuring exercise to diversify the group's activities and improve cash flow and profitability. 'The company was reorganising its operations and forming technical and strategic alliances to meet present and future challenges.' The restructuring programme included the strengthening of the company's human resources base and shedding the company's non-core business and a wide range of cost-cutting measures. The search for a technical partner is going to mark the group's first step in reducing reliance on one mineral. The most likely candidate for this partnership is an international mining company.

The same issue of the *Business Herald* reports on its first page on a multi-million (Zimbabwean) dollar (one US equalled 17 Z $ at that time) joint venture between a local paper and packaging firm and a similar South African firm. The new entity will be a major force in the printing and packaging industry. The reasons advanced for this international deal are on the one hand the company's need for finance to pay its debts, and to expand into export markets to cushion itself from the domestic problems caused by the fall in the Zimbabwe dollar. The partnership will bring the expertise required by the company to improve its products and stand up to the intense competition. The firm had been criticized for producing sub-standard packaging materials, which disadvantaged packaged products on international markets.

For similar reasons a large number of different forms of co-operation come into existence every day between companies in different parts of the world. The *Financial Times* (30 July 1998) announced for example that Philips in the Netherlands had bought a company in the United States which developed ultrasound for medical diagnostic technology applications. Such acquisitions are not limited to the industrial sector. The Netherlands KLM Airlines holds a 26 per cent stake in Kenya Airways and the South African listed Del Monte fruit cannery linked up with an Italian group with interests in dairy products, tomato paste and football (both in the *Financial Times* 14 July 1998). We learn from these examples that the combinations are sometimes unexpected and that the developing, as well as the developed countries can take a leading role, and that technology, finance or access to new markets seem to be the three major reasons to start a partnership.

CONCLUSIONS

Choice of technology is often discussed at very different levels. Economists tend to see it as a macroeconomic issue, determined by the prices of capital and labour. The appropriate technology movement tends to look at the meso level of markets and intermediaries. The question is: which technologies are known, made available and made attractive (Van Dijk, 1982)? Finally a number of micro-level studies tend to stress factors like the attitude of the entrepreneur, the opportunities arising and the exposure to certain examples (Trulsson, 1997).

Technological capacity is often developed from below, building on the level of skills of the workers, the training capacity in the country and the available institutions for technology adaptation and innovation diffusion. The science and technology, the research and development or direct innovation policies can have a beneficial impact on the local technological capability.

Donor organizations certainly play a role in the process of technology transfer and adaptation, although not always a positive one if tied aid leads to supply of inappropriate technologies. UNCTAD (1998) discusses new approaches to technology capacity building in developing countries, including a number of examples of enterprise co-operation. This indicates a change of thinking. Where we used to stress the role of the government in this process, now the emphasis is on what the private sector can contribute to technology development and innovation diffusion.

The challenge is to go from an approach stressing the transfer of technology to one stressing the development of local capacity to develop and adapt technology, possibly with some assistance in the framework of development co-operation. Private firms would be a major actor in this case, besides universities, local research and development organizations and the technical and practical skills available in the country. The latter are often available at the level of small and medium enterprises. Multinational companies can also play a role, in particular in the case of strategic alliances and in the case of multi-country production and distribution.[7]

Technology partnerships can contribute to the solution of a number of development issues. One type of partnership, namely one where financing is playing a key role, has received little attention until now and more needs to be learned from a large number of experiences. Research should start with identifying the stakeholders (their interests and the criteria they use to look at the project) and the shared values of the parties involved (which could help shared learning and the development of commitment). It should try to determine the impact of different cultural backgrounds of the partners involved and try to identify the factors that contribute to the success of these projects.

We have argued that there is a need to learn from the large number of experiences that have been going on in this field. A partnership is a shared learning experience. To allow the learning to take place in a systematic way, research institutes need to be involved and those parts of the private and public sectors involved need to take a more open approach to this kind of shared learning process.

RECOMMENDATIONS

What is the role of different institutes and levels of government in making available the necessary technologies for small and medium enterprises in developing countries? We would like to take a policy and development perspective: how to stimulate local technological capability. We will first mention examples of a local science and technology system, beneficial to small enterprise development (see UNCTAD, 1995 and 1996). Secondly, we shall look at the role of intermediary organizations in local innovation systems (for example, Lalkaka, 1994).[8]

Different types of technology partnerships can be distinguished and can play a role. For example, co-operation between the private and public sector in the framework of private–public partnerships (PPPs) and partnerships between private enterprises.[9] It is also possible to distinguish partnerships for a different purpose, besides a general partnership. In particular the distinction between technological, marketing and financial partnerships is important.[10] In the first two cases the objective is to gain access to a certain technology or to capture new markets. In public–private partnerships the management capacity of the private sector is often sought in addition to the financial support from this sector for a certain project.

Partnership is a generic term and the relationship may take on different legal forms, such as a joint venture,[11] a takeover, and a strategic alliance. Joint ventures with a technology component are announced regularly, for example in the *Financial Times*. Instead of seeking a partnership a company may prefer to build up a local subsidiary or use an existing sales outlet. In the case of technology, licensing and franchising are alternatives for technology partnerships.

Technology partnerships are important because technology is transferred in a reasonable way, without too much government interference. Governments, donors and non-governmental organizations (NGOs) could also be interested in developing technologies for basic needs, because that would establish a direct link with the situation poor people live in (cf. Singer, 1977).

Foreign investments may play an important part, and the way to make foreign investment in developing countries more attractive is to provide more up-to-date information to potential investors. In practice technology partnerships are often a necessary condition for entering certain markets. Government policies can enhance partnering by facilitating the development of local technological, managerial and organizational capabilities (UNCTAD, 1998).

The government may help to stimulate technology development and innovation diffusion. Science and technology policies could be directed towards developing products and to improving production methods of micro and small entrepreneurs. The government could help to develop centres of technology development and innovation diffusion, which would help micro- and small entrepreneurs to innovate, to produce different products in different ways. However, even in this case a maximum use should be made of existing technology development centres, for example the ones related to universities and the private sector. To assure a maximum use of these technology centres a business and technology support system needs to be put in place (Pedersen *et al.*, eds, 1994).

Entrepreneurship development programmes can be useful, particularly for female entrepreneurs and for enterprises that are blocked at a certain level and find it difficult to make the next step. Access to credit and government orders should be facilitated for entrepreneurs who co-operate and for those who participate in clusters and networks.

Barriers to entry should be diminished through deregulation and by facilitating administrative procedures. Information and assistance should be given to entrepreneurs on how to deal with existing formal requirements. Specialization should be stimulated through training entrepreneurs in changing designs, products, production methods and marketing channels.

Some of the major issues for developing countries are the consequences of globalization, capacity development and sustainable development. Ideas with respect to sustainable development have been discussed in the framework of the Rio conference in 1992. The major theme seems to be how capacity building can be improved by using partnerships and new forms of finance that have become available due to further globalization of the world economy. We are looking for possibilities for partnerships between enterprises of different sizes and how to create enabling policies and necessary mechanisms on the part of developed and developing countries to promote and provide incentives for such forms of co-operation.

The development of clusters, networks and different forms of co-operation should be stimulated to bring in new ideas in the business sector. Innovation and interfirm co-operation (in clusters or through subcontracting) are key words for this kind of development, as suggested by the flexible specialization paradigm. Providing space for economic activities, preferable at the same time for enterprises of different sizes can stimulate the creation of clusters of innovative entrepreneurs. Multipurpose equipment can help them to become more innovative. The development of clusters of economic activities should be stimulated, including the physical grouping of enterprises of different sizes. Subcontracting and other relations between micro, small, medium and large enterprises need to be developed.

NOTES

1. The relation between technology and employment is summarized in Turnham (1993).
2. The degree of labour intensiveness of a technology does not seem to count for the core technology (OECD, 1991).
3. Van Dijk (1995) undertook a study for UNCTAD on how to build up and reinforce the local technological capacity in two Least Developed Countries (LDCs), Bangladesh and Nepal. The emphasis was on identifying forms of technology co-operation that exist and on listing options for developing countries.
4. See case studies in Rasmussen *et al.* (eds) (1992).
5. In total, sixteen indicators were defined to operationalize flexible specialization in Dijkman and Van Dijk (1997). The entrepreneurs were scored on all these variables.
6. The research focused on the relation between household poverty and the economic activities of the members of the household. The analysis is based on 50 in-depth interviews in one neighbourhood of Accra (Abeka). Information has been collected also on 28 economic activities in which members of the households were involved. For comparative reasons data were also collected on another 24 economic activities taking place at the edge of Abeka, mainly along two important roads (Van Dijk, 1997).

7. Strategic alliances are defined as agreed co-operation between firms in a field where their knowledge or experience is complementary.
8. Lalkaka (1994) gives a description of incubators in economies in transition.
9. Bramezza (1996: 39) defines public–private partnerships as co-operative ventures between a public and a private party, whose aim is to realize common projects of which they share risks, costs and profit. She adds that they are mostly used by urban managers for financing projects, although they may also have the function of exchanging experience and knowledge.
10. Pietrobelli (1996) has defined an interfirm technology partnership and used different data sets to study them.
11. UN (1990: 69) defines joint ventures as one of the most important and acceptable instruments of foreign investment and technology transfer from transnational corporations, and also from medium-sized and small enterprises in industrialized countries to private and public sector enterprises in many developing countries.

REFERENCES

Abarnathy, W. and J.M. Utterback (1978), 'Patterns of industrial innovation', *Technology Review*, **50** (7), pp. 40–47.

Acs, Z.J., D.B. Audretsch and M.P. Feldman (1992), 'R&D spillovers and innovative activity', Milan: Italy, Conference on births and start-up of small firms.

Barnett, A. (1995), 'Technology and small-scale production', *Small Enterprise Development*, **6** (4), December.

Bramezza, I. (1996), 'The competitiveness of the European City and the role of urban management in improving the City's performance', Rotterdam: Tinbergen Institute, No. 109.

Calbrese, G. and S. Rolfo (1992), 'Factors leading to the introduction of products and process innovations in small firms', Stuttgart: EARIE conference.

Dijk, M.P. van (1982), 'The technology gap in the case of small enterprises development', in W. Riedijk (ed.), *Appropriate Technologies for Developing Countries*, Delft: University Press.

Dijk, M.P. van (1992), 'How relevant is flexible specialization in Burkina Faso's informal sector and the formal manufacturing sector?', in Rasmussen *et al.* (eds), pp. 45–51.

Dijk, M.P. van (1993), 'Industrial districts and urban economic development', *Third World Planning Review*, **15** (2), May, pp. 175–87.

Dijk, M.P. van (1995), 'Investment in technological capacity building in Bangladesh and Nepal', in UNCTAD (1995), pp. 39–61.

Dijk, M.P. van (1997), 'The economic activities of the poor in Accra, Ghana', in D. Bryceson and V. Jamal (eds), *Farewell to Farms, De-agrarianization and Employment in Africa*, Aldershot: Ashgate Publishing, pp. 101–17.

Dijk, M.P. van (2000), *Summer in the City, Decentralization Provides New Opportunities for Urban Management*, Rotterdam: HIS/Erasmus University.

Dijk, M.P. van (2001), *Is Nanjing's Concentration of IT Companies an Innovative Cluster?*, Jena: Max Planck Institute for Research in Economic Systems.

Dijk, M.P. van and R. Rabellotti (eds) (1997), *Enterprise Clusters and Networks in Developing Countries*, London: Frank Cass.

Dijkman, H. and M.P. van Dijk (1997), 'Opportunities for women in Ouagadougou's informal sector. An analysis based on the flexible specialization concept', in Van Dijk and Rabellotti (eds).

Galbraith, J.K. (1967), *The New Industrial State*, Boston: Houghton Mifflin.
Hoesel, R. van (1997), *Beyond Export-led Growth. The Emergence of New Multinational Enterprises from Korea and Taiwan*, Rotterdam: Erasmus University.
Kolnaar, A.H.J. (1999), 'Endogene groei en inkomensverdeling', in *Maandschrift Economie*, **63** (2).
Lalkaka, R. (1994), 'Incubating small entrepreneurial businesses in economies in transition', in *Small Enterprise Development*, **5** (3), September.
OECD (1991), *Managing Technological Change in Less-advanced Developing Countries*, Paris: OECD.
Pedersen, P.O., A. Sverrisson and M.P. van Dijk (eds) (1994), *Flexible Specialization. The Dynamics of Small-scale Industries in the South*, London: IT.
Pietrobelli, C. (1996), *Emerging Forms of Technological Co-operation: The Case for Technology Partnership*, Geneva: UNCTAD.
Pyke, F. and W. Sengenberger (1992), *Industrial Districts and Local Economic Regeneration*, Geneva: ILO.
Rasmussen, J., H. Schmitz and M.P. van Dijk (eds) (1992), 'Flexible Specialisation: a new view on small industry?', *IDS Bulletin*, **23** (3), July.
Rostov, W.W. (1956), 'The take-off into self-sustained growth', *The Economic Journal*, **66** (261), pp. 25–48.
Schmitz, H. (1992), 'On the clustering of firms', Rasmussen *et al.* (eds), pp. 64–9.
Schumpeter, J.A. (1942), *Capitalism, Socialism and Democracy*, New York: Harper.
Schutter, J. de and G. Bremer (eds) (1980), *Fundamental Aspects of Appropriate Technology*, Delft: University Press.
Singer, H. (1977), *Technologies for Basic Needs*, Geneva: ILO.
Solow, R. (1957), 'Technical change and the aggregate production function', in *Review of Economics and Statistics*, No. 39, pp. 312–320.
Trulsson, P. (1997), *Strategies of Entrepreneurship. Understanding Industrial Entrepreneurship and Structural Change in Northwest Tanzania*, Linkoping: Department of Technology and Social Change.
Turnham, D. (1993), *Employment and Development, a New Review of Evidence*, Paris: OECD.
UN (1990), *Joint Ventures as a Channel for the Transfer of Technology*, New York: United Nations.
UNCTAD (1995): *Technological Capacity Building and Technology Partnership. Field Findings, Country Experiences and Programmes*, Geneva: UN.
UNCTAD (1996), *Exchanging Experiences of Technology Partnerships*, Geneva: UNCTAD.
UNCTAD (1998), *Report on the Expert Group Meeting on the Impact of Government Policy and Government/Private Action in Stimulating Inter-firm Partnerships Regarding Technology, Production and Marketing*, Geneva: UNCTAD.

PART III

Innovation in Times of Economic Crisis

7. Innovation and competitiveness within the small furniture industry in Nicaragua

Mario Davide Parrilli

The importance of the furniture industry in Nicaragua is based on the country's comparative advantages: abundant natural resources and cheap labour. In fact, Nicaragua is a tropical country with a huge timber potential, since the growth rate of forests is much higher than for the majority of timber producing countries (4.3 million hectares of forest in 1990: Marklund and Rodriguez, 1993). Some Nicaraguan towns have a long tradition of skilled craftwork, the basis for the competitiveness of this industry. The Central Bank (BCN, 1998) estimates that there are about 2000 small furniture firms. The comparative advantage gains further strength from the geographical and sectoral concentration of small firms, which has recently become a model of development on the basis of several successful experiences with territorial or cluster development.

This chapter does not deal with the typical 'successful' case, as in many studies on clusters of small firms, rather it deals with an embryonic case. It does not represent the illustration of the elements that mainly spurred the evolution of a successful cluster; it rather acquires its relevance from being an analysis of one of the several unknown cases of potential development in developing countries. Indeed, it represents a very challenging task to participate in a process that will certainly take many more years, but which is a clear example of what development is not: an easy task.

One of the main problems of Nicaragua is the weak institutional and economic support given to this sector and to industry in general by the different governments that have ruled the country over recent decades. If one considers the level of gross value added or export value, one has to recognize that this sector, so beautifully endowed by nature, has been totally neglected by them. The Central Bank (BCN, 1998) shows the very low level of value added and exports of the sector. In 1995 the furniture industry generated 4 million dollars, with exports of 0.5 million dollars. It also shows the booming level of import of wood and wood products: more than 60 million dollars in 1997, mostly paper products. In terms of development, everything still has to be done. Natural and traditional resources are there and can be the basis for a significant and more sustainable development.[1]

Innovation is fundamental in order to produce competitiveness. In the context of a very poor developing country such as Nicaragua, innovation is a big word. This industry is still at the handicraft level: low productivity, limited mechanization, working for the local market and using family workers. In this case, it is hard to talk about innovation as production of 'absolutely new' products, processes or ways of doing things. It would be better to talk about imitation and learning about sustainable development, which has been tried in countries endowed as Nicaragua with wood, such as Scandinavian countries, Chile, Canada and some Asian countries. Innovative practices should be introduced in the country's entrepreneurial fabric and would set the basis for structural change in the competitiveness of this small industry.

The liberalization process is opening up the market, and small furniture firms in Nicaragua face new competition from Asia, the United States and even Latin American countries through increased imports. The high and middle class of the country want good products. The customers are willing to pay a good price for good quality imported goods. Open competition is the new drive of the market and increasing competitiveness is the key to match it. Competitiveness is not a black and white concept, rather something that can be achieved. It can be improved and also lost, depending on the effort from the enterprises and the institutional support. In this chapter, innovation is taken in a broad sense, as a key to improve the competitiveness of the small industry, and for its capacity to attribute new and attractive elements to the product, fostering its price structure and demand. In this sense, innovation presents several aspects: innovation of design, finishing, marketing and distribution, production inputs, technology, intra- and interfirm organization, and services.

Nicaraguan producers are just competing on the basis of low prices and low-cost workforce, which implies low-quality products and low returns. The main reason for such a 'low-road' of competition seems to be that Nicaraguan small industries produce only for the small local market. In fact, at that level innovation is not taking place. In this context, the main research question that this chapter tries to answer is about what kind of innovation is needed in order to develop. Once this question is answered, it becomes easier to answer a second question: what is the key to transform handicraft into a modern, small, competitive industry?

The solution to the problem of innovation and competitiveness of this sector (country) can also not be found at the enterprise level. Small enterprises cannot innovate on their own. Their resources are too limited and they can just follow a 'low-road' type of development, in which they compete through low prices, obtained by lowering the costs of production (wages, salaries, supply and subcontracting prices). This system does not spur development, since most of the actors in the chain (workers, suppliers, competitors, clients and final consumers) are worse off. On the basis of other countries' successful clusters, this chapter suggests the hypothesis that, in this context, a more systemic approach to innovation should be followed, which has the capacity effectively to spur a 'high-road' of development. This may happen when the enterprise system goes through an innovation path that ensures individual and collective efficiency, higher quality and a better market. All these aspects are part of the flexible specialization paradigm (Pedersen, Sverrisson and Van Dijk, 1994). Flexible specialization would be the key that stops the destructive competition in the local market, and focuses on more appropriate competition, which makes enterprises more competitive in international markets and able to achieve their growth potential.

In the following section it is suggested that the flexible specialization paradigm is relevant for Nicaraguan furniture industries. The theoretical framework suggested stresses the importance of intra- and interfirm relations and of private and public support institutions. The study is based on a qualitative and quantitative survey of 89 small industries in the six main clusters of the country. It suggests that innovation processes can promote the move of these clusters towards the high-road of competitiveness and development.

IN SEARCH OF SYSTEMIC INNOVATION

Competitiveness is the target of every enterprise and institution working for industrial development. It is a relative concept, which points to selling a product at a price that is comparatively lower than other firms' (and countries') price. However, consumers and markets are different everywhere; so are products. Two products of the same type can differ in price, but also in quality, style, availability and secondary characteristics. All these elements foster the interest of the customers in the product. Therefore, practising low prices is not the only way to be competitive. Quality and innovation of products and processes, marketing and increased efficiency can spur the competitive edge of an industry as much as low costs and prices. Such an approach to competitiveness is increasingly spreading around the world as the new and sharpest way to keep up with the competitive struggle that takes place in the arena of the globalized market (Best, 1990).

Innovation is one of the main factors of competitiveness. Usually, innovation is taken in the Schumpeterian sense of making money out of an invention. It is harder in developing countries to make inventions. In general, there is less capital available and fewer skilled people, and less is spent on

R&D. However, in developing countries there is a need for a broader type of innovation, which can be defined as 'imitation' (or adaptation) of successful experiences and models. It costs less, it is easier to reproduce, reflects better the present state of the developing economy and attains quicker results. In fact, 'a successful imitation, which is complemented with low cost labour, increases the competitiveness of developing countries' industry, allowing it a new margin in view of gaining new markets, inside and outside their own country' (Pissarides, 1997). In other words, in these contexts innovation should be oriented to replicate development paths or techniques 'which are mature in and of themselves and make them work in the local social context' (Pedersen, Sverrisson and Van Dijk, 1994).

Innovation within an individual enterprise does not result in general development if the remaining enterprises do not benefit. The Nicaraguan furniture sector does not involve large firms, rather just small and micro-enterprises. Hence industrial analysis should focus on the firms' territorial organization and development, such as sectoral networks, clusters, industrial districts and subcontracting networks. In Nicaragua innovation points to flexible specialization. In Nicaragua, neither the craft system, nor the Fordist paradigm about mass production can be valid strategies for sustained long-term development.

Furniture production is pure craftwork, which means a low quantity of production oriented to a local market for a 'localized' quality and style of goods, which family workers realize with a usually traditional technology. The new globalized market shows the weaknesses of such a production system. Producers are unable to catch up with increased orders and the standard of international quality and design furniture. The condition of the Nicaraguan furniture industry is far removed from well-known successful operations, which are based on competitive small and medium enterprises. Rather, it seems to be more similar to the informal sector, which usually consists of microenterprises. This sector represents a wide variety of conditions, as new theories about its heterogeneity recognize (Pérez Sainz, 1994). These firms frequently survive on the edge of the market (Tokman, 1992). In a few cases firms are linked to and exploited by larger enterprises, as Marxist theorists assert (Portes, 1997); in other cases, these firms just try to reduce the bureaucratic constraints and take up economic opportunities, as neo-liberal theorists affirm (De Soto, 1990). Nevertheless, none of the above-mentioned approaches takes the informal sector as a potential leader of development; rather, they consider it as a generally poor sector, which is not empowered to strike a radical change in the mode of production and competition, and to lead to sectoral and territorial development. Therefore, taking this stance means that we need to look for very tiny changes (or even none at all) in sectoral economic growth, and not be tempted to make this sector leader of economic territorial development. In the condition of a country that desperately needs quick and sustained growth, a different approach is needed to bring a well-endowed sector to a higher level of competitiveness.

The alternative industrial solution tried by socialist regimes of Asia and Europe and import substitution regimes of Latin America, is the Fordist mass production regime. This system is not appropriate in the context of an open economy. Indeed, the Fordist system cannot face the changing conditions of the globalized market. Today, international demand shows high variability: changing and personalized demand, segmented and niche markets, higher standards of quality, product and process innovation. These new requirements make it difficult to apply the mass production system. Invest-ment costs would be too high and not appropriate to respond to changing conditions. The workforce is often not skilled enough to increase productivity; the inventory costs would be too high to maintain low costs of production, and so on.

For these reasons flexible specialization is the most appropriate approach. It represents – in the two versions of the Third Italy and the Japanese models – a new production system, which combines a 'flexible' response to changes in market demand with the productive 'specialization' that makes a firm particularly capable of providing new high-quality and personalized goods in a very short period. Nowadays, the Japanese model is receiving more and more acknowledgement. But in Nicaragua it does not have many chances to succeed, since there are no large furniture firms. On the other hand, the Third Italy model of flexible specialization has a good chance given the long-standing existence of various clusters of small firms. Moreover, since in the furniture sector the majority of firms are microfirms, it seems appropriate to combine this model with the informal sector analysis, that recently recognized the heterogeneity of that sector. Indeed, even though the furniture sector only deals with small firms, the heterogeneity of these firms is higher. It reflects on the existence of firms with different rationalities, limits, potentials, which policy makers have to take into account when correctly planning future development. This is why, throughout this chapter, there will be differentiation based on the competitive answer for these different types of enterprises, namely: Competitive, Traditional and Subsistence firms.[2]

Within the flexible specialization framework, innovation is not monolithic, rather it presents several aspects: intra- and interfirm aspects that involve product design and finishing, process organization and technology, market and inputs search, vertical and horizontal interfirm relations of co-operation and competition, private and public support services. The development process can emphasize one or the other, depending on the priorities of the country or region that is analysed. In order to be effective and systemic, small enterprise development requires the involvement of the various actors of the economic chain: 'intrafirm actors' (entrepreneurs, family, workers), 'interfirm actors' (suppliers, subcontractors, other producers, traders and customers) and 'private and public support actors' (information/technology/transport services, municipality and so on). Once the innovation process moves, it is supposed to reinforce itself, since the actors realize the interdependence between a higher individual competitiveness and a higher systemic competitiveness. Such a consciousness spurs a change of mentality and a trend towards tightening up the linkages between the three types of relations: intrafirm, interfirm and support services.

THE FLEXIBLE SPECIALIZATION FRAMEWORK

The Intrafirm Level

At the intrafirm level, it does not seem too early to take into account techniques that are being implemented in industrialized countries, such as just-in-time production and total-quality-management. Researchers and consultants are adopting them in order to specify restructuring plans for clustered and smaller groups of enterprises in developing countries (Bessant, 1991; Murray, 1987; Kaplinsky, 1995).

Such techniques do not require huge technology investments, rather a change in the mentality of the entrepreneurs, which will certainly take some time (Messner, 1995). At the level of the individual small enterprise, the reduction of inventories of raw material, inputs, parts and finished products does not need specialized electronic or information technology, while the firm can reduce working capital and costs on credit, quality losses, warehouses and so on. The cellular organization, its system of team control and *kanban*[3] – instead of the craft or functional organization – certainly needs higher production levels than those realized at present. It does not require sophisticated or dedicated technology to be implemented. As a result, the intrafirm aspects of the flexible specialization approach will increase the fluidity of intrafirm relations, by reducing the necessary working capital, works-in-process, defects and wastes, reducing at the end the total costs of production and strengthening the quality and the price structure of the product.

In the new global market, there is no time to go at one's own pace; the market simply marginalizes the firms that are not competitive. This means that the innovation process must be fast enough to maintain some competitive edge in order to cope with international competitors. The alternative is for the market to be flooded by imported goods. These intrafirm innovations could soon be incorporated as an objective for a long-term development strategy, since learning time and the mentality change are likely to take time.

The Interfirm Level

At the interfirm level, relationships need to be changed in order to reap the benefits of producing in a sectoral cluster of small firms: more joint action (Schmitz and Musick, 1993). On the one hand, the presence of many firms of the same sector in the same geographic zone spurs externalities such as the presence of a skilled workforce; the flow of significant information about clients, technology, supply, services; the exploitation of infrastructural services and goods; the benefits coming from the division and specialization of labour among firms (Ghani and Stewart, 1991). It does not mean that wherever there is a cluster of firms, the externalities are fully enjoyed, rather it shows the potential benefits of such a productive configuration.

On the other hand, the presence of hundreds of firms can raise the potential of joint action, in order to reap benefits that a small enterprise could not achieve by itself: the access to export markets and to credit through consortia, the promotion of quality through local guarantee brands, the opportunity to share big orders through informal arrangements among a few firms, the opportunity to lobby in front of the local and central government for important initiatives such as the formation of industrial parks and so on (Schmitz and Musick, 1993).

In general, such an approach would help to overcome the narrowness of an approach that does not take into account the limits to competitiveness of the small enterprise itself. Furthermore, it emphasizes the need to abandon a destructive type of 'inside competition', substituting it for a brand 'new' and more competitive strategy of 'outside competition', which realizes that competing against one another (especially when the local market is small) means shaping a low-road of development (Pyke and Sengenberger, 1991). It involves a strategy of lowering costs and prices, hitting hard the weakest links of the productive chain, such as workers, suppliers, subcontractors and other less competitive firms. This competition leaves some winners and some losers, without any other aggregate changes for the sake of the country.

In this sense, there is the need to build up a different combination of competition and co-operation. Indeed, an innovative industrialization path would merge these two forces in a way that spurs the competitiveness of the whole industry. If competition is too strong, it hinders co-operation and overcomes typical problems that small individual firms face: access to credit, exportation, political lobbying, and so on. If competition is too weak, it does not spur a dynamic reaction of the entrepreneurial class in search of new competitive solutions. In this sense, the flexible specialization approach proposes such a type of 'high-road' strategy of local growth, which is mostly based on the result of a balanced mix of competition and co-operation and which emphasizes innovation of product and process, search for new markets, and better organization of existing resources within the firm and through the productive chain.

The Support Service Level

A broad approach to flexible specialization emphasizes the importance of a set of private and public service institutions for the small enterprise system.[4] The existence of a large number of sectorally and geographically specialized firms does not imply that these are competitive and developing. This system can only work if there are catalysts of development, such as private and public service firms and infrastructures. What could be done without roads and energy? What would be the benefits if there were appropriate and localized technical schools for furniture production? Would the benefits of the cluster with or without private service firms such as technological, mechanical, information, and transport firms be the same? What could be done without banks? And could one think of exporting if there were no trading companies? These are just some examples of the importance that territorial organization assumes in order to produce a competitive economic environment.

Better and denser relations are important between economic actors and the productive and institutional context. Successful cases of clusters and networks in Europe, Latin America and other continents show the relevance that ancillary private and public services have had for clusters' growth (Schmitz and Musick, 1993; Tendler and Amorim, 1996). The division of tasks between direct and indirect economic actors (subsidiary production such as raw material, parts supply and subcontracting, complementary services such as finance, trading, information, transport, education and training, technical and technological innovation and so on) is extremely important to increase the specialization and productivity of the cluster. At the same time, the demand that exists in such a specialized environment spurs the interdependence and reduces the risks of excessive investments. In fact, every actor just invests in a particular area of production and leaves the rest of the production tasks to others. In such an environment, risks and transaction costs shrink as a result of the continuous and denser work relations between the economic actors, which facilitate the generation of trust as a process-based socioeconomic outcome (Zucker, 1986).[5]

Obviously, the main point of such a structure is the co-ordination of the direct and indirect economic actors that operate in the cluster. It does not produce the same effects to organize a system of specialized actors that complement each other or to let the structure grow in a dispersed and unco-ordinated way. In this second case, the lack of mutual information would produce duplication and inefficiency in the efforts of the relevant public and private institutions. It would drastically reduce the positive effects of clustering. In contrast, the implementation of an organized effort of service institutions would increase efficiency and quality, because of the increasing mutual learning, interaction and co-operation in day-to-day activities. The successful experience of many Italian industrial districts is an example of the importance of such support (Best, 1990; Pyke and Sengenberger, 1991; Schmitz and Musick, 1993).

THE FURNITURE INDUSTRY IN NICARAGUA[6]

In the furniture industry, Nicaragua presents a particular configuration, since it is structured as clusters of small and micro enterprises. The main clusters are located in the capital Managua and five other towns that have between 100 and 200 small firms: Masaya, León, Chinandega, Estelí y Masatepe. In 1995, the total number of firms in the country were around 1500 (Banco Central de Nicaragua, 1998). If this information is compared with data from the Directory of the National Institute for Statistics and Census (2350 firms: MEDE, 1997) a few years before, it implies that many firms no longer exist. Therefore, the effects of the liberalization of the early 1990s have been that many workshops closed down. The new open competition allowed the high and middle-class of Nicaragua to buy more imported goods, which meant reducing the demand for national products. A second change is a restructuring of firms. In fact, the above-mentioned Directory includes 99.9 per cent of the firms in the category of firms with less than five workers. On the other hand, a recent survey shows that there are a number of small industries with more than 10 workers (16 per cent of the total, while 48 per cent have more than five: Parrilli, 1998a). It shows a trend towards a further concentration in the furniture industry, which underlines the heterogeneity of firms and the existence of a group of firms that have a good potential to grow. The six clusters studied are those that have more than 100 small enterprises and that, therefore, are more likely to present the critical mass needed to exploit the cluster's advantages. This is the first level that has to be taken into account in order to evaluate the basis for a feasible innovation process. We will first discuss intrafirm innovation dealing with the organization, process and product innovations.

Organization Innovation

The firm's organizational structure mostly reflects on production efficiency. The efficiency of small enterprises is double-faced. On the one hand, it is high as the level of inventories of finished products and of raw material and work-in-process is quite low. On the other hand, it is low, since capacity utilization is quite low. The first aspect depends on the type of work the craftsmen take, which is usually ordered by a final consumer. The furniture makers only work if there is a (small) order and on the basis of 50 per cent advanced payment, since they usually lack the working capital needed to buy the inputs of production. Firms with more than 10 workers, which are usually part of the Competitive category, have higher inventories. In general, these are organized in a functional way, which means that every worker performs a different type of operation, as in a typical Fordist factory. In fact, they also hold higher inventories compared to the rest of the industries (Parrilli, 1998b).

Table 7.1   Type of organization of production in the different types of small furniture firms

Types	Craft	Mixed*	Functional	Cellular
Competitive	No	No	Yes	No
Traditional	Yes	Yes	No	No
Subsistence	Yes	No	No	No
Total: %	60	13.3	25	1.7

Note: *'Mixed' means a mix between craft and functional organization, depending on the volume of the order. The qualitative data do not include one of the clusters.

Source: Author's survey, 1998.

In the three types of firms distinguished in Table 7.1, it is more frequent to observe craft organization, where every carpenter makes the whole product from the beginning to the end (helped by an apprentice). In this case, labour specialization and scale economies are still unknown.[7] This type of organization is so strongly incorporated in Subsistence firms that even in the few cases when these entrepreneurs share an order, they prefer dividing the number of products between themselves, rather than functions![8] Only in the event of big orders (Competitive and Traditional) do firms organize their production in series. The just-in-time organization has never been attempted, simply because it is still unknown both among support organizations and in the entrepreneurial environment. As an effect, efficiency is low as capacity utilization is quite low (less than 50 per cent of the installed capacity in more than 50 per cent of the national survey: Parrilli, 1998a). Despite this general outcome, which depends on the bigger sector of Subsistence firms, Competitive and, to a lesser extent, Traditional firms have a sufficient basis to adopt those techniques. Indeed, their used capacity, which reaches around 70–80 per cent in the case of Competitive enterprises, shows their much better management of productive and commercial activities (Parrilli, 1998b).

Until now, efficiency has not been considered as a problem, since the furniture production, on the whole, has not overcome the limits of craft (small and local) production. The way it is dealt with determines the growth of sectoral competitiveness. In this sense, a change in the mentality of several entrepreneurs is the necessary basis for passing from craft to just-in-time organization and total-quality management, which allow cost reduction and increase the quality of products. It can take place only when craftsmen leave their passive attitude of just waiting for the customers in their premises and start to take a more dynamic and organized attitude. They should increase production by improving the organization. In other words, it means leaving the old supply-based marketing and following a modern and more appropriate demand-based marketing approach. Interestingly, the adoption of such an approach has already been undertaken by Competitive firms, which realized how critical the shift from craftwork to industry is.

Product Innovation

The most traditional field of innovation is product innovation. In this case this refers mainly to style and quality. It rarely takes place in the furniture industry: the majority of the firms prefer repeating the same design and never innovate the design or the finishing technique. These firms – usually Subsistence firms – are specialized in the production of rocking chairs and rarely leave the production of the same types of chairs, kitchen tables and beds. At the same time, there are other small industries which show a high capacity to imitate new models: it just takes a week in order to check out the new product, imitate and sell it in the local market. In this case, the Schumpeterian monopolistic rent does not have enough margin to work. This reality demands a continuous production of repetitive styles and makes it hard to get beyond the local cheap products. The quality of products is generally low, since prices paid in the internal market are poor.

Leaving this general trend and analysing in detail the three types of firms, one observes consistent differences: Competitive, and to a lesser extent Traditional firms, are able to produce high quality furniture and diversify their products. They can make several types of high-price furniture (libraries, armchairs, bars, etc.). These producers present another face of this industry, which is able to perform qualitatively well for the highly sophisticated consumers of Europe and United States. Dynamizing marketing and technology purchase activities is a priority for these firms, in order to spur their high-quality production. It represents the alternative to imports. Moreover, this change reduces the investment cost of entering the market, since it pushes towards the purchase and adoption of a particular technology and labour skills, in which the firm benefits more from scale economies, wider production and better earning. A few cases, which mainly fit into the Competitive category, are firms that are looking for different kinds of niche markets, such as garden furniture, mirrors, doors and windows, cigar boxes. These and other cases show a higher tendency to change the design of the products often, in order to enter a higher-income segment of the national market. These cases are the most successful ones, both in terms of income and employment generation. In particular, the cluster of Estelí shows an interesting connection between cigar producers and woodworking firms: a first case of specialization and parallel growth of complementary branches. As a matter of fact, this is the cluster (together with Masaya) that shows the most interesting pattern of innovation and competitiveness.

Process Innovation

In general, small furniture enterprises are endowed with the same general-purpose machinery, which gives some sort of homogeneity to the industry itself. Frequently, these machines are old, due to the poor capitalization process of the firms and the low requirements in terms of quality level. This implies obvious limits to product and process quality. This obstacle does not affect sales in Nicaragua, but certainly is a problem in the international market. In the majority of the firms, the technical instruments are generally too simple and not provided with adequate control mechanisms to ensure the standardization of production. The lack of sufficient high-quality demand prevents the entrepreneurs from taking appropriate measures in order to improve the quality of the technological process. This general picture partially changes when the different types of enterprises are considered. In effect, Competitive firms and, to a lesser extent, Traditional firms are better endowed in terms of technology as they manage newer and more precise machinery. Nevertheless, it is still not industrial machinery, which implies that production takes longer and low productivity reduces their competitiveness. In this case, purchases of higher-capacity machinery could be taken into account for a gradual shift towards a faster rhythm of production.

Better machinery requires a higher participation of skilled labour. Apart from technical education, it points to particular work organization, such as cellular teamwork and sharper control of products and the production process. It would increase the productivity of labour and the quality of the product and process by reducing the number of defects, wastes and so on. Once again, this change would imply higher short-term costs for investment in technology and training, but also higher returns in the medium term. Competitive and Traditional firms, due to better capital accumulation, are the ones that can start such a process of technological upgrading. In the future, changes in the technological process are expected in order to bring Nicaraguan products up to international standards and raise productivity: for instance, by substituting the pure wooden furniture for sawdust and 'fibran' inputs.

INNOVATING INTERFIRM RELATIONS

In the furniture industry, interfirm relations are varied. On the one hand, interfirm horizontal relations are not well developed, since these are almost exclusively oriented to a low-road of competition: price competition within the same small local market. It obviously reflects its bad effects on the weak actors of the productive chain, such as weak enterprises and their workers, suppliers and subcontractors, by reducing their pay, wage, capital accumulation and, therefore, reducing their quality of work. Table 7.2 shows the forms in which this competition takes place at the horizontal level. On the other hand, interfirm vertical relations depend on the type of firm: Competitive and, to a lesser extent, Traditional firms show a different perspective about their suppliers and customers, trying to generate long-term and selected relations that help them raise quality and efficiency of work. Moreover, they do not emphasize the price aspect above the rest; rather they value the quality of raw material, inputs and information that those actors can bring them, which means accepting higher costs and prices, to produce a better product.

The Horizontal Level

The great majority of the small industries (80.6 per cent) experience an atmosphere of intense price competition. The few cases that do not feel it (13.4 per cent) are niche producers (garden furniture) or those who have experienced recent growth. Among the clusters, León is the exception, as 30 per cent of producers recognize the value of quality in order to gain on competitors. Usually, competition takes place as described in Table 7.2.

Table 7.2   Forms of competition in the small furniture industry

Clusters	None	Price	Quality	Finance	Responsibility	Product imitation
Total: %	10.4	80.6	8.9	1.5	1.5	8.9

Source: Survey, 1998. Multiple choice.

Somehow, even co-operation exists, but in these clusters it does not rank as well as in the past, due to the negative effects that liberalization and political instability had on the huge co-operative system, which grew in the 1980s. Nevertheless, there is a group of small industries that recognize the relevance of co-operation among enterprises (37 per cent). These are mainly the competitive firms. The majority of them experienced it in an informal way, such as obtaining loans for machinery and inputs, or informal chats taking place in the streets downtown. Still, the entrepreneurs do not mention formal activities of co-operation, such as export activities, credit access, input purchase, lobbying political activity, which could be realized through consortia, associations, chambers of commerce and industry. In the case of the furniture industry, these would therefore all be samples of an innovative practice of interfirm co-operation.

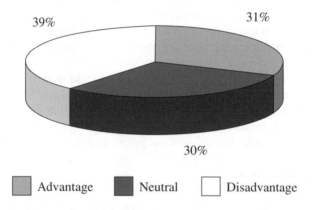

Figure 7.1   Opinion of small entrepreneurs on clustering

Referring to external economies, the consciousness of the benefits that living in a cluster of firms attributes to the participants (Ghani and Stewart, 1991) is quite differentiated. Therefore, it leads to different results in terms of the firms' appropriation of the possible benefits of aggregation. The vision on clustering shows big differences between enterprises in the evaluation of living in a cluster. In this case, the type of firm is not relevant for the perception of the entrepreneur. The biggest group observes the negative aspects of clustering, being the growing competition on the same small, local market (39 per cent). But there is also a similar group of producers who value the possible advantages of aggregation, recognizing the opportunity of obtaining new clients just by being localized in a high-density zone of furniture producers and through the possible co-operation that can take place there (31 per cent). In this sense, the cluster of Estelí constitutes the best performer (60 per cent), because of the above-mentioned production complementarity. It depends on the division of labour that this cluster is experiencing between the production of cigars and boxes. It could represent an interesting development model for other clusters and products.

A third group is made up of those who just think of their own workshop, and do not consider mutual relations with other small industries (30 per cent). In this and in the first case, the potential benefits of clustering are likely to remain 'potential', since awareness is the first step to interfirm division of labour. Division and specialization of labour between core firms, the existence of a skilled workforce, the flow of relevant information on supply of inputs, market and technology, the existence of common infrastructure facilities, the support of private and public services are possibilities that are not sufficiently valued by the entrepreneurs. At this level, innovation seems to mean information and training helping the entrepreneurs to develop their perception about the importance of firms' interdependence.

The Vertical Level

This level can be separated into forward and backward relations, where the first refer to supply relations of raw materials and inputs of production and the second to market relations. In the case of the supply system, the relations controlled by Subsistence firms, and to a lesser extent by Traditional firms, are still based on paying the lowest possible price for raw materials. These craftsmen tend to deal with several wood suppliers, as a function of the price and scarcity of wood. Scarce and bad wood (not dried, with nodes and flaws) affects the quality of the overall process and, in particular, of the final product. Nevertheless, Competitive firms show a different perspective, since they prefer to reduce the number of suppliers and to focus on a better quality of raw materials and inputs of production. In order to achieve this, they prefer to avoid purchasing wood from illegal traders. In this case, the supply relations are considered as good, while in the previous case these were considered as pure market relations, which are short-term oriented. Good relations have a longer-term orientation, which strengthens the constitution of high-trust relations that can increase efficiency and the quality of production by improving delivery times, terms of payments and prefinancing, technical assistance, common design and so on.

Again the approach depends on the type of firm. At the price and product level, Competitive firms show a 'high-road' approach. They concentrate on higher quality products for a higher segment of consumers that can pay a better price, rather than filling the cheap street market with cheap products that only guarantee low prices and earnings. In this sense, Subsistence firms usually produce the most common products such as beds and chairs, while Competitive firms prefer to diversify their production of armchairs, libraries, sofas, and other products of more sophisticated and high-income demand.

Traditional firms sometimes take the stance of Competitive firms and sometimes the stance of Subsistence enterprises.

In Nicaragua there is a clear need to open up the market in order to overcome the rigid constraint of the national demand. Indeed, national consumers number only 4.5 million people with a low annual per capita income of 480 dollars. How can they spur the level of production of 1500–2000 firms in China? Even the experience of successful industrial districts of much bigger countries shows that exporting is one of the key elements of expansion.[9] In the case of the six furniture clusters of Nicaragua, market diversification is still incipient: 70 per cent of the workshops sell their product in their premises or at the local cheap street market. It means that the price at which they sell is usually low.[10] Notwithstanding, a few enterprises – Competitive and sometimes Traditional firms – commercialize their products through specialized shops and also benefit from public procurement or contracts with other private firms. Sometimes these enterprises sell their products outside the local market, and even in export markets (both around 15 per cent). The cluster of Masaya shows an interesting indicator: 36 per cent of the entrepreneurs have exported. This figure does not refer to the total exported value, but to the producers who have experienced exporting; nevertheless, it represents a first step towards a new market perspective.

Table 7.3   Clients of the small furniture industry

Clusters	Final consumers	Private enterprises	Public institutions	Traders (retailers, wholesalers, exporters)
Competitive	Yes	Yes	Yes	Yes
Traditional	Yes	No	No	Yes
Subsistence	Yes	No	No	No
Total: %	73.1	8.9	10.4	44.8

Source: Survey, 1998. Mutiple choice.

Table 7.3 shows the characteristics of the commercialization process: craftsmen usually sell to consumers. On the whole, the intermediation chain, which usually has the capacity to expand the market and open up new opportunities to the industry itself, is still limited. Enterprises selling to traders, usually retailers of the local cheap street market, number 44.8 per cent. In this sense, the process of market expansion has a quite a long way to go, in order to leave the level of pure price competition. The national and international intermediation chain is still incipient (brokers, wholesalers).

Since it is a key to opening up new market channels, it should represent a fundamental target of a serious industrial policy. At the same time, public procurement, that somewhere else represented the first engine of local growth through production for schools, hospitals, public offices, is not much adopted, as only 10 per cent of the small industries have recently been incorporated in some public projects (Tendler and Amorim, 1996). On the positive side, in the last two years the public support agency (INPYME) has started to foster participation of private firms in Central American trade fairs, which could really be a first step in the direction of opening up the export market and of increasing the knowledge that entrepreneurs have about new trends in product, process and organization.

INNOVATING THE INSTITUTIONAL SUPPORT

At the level of services institutions, the survey shows the uncertain acknowledgement that private and public support institutions receive from producers. This substantially stems from the limited awareness of the small entrepreneurs about the usefulness of public and private services. Nevertheless, this seems to be the result of the low trust the craftsmen have in public support agencies. As a matter of fact, the only knowledge that local governments show about them concerns the tax registration office, which obviously underestimates the number of firms, due to the high informality of the economy. The fear of suffering from rising taxes, once they manifest their existence, represents a further obstacle to improving relations.

The different types of enterprises recognize different support agencies as their helpers. Subsistence firms indicate the support of public agencies and NGOs in training seminars. Traditional firms emphasize the credit support from NGOs, which is usually quite limited (less than 1000 dollars for a few months). Finally, Competitive firms highlight the support they receive from the formal bank system, which helps them with higher and longer credit lines, due to the higher guarantees they can provide. This outcome represents a stratification of the support system, which represents an obstacle to development. Indeed, it forces the enterprises to carry out a certain kind of economic activity and reduces their room for investment and capitalization. For instance, Traditional firms need more credit to modernize their activity, but at present they cannot adequately access it.

The survey shows an important percentage of entrepreneurs that cannot identify particular needs: 58 per cent at the national level. At the territorial level, the clusters with the oldest tradition of furniture production (Masaya and León) are the ones that most realize the importance of such services, but still at an incipient level. There are few private service firms in fields such as technology sale, information, international brokerage, repair shops, and inputs sales and their competitiveness is limited. At the public service level, there are some support activities, such as technical schools, innovation centres, information and technical assistance services, and infrastructures. The outcome of such a public effort is still limited. It also depends on the controversial way these public institutions have been working for the development of the small firms sector, which reduces the credibility of public services programmes.[11]

The lack of awareness and the reduced trust that small firms have in public and private services do not produce a significant lobbying activity *vis-à-vis* local governments, to increase all kinds of services. The entrepreneurs do not value the power they theoretically have to choose their own political representatives, which would allow them to reap the benefits of economic collaboration.[12] In this way, a whole set of external economies are neglected: all those referring to the presence of basic infrastructure (roads, energy, water), technical education and training for workers, national and international trade events, industrial parks, transport system, information services, technical assistance, innovation institutes and so on, that local governments could promote if properly pushed. At the same time, the strong individualistic entrepreneurial attitude, which is also a consequence of the atomizing liberalization process, does not push the rest of the society to build up complementary activities that would support the cluster's growth: local banks for industrial activity, technology and mechanical firms, information and commercial enterprises and so on. The weak interdependence between private and public service institutions and the producers makes the territorial environment much less competitive and attractive than it could be.

A radical change with the past is needed. Certainly, private services will join the cluster only when they see market and earning opportunities; but this should not be the position of the public support institutions. These have the unique capacity to join the local productive arena and offer services and infrastructure that would enhance the collective efficiency. Moreover, public service institutions could have the task of orienting systemic development by showing the relevance of the mutual complementarities existing between direct and indirect economic actors. This is out of the reach of the individual entrepreneurs. The action of the State 'facilitator' would attribute more co-ordination and effectiveness to the initiatives that the different actors realize in this context.

CONCLUDING AND PROSPECTING

The Nicaraguan furniture industry is still in its infancy. This industry, despite being organized in clusters of small firms, could be defined as 'unsuccessful' on the basis of its present outcome. If the idea is to push a productive sector to be leader of the territorial and national development process, this case only represents an embryonic case. Nevertheless, the challenge is there. Indeed, it is one of the higher potential sectors in the national economy for several reasons: huge potential of raw materials, low-cost and relatively skilled labour, sectoral and geographical concentration of small firms.

This chapter started by questioning the nature of innovation in the present poor sectoral context. The discussion stressed that if the country wants to leave the present 'low-road' competition, which only creates a destructive competition inside the country, it requires a systemic innovation. This means innovation that draws the whole sectoral and territorial economy in a process towards higher competitiveness, which is the key to development. In this sense, this chapter generates new prospects for sectoral development where there are still not significant results.

The discussion indicates that the flexible specialization approach of industrial development – within the small firms model – is appropriate in Nicaragua's economy. This is more likely to generate adequate and sustainable development than the several informal sectors' approaches, the Fordist and the Japanese systems of production. The critics of the appropriateness of the flexible specialization approach emphasize the present lack of success of the furniture sector and its distance from the model. On the whole, these small firms are indeed not quite yet successful and are still out of the international market and far away from the modern concept of competitiveness. Nevertheless, this research shows the heterogeneity of these firms, which present significant differences in terms of entrepreneurial economic rationalities, capitalization levels, bottlenecks and potential for growth. In particular, a group of firms (Competitive firms) already shows important aspects of 'high-road' competition and development, which are the fundamental basis of the flexible specialization approach. It means that some entrepreneurs already utilize a rationality which tries to incorporate a socio-economic perspective that emphasizes the co-ordination chain, in order to efficiently produce high-quality products that can be marketed to higher-income consumers inside and outside the country. This approach can be identified as the way out of the poor and static conditions of this sector, since it leads towards a type of development that emphasizes the competitiveness of systems of enterprises, rather than individual firms or restricted groups of large firms. It does so by highlighting the multiple aspects of an aggregate sectoral and geographic innovation and growth: product, process and organization at the intrafirm level; vertical and horizontal competition and co-operation at the interfirm level; private and public services at the support service level.

In this sense, the task to activate a high-road of development is rather great.

Structural change can be achieved only through multiple interventions at the level of the enterprise, the cluster and its environment. Nevertheless, an urgent task is to identify the key that can liberate the production system from the present low-road of competition so that it can move to a better system. This key seems to be the foreign market. Nicaragua exhibits a severe bottleneck in the internal market – due to low income and population – and the external market seems to be the best way to open up new opportunities. These consumers ask for different products and of better quality, but they are also capable of paying higher prices, which would allow Nicaragua's small industries a better pattern of capital accumulation. Recent studies on successful furniture clusters in developed countries (Forlí and Altamura, in Italy: Bertini, 1997) and developing countries (Jepara in Indonesia: Sandee, 1998) stress the fundamental importance of the export market in the growth of local economies. In fact, in these cases more than half of the entire production is exported. These studies show that international buyers play an important role in marketing the output of small enterprise clusters. Also these buyers are crucial in determining what products will be made in the future as they have the best insight into the preferences of overseas consumers.

Market innovation is the first step. Market reorientation could also be a catalyst for change, because of its capacity to activate the other aspects of the cluster's competitiveness. Through an increase in large orders, market innovation should give an incentive to the entrepreneurs to meet new standards by raising quality, efficiency and innovation/imitation of product, process and organization. It obviously needs a serious effort from public development institutions in order to facilitate the introduction of better practices (especially through a decentralized and effective system of technical assistance) that help overcome the qualitative and quantitative bottlenecks of the productive chain. This would result in a better organization and specialization of labour among the links of the chain and would probably help improve the sectoral competitiveness by increasing the quantity, quality and timing of input and product supply to producers and traders. A chain perspective makes it possible for small entrepreneurs to change their bad habits (low quality and slow process, repetitive styles, lack of timeliness and so on) and advance along the difficult path that takes them from craftwork to small industry.

In the case of weak and open economies such as Nicaragua's, the economic actors are still too individualistic and have limited experience of the competitive struggle that takes place in the market. That is why institutional support becomes critical. In the case of such an 'infant industry' as Nicaragua's furniture industry, public institutions should in fact work at two levels: first of all the policy level, to propose a long-term vision to direct and indirect actors (entrepreneurs and private services) and to provide co-ordination, coherence and consistence to the development process. Secondly, at the support level, to act on the frameworks of collective life and on the capabilities of civil society to allow the greatest possible number of agents to act effectively in the economic context. Indeed, in Nicaragua the market is not 'simply' there, rather 'it still has to be built up' (Bianchi, 1995). Systemic innovation is required to change the industrial profile of this sector effectively.

NOTES

1. The present deforestation rate is creating natural resource problems. The exploitation is due to forest burning and wood exporting companies that often break the law which limits the exploitation of endangered species. The craftsmen use no more than 1–2 per cent of the total cut wood, which means that they are not responsible for the extinction risks. Moreover, an appropriate reforestation programme would eliminate the risks of deforestation, since the rate of growth of the forest itself is extremely high in a humid tropical country.
2. This classification depends on the capacity of capital accumulation (zero, low and medium-high), which is based on their average net income. These categories also involve different economic rationalities, which are relevant for discussing the real development opportunities of this sector and to define type-specific development policies. In our survey, Subsistence firms represent the majority (64 per cent of the total), while the other two groups represent 18 per cent each (Parrilli, 1998b).
3. *Kanban* is the system by which each worker produces only on the basis of the order (card: *kanban* in Japanese) that the next worker gives him/her. It is demand that drives the working system of the factory. This results in a consistent reduction of the work-in-process, a better system at the work benches and, as a consequence, better quality and more efficiency.
4. Some scholars take a narrower view about the flexible specialization paradigm, limiting it to intrafirm and technological aspects (Pedersen, Sverrisson and Van Dijk, 1994) and distinguishing it from a broader view of development, called the new competition, which incorporates interfirm and institutional support aspects (Best, 1990).
5. Verbal contracts, easy communication of changes in the delivery programme, good feedback about consumers' reaction to the product are just some of the benefits that take place in this denser social economic network.
6. The quantitative data on which this chapter is based come from a survey of 67 small industries in the five major concentrations of small firms in the furniture sector: Masaya, Estelí, León, Chinandega, Managua. The qualitative data add another 22 cases from another cluster: Masatepe. These concentrations number between 100 and 200 firms; these have been chosen on the basis of the cluster approach, which requires a certain critical mass of firms in order to produce the benefits of externalities and joint action.
7. This characterization of the organization inside the workshop seems to be typical of developing countries. In fact, the Kenyan and Zimbabwean clusters studied by Sverrisson (1993) show the same characterization of small industries. Very few cases fit into a Fordist organization of production, almost none in the post-Fordist. The critical causes seem to be the size/type of market and the level of production.
8. This information comes from an interview with a British exporter who works with a group of six firms in Masaya and who identified this problem as a serious obstacle to reduce the costs of production.
9. The Italian cluster of Forlí is one of the clearest cases: it shows a sectoral GDP that ranks beyond 450 million US$, of which more than 50% refers to the export market (Bertini, 1997; Camera di Commercio di Forlí e Cesena, 1997). The Indonesian cluster of Jepara shows similar export features, since its recent production boom depends on the export market (from 3 to 127 millon dollars from 1989 to 1997: Sandee, 1998)

10. In most of the cases, a double bed made of real cedar costs between 50 and 100 dollars; a kitchen table of mahogany or cedar with 6 chairs is priced between 120 and 250 dollars.
11. Several craftsmen expressed disappointment in these organizations, that – in their opinion – have manipulated external co-operation for their own purpose.
12. This is one of the reasons for the economic success in industrial districts such as the Third Italy (Putnam, 1993).

REFERENCES

Banco Central de Nicaragua (BCN, 1996), *Directorio de las Empresas Manufactureras de Nicaragua*, Managua.

BCN (1998), *Datos de la Encuesta Manufacturera 1995*, Managua.

Bertini, S. (1997), *Il Settore del Mobile Imbottito a Forlí*, Milan: Nomisma.

Bessant, J. (1991), *Managing Advanced Manufacturing Technology: The Challenge of the Fifth Wave*, Manchester, NCC Blackwell.

Best, M. (1990), *The New Competition*, Cambridge: Cambridge University Press.

Bianchi, P. (1995), *Le Politiche Industriali dell'Unione Europea*, Bologna: Il Mulino.

Camera di Commercio di Forlí e Cesena (1997), *La economia regionale della provincia di Forlí e Cesena*.

De Soto, A. (1991), *Las Nuevas Reglas del Juego*, Bogota: Fundes.

De Soto, H. (1990), *The Other Path: the Invisible Revolution in the Third World*, New York: Harper and Row.

Dini, M. and W. Peres (1994), 'Sistemi di innovazione in America Latina: esperienze locali e sostegno delle istituzioni', *L'Industria*, October–December.

Kaplinsky, R. (1995), 'Technique and system: the spread of Japanese management techniques to developing countries', *World Development*, January.

Marklund and Rodriguez (1993), *Recursos forestales de Nicaragua en 1990*, Managua, Suedforest Consultancy/IRENA.

Messner, D. (1993), 'Shaping industrial competitiveness in Chile: the case of the Chilean wood-processing industry', in K. Esser (ed.), *International competitiveness in Latin America and East Asia*, London: GDI, Frank Cass.

Ministerio de Economia y Desarrollo (MEDE, 1997), *Desarrollo económico: libertad y democracia*, Managua.

Murray, R. (1992), *Flexible Specialisation and Agroindustry in Honduras*, Vienna: UNIDO.

Parrilli, M.D. (1998a), *La Competitividad de la Pequeña Industria de Muebles en Nicaragua*, Nitlapán-UCA, June.

Parrilli, M.D. (1998b), 'Una tipología de los productores de muebles en Nicaragua', mimeo, Nitlapán-UCA, December.

Pedersen, O., A. Sverrisson, M.P. van Dijk (eds) (1994), 'Introduction', in O. Pedersen *et al.* (eds), *Flexible Specialisation: a new Paradigm for the South*, London: Intermediate Technology Publications.

Pérez, Sainz (1995), 'Globalizacion y neoinformalidad en America Latina', *Nueva Sociedad*, n.135, February.

Pissarides, C. (1997), 'Learning by trading and the returns to human capital in developing countries', *World Bank Economic Review*, **11** (1).

Portes, A. (1995), *Ensayos sobre Teoria y Medicion de la Economia no regulada*, Mexico: FLACSO.

Portes, A. (1997), 'Neoliberalism and the sociology of development: emerging trends and unanticipated facts', *Population and Development Review*, **23**, pp. 229–59.

Putnam, R. (1993), *Making democracy work, civic tradition in modern Italy*, New York: Princeton University Press.

Pyke, F. and W. Sengenberger (1991), *Industrial districts and interfirm cooperation in Italy*, Geneva: ILO.

Sandee, H. (1998), 'The impact of the crisis on small-scale enterprises in Java, findings from selected case studies (Chapter 9, this volume).

Schmitz, H. (1995), 'Tale of a supercluster', *World Development*, January.

Schmitz, H. and B. Musick (1993), *Industrial Districts in Europe: Policy Lessons for Developing Countries*, IDS discussion papers n. 324.

Schumpeter, H. (1934), *The Theory of Economic Development*, Boston: Harvard University Press.

Stewart, F. and E. Ghani (1991), 'How significant are externalities for development?', *World Development*, **19**, pp. 659–591.

Sverrisson, A. (1993), 'Innovation as a collective enterprise: case studies of carpenters in Nakura, Kenya', Discussion paper no. 189, Research Policy Institute, University of Lund.

Tendler, J. and M. Alves Amorim (1996), 'Small firms and their helpers', *World Development*, March.

Tokman, V. (1992), *Beyond Regulation: The Informal Economy in Latin America*, London: ILO.

Zucker, L. (1986), 'Production of trust: institutional sources of economic structure', *Research and Organisational Behaviour*, **8**, pp. 53–111.

8. Why do(n't) they innovate? Explaining diverse SME adjustment strategies after an external shock

Regine Qualmann

Small and medium-sized enterprises (SMEs) are often assumed to adjust more easily to sudden changes in their economic environment than larger firms. Their responses to shifts in incentive structures are reported to be often flexible and innovative. In this chapter we assess a specific type of shift in incentive structures that are brought about by Structural Adjustment Programmes (SAPs). SAPs aim at changes in relative prices of tradables and non-tradables through stimulating trade liberalization and currency devaluation. Such measures are usually considered to be favourable for small enterprises. This applies in particular if SMEs rely on domestic inputs and labour to produce import substitutes or exportable goods.

Theory suggests a rather dynamic response of SMEs in the case of a major shift in incentives towards tradable goods. A series of World Bank studies analysing the adjustment of micro- and small enterprises[1] to liberalization in five African countries supports this notion (World Bank, 1995).[2] According to the World Bank studies, small enterprises adapted to relative price changes and increased import competition by changing their product line, upgrading their technology, introducing new products and entering export markets. The authors acknowledge great differences in adjustment behaviour at the level of individual enterprises, but the diversity of reactions within the same country and size group remain unexplained.

This chapter discusses small enterprise adjustment after the sharp devaluation of the CFA Franc in Senegal carried out in 1996. We argue that there is reason to be less optimistic regarding the outcomes of SME adjustment strategies compared with the World Bank findings (Qualmann *et al.*, 1996; Qualmann, 1997).[3] Real turnovers and profit margins of SMEs have on average declined during the first two years after the devaluation, as has also been observed in other CFA-countries, such as Burkina Faso (Camilleri, 1997), Cameroon (Hugon, 1996) and Côte d'Ivoire (Goreux, 1995). Our findings show that small enterprises react quite diversely to adjustment measures. The majority of the enterprises in our sample showed defensive reactions instead of dynamic or innovative strategies such as entering new markets or introducing new products or processes.

This chapter identifies different adjustment strategies of Senegalese SMEs in the post-devaluation period. In general, SMEs' reactions were neither as dynamic nor as homogeneous as might be expected according to neo-liberal theory. In this chapter we want to explain the diversity in reactions among small firms. Why do some SMEs adapt quickly and even change their products or production processes substantially when they are confronted with external shocks, and others do not? Why do some enterprises, even in periods of severe losses, sustain their production without actively trying to improve their situation? In short: why do some enterprises innovate and others don't?

The purpose of this chapter is to further our understanding of different firm-level responses to external changes. After a brief introduction of different conceptual approaches to analyse adjustment and innovation behaviour at the micro level in the second section, the findings on SMEs responses to the CFA Franc devaluation in Senegal are discussed in the third section. Four distinct patterns of SME adjustment strategies emerge from the discussion. An enterprise typology is derived from the observed adjustment strategies. The next section explores some of the determinants that may explain differences in strategic behaviour and various constraints on innovation. The discussion focuses on determinants related to the reduction of transaction costs and risk, and on patterns of technological learning. The final section concludes that innovation can be a very costly and highly contingent strategy in a setting characterized by high uncertainty and little co-operation.

DIFFERENT VIEWS ON SME ADJUSTMENT AND INNOVATION

There are a number of differing views on how small- and medium-sized enterprises (SMEs) react to adjustment programmes. In this section, I will briefly contrast the views proposed by the neo-classical, the neo-institutional, and the evolutionary approaches, considering the technological capabilities approach as a special type of the latter. The purpose is to bring out the factors that these distinct approaches consider most important to explain enterprise responses to sudden external changes.

The neo-classical approach suggests that enterprises react almost automatically provided that 'prices are right' and rational entrepreneurs seek the most efficient allocation of resources. The main determinants of enterprise behaviour are the new incentives after a shock which guide efficient resource allocation, for example mainly prices. Slow response or default is then explained partly by remaining market imperfections such as lack of infrastructure, and partly by the existence of 'good' and 'bad' entrepreneurs. Inefficient enterprises which fail to adjust will be forced to exit during the process. The main determinants of the pace and direction of enterprise adjustment reside, according to this neo-classical view, *outside* the firms.

World Bank studies on SME adjustment largely follow this conceptual approach. They do not only predict but usually also find overall positive outcomes of structural adjustment measures for small enterprises (Steel and Webster, 1992: 423ff; World Bank, 1995: 53ff.; World Bank, 1994a: 149ff.) It is argued that the type of market distortions which SAPs are presumed to reduce are particularly SME unfriendly. SMEs are consequently expected to prosper only when these obstacles are removed. If this was not the case, that is if it was found that SMEs failed to respond to liberalization or devaluation measures, it was most frequently blamed on the financial squeeze on SMEs following the malfunctioning of financial markets, lack of managerial competency or, more generally, on the absence of 'entrepreneurship' in the respective countries. The 'black box' of firm behaviour remained to a large extent untouched in these studies.

Steel and Webster (1992: 433) identify credit constraints and weak demand as major bottlenecks to firm growth. Their paper does not separate analytically adjustment processes and responses at the firm-level from enterprise performance, size-criteria or the managerial ability of the entrepreneurs: 'Sample entrepreneurs fell in two broad groups: dynamic, successful adapters with good prospects (found mostly among small-scale enterprises) and stagnant producers who had not adapted to the new competitive environment (found mostly among microenterprises)' (Steel and Webster, 1992: 423). Explanations of this type are of a rather tautological nature and do not add much to the understanding of firm behaviour and decision-making processes. The following quotation from a World Bank report that summarizes SME adjustment experience in five African countries reveals the same type of circular argument: 'Growing MSEs exhibited greater flexibility in adapting to the new environment. In particular, they were more likely than stagnant or declining MSEs to take advantage of the greater availability of imported inputs and to upgrade their equipment' (World Bank, 1995: 65).

The analysis of the most important enterprise-level constraints hardly goes further than the usual listing of firm problems as perceived by the respondents themselves. Such a list most often ranks access to credit and inputs as the most important obstacles to SME dynamics without questioning the firms' ability to spend additional capital on profitable investments. Thus, Steel and Webster

(1992: 433) conclude in the case of Ghana: 'In sum, the incentive side of the adjustment process was working – less efficient firms were being squeezed – but the financial side was not functioning adequately to enable more efficient firms to grow.' In the study on SME adjustment in five African countries, the underlying methodological problem is acknowledged. 'The focus of respondents on external constraints may be understandable given the interview nature of the survey instrument; entrepreneurs naturally identify limitations on their daily business operations that are outside their control, rather than internal management deficiencies' (World Bank, 1995: 59). Other supply-side constraints on enterprise responsiveness *within* firms, such as the acquisition of information or modes of technical learning, have only very recently been considered more thoroughly in some World Bank studies (Biggs *et al.* 1996: 107ff.).

Other supply-side problems, such as lack of relevant information or inability to process the available information, remain excluded from systematic analysis in these studies. Consequently, enterprises are not only expected to adjust more or less automatically to external changes but, moreover, to do so in a way that leads to a more efficient allocation of resources.

The New Institutional Economics (NIE) approach seeks to complement neo-liberal theory with an explicit analysis of institutions, organizations and transaction costs referred to as the 'costs of running the economic system' (Kenneth Arrow as quoted in Williamson, 1985: 19). Transaction costs are much more broadly defined than production costs. They emerge as transacting rests upon agreements (or, more formally: contracts) between different agents which have to be negotiated and enforced. Agents are assumed to be opportunistic, therefore much time and money has to be spent on seeking the necessary information to minimize the risk of being deceived by one's contract partner. The bulk of transaction costs is assumed to arise because 'information is costly and asymmetrically held by the parties to exchange' (North, 1995: 18). The purpose of the organizational form of the firm is to economize on production as well as transaction costs.[4] More generally, institutions determine the kind of performance that will pay off in a given economic, social and legal setting. Their formation and proper functioning will reduce transaction costs, in particular those arising from information problems: 'Information processing by the actors as a result of the costliness of transactions is what underlies the formation of institutions' (North, 1990: 107).

NIE employs price theory as an essential part of the analysis of institutions. Just like in the neo-classical approach, changes in relative prices are considered a major driving force for innovations (North, 1995). After a shift in relative prices, some activities pay off better, others less than before. But the agents of change are the decision makers in the organizations. Their subjective perceptions determine the choices they make, and they usually have to decide in a situation of uncertainty. According to transaction costs economics, in the presence of uncertainty firms will organize transactions in a way to minimize the risks incurred by bounded rationality and to safeguard against opportunism of other economic agents (Williamson, 1985: 32).

According to this approach, a firm has to take into account additional transaction costs when it plans to change input structure, production lines, modes of marketing or design. In other words, adjustment and innovation strategies involve not only access to externally available information, but also the costs of testing the validity of that information, of sharing it with the employees of the firm, drawing the right conclusions from it, establishing new personal relations with suppliers or intermediaries and so on. Thus we may think that entrepreneurs are passive (wait-and-see attitude) to changes, while, in fact, they are already involved in several processes that will lead to either adjustment or innovation. Moreover, it highlights the problem that an environment largely characterized by uncertainty and asymmetric information will increase the cost of innovation for individual firms. The risk of incurring 'sunk' transaction costs, which will not be recovered if the adjustment is not successful or not sustainable, is thus higher in an unstable setting.

While transaction cost economics thus significantly broadens the neo-classical scope of determinants of firm behaviour, it does not pay attention to how firms learn. Evolutionary economics and the technological capability approach take the argument of the costliness of firm adjustment further and complement it with valuable insights into the process of technical learning (Nelson and Winter, 1982; Nelson, 1987; Lall, 1992; Lall and Latsch, 1998). A micro-perspective of technical change and innovation is introduced to open up the 'black box' of enterprise-level decision making. Profit maximizing or opportunism are no longer regarded as the single or most dominant principle guiding a firm's strategic decisions (Nelson, 1987: 20). Nelson and Winter (1982) assume that actors operate according to a certain set of decision rules which they have learned over time in their continuous search to find better ways of doing things. These rules are called 'routines'. Routines determine operating procedures, investment behaviour and, most important for adjustment and innovation, 'the deliberative processes of the firm, its "search" behaviour' (Nelson, 1987: 22). By way of assuming different routines corresponding to different experiences and different abilities of individual firms it becomes possible to explain within the model why 'not all firms would be equally successful in thinking through what to do' (Nelson, 1987: 30) in response to external changes, such as shifts in relative prices.

A major contribution to innovation analysis is made by the writings of evolutionary economics on the processes of technological learning within and between firms. The learning process is cumulative and consequently path-dependent, which is explained by the existence of *tacit* elements of knowledge necessarily accompanying the ones embodied in technology (Dosi, 1988: 1126ff; Lall and Latsch, 1998: 445). Tacit knowledge cannot be passed on by blueprints or patents but involves experience, learning-by-doing and learning-by-interacting between the enterprise and its environment (for example, other entrepreneurs, consultants, intermediaries, suppliers or customers) as well as within the individual enterprise. The cost and risk of applying a new technology will decline with the level of technological and industrial development already reached in a firm's environment because of spill-over effects in terms of availability of skilled labour or specialized advice, as well as experience shared with other firms.[5] This is all the more relevant for SMEs lacking the resources for in-house training or R&D spending. The assumption that positive externalities are involved with technological learning and thus with enterprise adjustment and innovation has led to the conclusion that co-operation among firms, and among SMEs in particular, should significantly reduce information and transaction costs and consequently facilitate enterprise responsiveness to external changes.[6]

Three working hypotheses relating to SME adjustment strategies are derived from this brief discussion of conceptual approaches:

1. SMEs will not automatically adjust to shifts in relative prices that affect their production costs because their decision making is also guided by transaction costs;
2. transaction and in particular information costs are high in an environment of uncertainty, asymmetric information and low contract-enforcement;
3. the adjustment process of firms depends on their learning capabilities which are shaped by acquired routines while co-operation may accelerate learning.

DIFFERENT ADJUSTMENT STRATEGIES IN SENEGAL: SURVEY FINDINGS

The Pre-devaluation Phase

During the 1980s, characterized by growing flexibility of exchange rates throughout the world, the CFA franc zone, with its fixed parity against the French franc, became a much discussed special case (Qualmann, 1997). The competitiveness of the CFA countries, towed along by the European currency bloc, steadily deteriorated as a result of successive appreciations against the dollar.

Senegal's output and exports declined from the mid 1980s. By the end of 1993 it even had negative GDP growth rates (see IMF, 1996). Yet its government and also that of France feared the economic and political consequences of a parity alignment. The main risks were seen to be significant price rises due to high dependence on imports and major losses of purchasing power. Possible gains from a devaluation were being rated low given the low elasticities of demand for the main export products. The decision to devaluate the currency sharply was eventually taken under pressure from the Bretton Woods institutions, which doubted successful structural adjustment programmes without a large devaluation.

SMEs may be among those who gain from a devaluation. Their production is comparatively labour and natural-resource intensive, and, consequently, their factor costs will fall relative to those of foreign competitors and local large-scale competitors which are usually more dependent on imports. Unlike micro enterprises, SMEs typically manufacture traded goods and so benefit directly from a devaluation if they are producing substitutes for imports or are able to penetrate export markets. In addition, small firms are considered to adapt more quickly to changes in the market environment because production processes and decision-making practices are less complex than in larger firms (Parker *et al.*, 1995: 17).

Senegalese SMEs are on average much more import dependent than similar firms in other African countries (Parker *et al.*, 1995: 5). They compete mainly with imported goods on local markets with limited exposure on export markets. Therefore, devaluation should have had favourable effects on Senegalese SMEs. However, these positive effects could be mitigated by a reduction of local purchasing power, lowering overall demand. Consequently, it is expected that Senegalese SMEs would adapt processes or end products to changing consumer preferences and seize new export opportunities on regional non-CFA markets and abroad.

The Survey Sample

The findings are based on a survey carried out by five German Development Institute (GDI) researchers in the spring of 1996 (Qualmann *et al.*, 1996). The enterprise sample covers 45 SMEs in seven subsectors. Fish processing was treated as a separate category, and not as a part of food processing, because of its relative weight in Senegal's manufacturing and exports. Table 8.1 shows the distribution of the SMEs surveyed by size and sector. The enterprises were not selected randomly but we wanted the sample to reveal possible differences in adjustment due to input structure and marketing orientation. Our sample would make it possible to study any reallocation of resources from the non-tradables to the tradables sectors following changes in price incentives.

Table 8.1   Number of SMEs interviewed, by size[a] *and sector*

	5–9	10–49	50–100	Total	Per cent of SMEs interviewed
Fish processing	2	4	2	8	18
Textiles/clothing	2	4	2	8	18
Food processing	3	4	–	7	16
Metal working	3	3	1	7	16
Chemicals	1	4	–	5	11
Wood processing	2	2	–	4	9
Printing	–	3	1	4	9
Other	–	2	–	2	4
Total	13	26	6	45	100

Note: a. Related to the number of permanent employees, including apprentices.

Source: Survey data.

Changes in Prices

The Senegalese government succeeded in quickly curbing inflation after the devaluation by pursuing a restrictive monetary policy. Inflation reduced from 32 per cent in 1994 to 8 per cent in 1995. The real devaluation effect was thus lowered, but still estimated at 20 to 30 per cent. In Senegal, however, the difference between the relative prices of traded and non-traded goods – and consequently the incentive for producers to improve factor allocation – remained far less pronounced than expected (Goreux, 1995: 18, 21f.). Although the reduction in tariffs and taxes and the fixing of the prices of certain imported goods, such as basic foodstuffs, fuels and medicines, had the effect of checking inflation, they also greatly reduced the competitive advantage of local factors of production and end products.

Regarding wages, most private enterprises including SMEs were as usual guided by the public sector, where wages were raised by an average of about 15 per cent in April 1994.[7] The next round of wage negotiations did not take place until late in 1995; wages in the private sector then rose by an average of 4 per cent at the beginning of 1996. The resulting decline in real wages over the two years inevitably led to considerable losses of purchasing power. Given the low level of productivity, wages in the formal manufacturing sector must nonetheless be regarded as high by international standards, and the incentive for labour-intensive factor re-allocation remains limited.

The price increases of certain utilities remained slightly below the average rate of inflation. It should be noticed, however, that the initial level of these factor costs was already high by regional standards and still cannot be regarded as competitive after the devaluation. There were above-average increases in transport costs, which are largely determined by the private sector. Overland transport became 80 to 100 per cent more expensive, while the cost of air and sea transport more than doubled in CFA francs in some cases. Both factors reduced the new incentive to export.

Increases in the Cost of Inputs

Immediately after the devaluation the government froze the prices of some goods, including food and rents, in order to curb inflation. Substantially reduced standard import duties and turnover tax rates were introduced just after the devaluation to compensate for upward pressure on import prices. Of the SMEs interviewed, over half were importing more than 50 per cent of their inputs (see Table 8.2) and one third even more than 80 per cent. This shows that SMEs are far more dependent on imports than is often assumed.

Table 8.2   Number of SMEs interviewed in various sectors, by origin of important inputs

	More than 80 per cent of local origin	50–80 per cent of local origin	50–80 per cent imported	More than 80 per cent imported
Fish processing	8	–	–	–
Textiles/clothing	2	3	2	1
Food processing	3	2	1	1
Metal working	–	1	4	2
Chemicals	1	–	–	4
Wood processing	–	–	3	1
Printing	–	–	–	4
Other	1	–	–	1
Total	15	6	10	14

Source: Survey data.

According to the survey results, production costs rose by 10 to 200 per cent. Surprisingly, the rise in the prices of imported inputs was not significantly higher than the rise in the prices of local inputs. Government price policies and cheap imports (textiles, foodstuffs) and the limited availability of local inputs (fishing, construction industry) have eroded the impact of the devaluation and reduced the incentive to substitute local for foreign inputs.

Prices of Outputs

Most SMEs in our sample produce for local markets, where they compete with imports or brand products made locally under licence. SMEs enjoy some protection against imports because they manufacture a specific range of locally consumed products and because transport costs for importers are high. Very few Senegalese SMEs – primarily those processing fish and a small number of clothing manufacturers – were export oriented before the devaluation. Exporting enterprises are slightly over-represented among the SMEs interviewed (see Table 8.3).

Table 8.3   Number of SMEs interviewed in various sectors, by marketing orientation

	More than 80 per cent marketed locally	50–80 per cent marketed locally	50–80 per cent exported	More than 80 per cent exported
Fish processing	–	–	1	7
Textiles/clothing	5	2	1	–
Food processing	5	1	–	1
Metal working	7	–	–	–
Chemicals	5	–	–	–
Wood processing	4	–	–	–
Printing	4	–	–	–
Other	2	–	–	–
Total	32	3	2	8

Source: Survey data.

In the product markets, too, the greater protection against imports after devaluation was partly cancelled out by the almost simultaneous reduction in import charges introduced by the Senegalese government. Some international suppliers also reacted to the devaluation by lowering their foreign exchange prices in the franc zone markets. In Senegal this was particularly true for clothing, footwear and foodstuffs, where smuggled and second-hand goods also depress the prices of imported products. Even after the devaluation there was little improvement in price competition with imports.

In the case of goods traded predominantly in local markets the competitive pressure from micro-enterprises increased for SMEs (textiles, furniture, printing), because buyers changed to cheaper, lower-quality products. Higher costs could be passed on in selling prices in these markets only when SMEs were successful in bidding for public procurement contracts (clothing, construction industry) or in selling to larger customers with considerable purchasing power.

In markets outside the CFA franc zone it was possible to raise selling prices in CFA francs sharply or even double them after the devaluation, which more than compensated for higher production costs. Some Senegalese exporters were also able to reduce their foreign exchange prices and so increase their sales volume. However, the situation for the (exporting) fish processing SMEs deteriorated significantly in the second year, when input costs rose sharply because of a shortage of fish, and when selling prices simultaneously came under heavy pressure in the European markets. All in all, however, the relative reduction in the cost of Senegalese products in established export markets was enough to improve their international competitiveness.

Conclusions on Shifts in Price Incentives

Relative prices did not always shift in the direction and quantities originally expected. Some conclusions on the shifts of price incentives are as follows: first and most clearly, exporting became more profitable in almost all of the surveyed branches. Sporadic exports by other sample enterprises to CFA and non-CFA countries in the region support this finding. Second, demand for non-essentials (for example, printing matter, furniture) on local markets dropped drastically. Selling prices often did not cover production costs and hardly yielded a profit. Third, price increases for imported inputs were more pronounced than for locally or regionally (CFA countries) available resources in the cases of textiles, wood, construction materials, and some foodstuffs. Fourth, profits in local markets characterized by high purchasing power and growing demand remained unchanged or rose as selling prices could be raised due to higher production costs.

SMEs' Perceptions

The majority of small-scale producers rated the effects of the devaluation negative. Others were ambivalent, even when the development of their enterprises had been positive. This view reflects the shock and uncertainty felt after the devaluation. In the first two years after the parity alignment only a few of the enterprises undertook extensive adjustment measures or changed business strategies fundamentally. Many SMEs felt they had very little leeway in view of the relative increase in the prices of inputs, the lack of substitution options, the decline in purchasing power and their inability to obtain credit.

Co-operation of SMEs

There is little horizontal and vertical co-operation among enterprises in the same sector in Senegal and considerable distrust of institutions because of past experiences and prejudices. Many enterprises concentrate their firm development strategies on personal contacts with people they have known before but who are often unfamiliar with the sector. In addition, they focus on people considered to be influential and, less frequently, customers. Very little of the information and advice offered by the formal institutions is geared to SMEs' needs, and, for example, most export promotion measures are only accessible to large firms.

Adjustment Strategies

Both the direct impact of the devaluation and the reactions and adjustment strategies of the SMEs varied widely, even within the same sector. Changes in prices, the competitive situation and the trend in purchasing power in a given market influenced the individual enterprise's room for manoeuvre. Firm adjustment strategies depend much on the individual entrepreneur's access to information and his ability to process the information appropriately for his needs. Access to information was very often of an informal, personalized type rather than formal institutional support. Distrust in validity and reliability of sources of formal information was regularly articulated in the interviews. Some of the enterprises had regular orders from the same client but none of them could be regarded as a regular subcontractor in a supply chain. Therefore, most enterprises can be considered 'independent' in pursuing their own adjustment strategies.

The term 'innovation' in this chapter refers to all measures taken by an enterpreneur in order to produce and sell a superior product at competitive prices. It includes product innovation through improvements of the product design (or introduction of a new product), and process innovation by making an existent product at lower cost through changes in the production process. Innovation refers also to incremental changes in quality of output and/or production processes. African SMEs are mostly 'adaptive imitators' rather than innovators. In this chapter, SMEs are considered innovative if they are the first to introduce a locally new product design, use and slightly adapt a new technology, or substantially reorganize their production process.

Enterprise reactions followed four adjustment patterns:[8]

- *active or innovative adjustment*: substitute inputs or end products, diversify markets or price products strategically.
- *delayed, client oriented adjustment strategies*: minor adjustments to products or processes without actively seizing new market opportunities.
- *defensive but of a belt-tightening nature*: continue executing certain activities though they are temporarily unprofitable;
- *passive behaviour* despite severe losses.

Active adjustment responses

Of the 45 SMEs interviewed, nine competing with imports or locally manufactured brand products had adopted active strategies of adjustment and innovation. This entails the substitution of locally manufactured inputs for imported inputs. In addition, it includes improved marketing and after-sales service. Examples include the start of in-house processing of palm oil in a soap producing enterprise which had previously imported it. This resulted in the enterprise producing a much less expensive end-product than competing large brandname firms. Another example concerns a food processing enterprise that reduced its unit sizes sold and developed direct delivery to several markets through its own distibution network instead of wholesale outlets.

Delayed adjustment in spite of new opportunities

The majority of the SMEs interviewed reacted to the new situation with a delay of up to two years. For example, a wood processing firm had just established new supplier contacts for wood supply from CFA-country origin (instead of regional non-CFA suppliers) at the time of the interviews. Other SMEs started to benefit from the more indirect effects of the devaluation and prepared for the new opportunities by purchasing new technology. Some metal working and wood processing SMEs benefited from the post-devaluation boom in the construction sector. Many entrepreneurs doubted the duration of the increase in demand, a response found especially in fish processing and some metal working enterprises. Consequently, they did not have plans for innovation in spite of high levels of capacity utilization, but they relied chiefly on increasing working hours and hiring additional (casual) labour.

Most exporters and SMEs serving large public or private customers were able to pass on their increased production costs by raising their selling prices without risking their market share. These firms did not undertake additional active measures, however, to seek new opportunities or to expand their market share. Only two exporting SMEs (high-class textiles and furniture) succeeded in increasing their shares in niche export markets. In these cases, active measures included the development of new designs, expansion of production, and improved marketing through trade fairs and intermediaries in Europe. Remarkably, not a single firm that had not exported before managed to become an exporter after the devaluation.

Defensive reaction despite perceived negative effects
In local markets the decline in purchasing power led to a shift in demand towards cheaper products, which resulted in declining profits and market shares for about a third of the SMEs. Measures taken by these enterprises include reducing the size of product units. However, this frequently resulted in even fiercer competition, especially among micro enterprises. This trend was most visible in the wood and food processing, metal working and printing sectors. These enterprises were unable to adjust 'upwards' or to move to other, higher quality markets. However, these entrepreneurs had succeeded in largely stabilizing their firms' situation, although at a lower level than before the devaluation.

Passive behaviour
Some enterprises remained completely passive even in a situation when survival of their enterprise was at risk. These entrepreneurs had very little knowledge of the activity and markets they were engaged in (fish processing) or were using extremely outdated technology (printing, food processing). Their survival appeared to be at risk at the time of the survey.

Table 8.4 summarizes the survey results in a typology concerning enterprises' strategic responses to devaluation. It focuses on their capabilities to acquire and process information and their experience or willingness to co-operate with institutions (that is, chambers, business services, banks, consultants, and private business associations) and other enterprises. Remarkably, most of the best-performing SMEs were very reluctant to co-operate within formal networks and almost exclusively relied on personalized contact with friends or family members. In contrast, type 2 enterprises were more likely to seek institutional support, though clearly preferring private associations to public institutions.

EXPLAINING THE ADJUSTMENT RESPONSES OF SMES

We need to look at a number of interacting factors in order to explain enterprise behaviour. The shift in relative prices was an advantage for various types of firms, namely those who had been exporting prior to the devaluation, who relied less on imported inputs and whose local markets suffered less from the overall contraction due to losses in purchasing power. Reactions were

Table 8.4 Enterprise typology

Type of enterprise strategy	Type 1: innovative	Type 2: defensive, client oriented	Type 3: defensive, belt tightening	Type 4: passive up to risking exit
Strategic responses to devaluation	Active strategies of import substitution, product diversification, and targeted marketing; investment in new technology	Minor and delayed adjustment of products and processes, such as size or quality reduction, use of idle capacity for expansion of production	Delayed, often defensive reaction, such as forced price reduction, idle capacity and temporary loss of profit	Completely passive behaviour, despite negative development of enterprise
Internal information processing and technological learning concerning adjustment	Capable of recognizing internal problems and of making changes themselves	Capable of recognizing internal problems and willing to make changes, often seeking external advice	Often unable to identify or articulate problems and need for advice, but not systematically seeking it	Unable to identify need for assistance and hardly able to take advantage of external support
Access to information and experience/ willingness to co-operate	Moderate; sceptical of institutions and other firms; preference for making use of personal information sources and contact	Moderate; some scepticism, especially of public institutions, but mostly members of business associations	Little access to formal information; little or unfavourable experience of co-operation	Limited; little experience of co-operation
Output markets:				
Local	9	17	5	1
Exports	4	5	–	4
Reg. distribution:				
Dakar	10	15	2	3
Regional towns	3	7	3	2
Total	13	22	5	5

sometimes different within subsectors too. However, in some subsectors the overall picture was quite clear. There were gains in the fish processing branch while there were clear losses in printing. Other sectors did not show such a clear pattern because of product market segmentation. Some products encountered high income and price elasticities (such as textiles, non-basic foods, printing matter), while others could be sold at higher prices (basic foods, textiles for public procurement) or even grow in demand (metal and wood working).

These shifts in relative prices need to be understood in terms of opportunities for some firms and increasing pressure for others. However, they did not automatically trigger responses one way or the other. The finding that the majority of the enterprises in the survey hesitated with their adjustment or did not show any strategic behaviour at all shows that there are constraining factors at work, both outside or within the firms. Our survey was executed two years after the devaluation, which may have been too soon to register adjustments. We need to take into account the learning procedures that take place in SMEs that are characterized by trial-and-error practices.[9]

There are, however, constraints other than just the time factor. First, small entrepreneurs appear to have misconceptions and a generally negative assessment of the devaluation impact. This was found to be very common, even if an enterprise did quite well after the devaluation. Entrepreneurs lack information – the government had for example prevented business associations from discussing the effects of a possible devaluation in late 1993. Of course, they had never experienced a devaluation before and did not always know how to cope with it. This is confirmed by the finding that entrepreneurs with working experience abroad were more self-confident when they were confronted with the new situation.

Uncertainty about the future development of demand and perceived risks of sunk costs also played a major role for delaying adjustment measures, especially those involving investment in new technology. There was clear evidence for widespread distrust regarding the general business environment. The transaction costs approach is relevant here. A high-risk environment with little access to reliable information, coupled with bounded rationality and opportunistic behaviour of the agents, increases transaction costs and thus prevents firms from taking the measures which would be expected when only calculating with production costs.

While these constraints apply almost equally to all firms in our sample, we found several remarkable exceptions. The successes of these firms (and failures of others) can be well explained by an evolutionary approach. Those firms who succeeded in implementing, albeit small, changes in their product or production processes had good technical knowledge or were technical engineers. Therefore, in a more or less systematic and formal way (trial-and-error or targeted adaption of well-selected imported technology), they were able to adjust the technology they mastered to their new needs.

In addition to technical skills, this group of enterprises stands out, together with those who were successful in expanding their markets by improved marketing or new distribution networks because of their modes to seek information and to co-operate with other agents. Contrary to much recent analysis on co-operation among SMEs and between firms and support services, the firms in our sample hardly showed any signs of formal co-operative relations. Instead, most of them, and particularly the successful adjusters among them, prefer rather informal, very personalized types of contacts, be it with intermediaries, final customers or people whom they ask for technical or financial support. This finding is supported by the view that African SMEs in particular have to cope with a problem that has been termed the 'missing middle phenomenon'. The comparatively small number of enterprises that has outgrown the informal sector with all its social networks has to face the constraints of formality without having the same access as large firms to formal support institutions and especially finance. Entrepreneurs confirmed this by describing their dependence on large suppliers and their unsuccessful efforts to submit the necessary documentation to commercial banks.

Seeking information on new technology and on new markets is highly contingent because it depends on the coincidence of skills and personal relationships. It is remarkable, however, that, in the eyes of the entrepreneurs, this is still somewhat less contingent than co-operating with formal support institutions such as chambers. In any case, we have to conclude from this that systematic acquisition of information and technical learning from external sources is quite limited. Successful adjustment and innovation are based on the enterprises' capabilities regarding technological learning. When SMEs cannot rely on information sources external to their firm, adjustment depends all the more on the abilities already accumulated within the firm, most importantly technical but also organizational skills. Even good skills, however, will seldom allow quality leaps by a single firm. In an environment characterized by limited co-operation we have to expect incremental adjustment strategies that are based on often inefficient trial-and-error learning processes within individual firms (Romijn, 1998: 18).

CONCLUSIONS

The analysis of firm behaviour after the devaluation in Senegal revealed a diverse picture of adjustment and innovation strategies by SMEs. The neo-classical approach which abstracts largely from behavioural notions and expects all firms to adjust instantaneously to new price incentives cannot explain micro-level differences between similar firms confronted with similar changes such as new price incentives. The most dynamic reactions came from those enterprises who were directly favoured by the shift in relative prices and gained more 'room for manoeuvre'. In contrast, firms with high import dependency and producing output with significant price elasticities felt trapped by the new situation. Generalizations as to the favourable effects of the relative price changes on SMEs do not seem justified.

The analysis of firms and their behaviour towards external changes is broadened by the transaction costs approach based on the assumptions of opportunism and bounded rationality. It points out that in a world of limited and asymmetric information and uncertainty firms will face transaction costs which largely exceed production costs. Measures such as adjustment and innovation of products or production processes require complex transactions among various agents that need to be negotiated and enforced. All this involves costs which may well be higher for an SME than the (maybe temporary) losses that have to be faced after an external shock such as the devaluation. Thus, much of the defensive behaviour observed may be explained along these lines.

Following the evolutionary approach, we were able to analyse more systematically the different adjustment strategies identified in the enterprise survey. Innovative responses and successful adjustment could largely be explained by different capabilities in technological learning. The findings support the view that while technical and organizational skills play an important role for individual enterprises to find and adapt technical solutions to their needs, there is also a need for more systematic external support for information acquisition and processing. In a setting characterized by high uncertainty and little co-operation among enterprises and between them and institutions, the learning process depends largely on internal firm processes. Even incremental improvements are therefore often only achieved after inefficient experimental processes, and quality leaps are highly improbable. SME support policies should be more systematically geared towards this type of learning process taking place within and between firms. However, we have to face the fact that it will not be easy to overcome the 'routine' of unco-operative behaviour widely in use among African SMEs. 'Clustering blueprints' will not serve much more than technical ones in this respect. Rather, it seems that a joint step-by-step learning process of SMEs, support institutions and donors has to be gone through.

Transaction costs and evolutionary economics have enlarged economic theorizing on firm behaviour, but it seems that other concepts more open to the social traits of economic interaction such as loyalty, motivation, trust and co-operation are necessary to complement the study of adjustment and innovation abilities of firms. More thorough empirical analysis is certainly needed to complement the theoretical debate.

NOTES

1. Micro-enterprises in these World Bank surveys comprise firms with 1–5 workers, small enterprises are those with 6–49, see World Bank (1995: 13).
2. The five countries covered in the survey are Ghana, Malawi, Mali, Senegal, and Tanzania. The interviews were carried out between 1989 and 1991; major parts of the SAPs were introduced in the different countries around the mid 1980s, the adjustment period for the enterprises thus covering between three and five years.
3. In addition to qualitative criteria, SMEs in this study were also defined by the employment criterion and comprised firms with between 5 and 100 workers (Qualmann *et al.*, 1996: 6).
4. More fundamentally even, firms are assumed to emerge precisely because the cost of transacting through the market (that is using the price mechanism) is higher than the cost of co-ordinating the same transactions within the firm (Coase, 1990: 38 f.).
5. These are the type of external economies first mentioned by Alfred Marshall (1927: 266f.) which formed the basis for the theoretical discussion on industrial districts.
6. Empirical support of this theoretical argument comes from the vast literature on clustering and industrial districts. For an early overview of the discussion on clustering in developing countries see the contributions in *World Development*, **23** (1), 1995.
7. In the public sector, wages had been reduced by 15 per cent in November 1993 as part of an emergency programme which aimed at preventing the devaluation.
8. Helmsing derives five very similar categories from 16 different responses of Zimbabwan enterprises reacting to competitive threats emanating from SAP measures like external trade and internal market liberalization (Helmsing, 1998: 6ff.).
9. Romijn (1998) gives very illustrative examples of the process of building technological capability in small enterprises.

BIBLIOGRAPHY

Bates, R.H. (1995), 'Social dilemmas and rational individuals. An assessment of the new institutionalism', in J. Harriss, J. Hunter and C.M. Lewis (eds), *The New Institutional Economics and Third World Development*, London: Routledge, pp. 27–48.

Biggs, T., M. Miller, C. Otto and G. Tyler (1996), 'Africa can compete! Export opportunities and challenges for garments and home products in the European market', World Bank Discussion Paper, No. 300.

Biggs, T., G.R. Moody, J.-H. van Leeuwen and E.D. White (1994), 'Africa can compete! Export opportunities and challenges for garments and home products in the U.S. market', World Bank Discussion Papers. Africa Technical Department Series, No. 242, Washington, DC.

Camilleri, J.-L. (1997), 'The impact of devaluation on small enterprises in Burkina Faso', *Small Enterprise Development*, **8** (4).

Coase, J. (1990; reprint of 1937): 'The nature of the firm', in *The Economic Journal*, **47**, November, pp. 713–19.

Daniels, L. (1994), 'Changes in the small-scale sector from 1991 to 1993: Results of a second nation-wide survey in Zimbabwe', GEMINI Technical Report No. 71.

Dawson, J. (1990), 'The wider context: The importance of the macroeconomic environment for small enterprise development', *Small Enterprise Development*, **1** (3).

Devarajan, S. and L.E. Hinkle (1994), 'The CFA franc parity change: an opportunity to restore growth and reduce poverty', *Africa Spectrum*, **29** (2).

Dosi, G. (1988), 'Sources, procedures, and microeconomic effects of innovation', in *Journal of Economic Literature*, **26**, Sept., pp. 1120–71.

Goreux, L. M. (1995), 'La dévaluation du Franc CFA. Un premier bilan en décembre 1995' (draft report).

Helmsing, A.H.J. (1998), 'Competitive response, innovation and creating an innovative milieu. The case of Bulawayo, Zimbabwe', paper presented at the EADI Working Group on Industrialization, The Hague, 18 and 19 September.

Hettige, H., W.F. Steel and J.A. Wayem (1991), 'The impact of adjustment lending on industry in African countries', Industry and Energy Department Working Paper, Industry Series Paper, No. 45.

Hodgson, G.M. (1998), 'The approach of institutional economics', *Journal of Economic Literature*, **26**, pp. 166–92.

Hugon, P. (1996), 'Le Cameroun dans l'entre deux', *Politique Africaine*, June.

Humphrey, J. and H. Schmitz (1998), 'Trust and inter-firm relations in developing and transition economies', *Journal of Development Studies*, **34** (4), pp. 32–61.

IMF (1996), 'World economic outlook', Washington, IMF.

Lall, S. (1992), 'Technological capabilities and industrialization', *World Development*, **20** (2), pp. 165–86.

Lall, S. (1995), 'Structural adjustment and African industry', *World Development*, **23** (12), pp. 2019–31.

Lall, S. and W. Latsch (1998), 'Import liberalization and industrial performance: the conceptual underpinnings. Development and change', *Institute of Social Studies*, **29** (3), pp. 437–65.

Liedholm, C. (1992), 'Small-scale industry in Africa: dynamic issues and the role of policy', in Stewart *et al.* (eds), *Alternative Development Strategies in Sub-Saharan Africa*, London. Liedholm Ann Arbor: Michigan State University.

Marshall, A. (1927), *Principles of Economics*, Reprint of the 8th edition of 1920, London: Macmillan.

Mead, D.C. and C. Liedholm (1998), 'The dynamics of micro and small enterprises in developing countries', *World Development*, **26** (1), pp. 61–74.

Meier, G.M. and W.F. Steel (1989), *Industrial Adjustment in Sub-Saharan Africa*, Washington, World Bank.

Nabli, M.K. and J.B. Nugent (1989), 'The new institutional economics and its applicability to development', *World Development*, **17** (9), pp. 1333–47.

Nelson, R.R. (1987), 'Understanding Technical Change as an Evolutionary Process', *Theory, Institutions, Policy*, Vol. 8.

Nelson, R.R. and S. Winter (1982a), *An Evolutionary Theory of Economic Change*, Cambridge University Press, MA.

North, D.C. (1990), *Institutions, Institutional Change and Economic Performance*, Cambridge University Press.

North, D.C. (1995), 'The new institutional economics and third world development', in J. Harriss, J. Hunter and C.M. Lewis (eds), *The New Institutional Economics and Third World Development*, London: Routledge, pp. 17–47.

North, D.C. and J.J. Wallis (1994), 'Integrating institutional change and technical change in economic history. A transaction cost approach', *Journal of Institutional and Theoretical Economics (JITE)*, **150** (4), pp. 609–24.

Parker, R.L. and W.F. Steel (1992), 'Small enterprises under adjustment in Senegal', World Bank Industry and Energy Department Working Paper, Washington, DC.

Parker, R.L., R. Riopelle and W.F. Steel (1995), 'Small enterprises adjusting to liberalization in five African countries', Washington: World Bank Discussion Paper, No. 271.

Pedersen, P.O. (1998), 'The dynamics of small and medium-sized enterprises in developing countries – the case of Zimbabwe', Copenhagen, unpublished manuscript.

Qualmann, R. *et al.* (1996), *Die Klein- und Mittelindustrie nach der Abwertung des Franc CFA. Eine Untersuchung der Auswirkungen, Reaktionen und Potentiale in Senegal*, Berlin: GDI.

Qualmann, R. (1997), 'SMEs adjusting to the CFA franc devaluation in Senegal', *Small Enterprise Development*, **8** (3), pp. 26–34.

Recensement Industriel (1995), 'Présentation du synthèse des résultats provisoires au 31/12/95', Dakar: Direction de la Statistique.

Romijn, H. (1998), 'Small enterprise development in developing countries: innovation or acquisition of technological capability?', Chapter 2, this volume.

Siggel, E. (1994), 'Trade and industrial policy reform in Senegal: 1986–90', in *Development, Trade and the Environment*, Basingstoke.

Steel, W.F. and L.M. Webster (1992), 'How small enterprises in Ghana have responded to adjustment', *The World Bank Economic Review*, **6** (3), pp. 423–38.

Stein, H. (1992), 'Deindustrialization, adjustment, the World Bank and the IMF in Africa', *World Development*, **20** (1), pp. 84–95.

Stein, H. (1994), 'Theories of institutions and economic reform in Africa', *World Development*, **22** (12), pp. 1833–49.

Stone, A., B. Levy and R. Paredes (1996), 'Public institutions and private transactions: a comparative analysis of the legal and regulatory environment for business transactions in Brazil and Chile', in L.J. Alston (ed.), *Empirical Studies in Institutional Change*, New York: Cambridge University Press, pp. 95–128.

Toye, J. (1995), 'The new institutional economics and its implications for development theory', in J. Harriss, J. Hunter and C.M. Lewis (eds), *The New Institutional Economics and Third World Development*, London: Routledge, pp. 49–68.

Williamson, O.E. (1985), *The Economic Institutions of Capitalism*, New York: Free Press.

World Bank (1994a), *Adjustment in Africa: Reforms, Results and the Road Ahead*, New York.

World Bank (1994b), *Adjustment in Africa: Lessons from Country Case Studies*.

World Bank (1994c), *Senegal. Private Sector Assessment*, Washington: IBRD.

World Bank (1995), 'Small enterprises adjusting to liberalization in five African countries', World Bank Discussion Papers. Africa Technical Department Series, No. 271, Washington.

9. The impact of the crisis on small-scale enterprises in Java, findings from selected case studies

Henry Sandee

The importance for poverty alleviation of the small-scale sector in Indonesia was proven after the 1997–98 economic crisis. Since much of the modern sector contracted sharply during the crisis, the capacity of the small-scale enterprise to adjust to the crisis and maintain jobs or even expand employment has been critical for averting widespread unemployment and poverty. This chapter concentrates on small-scale *industries*, and, in particular, we concentrate on so-called small-scale industry *clusters,* defined as a geographical concentration of similar enterprises. In rural Java we can observe a large number of villages which are specialized in the manufacturing of specific products such as palm sugar, tahu and tempe, tile and bricks, and furniture.

This chapter presents evidence from three small-scale enterprise clusters in Central Java that concentrate respectively on roof tile, brass handicrafts, and furniture production. All clusters were already subject to study many years prior to the crisis. In 2000 we have returned to these clusters to do new field work. The aim of this chapter is to assess the impact of the crisis on selected clusters. Our new study was inspired by the impression that small-scale enterprises have been weathering the crisis better than larger companies because they are less reliant on formal markets, and less reliant on now far more costly borrowed funds. We wanted to understand whether this is also true for our cases, and what explains this good performance.

This chapter is structured as follows. In the next section we will discuss the importance of clustered small-scale industry in the province of Central Java. The third section provides an overall assessment of the impact of the economic and financial crisis on small-scale industries in Indonesia with special reference to clusters. The following two sections discuss the findings from our own studies. An important conclusion is that our selected small-scale industry clusters have been doing well, both during Indonesia's period of rapid growth and during the present crisis. It is suggested that we cannot understand this good performance when we concentrate the analysis on individual small-scale entrepreneurs only. Insight into collaboration among small-scale producers and the role played by traders are crucial in discerning the dynamics of small-scale enterprises.

THE IMPORTANCE OF SMALL INDUSTRY CLUSTERS IN CENTRAL JAVA

Recent research on small-scale industries has been inspired by the tendency of small-scale enterprises to group together. It is argued that clustering may help small enterprises to overcome growth constraints and compete in distant markets. Clustering offers possibilities for joint action among producers; it makes it possible to adopt costly new technology together and, consequently, to share the costs and risks associated with innovation adoption. Furthermore, clustering is of interest to traders who are in a position to buy large amounts from various producers on a single visit (Schmitz and Nadvi, 1999).

In rural Java there are many villages which specialize in the food processing of palm sugar, tahu, tempe, and so on. Other examples of clusters which process local resources include the production of bamboo mats, or tile and brick manufacturing. There are also clusters where the producers do not process local resources, but where resources are 'imported' into the cluster, such as footwear and garments. Traders or large-scale producers from urban areas contract out orders to clusters in rural areas. In Table 9.1 estimates are given of the share of clustered employment in different industrial subsectors of Central Java.

The table suggests that some 50 per cent of manufacturing employment in Central Java is concentrated in clusters. Clustered employment is particularly important in wood products, structural clay products, and basic metals subsectors. Clustering provides between 40 and 50 per cent of employment in food processing, textiles, and footwear, and the fabricated metal subsectors. Clustering is not important in subsectors such as paper products and chemicals, where economies of scale in production are prominent.

There is a whole spectrum of small industry clusters in Java. At the one extreme lie dormant clusters that show little dynamism, and which produce basic products for poor consumers. In such clusters the involvement of the rural population may be a sign of distress as it could be explained by the lack of access to better-paid alternative employment. Consequently, growth of the number of small producers may easily turn to severe price competition, which undermines the existence of individual firms, and leads to payment of lower wages. However, such clustering may be of interest to traders, as it lowers transaction costs, when they collect and sell output to market towns. At the other end of the spectrum, there are dynamic clusters with strong interfirm

Table 9.1   Clustered manufacturing employment in Central Java, 1986 and 1989

ISIC	Manufacturing employment 1986	Share of clustered employment (%) 1989
31. Food processing, beverages, tobacco	631 823	49.2
32. Textiles, garments, leather, footwear	164 616	49.0
33. Wood products, furniture	225 896	75.2
34. Paper products, printing, publishing	14 358	0.0
35. Basic chemicals, rubber products, plastic products	31 395	9.8
36. Ceramics, glass products, cement products, structural clay products	112 967	78.0
37. Basic metals	444	100.0
38. Fabricated metal products, transport equipment	36 744	41.0
39. Misc. manufactures	149 536	14.1
All industries	1 370 761	50.4

Source: Sensus Ekonomi 1986, Daftar Sentra Industri Kecil 1989.

linkages, which have been able to break into national or even international markets. The advantages associated with clustering can be quite substantial, for example specific technology can be adopted that could not have been acquired profitably by individual enterprises. The developments in dynamic clusters are frequently 'buyer-driven' in the sense that traders and other (market) agents play a decisive role in their patterns of growth. Interestingly, we note that traders and other buyers connect clustered producers to markets. They play an important role in linking small firms to distant markets, and they provide information on the (changes in) consumer preferences.

The Indonesian government has long recognized the importance of clustered industry. This has resulted in the execution of a targeted development programme. Stimulating innovation is a high priority in the strategy of the programme. It is believed that, without process and product innovations, the majority of small-scale enterprise clusters will not be able to participate in the changing economic environment, and, consequently, they will be threatened in their existence. Technical assistance consists of courses provided by extension workers and the introduction of new equipment to demonstrate to the producers the advantages of technological change. Budgets for interventions are approximately Rp. 2–3 million per cluster. The assistance provided by Bimbingan dan Pengembangan Industri Kkecil (BIPIK, a project for SME development) is non-recurring, given the fact that so many clusters have not yet received any assistance at all. Impact studies have shown that cluster development programmes have not been effective in dormant clusters. This is mainly because technical assistance aimed at innovation adoption is not effective when there is no access to those market channels that are interested in the new product. Assistance is more relevant in dynamic clusters where there is demand for technical and financial assistance to accommodate growth processes that were initiated by buyers and producers (Sandee, 1998).

SMALL INDUSTRIES IN INDONESIA DURING THE CRISIS

There are a number of nationwide surveys that provide insight into the impact of the crisis on various sectors of the Indonesian economy (Sumarto *et al.,* 1998: Suryahadi *et al.,* 1999). The results from a nationwide *Kecamatan* survey indicate that urban areas have been harder hit by the crisis than rural areas. Further, it is noted that the impact of the crisis is very diverse, with some regions experiencing great difficulties and others doing relatively well. In general, it was found that both rural and urban areas on Java have been hit hard by the crisis while on some other islands the impact has been much less severe. Finally, the surveys found that there is little connection between the initial poverty levels and the extent to which an area has been hit by the crisis (Sumarto *et al.,* 1998).[1] Evidence from an update on the impact of the crisis, using data from the '100 villages survey', suggests that some easing off of the impact of the crisis has taken place since August 1998. This follows a massive deterioration that took place in the period from May 1997 to August 1998. Nearly all areas are still worse off than before the crisis. In addition, caution is warranted considering that some regions are still experiencing continuous deterioration, even after August 1998 (Suryahadi *et al.,* 1999). These findings also suggest that the impact of the crisis on small-scale enterprises is likely to be quite diverse. Our fieldwork concentrates on small-scale industries in Central Java, which have been hit hard by the crisis. We have studied various types of clustered small-scale enterprises that aim at very different markets, and, consequently, we may assume that the impact will be diverse.

There is, however, a widespread impression that small-scale enterprises have been weathering the crisis better than larger companies (Cameron, 1999). Two distinct explanations for the resilience of small-scale enterprises in the current period of economic distress have been suggested. First, Jellinek and

Rustanto (1999) argue that there has been an unprecedented upsurge of the small-scale sector, with new economic opportunities in, for example, blacksmith communities, furniture making, fishing, agricultural tools, brick and tile making and small-scale vending activities. They judge that the economic crisis is a 'blessing in disguise' to the small-scale sector that was gradually losing ground during the New Order period. Jellinek and Rustanto view the crisis as a policy correction which has created growth prospects for 'communal-capitalist' systems that are currently created by the people themselves. Jellinek and Rustanto concentrate on the emergence of *new* enterprises that have mushroomed as a consequence of the crisis. Many of these are microenterprises that offer 'last resort' employment to persons that have lost better-paid jobs elsewhere or which are in dire need of work to compensate for the loss of income of their household members. A second explanation stresses that their good performance during the crisis should be seen in conjunction with the fact that many small-scale enterprises were already doing well *before* the crisis. According to this view, small-scale industries, and especially clusters, are resilient and able to adjust flexibly and quickly to changes in the economic and policy environment. There is evidence of small industry clusters doing well in the furniture, roof tile, cloth weaving, and metal casting industries (Berry *et al.,* 1999). In the following sections of this chapter we will present three case studies, on roof tile, brass handicrafts, and furniture clusters, that will allow us to gain insights into the relevance of the various explanations mentioned above.

CASE STUDIES: ROOF TILE, BRASS HANDICRAFT, AND FURNITURE CLUSTERS

The Baseline (pre-crisis): Micro and Small Enterprise Clusters

The roof tile cluster included in this study is located in the semi-urban village of Karanggeneng, which is situated on the outskirts of Boyolali city. In 1987, the cluster, with some 120 small enterprises, concentrated on the production of traditional output that was sold to rural areas and nearby urban centres in Central Java. In traditional tile production, the preparation of clay is done by pounding feet while simple moulds are used for printing tiles. A kiln is used for firing the tiles. Traditional producers make use of both family and paid labour. Most traditional enterprises in Karanggeneng employ some 3–5 workers. Female workers are especially used for printing tiles while men are dominant in the other stages of the production process. Waged work in the industry is heavy but it pays relatively well. It is especially popular among school-dropouts that do the work for some years before they search for long-term employment outside their communities. There are only a few female entrepreneurs, and most of these take care of businesses while their husbands are working elsewhere.

We found that traditional producers with direct access to markets do not only sell more tiles than the producers who sell through intermediaries, but they also sell their tiles at higher prices. Consequently, access to markets is a crucial variable explaining success in the small business. Our survey revealed that direct sales by small-scale enterprises to consumers occur much less frequently than is generally assumed. It also appeared that producers with direct access have invested more in their businesses than others. They are also older, suggesting that producers develop and strengthen their enterprise gradually over the years. To some extent, producers will be able to build up their own clientele over several years, and direct access is gradually earned when small producers are able to deliver good products according to agreed delivery schedules. Table 9.2 summarizes some main findings of our sample of the situation in Karanggeneng in 1987.

Table 9.2   Comparison of traditional tile producers and marketing chain in Karanggeneng 1987

	Sales to intermediaries ($n = 23$)	Direct sales to consumers ($n = 11$)	All producers ($n = 34$)
Tiles output	62 400	67 100	63 900
Price (Rp.)	20.4	29.5	23.3
Industrial capital (Rp.)	264.6	695.7	392.4
Age of entrepreneur	32	47	38

Source: Own fieldwork.

Clustering of traditional tile enterprises allows co-operation in the execution of large orders such as tiles for schools and market shelters. Contracting-out of work is, in such cases, very common. It takes place mostly in family networks. Producers with direct access take large orders and distribute the work among their family members who are also involved in the tile business but who do not have direct contacts with customers. There is also exchange of workers among enterprises belonging to the same extended family in accordance with the needs of individual firms. Relatives may also be an important source of finance for working capital. Likewise network leaders give advice and offer apprenticeships to members of their extended family. Clustering makes it possible to develop a specialized casual labour force for specific jobs, such as clay processing and firing tiles, heavy jobs that are generally carried out by paid workers who come from poor regions in Central Java. Traditional tile clusters consist of several extended family networks in which production and marketing are organized. Some families have leading roles and control access to markets while others concentrate on production.

In the case of Karanggeneng, technological change was initiated in the late 1980s. Pioneer adoption was initiated by a small group of leading traditional entrepreneurs. Successful pioneer adoption in the tile cluster is explained by two factors. First, access to information on more productive technologies was needed. It took a trip to other clusters to give producers a chance to actually see the improved (hand press) technology with their own eyes, and assess together whether they were technically and financially able to adopt this new technology. Second, these leading producers needed to be able and willing to step out of their traditional extended family networks and to develop joint action with their competitors to tackle the technological indivisibilities and risks associated with innovation. This is a substantial break from the past, and it exposes leaders to criticism of their family members because they are forging new paths. However, as we shall see below, this break turned out to be only temporary and innovations become embedded in traditional family networks as soon as possible.

Innovation adoption implies the introduction of the hand press. Pressing such tiles requires a better clay mixture that is obtained through the introduction of a diesel-driven clay mixer. This mixer is expensive and its capacity far exceeds the need of individual pioneer adopters. Consequently, there is a need for joint action to tackle the high costs (and also risks) of technological change. We found that pioneer adopters do not feel comfortable taking risks and bearing the costs associated with innovation adoption while relying on their own networks. Instead, collaboration *among* pioneers is preferred to tackle the uncertainties.

The number of adopters increased rapidly. In the beginning of 1997 virtually all producers in the cluster had adopted the hand press technology. The pattern of innovation diffusion of the new technology in the cluster cannot be fully understood by 'standard' economic analysis only. Such analysis would assume that innovation diffusion is explained by variables such as access to markets and/or access to human and capital resources of the individual small enterprises. Our findings suggest that the social network in which producers operate matters as well. We mentioned above that early adoption has transcended traditional networks. However, there is evidence of relatively early adoption by producers who played subordinated roles in traditional production patterns. We found that as soon as possible, when risks and costs of innovation adoption appear to be manageable, leaders aim at stimulating innovation adoption by their family network and they give up their collaboration with other pioneers as this network is no longer needed.

The introduction and widespread diffusion of the press tile technology has not resulted in important shifts in the structure of employment. Women remain assigned to certain tasks of the production process only. The scope of women's work has become somewhat narrower as they are not invited to participate in those parts of the production process that have become mechanized. Female entrepreneurs with press technology remain exceptional. Payments systems have also changed gradually with piece rate systems becoming more important over the years. Marketing patterns have not changed much as a consequence of technological change in Karanggeneng. Press tiles are sold mainly to urban areas and it remains true that only a limited group of producers have direct access to markets. The majority remain involved in subcontracting relationships, and they sell their output either to leading producers or to intermediaries.

The brass handicraft cluster is also located in the Boyolali regency. It is situated in the village of Tumang on the slopes of the mountain Merbabu in Central Java, relatively isolated from urban centres. Surprisingly, however, Tumang has a long tradition in brass handicraft manufacturing, using copper as its main input. Copper is purchased in nearby urban centres like Solo and Semarang by specialized traders. These traders sell the copper to middlemen who operate at the Tumang city market. There are some 400 small-scale enterprises in the cluster. Traditionally, the cluster concentrates on the production of basic kitchen utensils with cooking pots as its main output. These pots are sold mainly to rural markets. There are specialized traders in Tumang that are taking care of the marketing of traditional output.

Traditional brass handicraft production is almost exclusively a man's job. In addition, there is very limited use of non-family labour. Most traditional enterprises are household enterprises where copper handicraft production is embedded in the household economy. Incomes from traditional production are low and dependent on the availability of family labour. Large families are able to produce more and, so far, any additional supply can be absorbed by the market. Traditional tile and copper handicraft clustered enterprises have characteristics that are typical for cottage industry clusters in Java. Such clusters consist of household enterprises that operate with family labour. The activities are subject to seasonal fluctuations. The clusters operate with traditional technology that has not changed much through time. As in the roof tile cluster in Karanggeneng, most household enterprises do not have direct access to markets. Many of them are producing exclusively for certain middlemen who collect their daily output at the village market. Clustering of traditional copper producers in Tumang is to the advantage of suppliers of inputs (especially copper) and the traders of output. Both are able to achieve lower transaction costs when they buy in bulk rather than from dispersed small producers. Suppliers and traders have a strong influence on the organization of the small-scale and cottage industry sector.

In the beginning, innovation adoption in Tumang was concerned with the introduction of new designs. Instead of manufacturing traditional kitchen utensils, pioneer adopters concentrated on 'modern handicrafts' such as vases, wall decorations, and statues. Gradually, the concentration on new designs resulted in the introduction of improved equipment and better materials. This allowed further improvements of designs and quality. Innovation adoption is a gradual process; it is possible to add new tools, equipment, and designs through time when adopters gain experience. Innovation adoption resulted in a very new type of output that could not be marketed through traditional channels. It required the development of new marketing strategies to penetrate urban market segments, as modern handicraft demand comes mainly from consumers in cities. Marketing became the responsibility of a new group of traders that did not have links with the cluster previously.

Most adopters manufacture ready-made products on order from urban traders. In addition, there are selected producers who manufacture semi-finished products that are processed further by large firms in the cities. Occasionally, Tumang adopters produce for foreigners and export their output. In Tumang adopters have developed their business on a much larger scale compared with Karanggeneng. There are few examples of sharing equipment among adopters similar to the joint action that was a key to successful adoption in the tile cluster discussed above. Most adopters have gradually expanded their own capital goods and equipment, with few signs of collaboration among firms.

In the beginning of 1997 there were some 25 adopters in Tumang. Modern firms in Tumang make use of paid labour on a relatively large scale. On average adopters employ some 20 workers. Workers are often young men who originate from elsewhere, sometimes from quite far (for example, Gunung Kidul). Adopters profit very much from the proximity of traditional producers. Clustering allows the adopters to employ traditional producers as waged workers whenever there are large orders. It does happen that more than 100 producers become part-time waged workers. This flexible access to skilled workers would not be possible in the absence of large numbers of traditional producers that operate in the same village. This has made it possible for adopters to participate in profitable but highly fluctuating markets. Such markets are characterized by very high demand during rather unpredictable periods of the year while it may be much lower normally. For example, adopters in Tumang were very busy with the manufacturing of brass handicrafts for the expansion of the Soekarno-Hatta airport. During this period, many traditional producers in the cluster assisted adopters in the production process.

The Baseline (pre-crisis): Small- and Medium-scale Enterprise Cluster

Our next case study discusses a furniture cluster in Jepara that is substantially larger than the roof tile and brass handicraft clusters discussed above. Schiller and Martin-Schiller (1997: 2) summarize the main features of the cluster as follows:

> the industry has transformed Jepara from being a sleepy town into a thriving commercial centre with a five-mile avenue of furniture showrooms and factories, modern hotels, new banks, supermarkets, mobile phones, fax machines, karaoke bars, European restaurants. Local wages have risen, immigration is occurring and housing rentals are said to be higher than in the provincial capital.

Estimates are that in 1996 the cluster employed some 60 000 workers in more than 2000 small enterprises and more than 100 medium- and large-scale firms. The cluster contributes substantially to regional employment generation and provincial income. Some 80 villages in the region are involved in the industry through subcontracting linkages. In these villages, farming households are increasingly gaining access to additional employment by part-time involvement in the furniture industry. Employment in furniture manufacturing is chiefly restricted to men, and there are few women involved.

In Jepara there is a sharp distinction between domestic-oriented and export-oriented networks. Domestic producers operate with basic technology and concentrate on traditional products that are still widely in demand throughout Java. The nature of domestic demand has changed little through time which has allowed producers to manufacture for stock. The domestic industry is a craft industry with small-scale entrepreneurs and their workers operating businesses and technologies that have remained unchanged in decades. Subcontracting exists with some producers putting out (part of) orders to their colleagues in the cluster. Production for domestic markets is sold both through showrooms in Jepara and through a vast network of furniture shops in the province.

The furniture export industry in Jepara has grown out of the domestic manufacturing. A major breakthrough has been the participation of Jepara furniture producers in various trade fairs in Bali. This has fostered close links between producers and foreign buyers. Presently, there are many foreign buyers in the cluster who order large amounts of semi-antique and modern furniture for Western clients. Some foreign buyers own companies in Jepara that collect and further process products made by small subcontractors. Foreign participation in furniture production is motivated by the desire to have better control over the quality of exported output. Thus small firms are involved in the export trade as subcontractors only. Many small firms pass on (parts of) orders to others, and this has resulted in the development of multi-layered subcontracting relationships. The participation of small firms in export networks required substantial adaptations like working with new equipment, producing new designs, stricter supervision of quality, quality control, the need to pay attention to standardization of output, and so on.

There are large numbers of mobile skilled craftsmen in Jepara who offer their services to various leading producers and subcontractors. The presence of such craftsmen is very important for the development of the cluster. It allows firms to employ relatively small steady labour forces. However, the firms can be assured of access to additional *skilled* workers whenever demand is booming. Wages for skilled craftsmen are between Rp. 10 000–20 000 per day; this is significantly higher than average provincial wage levels. It shows that such skilled workers are scarce.

Table 9.3 summarizes selected indicators of the development of the Jepara furniture industry prior to the crisis, with particular reference to exports. The table shows a steady growth of the industry. In particular, it shows a significant growth of exports. The number of foreigners has increased rapidly throughout the years. There are both foreign buyers and companies in the region; they come from various countries such as Japan, Korea, Australia and Europe. The table shows that the value of exports per cubic metre has almost doubled between 1989 and 1996 which suggests that there has been a steady upgrading of output over time with exports shifting to products of higher quality.

The table refers to all types of enterprise in the clusters, and it does not make a distinction between small and large firms. Our estimation is that the number of large firms in Jepara is less than 100, and the fast growth of the total

Table 9.3 The development of the Jepara furniture industry 1989–96

	1989	1990	1991	1992	1993	1994	1995	1996
Enterprises	675	1902	1973	2097	2110	2145	2216	2347
Employment	8400	20 964	22 104	27 104	29 258	29 882	32 624	25 234
Registered foreigners	20	26	49	63	70	76	112	154
Volume exports (m³)	1160	1597	1628	7938	12 133	8516	11 004	16 403
Exports $'000	3852	2926	4449	23 957	47 612	48 716	61 621	97 431

Source: Jepara office Ministry of Trade and Industry.

number of enterprises is mainly caused by the expansion of small enterprises. As mentioned above, small enterprises are embedded in various networks and they do not have direct access to markets. Consequently, their trajectories of development are determined by the networks in which they participate; domestic networks concentrate on traditional and relatively cheap designs to serve a growing Indonesian middle class, while export networks stress quality and on-time delivery in accordance with the priorities of consumers in Western countries.

THE IMPACT OF THE CRISIS ON SELECTED CLUSTERS

Micro and Small Enterprise Clusters[2]

The crisis has little impact on traditional tile producers in the Karanggeneng cluster. Table 9.4 summarizes some findings on the impact of the crisis in the tile cluster. The table shows that prices and production of traditional tiles have gone up. There are, however, no changes in employment levels or marketing patterns. The table shows that the tiny group of traditional producers appear to be unaffected by the crisis so far. They are still selling their traditional output to poor households in the rural areas surrounding Boyolali city.

Table 9.4   Impact of the crisis on tile cluster in Karanggeneng. Comparison August 1997-98

Changes	Traditional ($n=5$)	Press ($n=37$)
Price	53%	84%
Output	9%	-2%
Employment	0%	5%

Source: Fieldwork.

Table 9.4 shows that press producers in the cluster have maintained production levels. Higher prices for inputs were compensated by increases of output prices. Employment levels have gone up slightly, and this is explained by the absorption of members of Karanggeneng households who have lost their jobs in the cities. In this sense, the tile industry functions in a similar way to the agricultural sector in Central Java: it is a social safety net for relatives who have lost their jobs elsewhere. Wage levels have increased only slightly in Karanggeneng, and, on average, workers received in 1998 Rp. 6000 per day compared with Rp. 5000 previously. Consequently, their wages declined substantially in real terms. Interestingly, there have been important changes in the marketing of press tiles. Before the crisis press tiles were sold chiefly through middlemen to urban markets in Central Java. Recently, sales to rural markets have become much more important.

There has also been a change in both marketing channels and areas. Rural areas have become more important. Tile producers argue that this change in marketing is explained by the increased incomes of many farming families while, in contrast, demand from urban areas, especially from large-scale building projects, has almost come to a standstill. Tile producers stress that farmers have been better able to adjust to the economic adversities than urban households. Demand for their agricultural products has remained high during the crisis; this is explained by the fact that demand for basic necessities is less subject to economic adversities compared with manufacturing products and services.

The impact of the crisis in traditional and modern brass handicraft production in Tumang is summarized in Table 9.5. The table shows that the crisis does not have a negative impact on traditional production in the cluster. Producers were able to compensate for higher input prices by increasing the prices of outputs. Traditional output, kitchen utensils, is very much a basic necessity sold to rural households. There are few complaints from traditional producers about marketing: they continue to produce for rural markets. Consequently, there are no changes in employment in the traditional brass handicraft industry. Since the outbreak of the crisis wage levels have risen slightly in nominal terms in a similar way to the tile cluster discussed above. Developments in the traditional tile and brass handicraft industries are rather similar. In both cases traditional producers have hardly been hit by the crisis; they remain producing for rural consumers who continue buying these products.

The situation is rather different for modern producers in this brass handicraft cluster. Table 9.5 indicates that these producers have not been able to compensate for the price increases of inputs by raising the prices of their

Table 9.5   Impact of the crisis on brass handicraft production in Tumang, August 1997-8

Changes	Traditional ($n = 37$)	Modern ($n = 23$)
Price	49%	23%
Output	2%	−15%
Employment	1%	−34%

Source: Fieldwork.

outputs. This is especially true for copper which is imported and which has been subject to very substantial price increases. We found that output and employment levels in the modern brass handicraft industry have declined. Modern brass products are sold mostly to the urban middle class who have been severely hit by the crisis. Before the crisis modern producers in Tumang exported their output occasionally. In principle, the crisis might offer interesting new export opportunities as, because of the devaluation of the Rupiah, their products have become much cheaper on international markets. However, there is no evidence of more exports since the crisis. The Tumang producers themselves do not have access to international markets, and there was no sign of Indonesian or international traders profiting from this market opportunity. Employment levels have declined more than output in the modern industry because entrepreneurs are anticipating further declines in demand, and have reduced their number of steady workers more than proportionally. We need to keep in mind that these entrepreneurs know that they can always rely on the presence of traditional producers who can be employed as casual workers whenever this is necessary.

Modern firms in Tumang do not function as a social safety net as they do in Karanggeneng. Many paid workers come from outside Tumang, and, consequently, it is relatively easy to dismiss them. The situation is different in the tile cluster where the majority of the labour force was born in the village. Presently, subcontracting is less important in the cluster as modern producers are scaling down production. Traditional producers have less chance of gaining additional income through casual work. They can still rely on the markets for their traditional output but their total household income is likely to have suffered as a consequence of the crisis.

Small- and Medium-sized Enterprise Clusters

Recent developments in the Jepara furniture cluster are presented in Tables 9.6 and 9.7.[3] Table 9.6 gives an overview of the development of the industry

Table 9.6   Development of the Jepara furniture industry during the crisis

	1996	1997	1998
Enterprises	2347	2507	3008
Employment	35 234	39 426	43 916
Registered foreigners	154	n.a.	n.a.
Volume of exports (m³)	16 403	n.a.	n.a.

Source: Jepara office of Ministry of Trade and Industry; newspaper *Suara Merdeka*.

Table 9.7   Average monthly turnover of firms in the Jepara cluster

	Monthly turnover July–Sept. 1997 (US$ '000)	Number of observations	Change of turnover compared with July–Sept. 1997 (%)	
			Oct.–Dec. 1997	Jan.–March 1998
Indonesian exporters	39 445	5	34.4	27.7
Joint ventures	36 074	9	12.3	16.5
Domestic firms	13 740	7	22.3	3.0
Subcontractors	9 815	21	24.1	16.3

Source: Andadari *et al.* (1999: 28) processed.

during the crisis. It shows that the industry has been growing steadily during the crisis. Registered employment and the number of enterprises continue to expand, and the dollar value of exports continues to rise. Table 9.6 suggests that the number of new enterprises has been accelerating since the outbreak of the crisis, suggesting that the industry is booming.

The impact of the crisis is very different when the domestic and export market segments are compared. The *domestic* industry is confronted with a stagnation of demand for furniture in Indonesia. Domestic producers are confronted with large amounts of stock that cannot be sold without substantial price discounts. Domestic producers attempt to market directly and rely less on the services of traders and furniture shops throughout Java in order to compensate for lower profit margins.

Table 9.7 compares the performance of domestic *vis-à-vis* export producers. It is based on a limited survey among large and small firms in the cluster (Andadari *et al.*, 1999). The table shows how different groups of producers have reacted to the crisis.[4] In the table we have presented the data on turnover not in rupiah but, instead, we have used the US dollar value for the various periods under review.

Table 9.7 shows the growth of Indonesian and joint ventures that concentrate on export markets. It suggests that Indonesian exporters are doing relatively well during the crisis in spite of their complaints about the growing and unfair competition from foreigners in the cluster.[5] Our table, which is based on a limited sample only, suggests that Indonesian exporters seem to profit from the depreciation of the Rupiah. Joint ventures have also been able to profit from the new export opportunities. Domestic firms were able to keep up their sales right up until the beginning of 1998. Scattered evidence suggests that domestic demand has continued to contract since the execution of our survey but there has not been a total collapse of the domestic market. Table 9.7 shows that subcontractors are doing well. On the one hand, this refers to small firms who were already involved in export networks prior to the crisis, and who are currently getting more orders. On the other hand, this group also includes small firms that were previously involved in domestic trade networks but that have recently switched to the export sector. We need to keep in mind though that Table 9.3 refers to existing firms only. Exits from the industry were not taken into account. In principle, the latter may counterbalance the growth of employment and exports of existing firms. Table 9.3 suggests, though, that there has been overall growth in the industry.

The exporting firms' first reaction to the widened export opportunities was to expand existing networks and to make more intensified use of qualified subcontractors. Expansion took place also through hijacking of skilled employees from domestic firms. To counter these developments, strategies were developed to avoid hijacking; subcontractors are offered long-term contracts with guarantees concerning minimal monthly demand for their services and products. Previously, many subcontractors sold part of their products on their own account but since the crisis this option has become less important as involvement in the networks of leading exports takes up most of their time. The growth of the export market also attracted the attention of domestic firms. Most firms cannot penetrate export markets successfully on their own because of unfamiliarity with specific requirements regarding quality, design, delivery schedules, and so on. There is a tendency for these firms to become subcontractors to well-established exporters.

Since the crisis, prices of wood and, of course, imported inputs have gone up considerably. Wood prices have gone up also because the export ban on logs has been revoked in the framework of the agreement between Indonesia and the IMF. This has increased competition for good quality wood. Uncertainty about input prices has stimulated large firms to secure long-term access by buying large amounts and developing a stock. Other companies have tried to purchase cheaper inputs by replacing expensive mahogany and teak. Wages have also gone up considerably during the crisis. This is especially true for skilled workers, and their wages have reached Rp. 30 000 per working day from around Rp. 15 000 prior to the crisis. Wage costs in dollar terms were still lower than before the crisis, which partly explains why the industry has become more competitive internationally. Unskilled wages have remained stable at Rp. 8500 in the same period, which implies a substantial decline in dollar terms. Cash has replaced credit in many transactions due to the uncertainties in the banking sector. The uncertainty about the Rupiah exchange rate, the very high interest rates, and inflation has created a business environment in which credit from Indonesian banks plays a limited role. Foreigners have become increasingly important in financing production in the cluster, and this has stimulated firms to develop closer links with the foreign community in Jepara.

The number of containers that are exported has gone up from 500 per month in 1996, to 800 in 1998 to 1000 in 1999 according to the Ministry of Industry and Trade and provincial newspaper reports. Data may not be fully accurate but they also suggest fast growth of the export industry. The costs of container transport have gone up considerably which has stimulated the export of products with higher value added. Recently, the costs of container transport have risen explosively. The depreciation of the Rupiah has caused a substantial decline of imports to Indonesia and, consequently, there are fewer containers coming into the country. In the period 1997–9, the container costs of the industry for transports to Europe went up by some 100 per cent.

Small firms that were involved as subcontractors in export networks before the crisis are doing well presently. These firms are now more closely tied to large firms than previously, and they have lost their direct access to markets. In general, however, these small firms do not complain as their profits and turnover have become substantially higher. Small firms that do not have previous experience in the export trade have become 'second-tier sub-contractors', receiving orders from their counterparts who are already embedded in export trade networks. Furthermore, there are firms with little export experience that collaborate with foreign tourists who want to reap quick profits from the current low value of the Rupiah. In Jepara there are complaints about these new 'joint ventures' as their output is of low quality, and it is feared that it may be detrimental to the development of the industry in the long run.

Most recent developments indicate that the prospects of the export industry remain uncertain due to political instability. During the Indonesian election period many foreigners withdrew temporarily from the Jepara cluster as there was fear of violence. This caused a temporary setback for the development of the export industry. The industry picked up quickly after the elections but in the second half of 1999 anti-Western sentiment in the region has caused once more an upheaval in the export industry. The stabilization of the Rupiah at some Rp. 8000 to the US dollar has resulted in a decline in interest for furniture exports from 'tourists'. In October 1999 Indonesia elected a new president and vice-president, and more political stability in the future is expected. The exchange rate of the Rupiah has improved substantially. The rate was below Rp. 7000 at the end of October. This is not good news for many Indonesian and foreign exporters in Jepara because it increases the price of their products on international markets in the short run. It also means that more attention needs to be paid to quality of output in order to secure a place in international furniture markets in the longer run.

At the national level, the policy environment has become more favourable for foreign business and exports. The agreement between the Indonesian government and the IMF has simplified the entrance of foreign producers and traders in the industry. We have mentioned above that the agreement has also driven up the price of wood as logs can now be exported again. Provincial and local government agencies are mainly involved in administrative matters, and some progress has been made recently in streamlining export permits. Government agencies have recently stepped up their monitoring of foreigners in the industry, and those who do not have the right permits are threatened with expulsion. In general, however, it seems that the export boom is not related to particular export interventions, and there are no examples of particular types of government support that have contributed to the growth of the export industry.[6]

CONCLUSIONS

In this chapter we have discussed the developments in selected small industry clusters before and during the crisis. Our case studies concern clusters that have developed well during Indonesia's period of rapid economic growth. Innovation adoption has contributed significantly to growth of small enterprises in these clusters. Technological upgrading has allowed small producers to adjust to changes in demand, so that they are able to accommodate to changes in consumer preference. This chapter has made it clear that successful adjustment is not something that small firms can do individually. First, collaboration among small firms is crucial in order to share the costs and risks associated with technological change. Second, networks of firms are important. Such networks facilitate the development of sub-contracting relations that allow adopters to operate flexibly. Finally, growth of the clusters is associated with participation in wide trade networks that allow sales beyond local markets. Traders play a substantial role in the development of small enterprises. Collaboration of firms, subcontracting, and participation of traders is realized best in clusters where small enterprises flock together. This may explain why clusters appear to have done well in the (census) period 1986–96.

Our findings suggest that the selected clusters are also performing well during the crisis. This is especially true for the well-organized furniture industry that has profited from its involvement in international trade networks and the depreciation of the Rupiah. To a lesser extent it appears also to be true for the roof tile and brass handicraft clusters that were studied. In these cases the clusters attempted to adjust to changes in the structure of demand, and they have geared production partially towards rural markets that appear to be hit less by the crisis. We noted, however, that in the case of brass handicraft production loss of urban markets could not be compensated, and this caused a loss of jobs for poor migrants in the industry. In general, however, clustered small enterprises appears to have been weathering the crisis better than their dispersed counterparts.

NOTES

1. There is an important policy implication to the lack of connection: it implies that crisis impact targeting and poverty alleviation targeting are two, quite different exercises.
2. Data were recently collected by Jelle de Rooij, Chantal Quinten and Bayu Wijajayanto.
3. We have been able to do more research in Jepara than in the other clusters. Therefore, our analysis of the impact of the crisis is most comprehensive in the case of this furniture cluster.
4. Unfortunately, Andadari *et al.* (1999) were not able to include foreign firms in their small sample.
5. Indonesian exporters complain about the large number of foreigners who do business while using a tourist visa. Foreigners use this visa frequently because applying for an official business visa is time-consuming and sometimes it is not issued at all. Recently, some foreigners have been deported for doing illegal business. A leading Indonesian exporter mentioned to a regional newspaper that 'we should be the owners of businesses in our own country, and not become employees of foreigners' (Suara Merdeka 31/7/1998).
6. Cole's findings on the role of government agencies in the development of the Bali garment industry are very similar. He found that '...the role the government played seems more positive in its absence than in its actions. The forbearance of the provincial government ... was a critical factor in the success of the industry. Local government took an essentially tolerant, hand-off attitude to the development of the garment industry, despite what may have appeared to be highly undesirable characteristics during the early stages (the high-profile role of foreign entrepreneurs, the highest returns clearly going to the foreigners...) (Cole, 1998: 277).

REFERENCES

Andadari, R.K., S. Sulandjari, I. Ibty and Muslichin (1999), 'Dampak Krisis Moneter pada Usaha Mebel Kayu Jepara', Fakultas Ekonomi, Universitas Kristen Satya Wacana, Salatiga.

Berry, A., E. Rodriquez and H. Sandee (1999), 'Firms and group dynamics in the role of the SME sector in Indonesia and The Philippines', paper presented to the World Bank Project on 'The Role of Small Enterprises in Development', Chiang Mai, Thailand.

Cameron, L. (1999), 'Survey of recent developments', *Bulletin of Indonesian Economic Studies*, **35** (1), pp. 3–40.

Cole, W. (1998), 'Bali's garment export industry', in H. Hill and Thee Kian Wie (eds), *Indonesia's Technological Challenge*, Institute of Southeast Asian Studies, Singapore, pp. 255–78.

Jellinek, L. and B. Rustanto (1999), 'Survival strategies of the Javanese during the Economic Crisis', Consultancy Report to the World Bank, Jakarta.

Sandee, H. (1998), 'Promoting small-scale and cottage industry clusters in Indonesia', *Small Enterprise Development*, **9** (1), pp. 52–8.

Schiller, J. and B. Martin-Schiller (1997), 'Market, culture and the state in the emergence of an Indonesian export furniture industry', *Journal of Asian Business*, **13** (1), pp. 1–23.

Schmitz, H. and K. Nadvi (1999), 'Clustering and industrialization: introduction',

World Development, Special Issue on Industrial Clusters in Developing Countries, **27** (9), pp. 1503–14.

Suryahadi, A., S. Sumarto and L. Pritchett (1999), 'Update on the impact of the Indonesian crisis: results from the December 1998 Round of 100 Village Survey', Worldbank Office, Jakarta, mimeo.

Sumarto, S., A. Wetterberg and L. Pritchett (1998), 'The Social impact of the crisis in Indonesia: results from a Nationwide *Kecematan* Survey', Worldbank Office, Jakarta, mimeo.

PART IV

Mechanisms for Innovation Diffusion

10. Enhancing innovation capabilities in SME clusters: evidence from a service centre in Spain

Manuel Albaladejo

Many have acknowledged that innovation is an essential factor in order to compete in the knowledge-driven economy. Under this scenario characterized by the fast development and the relative cheapness and accessibility of information technologies, economic actors have had to restructure their production systems towards greater decentralization and specialization in order to cope with new competitive pressures. Small- and medium-sized enterprises (SMEs) have faced even more constraints when competing in 'high-street' markets with innovative and quality products due to their lack of resources. In this context, research has shown that geographical proximity and institutional support could play a key role in helping SMEs to build up technological competence and innovation capabilities.

This chapter looks at the case of the 'Toy Valley' cluster in the Spanish region of Alicante, and the AIJU (Toys Institute), a local service centre that provides technical services to toy-related SMEs. This case study provides a very interesting example of institutional support for SMEs who faced new competitive pressures through more innovative and quality conscious products. The main aim of this chapter is to draw up policy recommendations to enhance innovation capabilities of SME clusters in the developing world.

The chapter has five sections. The next section sets up the conceptual debate presenting current issues concerning globalization, flexible specialization, clustering and provision of technical services. The third section introduces the case study: 'Toy Valley' and the Toys Institute (AIJU). The main findings of this exercise are presented in the fourth section. Using primary date gathered in the field, we explore how toy-related SMEs have faced globalization and AIJU's role in supporting companies to innovate and improve quality. The final section states the conclusions and draws policy lessons concerning the enhancement of innovation capabilities of SME clusters in developing countries.

THEORETICAL UNDERPINNINGS: POST-FORDIST RESPONSES TO GLOBALIZATION

It is evident that in recent decades markets have become more segmented and diversified. Price is no longer seen as the decisive purchasing factor that it used to be in the mass production era. The spread of a 'quality culture' has brought other purchasing factors such as innovation, originality, quality, and fashion into the game. The rise of new information technologies, improvements in communication and transport, together with the massive decline in their cost, have given companies new ways of looking at innovation processes and organization of production.

This new scenario has contributed to the speeding up of the shift from mass production to post-Fordist forms of industrial organization. Best (1990) argues that economic actors now operate under the 'New Competition', characterized by the development of market-shaping activities as opposed to market-reacting responses typical of Fordist times or the 'Old Competition'. The whole concept of competitiveness has changed from static to dynamic, which implies the ability to constantly supply market niches with the right product at the right time. These new market demands have forced companies to decentralize production, forge new and more intense collaborative relation-ships with suppliers, subcontractors and clients, and specialize in particular phases of the production process (Piore and Sabel, 1984).

Undoubtedly, the globalization process has opened up market prospects for most companies, but the changes imposed by this new scenario have also posed new challenges for SMEs since they lack the capacity and resources of large companies and multinational corporations. As innovation and incremental quality improvements are considered essential factors when competing in the new international context, the current debate is about the high costs of such a restructuring process.

Which sort of mechanisms or industrial strategies can help SMEs to cope with increased international competition? As stressed by Sengenberger and Pyke (1991), the problem of many small firms is not their size but rather their isolation. Ongoing research shows that clustering – understood as a group of firms geographically and sectorally concentrated (Schmitz, 1994) – represents a post-Fordist form of industrial organization, which can help SMEs to raise their innovation capacity, taking advantage of the external economies and joint action induced by spatial proximity.

Unlike the European experience, where industrial clusters have been able to compete successfully in quality markets, many SME clusters in developing countries have remained stagnant and have not exploited the enormous benefits of spatial agglomeration (Nadvi and Schmitz, 1994). Although these SMEs have exhibited organizational changes, mainly increases in subcontracting arrangements and decentralization of production, their low technological capabilities have led them to a 'race to the bottom' where price remains the main competitive factor.

Previous research in Europe has shown that institutional support can strongly contribute to enhance the technological capabilities and competitiveness of SMEs (Pyke, 1992, 1994; Brusco, 1992). A review of the same literature in the Third World shows that weak institutional support – both private and public – seems to be one of the major causes of the relatively poor technological performance of many SME clusters. The provision of technical services in the developed world (Pyke, 1994; Brusco 1992; Julien, 1992) has been considered in the 1990s as one of the most successful government interventions to support those SMEs aiming at increasing their innovation capabilities and quality standards. It involves supplying companies with those technology-oriented services which, for reasons of scale, they are unable to provide for themselves. Service centres and technology institutes are in charge of providing these technical services and their success in Europe seems to lie in their customer-oriented, collective and cumulative policies (Humphrey and Schmitz, 1996). These centres focus on collective needs rather than individual needs.

Although the nature of these services might change from country to country and from sector to sector, a common feature is that these services tend to offset the main structural constraints faced by SMEs, encouraging them to compete through continuous innovation and quality upgrading.

Zeitlin (1992) classifies the range of technical services provided by service centres in the following categories: services concerned with marketing, from information gathering and research to co-operative sales initiatives; services concerned with production, from technological information and consultancy to co-operative R&D and joint operation of large-scale equipment such as CAD/CAM systems; and services concerned with key inputs such as raw material purchasing and testing, or training of skilled workers and technicians.

THE SPANISH TOY VALLEY AND THE TOYS INSTITUTE

The geographical area known as the 'Toy Valley' is located in the region of Alicante, in the Southeast of Spain. It has a total area of 322 km^2 and comprises four main villages: Ibi, Onil, Castalla and Biar. Toy production is the most important industrial activity in the valley giving work to 57.7 per cent of the local population. More than 57 per cent of the national toy producers stay in the cluster, producing around 45 per cent of the total national output.

The Spanish Association of Toy Producers (AEFJ, 1998) points out that there are about 250 toy-related companies operating in the cluster, 103 of which are product finishers, the rest being subcontractors who specialize in specific stages of the production process (aluminium mould artisans, plastic and metal injectors, graphic arts designers, electricians and others). The majority of these companies are family-owned, employing less than 20 workers, though two large and around 10 medium firms account for 66.4 per cent of the total local production. The Toy Valley specializes in the production of traditional toys (dolls, bicycles, plastic toys, and so on) with low content of electrical components.

Globalization has been felt by Spanish toy producers whose competitiveness has been eroded by the massive penetration of cheap imitations of traditional low-tech toys produced in China. Although Chinese toys were already present in the Spanish market from the early 1980s, imports rose from 15.5 per cent in 1998 to 56 per cent in 1996. This was the main reason for the negative trade balance of the Spanish toy sector, a situation that still persists in the late 1990s (AEFJ, 1998). This period of crisis was particularly damaging for those small and very small companies that could not restructure their production system to cope with those pressures. Thus, the number of very small producers fell from about 200 in 1988 to 100 in 1995. This had serious implications for the local economy since many jobs related to the sector were lost.

Since price could no longer be seen as the main competitive factor, a restructuring process based on enhancing innovation, increasing quality, and upgrading technology began in the cluster in order to distinguish their products from the Chinese toys. Overall, companies in the 'Toy Valley' have faced international pressures by adopting post-Fordist forms of industrial organization – that is, increasing co-operation and subcontracting arrangements, decentralizing production and specializing in concrete phases of the production process – which have been facilitated and strengthened by geographical proximity.

In line with these reforms and due to the limited capacity and resources of the SMEs operating in the 'Toy Valley', the Institute for the Promotion of Small- and Medium-Sized Firms in the Valencian Region (IMPIVA) and the Spanish Association of Toy-producers contributed to the creation of AIJU (the Toys Institute), a service centre which would provide technical services to toy-related companies. The principal objective of this non-profit technology institute is to raise the competitiveness of the cluster by supplying companies with technology-oriented services to strengthen their innovation capabilities. AIJU is trying to foster innovation adoption and technological upgrading by small-scale firms in the following ways:

- AIJU plays an intermediary role between local toy-producers and technology development world-wide. It participates in international technology fairs and brings to the cluster new machinery that could improve the innovativeness of small producers and subcontractors. Obviously, SMEs could not afford to do this themselves. Thus, AIJU contributes to the technological diffusion and upgrading in the cluster.
- Testing of toys and raw materials in the laboratory is the principal service provided by AIJU. This is because EU norms require a range of qualities – including controls in toxicity, durability, flammability, and so forth – if the product has to be exported. With this service, AIJU is indirectly influencing firms to take the 'high road' towards higher quality and safer toys. Thus, low quality toys will not pass laboratory testing and will not obtain the 'EU' label to be legally sold in European markets.
- AIJU has a yearly competition to award the most innovative toys produced by its members. AIJU also produces a catalogue with the best local toys, which is commonly used by external buyers.
- Apart from machinery, the innovation process also requires the upgrading of technical knowledge. Training courses are given high priority at AIJU. These are determined by the demand of member firms and comprise fields such as firm management, administration, information technology, technology and design, product commercialization, and others.
- Innovation can also be fostered by identifying market niches for new products so producers feel that their investment is worthwhile. AIJU also offers a market information service and a marketing research service. It has a database, scientific and technological publications, norms related to the toy sector, catalogues of exports, imports and production, and many other information sources to be used by its members. Another aspect of market research is the use of a toy-testing room where toy producers can leave their brand new products and observe whether children like them or not. This system reduces the risk when commercializing the product.

To sum up, AIJU is a local service centre that acts both as 'industry leader', providing services for SMEs to improve their technological capabilities according to its own perception of 'best practice', and as an 'industry-driven' institution, reflecting in its services the main external and internal constraints faced by toy-related SMEs.

ENHANCING INNOVATION CAPABILITIES IN
TOY-RELATED SMEs: THE ROLE OF AIJU[1]

Generally speaking, the changes imposed by the restructuring process, which most of the companies have experienced in the cluster over the last few years, seem to be having a positive impact on their overall performance. After the crisis, the general picture is that a stabilization process is occurring in the cluster. For instance, most companies – 73.6 per cent and 68.4 per cent – reported increases in the average quality of their products and speed of delivery over the last five years (Table 10.1). These improvements in quality and service have led firms to boost their annual sales and net profits. It is also clear that SMEs in the 'Toy Valley' are not primarily export-driven, and that the national market is still the major outlet. As the table shows, this trend has not changed significantly in the last five years.

Table 10.1   Changes in performance of SMEs, 1993–98 (% of reported answers)[2]

	Increase	No change	Decrease	Sample size
Output	60.5	18.4	21.1	$N = 38$
Annual sales	59.2	25.9	14.9	$N = 27$
Percentage exported	27.0	56.7	16.3	$N = 37$
Average price	36.8	50.0	13.2	$N = 38$
Average quality	73.6	26.4	0	$N = 38$
Speed of delivery	68.4	31.6	0	$N = 38$
Number of workers	39.4	36.8	23.8	$N = 38$
Net profits	55.2	26.3	18.5	$N = 38$

Source: Author survey.

Despite the economic improvements experienced by toy-related companies, empirical evidence shows that weak managerial skills and market information seem to be the main obstacles to innovation (Figure 10.1). As shown in the figure, 52.2 per cent and 47.8 per cent of firms ranked themselves as having low managerial skills and market information respectively. Many entrepreneurs in the 'Toy Valley' acknowledged that the problems associated with poor management have traditionally been handed down from one generation to the other. In words of one interviewee, 'my father taught me how to make toys, but never taught me how to sell them or even how to run a business simply because his father did not teach him either' (interview carried out 16 June, 1998). However, a new and more educated generation is taking

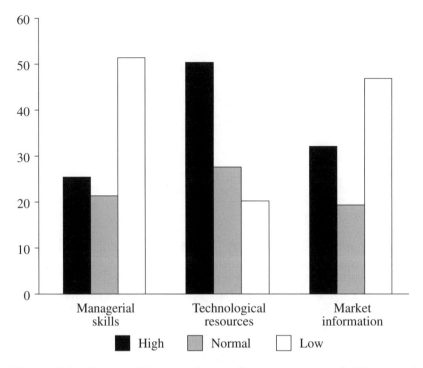

Figure 10.1   How would you rank your firm concerning...? (% reported answers)[3]

over and putting more emphasis on the importance of innovation and good management for the overall success of their companies.

But what has been the role of AIJU in recent improvements experienced by toy-related SMEs in the cluster? To what extent has AIJU helped member companies to overcome their internal constraints for innovation? Is there a relationship between AIJU's support and firms' performance? All these questions will be tested by looking at the significant differences between AIJU members and non-members, concerning constraints, market strategies, and economic performance, and then by asking member companies to evaluate whether AIJU's provision of technology-oriented services has reinforced the differences found between members and non-members.

Although shortages of managerial skills and market information seem to be the main constraints affecting SMEs as a whole, significant differences are found when splitting up firms by AIJU membership (Table 10.2). Members tend to have more capabilities regarding firm management and market information than non-members. For instance, 30.3 per cent and 32.6 per cent of AIJU firms ranked themselves high concerning managerial skills and

Table 10.2 Main constraints ranked by members and non-members (% of reported answers)

AIJU membership	Members N=33		Non-members N=13		Pearson value and significance test	Sample size
	High	Low	High	Low		
Managerial skills	30.3	42.2	15.4	76.9	4.567 (.090)	N=46
Technological resources	51.3	20.5	54.5	27.3	0.918 (.631)	N=39
Market information	32.6	47.8	7.7	84.6	9.883 (.007)	N=46

Note: Columns for the value 'normal' are not shown in the table.

Source: Author survey.

market information, compared with only 15.4 per cent and 7.7 per cent for non-members, with Pearson's value statistically significant at 0.090 and 0.007 respectively.

Pearson's significance test also shows two clear trends concerning market strategies between members and non-members (Table 10.3). Despite the restructuring process in the 'Toy Valley' towards increased quality and innovation, almost 77 per cent of the non-members report that price constitutes their main market strategy. On the other hand, AIJU members report that their competitiveness is chiefly based on quality and service.

Table 10.3 Main market strategies by AIJU membership (% of reported answers)

AIJU membership							
Members N=33			Non-members N=13			Pearson value and significance test	Sample size
Price	Quality	Service	Price	Quality	Service		
6.1	69.7	24.2	76.9	7.7	15.4	25.160 (.000)	N=46

Source: Author survey.

Market strategies definitely determine the nature of the co-operation ties between companies. Thus, firms that accept the challenge of producing at lower prices tend to have weak and less fruitful co-operative ties since price determines the nature of the relationship with clients, subcontractors and input suppliers. On the other hand, a quality strategy forces toy producers to strengthen their relationship with subcontractors and input suppliers in order to obtain an improved product to satisfy their clients. Evidence from the survey shows that, though co-operation has not practically changed over the last five years, AIJU members co-operate more with clients and input suppliers for innovation purposes than non-members. This finding confirms the difference in the nature of the supply chains between member companies and non-members.

How does this affect firms' economic performance? Empirical evidence confirms that AIJU members have performed better than non-members during the last five years (Table 10.4). Such differences are statistically significant in the case of percentage exported, average price, average quality, speed of delivery and number of workers. There are two key aspects to be read from this table. First, findings of this table confirm that AIJU firms are more likely to follow the 'high road' path since they have increased both quality and price in order to distinguish their products from Chinese toys. On the other hand, non-members tend to maintain quality, and compete by reducing prices. Price reduction is the consequence of high competition within the cluster: 92 per cent of the non-members say that their main competitors are located in the 'Toy Valley'.

Second, whilst AIJU firms have increased their exports in recent years, non-members have even decreased their percentage exported. The plausible reason is that EU markets are demanding even greater quality and safety certificates for products to be sold at European borders, and non-members may not be able to restructure their productive systems to meet such quality requirements.

Table 10.4   Changes in performance by AIJU membership 1993-98 (% answers)

AIJU membership	Members (33)		Non-members (13)		Pearson value and significance test	Sample size
	+	–	+	–		
Output	64.3	17.8	50.0	30.0	0.782 (.676)	$N=38$
Annual sales	66.7	14.3	33.3	16.7	2.617 (.270)	$N=27$
Percentage exported	35.7	10.7		33.3	5.568 (.061)	$N=37$
Average price	46.4	7.1	10.0	30.0	5.851 (.053)	$N=38$
Average quality	85.7		40.0		7.941 (.004)	$N=38$
Speed of delivery	78.6		40.0		5.073 (.020)	$N=38$
Number of workers	42.9	14.3	30.0	50.0	5.321 (.069)	$N=38$
Net profits	60.7	10.7	40.0	40.0	4.208 (.121)	$N=38$

Notes: + is increase in performance, – is decrease, and no change values are not shown in the table.

Source: Author survey.

But since AIJU focuses on technical services and improving efficiency, could it not be possible that it only attracts the more capable entrepreneurs who feel that they can respond to the crisis? Could it not be reasonable to think that the better-off and more efficient firms join AIJU because of social obligation or because their clients see it as an indicator of competence and trustworthiness? How can we now prove that AIJU has contributed to improve the capacity and performance of its members? We have partly solved this causality problem by asking members to report about the specific benefits of membership, in terms of economic performance and constraint easing.

Company members were asked to report about the effects of AIJU's services on their economic performance. Many interviewees agreed that AIJU's services greatly contribute to their performance in an indirect way. In words of one respondent, 'AIJU cannot have a direct impact on my performance because it does not take key decisions on my behalf. AIJU is behind the sector offering services that we would not get by ourselves. If you asked me about AIJU's indirect contribution to my performance, I would say a lot' (interview carried out on 29 June, 1998).

Out of the 33 AIJU members interviewed, 66.7 per cent report that the economic situation of their companies would have deteriorated if AIJU did not exist, while the remaining companies argued that their economic performance would not have changed at all. In the perception of many companies in the 'Toy Valley', the non-existence of AIJU would have meant extra costs to get the sort of services that the institute is offering today.

These services are directed to offset the basic constraints that SMEs face in order to innovate, that is managerial skills, technological resources, and market information. The majority of firms (69.7 per cent) report that AIJU's training courses have contributed a great deal to improving their management and to tackling the technological bottlenecks in production (Table 10.5).

Surprisingly, 75 per cent of the member companies report that AIJU has hardly contributed to their market information. According to one AIJU executive, 'companies do not use our information services due to the lack of

Table 10.5 AIJU's contribution to constraint easing (% of reported answers)

	A lot	A little	Nothing	Sample size
Managerial skill formation	69.7	6.1	24.2	$N=33$
Technical assistance	69.7	12.1	18.2	$N=33$
Market information assistance	6.1	18.2	75.7	$N=33$

Source: Author survey.

entrepreneurial culture in the "Toy Valley". There is still the belief of seeing information as something volatile and untouchable that cannot generate profits' (interview carried out on 30 June, 1998).

As far as co-operative ties are concerned, and though AIJU does not have any specific service to promote them, 43 per cent of members acknowledge that AIJU has contributed to improve their vertical co-operation ties. This is mainly due to the creation of three technological commissions, where toy producers, subcontractors and scientists work together in order to identify common needs and to solve production and technology bottlenecks.[4] This practice has often resulted in working opportunities for both toy producers and subcontractors.

Overall, the findings of this study seem to confirm that there is clear evidence to support the hypothesis that AIJU's services have to a great extent contributed to building up innovation capabilities in its member companies. AIJU does not trigger off change and growth but rather stays behind the toy sector, facilitating and strengthening processes already on their way. AIJU is supporting SMEs in overcoming companies' constraints by offering services directed to enhance competitiveness based on innovation and quality rather than price. These factors seem to be explanatory reasons for the difference between members and non-members concerning innovation capabilities and economic performance. Although these findings do not fully resolve the causality problem between membership and greater efficiency, they do confirm the belief that members have greatly benefited, regardless of their economic status and technological capabilities when they joined AIJU.

CONCLUSION

This chapter has shown how the globalization process has posed further problems for SMEs and how institutional support can play a crucial role in helping them to face new competitive pressures. Indeed, service centres in developed economies have shown to be an effective way of fostering innovation processes in small-scale businesses since they can play a major role in technology diffusion, technical knowledge acquisition, identification of niche markets, and interfirm co-operation promotion. Service centres are responsive of the industry's demands, reacting to the needs of their customers, but also acting as 'industry leaders', encouraging firms to change their technology and organization according to their perception of 'best practice'. Although service centres are not directly responsible for the overall performance and innovation capacity of SME clusters, they still play a significant role in acting as intermediary agents to facilitate and strengthen growth and change trends that are already on their way.

One of the main questions in industrial policy is whether successful models of institutional support can be exported to developing countries where conditions for SME development are tougher. We do not think that the AIJU model could be replicated elsewhere since it has been the result of concrete historical, cultural, social and economic circumstances. However, the AIJU experience provides some interesting policy lessons that could be taken into consideration for policy makers aiming at enhancing the innovation capabilities of the SME sector in developing countries.

Being aware of the technological limitation within clusters, services centres should foster the innovation capabilities of local firms making good and rational use of external sources (for example bringing to the cluster the right technology required for SMEs to take the 'high road' path). But innovation processes are uncertain, costly and very risky, especially in the case of SMEs, since it is not easy for them to find the appropriate physical capital as well as to accumulate technological learning to use the machinery efficiently. From the AIJU experience, service centres in developing countries should learn to reduce these 'limitations on innovation' by doing the following:

- Designing support services on the basis of the indigenous capacities of local firms and the spread of technologies through a process of inter-enterprise learning (ILO, 1998: 17). Service centres should act as intermediary agencies contributing to the technological diffusion and upgrading in the cluster rather than triggering off change and growth. The challenge must come from the private sector while supporting institutions facilitate and strengthen processes already on their way.
- Focusing on R&D-intensive services to encourage SMEs to move towards more innovative and therefore higher value-added products. For instance, service centres can encourage this by having a yearly competition to award the most innovative firm, or produce a catalogue with the most innovative local products.
- Putting science on the shop floor by having technological commissions where scientists and entrepreneurs work together. The AIJU experience shows that this is one of the most practical and efficient ways to increase innovation within firms.
- Innovation means nothing if there is no niche market where the new product can be sold. Otherwise, there is no incentive for entrepreneurs to improve quality, invest in fashion and design and so on. Thus, service centres should not forget the final stages of the production process (that is, marketing and commercialization), and marketing research should be encouraged in SMEs to find out about the viability and prospects of new innovations.

NOTES

1. A questionnaire survey was conducted with 46 SMEs in the 'Toy Valley' during June and July 1998. In order to achieve a representative sample, the study targeted 19 toy producers and 27 subcontractors, 33 of which were AIJU members.
2. Eight interviewed firms were less than five years old and therefore trends in performance could not been analysed. This is the reason why the sample size for many variables is 38 instead of 46. In the case of annual sales, the sample size goes down to 27 since most of the subcontracting firms do not sell their product to final buyers. They only deal with toy producers.
3. The sample size for the technological resources variable is only 39 because many toy producers subcontract all production stages and therefore do not need machinery.
4. The three Technological Commissions are linked up to AIJU's main departments: laboratory R&D, engineering, and human resource formation. Each commission is made up of between 5 and 10 people including firm representatives and AIJU scientists.

BIBLIOGRAPHY

AEFJ (1998), *Memoria 1997*, Ibi, Alicante, Spain.

Beccatini, G. (1990), 'The Marshallian industrial district as a socio-economic notion', in F. Pyke *et al.* (eds), *Industrial Districts and Inter-firm Co-operation in Italy*, pp. 37–51.

Benton, L. (1992), 'The emergence of industrial districts in Spain: industrial restructuring and diverging regional responses', in F. Pyke *et al.* (eds), *Industrial Districts and Local Economic Regeneration*, Geneva, International Institute for Labour Studies, pp. 48–86.

Best, M. (1990), *The New Competition: Institutions of Industrial Restructuring*, Cambridge: Policy Press.

Bianchi, P. (1993), 'Industrial districts and industrial policy: the New European perspective', *Journal of Industry Studies*, **1** (1).

Bianchi, P. (1996), 'New approaches to industrial policies at the local level', in F. Cossentino *et al.* (eds), *Local and Regional Response to Global Pressure: The Case of Italy and its Industrial Districts*, Research Series 103, Geneva: International Institute for Labour Studies, pp. 195–206.

Brusco, S. (1992), 'Small firms and the provision of real services', in F. Pyke *et al.* (eds), *Industrial Districts and Local Economic Regeneration*, pp. 177–96.

Curran, J. and R. Blackburn (1994), *Small Firms and Local Economic Networks: the Death of the Local Economy?*, London: P.C.P. Paul Chapman.

Humphrey, J. and H. Schmitz (1996), 'The triple C approach to local industry policy', *World Development*, **24** (12), pp. 1859–77.

ILO (1998), 'Business development services for SMEs: preliminary guideline for donor-funded interventions', summary of the Report to the Donor Committee for Small Enterprise Development, Washington, DC, January 1998.

Julien, P-A. (1992), 'The role of local institutions in the development of industrial districts: the Canadian experience', in F. Pyke *et al.* (eds), *Industrial Districts and Local Economic Regeneration*, Geneva: International Institute for Labour Studies, pp. 197–214.

Kristensen, P. (1990), *Industrial Districts in West Jutland*, Geneva: International Institute for Labour Studies.

Loveman, G. and W. Sengenberger (1990), 'Introduction – economic and social reorganisation in the small and medium-sized enterprise sector', in W. Sengenberger *et al.* (eds), *The Re-emergence of Small Enterprises*, Geneva, International Institute of Labour Studies, pp. 1-61.

Murray, R. (1992), 'Flexible specialisation in small island economies: the case of Cyprus', in F. Pyke *et al.* (eds), *Industrial Districts and Local Economic Regeneration*, pp. 255-76.

Nadvi, K. (1997), 'The cutting edge: collective efficiency and international competitiveness in Pakistan', IDS Discussion Paper 360, July 1997.

Nadvi, K. and H. Schmitz (1994), 'Industrial districts in less developed countries: review of experiences and research agenda', IDS Discussion Paper 339, January 1994.

Piore, M. and C. Sabel (1984), *The Second Industrial Divide: Possibilities for Prosperity*, New York: Basic Books.

Pyke, F. (1992), *Industrial Development through Small-firm Cooperation. Theory and Practice*, Geneva: International Labour Office.

Pyke, F. (1994), *Small Firms, Technical Services and Inter-firm Cooperation*, Geneva: International Institute for Labour Studies, research series 99.

Schmitz, H. (1982), 'Growth constraints on small-scale manufacturing in developing countries: a critical review', *World Development*, **10** (6), pp. 429-50.

Schmitz, H. (1994), 'Collective efficiency: growth path for small-scale industry', *Journal of Development Studies*, **31** (4).

Schmitz, H. (1995), 'Small shoemakers and Fordist giants: tale of a supercluster', *World Development*, **23** (1), pp. 9-28.

Sengenberger, W. and F. Pyke (1991), 'Small firm industrial districts and local economy regeneration: research and policy issues', *Labour and Society*, **16** (1).

Sengenberger, W. and F. Pyke (1992), 'Industrial districts and local economic regeneration: research and policy issues', in F. Pyke *et al.* (eds), I*ndustrial Districts and Local Economic Regeneration*, pp. 3-30.

Zeitlin, J. (1992), 'Industrial districts and local economic regeneration: overview and comment' in F. Pyke *et al.* (eds), *Industrial Districts and Local Economic Regeneration*, pp. 279-94.

11. Linkages between small and large firms in the Kenyan food processing sector

Dorothy McCormick and Rosemary Atieno[1]

Firms link to achieve ends that would be difficult or impossible to attain alone. Large manufacturers develop networks of small suppliers to provide them with a wide variety of needed inputs. Service providers, such as tour operators, assemble lists of foreign and domestic contacts to expand their markets and enhance their service. Small traders co-operate with larger ones to ensure that they have access to the goods their customers want. Firms of all types contract out specialized activities ranging from security services to technology-intensive manufacturing of component parts. They form associations to address common concerns and tap their informal networks when faced with particular challenges. This chapter examines these and other types of interfirm linkages, focusing in particular on those between large and small firms within the food processing sector in Kenya.

We will first discuss the theory relating interfirm linkages to firm performance. Kenya's food processing subsector is then described, as well as the research methodology. Subsequently a profile of the industry's linkages is given and firm linkages are related to performance.

INTERFIRM LINKAGES AND FIRM PERFORMANCE

Linkages between firms are not new to economic analysis. The industrial organization paradigm recognizes that buyers and sellers may co-operate in matters ranging from pricing to research and development (Scherer, 1980). Institutional approaches emphasize both the nature and the potential costs of the interactions between key economic actors (Williamson, 1975; North, 1990; Granovetter, 1985). Before exploring the relationship between linkages and performance, it is helpful to clarify the meaning of this term and examine sources of linkages and their most common forms.

Interfirm Linkages

Interfirm linkages have been approached from two slightly different perspectives. Network theorists tend to see any linkage as part of a larger network of social relationships (Mitchell, 1969; Knoke and Kuklinski, 1982; Johanson and Mattson, 1987; Rasmussen, 1992). The networks themselves have been conceptualized in various ways, but all are thought to be based more on personal relations, trust, and reciprocity, than on pure market or power relations (Pedersen, 1996). All are also multilateral, that is they have a large number of participants. Networks can be analysed in terms of their overall interaction patterns or according to the nature of the links among the participants (Mitchell, 1969).

The second way of looking at interfirm linkages takes a narrower focus. Linkages are considered individually, rather than seen as part of an entire network. In this sense, a linkage is a connection between persons and/or organizations. It may be a market connection, a contractual relationship, or an ownership tie (Harrigan and Newman 1990; Mead, 1994), or it may be the social bond linking members of the same family or ethnic community, friends, co-workers, or former schoolmates (Grabher, 1993; McCormick, 1996). The notion is sometimes narrowed still further by limiting linkage content to economic transactions (Meyanathan and Munter, 1994).

While we draw on the insights of network theorists, we focus on the linkages among the firms without attempting to piece together a given firm's full network of connections and contacts. In this sense, we take the narrower focus. We do not, however, limit linkages to purely economic transactions. Both theory and empirical evidence strongly suggest that economic activity is informed and affected, not only by the underlying social, political, and cultural systems, but also by particular social relations (Granovetter, 1985; Whitley, 1992; Evans, 1995; Barr, 1995). We therefore define an interfirm linkage as *any type of continuing relationship between enterprises.*

Designating these linkages as *interfirm* linkages means that the firm as an organization is the central actor. This is important because the links forged between organizations can outlast particular individuals. In the smallest firms and in some of the larger ones, however, the distinction between organizational and entrepreneurial linkages has little practical importance because of the close identification of the entrepreneur with the business. In such cases, the firm's linkages are drawn mainly from the interlocking social and professional networks of the business owner.

Why Firms Link

Co-operation enables organizations to attain ends that they cannot achieve alone (Harrigan and Newman, 1990). This is important in any context, but especially so in the circumstances faced by firms operating in developing countries. Industry in developing countries suffers from poor physical infrastructure, lack of relevant information, weak technological capacity, lack of finance, weak or missing economic institutions, and unstable political systems. By linking together, firms can overcome at least some of the constraints on industrial development.

Although these problems are common to industry in general, firms experience them in varying degrees. A fish processing firm that requires a constant flow of electricity to keep its cooling machinery running may suffer more from erratic power supply than a wholesale dry goods trader. A firm manufacturing for export may find the lack of published market information more constraining than one producing for a narrow local market that is already well known. More generally, the nature of the industry – especially its input and product markets, its production technology, and the way firms are financed – can be expected to give many clues as to which linkages are likely to form.

The sources of inputs and factors determining their choice are important for assessing the potential linkages between firms. In most cases, small firms buy their inputs from sources different from large firms. Linkages between firms for the procurement of inputs may allow small firms to access a different set of suppliers, thus enabling them to reap immediate gains in terms of price, variety, and, sometimes, service. Product markets offer another arena for inter-firm linkages. Firms may link to tap a market that individual firms could not penetrate alone. This is especially true of export markets, but may also apply to niche markets or broad national markets.

Technology is a particularly important area of linkages for developing country firms. Bell and Pavitt (1995) point out that the complex structure of interactions among firms is a critical component of industrial technological change. This structure often depends heavily on the capabilities of leading firms within emerging networks. It is important to note that technological issues are relevant not only to manufacturing, but also to services and trade. Technology ensures that firms remain economically viable in the midst of competition. It also has strong interrelationships with employment, firm incomes and sectoral growth.

In the long run, technological growth in any sector should redistribute national technological endowments towards indigenous entrepreneurs and improve the quality, volume, and range of firm products. A number of forward linkages like export development, lower producer prices, and increased accessibility to consumer and capital goods in rural areas can be achieved from technological growth in small firms. The ability of small firms to diversify both their products and processes to meet the varied consumer tastes has been noted as a key source of technological development (Abuodha and King, 1993).

Another potential area for linkages between firms concerns finance. It is well known that small firms are frequently constrained by lack of working and investment capital. Linkages between firms can ease such constraints by reducing the amount of fixed capital required. Vertical linkages between producers and their suppliers may bring credit that reduces working capital requirements. Linkages may also provide access to new sources of capital. An obvious example is membership in group lending schemes. In such schemes, a group of micro enterprises join together to guarantee one another's loans (Aleke-Dondo, 1991). Without such linkages most of these firms would be unable to borrow.

Industry structure, including the size distribution of firms and their degree of vertical integration, also affects both the need and the scope for linkages. Of course, industry structure is not fixed, and the argument has been made that creating a better environment for linkages can change the existing structure (Meyanathan and Munter, 1994). The structure and operational patterns of particular industries also vary from one national business system to another. In construction, for example, contracting systems are common to both Britain and France, but the organization of these systems and the roles played by different system participants are quite different in the two countries (Winch, 1996). Industry structure is, however, unlikely to change significantly in the very short run, so this study takes the existing structure of the food processing industry as given.

Lall (1990) notes that while it is often assumed that such linkages automatically occur as a result of market forces directing interfirm and inter-industry transactions, this is frequently not the case since markets are often fragmented, narrow and incapable of providing the environment needed to stimulate linkages. The setting up of linkages, therefore, requires sustained effort and special skills on the part of the firm involved, and the country in general, to encourage linkages among enterprises (Meyanathan and Munter, 1994).

Forms of Linkages

As defined, interfirm linkage refers to all possible forms of relationships or connections between firms operating in an economy. For purposes of empirical investigation, we have chosen to limit the possibilities in two ways. *First*, we have concentrated on interactions between large and small firms, and, *second*, we have limited the forms of interaction to four: subcontracting, collaborations, informal contacts, and membership in formal associations.

As countries industrialize and liberalize their trade, small firms can be pinched by the 'double development squeeze' of rising wages and falling product prices (Snodgrass and Biggs, 1996). As a result, many small firms disappear. Those that survive usually have superior management capability, access to finance, and good information about markets and technology. Observers have argued that connections with large firms can help small ones obtain these ingredients that are critical to survival and success (Meyanathan and Munter, 1994; Snodgrass and Biggs, 1996).

Subcontracting is one form of a broader category of contractual linkages. Subcontracting is the contracting out of certain activities. Firms subcontract both core production activities and auxiliary services. Typically the motives for subcontracting fall into one or more of the following categories: lowering labour costs, reducing risk by lowering fixed costs, need for specialized products or services that would be difficult or expensive to produce in-house, avoiding labour conflicts, keeping a business small and controllable (Beneria, 1989).

Collaborations are formal or informal agreements to work together. Formal collaborations include joint ventures, industrial co-operation, and franchising relationships. Firms also collaborate informally. For example, an international distributor may help a small company master different banking systems, business systems, or cultures (Kantor, 1995). For this research, the term was kept purposely broad to enable us to capture all kinds of relationships that a more restrictive definition would not have revealed.

Contacts differ from collaborations in that they need not have an immediate aim of working together. Interfirm contacts are often for information sharing, as when an entrepreneur calls a former workmate in the same industry to discuss common problems. Contacts, even those with no explicitly business content, may build trust and mutual respect that can be drawn on for business purposes at some later date.

The final form of linkage investigated in this research – association membership – is multilateral, rather than bilateral. Business associations are groups of individuals and firms that come together usually for a rather generalized purpose of fostering business activity. Once formed, they provide a structured setting for co-operation on specific issues facing the business community as a whole or some part of it.

Linkages and Performance

Linkages are believed to improve firm performance in at least four ways: first, by reducing market friction and its resulting costs; second, by allowing firms to maintain a greater degree of flexibility than would be otherwise possible; third, by improving skills and encouraging the diffusion of technology; and, fourth, by facilitating the sharing of market information (Meyanathan and Munter, 1994; Lall, 1990).

Market frictions are reduced as repeated interactions between firms lower the transaction costs of obtaining and acting upon information. As firms link and work together over time, the friction created by discrete transactions is gradually replaced by a smooth system of relationships with significantly lower costs per transaction (see Williamson, 1985).

Linkages also enhance flexibility. This happens most directly by allowing firms to reduce fixed costs. For example, the firm with good linkages can gain access to equipment without the high cost of ownership, or buy in specialized services instead of keeping the specialists on the payroll. Small firms with good linkages can specialize in one aspect of production or service provision, and sell its products to other, often larger, firms. Such market linkages have been widely discussed under the heading of 'flexible specialization' (Piore and Sabel, 1984; *IDS Bulletin*, 1992; Pedersen *et al.*, 1994).

Technology acquisition is a major challenge to developing country industry, partly because of low education and skill levels, and partly because of the weak communications infrastructure that blocks information dissemination. The problem affects firms of all sizes, but is especially critical for small enterprises. A recent study of technological capabilities in Africa suggests that connections with larger firms, both local and foreign, improves small-firm access to technology information (Biggs *et al.*, 1995). One of the most beneficial forms of such linkages is the supply of technology-intensive products by small to larger firms (Meyanathan and Munter, 1994). As such interfirm relationships are repeated, the small firm gains a valuable skills upgrade and the technology that was formerly lodged in the larger firm becomes more widely available.

Finally, certain kinds of linkages facilitate the sharing of market information. Horizontal linkages, especially multilateral linkages such as membership in sectoral associations, seem particularly useful in this regard (Nadvi and Schmitz, 1994).

Despite considerable agreement on the potential benefits of firm linkages and networks, scholars have also underscored the risks involved in entering into various types of linkages. Large firms stand to lose considerably if inputs of poor or uneven quality threaten the quality of their final product. Large firms may also doubt a small firm's ability to deliver parts on time (Masinde, 1996). Since a considerable amount of expense may be incurred in developing safeguards against such risks, the costs may outweigh the benefits of particular linkages, especially in countries where the institutional framework for business activity is poorly developed (Lorenz, 1991; Fafchamps, 1996; Kimuyu, 1997).

Forging interfirm linkages also has risks for small firms, especially if the partner is a larger, stronger enterprise (Beneria, 1989). The small firm runs the risk of becoming overdependent or, at worst, suffering exploitation at the hands of a large enterprise. Subcontracting, particularly in cases where the small firm acts exclusively as a subcontractor and has no markets of its own, seems more likely than other types of linkages to result in loss of small-firm autonomy.

Performance as Growth

The most basic performance indicator for any business firm is profitability. This is true whether profits are measured absolutely or relative to sales or investment, and whether the yardstick used is the firm's own past performance or some external standard. The trouble with profitability as a measure of performance in any study involving small enterprises in developing countries is that it is extremely difficult to quantify. The reasons for this are well known: the smallest firms do not keep records; even when records are kept, entrepreneurs fear sharing income information lest it lead to taxation; even medium and large firms are likely to be family businesses that do not easily share financial information.

These problems have led researchers to search for alternative performance measures. The most common is some sort of measure of firm growth. Growth is clearly related to profitability in that most growing firms finance their expansion at least partially through retained earnings. Nevertheless, growth is not the same as profitability. Many profitable firms do not grow. Instead their owners diversify into other activities, either to avoid risks or for better management of cash flow (McCormick, 1993; Ærøe, 1992). Despite the problems, however, firm growth is often the only performance measure available. Its use in such cases can be justified, especially in studies such as this one, which are designed to provide a first look at linkage patterns and consequences.

Linkages and Firm Growth: An Analytical Framework

The theoretical discussion, which has ranged over a number of issues, needs now to be summarized into a framework for analysing Kenya's food processing sector. Interfirm linkages have been defined as continuing relationships between enterprises. Firms form such linkages to attain ends that they cannot achieve alone, thus improving the performance of the firm. Both the linkages and the reasons for forming them are likely to vary from one industry to another. Differences in input and product markets, production technology, financing, and industry structure are largely responsible for these variations.

Linkages are believed to improve firm performance in at least four different ways: by reducing market friction and related costs, by enhancing flexibility, by improving skills and diffusing technology, and by facilitating the sharing of market information. In this study, firm growth is taken as a proxy for performance. Various indicators can be used to measure the growth of firms. These include employment, sales and physical assets. In most cases, however, historical sales data have been found to be unreliable since the absence of records means that the data are only as good as the respondents' recall (Departments of Economics, 1994). Employment data have therefore often been used in such cases. This approach has been used in this study.

The discussion has thus far not defined small, medium, or large firms. In the initial stages of the research, an employment-based definition such as that used in the GEMINI studies seemed appropriate.[2] In these studies, a *small* enterprise has 1–10 workers, a *medium* enterprise has 11–50 workers, and a *large* enterprise has more than 50 workers. Useful as employment-based size categories are generally, they are problematic when applied to certain industries (McCormick and Atieno, 1997). A 'small' retailer will, for example, often have fewer employees than a 'small' hotel. Within manufacturing, technology and the level of investment are at least as important as the number of employees in establishing the size of the enterprise. For this study, therefore, we chose not to use employment categories, but to classify firms as small, medium, or large, based on what they said about themselves. Details of the size distributions of the industry will be provided.

Kenya's Food Processing Subsector

The importance of the food processing sector in the Kenyan economy draws from the sector's direct linkage to agriculture which is the major player in the country's economy. The sector has been an important contributor in the country's industrialization process, being one of the sectors to emerge early in the country's industrialization. Its contribution in terms of value added and employment has been considerably above the national manufacturing average. Food processing currently represents about 46 per cent of manufacturing sector output (Republic of Kenya, 1995). The sector's importance in the economy is also reflected in its employment creation, income generation, foreign exchange earnings and the stabilization of farm incomes through the processing of perishable agricultural products.

The sector is characterized by a high level of diversity, reflected in the large number of subsectors and the many firms in each subsector. The main products are meat and meat products, grain mill products, edible oils, sugar, dairy products, canned fruits and vegetables, bakery and confectionery products. Most firms in this subsector produce a variety of products, using a range of production technologies, from simple labour-intensive to highly sophisticated capital-intensive methods of production (Department of Economics, 1994). One main characteristic of the sector is its direct dependence on agriculture for raw materials, making it highly susceptible to factors affecting the agricultural sector. This is also reflected in the seasonality of its production, and the location of firms in the sector.

It has been argued that due to lack of appropriate policies addressing the growth needs of the sector, it has tended to be inward looking and stagnating. Most firms in this sector cater only for the domestic market, which shields them from world market competition, and has contributed to the low quality of their products. A majority of the firms are owned by Kenyans with few multinational corporations (MNCs) mainly in soft drinks, canning and the manufacture of fats and oils.

At the local level, the inability of medium and large firms to compete provides an opportunity for small-scale and micro firms to increase their market share due to their low overhead costs and cheaper packaging (Department of Economics, 1994). The large number of firms in the industry makes it relatively more competitive than other sectors, though this varies somewhat from one subsector to another. The production technology is labour intensive, and local firms, in particular, employ mainly unskilled labour (Department of Economics, 1994).

As is the case with most Kenyan manufacturing, technology is mainly embodied in machinery and equipment (Teitel, 1993). The more techno-logically sophisticated firms, however, tend also to have employees with technical and professional skills. Food processing firms' technological performance appears closely related to the size of the enterprise, with larger firms scoring higher than small or medium ones on most measures of technological competence. Three subsectors within the food processing sector were selected for the Kenyan country study.[3] These are grain milling, fruit and vegetable canning and dairy processing. Each is described briefly below.

Grain Milling Subsector

Grain milling was chosen because of the importance of grains in the country's food policy. The major one, maize, is a staple commodity for a large percentage of the country's population. Grain milling also accounts for the largest number of firms in the food processing sector. The recent liberalization of grain marketing in the country has provided new opportunities and potential for the development of the sector and its contribution to the overall economy, especially through the development of private enterprises (Depart-ment of Economics, 1994).

Although dominated by a few large firms, the grain milling industry has seen an increase in the number of private traders and millers, especially in maize milling in recent years, mainly because of the liberalization of the grain marketing subsector. The large firms use a fairly capital intensive technology, both for the milling process itself and for moving grain from silos to the mills (Ikiara *et al.*, 1995). In contrast are Kenya's thousands of small-scale *posho* mills that typically employ 1–5 persons.[4] In the past these mostly combined service production with contract work for local schools and hotels. With liberalization, many are venturing into market production.

Ikiara *et al.* (1995) identify four categories of trader in the sector: transporters–distributors; large market traders; retailers and small market traders; and 'brokers'. One of our key informants stressed the importance of the first of these, pointing out that the lorry transporters control the bulk of the traded grains, especially interdistrict, trade (NCPB key informant interviews). They normally sell either directly to the millers, or to retailers who then sell either to millers or to final consumers.

This study hypothesizes that linkages are important to the growth of private enterprises. Hence it is important to trace the actual and potential links of firms in this subsector to other food processing firms and to firms in other sectors. According to information obtained from the NCPB (Key informant interviews), the potential for the development of linkages is much stronger in the wheat than the maize market. Associations formed by large-scale wheat farmers control the farm gate price of wheat by restricting the quantity they release to the market. The large wheat farmers are able to do this because of their ability to maintain the quality of the product through cleaning, storage and contract with millers. In the context of business relations, it is worth noting that initially the multiplication of small *posho* millers threatened the large-scale millers mainly because of the variety of milled products they were able to offer in response to the existing market demand. The large millers, in contrast, offered only one or a very few products. The large-scale millers have, however, responded to the situation by diversifying their products to recapture some of the market share. Nevertheless, the large-scale millers still recognize the small *posho* millers as formidable competitors because of their flexibility, and range and quality of products which have strong appeal for certain categories of consumers.

Fruit and Vegetable Canning Subsector

Fruit and vegetable canning was chosen mainly because of the emerging importance of horticultural farming as a source of non-traditional exports and foreign exchange. With trade liberalization, the sector has been exposed to new dimensions of competition especially from imports. Due to the diversity in its production activities, the opportunities for small scale and micro development could be explored. The fruit and vegetable canning subsector has few firms and is dominated by large enterprises, mainly subsidiaries of multinational corporations. The industry faces strong competition from exporters of horticultural products who bid up farm gate prices for raw materials.

A major constraint noted in this subsector is lack of raw materials and this has led to the closure of some of the canning factories. Some firms have addressed this problem by having their own farms to supply their factories. Potential competition between the canners and fresh produce exporters for raw materials has been reduced by the contractual arrangements for the supply of raw materials. Firms in this subsector have diversified their products, mainly to increase the utilization of their existing capacity. Seasonal fluctuations in the supply of raw materials could result in periods of capacity underutilization. Diversification of products therefore enables the firms to adjust their production lines depending on the availability of raw materials, thereby increasing their rate of capacity utilization.

Dairy Processing Subsector

The dairy sector is an area of high priority within the agricultural sector, making dairy processing one of the most important agro-based industries in the country. Its importance lies in its potential for creating employment, especially in processing and distribution of dairy products. The country also has a competitive advantage in the production of dairy products in the East African region (Republic of Kenya, 1997). The sector faces problems of cyclical fluctuations in the supply of milk. The country currently produces only 2.2 billion litres annually, despite having a production potential of 4 billion litres annually (Republic of Kenya, 1997). For many years the subsector was dominated by the Kenya Cooperative Creameries (KCC) Ltd., which has ten factories and seven cooling centres spread all over the country (Departments of Economics, 1994).

Inadequate milk storage facilities to minimize losses and increase the milk available for processing, in addition to poor rural infrastructure, government interventions and the dominance of the market by one single player are some of the constraints to the development of the dairy industry (Department of Economics, 1994; Mwaniki Associates, 1997; Republic of Kenya, 1997).

Liberalization has brought several new market developments to the dairy sector. A number of private processors have entered the market. Many have their own farms to supply the milk, while others have subcontracted dairy farmers to provide milk. Most would be categorized as medium-sized firms which use the same capital-intensive technologies as KCC. Smaller players, also lured into the field by liberalization, include middle-scale distributors supplying milk bars and restaurants, and small-scale vendors mainly selling to households. Many of these sell raw milk. Those that process the milk either boil it or use very simple pasteurisers (Mwaniki Associates, 1997).

METHODOLOGY

The research into Kenya's food processing sector is part of a larger study of interfirm linkages in four African countries. Countries were given some latitude to choose sectors and develop the methodologies to suit local conditions. The Kenya study investigated three sectors – food processing, tourism, and construction – using a common methodology. Although the study examined linkages between foreign and domestic firms, as well as those between large and small firms, this chapter presents only the results of the investigations into linkages between large and small firms. As will be discussed later in the chapter, firm size is based on the entrepreneurs' perceptions of the size of their firms.

The selection of the three sectors to be included in the research was guided by the overall objectives of the three-country study. Food processing was common to the three countries. The narrowing of each sector to particular subsectors was determined by the structure of the industry in Kenya. Thus three subsectors of food processing were selected, namely fruit and vegetable canning, grain milling, and dairy processing. The choice of the study sites was determined by the geographical distribution of the food processing firms in the country, and agricultural production which forms the source of raw materials for the firms studied. The survey was therefore carried out in the major towns of Nairobi, Mombasa, Eldoret, and Nakuru.

Different sources of information were used in constructing the sampling frame. For the food processing industry, the primary source was a listing of registered (mostly medium to large-scale) enterprises in the named activities and locations provided by the Central Bureau of Statistics (CBS). This was augmented by a quick survey of relevant items stocked on the shelves of 20 supermarkets in Nairobi and 10 in Mombasa to identify local manufacturers not included in the CBS lists. We also added firms listed in the various business directories but not appearing in the CBS lists. Finally, we visited various government offices, including the Ministry of Agriculture and trade licensing offices in the study areas.

Systematic sampling was used to select firms from the lists within each subsector. Additional firms were also selected to serve as alternatives if the sampled firms could not be located or were otherwise unavailable for interview. Thirty-one very small firms were chosen by the research assistants in the field. In order to avoid interviewer selection bias, very specific instructions on how to select these firms were given to the research assistants.

In food processing, a total of 68 firms were sampled, but only 59 were successfully interviewed. The discussion that follows is therefore based on the analysis of results from these 59 firms. The distribution by subsectors was 34 in grain milling, 18 in dairy processing and seven in fruit and vegetable canning. Due to the small number of the firms successfully interviewed in the fruit and vegetable canning, the subsector could not be analysed separately. Hence for purposes of analysis, dairy processing and fruit and vegetable canning firms were sometimes grouped together.

In addition to the survey of individual firms, key informant interviews were also conducted with institutions and persons, with more in-depth information in the specific subsectors. For the food processing sector, the key informants were the Kenya Association of Manufacturers (KAM), the Kenya Dairy Board, and the National Cereals and Produce Board (NCPB).

LINKAGES AND FIRM PERFORMANCE

The study hypothesized that linkages should have a positive effect on firm performance. More specifically, it proposed that firms with more linkages would grow more, with growth measured in terms of increased employment. This section presents the results of the analysis. The following sections provide basic data on firm size and growth, the market, and the various types of linkages. The final section discusses the relationship between linkages and firm growth.

Firm Size and Technology

The industry has firms of varying sizes. As explained above, the study adopted size designations based on what the owners said about the size of their firms. Over half (33 firms, or 55.9 per cent) considered themselves small, while 32.2 per cent said they were medium, and 10.3 per cent, large (Table 11.1).[5]

Discussions of these size designations with knowledgeable industry sources revealed that for most firms in the food processing sector, the level of employment is not the major criterion used by manufacturers in determining the size of their firms. Rather in dairy processing, firm size is mainly determined by a firm's production capacity; in fruit and vegetable canning, it is determined by production capacity and employment; while in grain milling size is determined by milling capacity.

The few large firms, especially those in dairy and grain milling, tend to have production facilities in various parts of the country. Some of the medium-sized firms also have multiple branches, but most of the medium-sized and all of the

Table 11.1   Firm size distribution by entrepreneurs' designation

Size	Total sample		Dairy, fruit and vegetable canning		Grain milling	
	Frequency	Percentage	Frequency	Percentage	Frequency	Percentage
Small	33	55.9	13	52.0	20	58.8
Medium	19	32.2	9	36.0	10	29.5
Large	6	10.2	3	12.0	3	8.8
Missing	1	1.7	0	0.0	1	2.9
Total	59	100.0	25	100.0	34	100.0

Source: Survey data.

small producers operate from a single location. In describing their technology, five out of six (83.3 per cent) of the large firms referred to 'computerization', 'modern machinery', or 'the latest technology'. Among the small firms, nearly one-third (30.3 per cent) said that they had 'no technology', while just over one-third (36.4 per cent) reported 'modern machinery' or 'computerization'. Clearly, as in Kenyan manufacturing as a whole, size is related to technology in the food processing subsector.

Firm Growth

Firms generally increased their employment between 1990 and 1996 (Table 11.2). The level of increase varied significantly, both according

Table 11.2   Mean employment growth according to self-designated firm size 1990-6

Firm size	Total	Grain milling	Dairy processing
Large	10.21	0.35	12.56
Medium	3.21	6.40	2.05
Small	0.45	0.17	0.60
P	0.0005	0.0075	0.0085
N	54	32	18

Source: Survey data.

Note: Five cases were missing.

to the size of the firm and its activity. Looking at the total sample, large firms appear to have grown more in employment than both medium and small firms, with the difference in growth being statistically significant. Among the grain milling firms, however, medium-sized firms had the highest growth, while small-scale firms grew least. For the dairy processing firms, those in the large-scale category grew most, and the small ones grew least.

The results can be interpreted in a number of ways. One important aspect is the changing market situation for both sectors over this period. Both grain and dairy markets were liberalized after 1990, giving new openings for private firms to enter into these activities. In the grain milling subsector large firms had been the main players prior to liberalization of the markets. This situation has now changed, and small- and medium-sized firms are increasing their share of the market. In the dairy subsector, the private processors that have entered the market to compete with the former monopoly of Kenya Cooperative Creameries (KCC) fall mainly into the large-scale category, and their high growth can be seen as a reflection of the rate at which they are increasing their market penetration.

The Market and Competitive Relations

With liberalization, markets have become increasingly competitive. Firms compete both with firms that are larger and those that are smaller than themselves. All producers were able to identify their direct competitors, and most could also state whether these firms were larger or smaller than themselves. The responses with respect to firm size show that 69.5 per cent of the firms are competing directly with larger firms, while 28.8 per cent were in direct competition with smaller firms, and one firm could not classify its competitors.

The main basis for competition also varied between different firms and activities (Table 11.3). Price alone was the main basis for competition for only about one-fifth (20.3 per cent) of the firms. For other firms, other factors, either alone or in combination with price, determined competitiveness. Product quality and design was a basis for competition for up to 23.7 per cent of the firms, while 27 per cent of the firms saw both price and product quality as a main basis for competition. When asked to describe the particular quality and design requirements of their customers, firms mentioned aspects such as flavour, freshness, packaging, and standard grades. For firms in the dairy, fruit and vegetable canning sub-sectors, competitiveness rested on both price and quality, while for grain milling, product quality and design were the leading bases for competition.

Table 11.3   Distribution of main basis for competition by subsector

Basis for competition	Total sample		Dairy, fruit and vegetable canning		Grain milling	
	Frequency	Percentage	Frequency	Percentage	Frequency	Percentage
Price	12	20.3	3	12.0	9	26.5
Product quality and design	14	23.7	2	8.0	12	35.3
Availability/ accessibility	4	6.8	4	16.0	0	0.0
Both price and quality	16	27.1	7	28.0	9	26.5
Both quality and availabity	1	1.7	1	4.0	0	0.0
Price and availability	1	1.7	1	4.0	0	0.0
Price, quality accessibility	8	13.6	6	24.0	2	2.9
Missing	3	5.1	1	4.0	2	5.9
Total	59	100.0	25	100.0	34	100.0

Source: Survey data.

Linkages

Subcontracting arrangements

Apart from the backward linkages into agriculture which this research did not consider, subcontracting appears not to be common in Kenya's food industry. Most firms (52, or 88 per cent) responded that they do not subcontract any of their activities. The seven subcontracting firms contract out activities outside their main line of activity, mostly services. The frequency and percentage distribution of the main activities subcontracted are given in the Table 11.4.

Out of the seven firms which subcontracted, five were in grain milling and two in fruit and vegetable canning. The main activities subcontracted by these firms were transportation of commodities, sales and distribution, and grain milling which was subcontracted by five firms. Differences among the subsectors in type of activity subcontracted were not statistically significant. Firms subcontracted because of seasonal fluctuations in supplies (43 per cent of those subcontracting) and lower costs (57 per cent). Other reasons given for subcontracting out activities included lack of skilled personnel by firms and the occasional heavy work load.

Table 11.4   Subcontracted activities

Subcontracted activity	Total sample	
	Number	Percentage
Subcontracting	51	86.4
Transportation	1	1.7
Sales and distribution	1	1.7
Grain milling	5	8.5
Missing	1	1.7
Total	59	100.0

Source: Survey data.

Firms identified additional activities suitable for further subcontracting, such as flour packaging, grain milling during peak season, and extraction of maize jam. Four of the seven firms currently subcontracting saw no other activity suitable for subcontracting. When asked whether they receive subcontracts, only 12 firms (20.3 per cent) responded positively. For these 12, the main activities performed on contract were: removing dirt from raw maize, quality testing, milk processing, and packaging. Eight of these firms were in grain milling. Only five firms saw any additional activities suitable for subcontracting. Grain milling firms saw opportunities in grain milling and transportation; dairy firms thought that packaging and quality analysis could be subcontracted.

Although the proportion of firms presently receiving subcontracts is small, most (39 firms or 66.1 per cent) would like to receive more subcontracts. Nearly half (42.4 per cent) of them expected to increase their production and revenue through subcontracting, while an additional 16.9 per cent hoped for better utilization of their available capacity.

What emerges from the responses to questions about the giving and receiving of subcontracts, is a fairly clear picture of an industry with excess capacity. Firms seem to be able to expand their activities without increasing their investment. Subcontracting is most common in grain milling, where it is nearly all capacity based (Table 11.4). Future possibilities for subcontracting may be limited in both grain milling and dairy because the markets for their products have become extremely competitive. The liberalization in the marketing of agricultural commodities, especially grains and dairy products, has encouraged many new businesses to enter the market. Demand, however, has grown slowly, so the larger number of firms is competing for essentially the same market, leaving little need for capacity based subcontracting.

None of the subcontracting appears to be technology based. There was no case of a small firm presently supplying technology-intensive products to larger firms, nor do firms envision such subcontracting in the future.

Collaborative relationships

Almost half (49.1 per cent) of the firms collaborate in some way with other firms in the industry. The rest have no collaborative arrangements of any type. Of those with collaborations, 30.5 per cent collaborated with larger enterprises. Collaboration took different forms as shown in Table 11.5 below.

Table 11.5   Forms of collaboration in the same subsector

Nature of collaboration	Total sample	
	Number	Percentage
No collaboration	29	49.2
Acquisition of raw materials	9	15.3
Exchange business related ideas	3	5.1
Subcontracts	3	5.1
Consult on technology	6	10.2
Price setting	8	13.6
Missing	1	1.7
Total	59	100.0

Source: Survey data.

Acquisition of raw materials and price setting are the most important forms of collaboration (Table 11.5). While acquisition of raw materials was most important for dairy and fruit and vegetable canning, for grain milling price setting appeared to be the most important reason for collaboration. Such differences among the subsectors were, however, not statistically significant.

Association Memberships and Informal Contacts

Association memberships and informal contacts offer businesses ways of extending their networks and obtaining specific services. The industry does not appear to have strong associational links. Only 19 firms (32 per cent) belonged to at least one association. The remaining 40 firms (68 per cent) had no association membership. Business owners reported a variety of purposes for these associations, ranging from financing of business and personal expenses, to offering training. Most association members (84 per cent) indicated that they attend meetings called by the association, but many seemed not to use the associations' services. It seems that, although association members are willing to attend meetings, the associations had either failed to develop mechanisms for benefiting the members, or had not communicated well about the benefits they offered to their members.

The study investigated contacts with business people who were neither customers nor suppliers (see Table 11.6). On the whole, such contacts are infrequent and tend to be with smaller firms. Only 10 firms (17.3 per cent) reported frequent contact with firms larger than themselves and in the same line of business. Over two-thirds of the businesses have no contact with larger firms of any type. Contact with smaller firms is more common. Over a third (39.3 per cent) report frequent contact with smaller firms in the same line of business, while a quarter (26.8 per cent) have frequent contact with smaller firms in different lines of business. The contacts were based on a variety of factors. In some cases the entrepreneurs went to school together or worked together; in others, they belong to the same association, come from the same locality, or are relatives. These kinds of relations were observed to cut across all firms.

Both formal and informal linkages were viewed as being equally important by a majority of firms interviewed. An investigation of the importance of both formal and informal contacts showed that 32 firms (54.2 per cent) considered formal linkages to be important to the progress of their business, and 27 firms (45.8 per cent) considered informal linkages to be important to the success of their business.

Table 11.6   *Distribution of frequency of contacts with firms in the same industry (neither customers nor suppliers)*

Type of firm	Frequent	Infrequent	*N*
Larger firms, same line	10	46	56
Smaller firms, same line	22	36	58
Larger firms, different line	12	44	56
Smaller firms, different line	15	41	56

Notes:
Contacts are *frequent* when made daily, weekly, or monthly.
Contacts are *infrequent* when made yearly or never.

Source: Survey data.

THE RELATIONSHIP BETWEEN LINKAGES AND FIRM GROWTH

In the preceding sections, we have observed that the Kenyan food processing sector has few interfirm linkages. The theory laid out at the beginning of the chapter leads us to hypothesize that the minority of firms that are well linked should have experienced greater growth than the majority without such linkages. To test this, we have analysed the growth in employment for firms with and without each major type of linkage (Tables 11.7 and 11.8).

Among the contractual and collaborative linkages, only the giving of subcontracts and association membership show positive and significant relationships to employment growth (Table 11.7). Firms that give subcontracts experienced a bigger change in employment (42.7 employees) than those which did not (10.17 employees) and the difference is significant. Association membership also appears important. Firms that belong to associations (19 firms) experienced a significantly higher growth in employment (28.47 workers) than those that do not (7.17 employees).

Table 11.7   Contractual and collaborative linkages and employment growth 1990-6

Type of linkage	Yes	No	N	P
Give subcontracts	42.71	10.17	59	.0202
Receive subcontracts	27.75	10.53	59	.1314
Collaborate with large firms	9.72	14.87	57	.6091
Collaborate with small firms	8.62	15.94	57	.4496
Association membership	28.47	7.17	59	.0285

Source: Survey data.

The relationship between informal contacts and firm growth was also investigated. The results of employment growth for firms which had this relationship compared to those which did not are presented in Table 11.8. In all cases except for contacts with small firms in the same line of business where firms with contacts grew less than those without, firms with informal contacts grew more than those without. However, the differences in all cases were not statistically significant.

When considered in terms of the subsector, the same pattern emerges whereby those with contacts increased employment more than those that did not, but the differences were not statistically significant. Neither grain millers nor dairy processors who had contact with firms either in the same line or

Table 11.8   Informal contacts and employment growth, 1990-6

Type of contact	Frequent	Infrequent	N	P
Small firm, different business line	14.60	12.63	56	.8552
Large firm, different business line	21.58	10.86	56	.3546
Small Firm, same business line	8.81	17.11	58	.3925
Large firm, same business line	15.60	12.63	56	.8115

Notes:
Contacts are *frequent* when made daily, weekly, or monthly.
Contacts are *infrequent* when made yearly or never.

different lines of business had any significant growth beyond those that lacked such contacts.

SUMMARY AND CONCLUSIONS

The findings can be briefly summarized. Firms in the food processing sector are not well linked. Very few give or receive subcontracts. Only about half collaborate with other firms. Informal contacts are mostly infrequent, and seem not to involve larger firms in any significant way. Only about one third of the firms belong to any association. Yet certain types of linkages appear to be associated with firm growth. Firms that give subcontracts grew more than those that do not, and firms that belong to associations also grew more than non-members.

The type of technological linkages believed to offer opportunities for small firms to improve their technological capacity are entirely missing. Fostering these might be difficult, in part because the integrated technology used by larger firms does not easily lend itself to separation of activities. Furthermore, small firms in Kenya are typically undercapitalized and might, therefore, be unable to invest in the equipment needed to supply technology-intensive products.

An obvious question raised by these findings is whether linkages between and among firms are desirable and should be actively encouraged. On the positive side, we see that subcontracting, especially of non-core activities, should allow firms to operate more efficiently and thus become more competitive on both domestic and international markets. Association membership also offers important benefits to firms. Sectoral associations can be effective means of disseminating information, offering training and advisory services, gathering market information, and providing cost effective sourcing of materials. Broad-based associations such as the Kenya

Association of Manufacturers might be able to facilitate contacts between larger firms in the industry and small firms desiring to develop suitable subcontracting arrangements.

On the other hand, the lack of linkages may mean that this industry is simply not conducive to linkages and may therefore not encourage their development. A number of factors influence the emergence and development of interfirm linkages. An industry's internal operations and links with the world market may affect the pattern of linkages. The nature and size of the markets faced by the firm will determine whether linkages develop, and will affect the likely linkage partners and the types of relationships between them. In the food processing sector, the nature of the industry does not encourage interfirm linkages within the sector. The technology used by larger firms, especially in dairy and fruit and vegetable canning, does not lend itself to subcontracting or other direct production linkages. The industry's current excess capacity further discourages capacity-based subcontracting.

There is, however, potential for the development of linkages with firms outside the sector (a good example being the transport sector), and direct backward linkages with farmers. This suggests that in addition to looking at the relationship between linkages and firm growth, it is important to consider whether there is any potential for development of such linkages and whether they are even desirable.

At least two cautionary notes must be sounded. First, although this study provides empirical evidence to support the theoretical links between certain types of linkages and firm growth, the size of the food sector sample may have been too small to be fully reliable. The second caution concerns the direction of causality. The theory suggests that the existence of linkages enables firms to grow and to prosper. The reality could, in fact, be the other way around. It may be that the more profitable, growing firms are those giving subcontracts and joining associations. If this is the case, then efforts to foster linkages will do little to promote firm growth.

Further research in this area is clearly needed. A follow-up study with a larger sample, possibly including a wider range of food processing activities, is needed to confirm these findings. Ideally such research should incorporate additional measures of firm performance such as growth in profits, investment, or efficiency. Supplementing the basic survey with more qualitative approaches could be helpful in establishing the true cause and effect relationships between linkages and firm performance.

NOTES

1. The authors are grateful to the International Centre for Economic Growth (ICEG) for the financial support that made this study possible. The chapter has also benefited from

comments of participants at conferences in Nairobi, Kenya and Dar es Salaam, Tanzania, where preliminary results were presented in 1997, in informal workshops within the Institute for Development Studies, University of Nairobi, and at the workshop organized by the European Association of Development Institutes in The Hague, Netherlands, in September, 1998. We, of course, remain responsible for errors and omissions.

2. The Growth and Equity through Microenterprise Investments and Institutions (GEMINI) studies, sponsored by the United States Agency for International Development were baseline studies of micro and small enterprises that have been conducted in a number of African countries, including Kenya, Zimbabwe, Swaziland, Malawi, Botswana, and Lesotho, using a methodology developed at Michigan State University (USA).

3. The main subsectors of the food processing industry in Kenya are: (a) meat and meat products, (b) dairy products processing, (c) fruits and vegetable processing, (d) grain milling, (e) bakery products, (f) sugar processing, (g) confectionery, and (h) others, such as beverages, honey refining.

4. *Posho* is the Swahili word for grain.

5. This sample probably contains a larger share of medium and large firms than the population of all food processing firms.

REFERENCES

Abuodha, C. and K. King (1993), 'The building of an industrial society: change and development in Kenya's informal (*Jua Kali*) sector, 1972–1991', DP No. 292, Institute for Development Studies, University of Nairobi.

Ærøe, A. (1992), 'Rethinking industrialisation – from a national to a local perspective: a case study of the industrialisation process in Tanzania with particular emphasis on the construction industry', CDR Project Paper 92.3, Centre for Development Research, Copenhagen.

Aleke-Dondo, C. (1991), 'Survey and analyses of credit programmes for small and micro enterprises in Kenya', K-REP Research Paper No. 2, Kenya Rural Enterprise Programme, Nairobi.

Alila, P.O. and D. McCormick (1997), 'Firm linkages in Kenya's tourism sector', paper prepared as part of multi-country study of private enterprise development, Kenya Case Study, Institute for Development Studies, University of Nairobi.

Atieno, R. (1997), 'Firm linkages in Kenya's food processing sector', paper prepared as part of multi-country study of private enterprise development, Kenya Case Study, Institute for Development Studies, University of Nairobi.

Barr, A.M. (1995), 'The missing factor: entrepreneurial networks, enterprises and economic growth in Ghana', Centre for the Study of African Economies Working Paper WPS/95-11. University of Oxford, Oxford: CSAE Publishing.

Bell, M. and Pavitt, Keith (1995), 'The development of technological capabilities', in Irfan ul Haque (ed.), *Trade, Technology, and International Competitiveness*, Washington, DC: Economic Development Institute of the World Bank, pp. 69–102.

Beneria, L. (1989), 'Subcontracting and employment dynamics in Mexico City', in Alejandro Portes *et al.* (eds), *The Informal Economy: Studies in Advanced and Less Developed Countries*, Baltimore: Johns Hopkins University Press.

Daily Nation (1998), Nairobi.

Biggs, T., M. Shah and P. Srivastava (1995), 'Technological capabilities and learning in African enterprises', Technical paper no. 288, African Technical Department Series, World Bank, Washington, DC.

Department of Economics, University of Nairobi, and Department of Economics University of Gothenburg (1994), 'Limitations and rewards in Kenya's manufacturing sector: a study of enterprise development,' Nairobi and Gothenburg.

Evans, P. (1995), *Embedded Autonomy: States and Industrial Transformation*, Princeton: Princeton University Press.

Fafchamps, M. (1996), 'The enforcement of commercial contracts in Ghana', *World Development* **24** (3), pp. 427–48.

Grabher, G. (1993), 'Rediscovering the social in the economics of interfirm relations', in G. Grabher (ed.), *The Embedded Firm: On the Socioeconomics of Industrial Networks*, London: Routledge, pp. 1–31.

Granovetter, M. (1985), 'Economic action and social structure: the problem of embeddedness', *American Journal of Sociology*, **91**, pp. 481–510.

Harrigan, K.R. and W.H. Newman (1990), 'Bases of inter-organizational co-operation: propensity, power, persistence', *Journal of Management Studies*, **27**, pp. 417–34.

IDS Bulletin (1992), Special issue on 'Flexible specialisation: a new view on small industry?', **23** (3).

Ikiara, G.K., M. Jama and J.O. Amadi (1995), 'The cereals chain in Kenya: actors, reforms and politics', in P. Gibbon (ed.), *Markets, Civil Society, and Democracy in Kenya*, Uppsala: Nordiska Afrikainstitutet, pp. 31–68.

Johanson, J. and L.G. Mattsson (1987), 'Interorganizational relations in industrial systems: a network approach compared with the transaction-cost approach', *International Studies of Management and Organisation*, **17** (1), pp. 34–48.

Kantor, R.M. (1995), *World Class: Thriving Locally in the Global Economy*, New York: Simon & Schuster.

Kenya, Republic of (1992), Sessional Paper Number 2 of 1992 on Small Enterprises and JA Kali Development in Kenya, Nairobi: Government Printer.

Kenya, Republic of (1995), *Statistical Abstract 1995*, Nairobi: Government Printer.

Kimuyu, P. (1997), 'Enterprise attributes and corporate disputes in Kenya', Discussion Paper No. DP 001/97, Institute of Policy Analysis and Research, Nairobi.

Kinyanjui, M.N. (1998), 'Vehicle repair clusters in Kenya: alternative strategy for small enterprise development', report prepared in connection with research on Enterprise Clusters in Africa, University of Nairobi, Institute for Development Studies, Nairobi.

Knoke, D., and H.J. Kuklinski (1982), *Network Analysis: Basic Concepts*, Sage University Paper series on Quantitative Applications in the Social Sciences, paper no. 18, Beverly Hills: Sage Publications.

Lall, S. (1990), *Building Industrial Competitiveness in Developing Countries*, Paris: Development Centre of the Organization for Economic Cooperation and Development.

Lorenz, E.H. (1991), 'Neither friends nor strangers: informal networks of subcontracting in French industry', in Grahame Thompson *et al.*, *Markets, Hierarchies and Networks: The Coordination of Social Life*, London: Sage.

Masinde, C. (1996), 'Small enterprise development: production and distribution in Kenya motor industry', in D. McCormick and P.O. Pedersen (eds), *Small Enterprises: Flexibility and Networking in an African Context*, Nairobi: Longhorn Kenya.

McCormick, D. (1988), 'Small enterprise in Nairobi: golden opportunity or dead end?', Ph.D. dissertation, Johns Hopkins University, Baltimore.

McCormick, D. (1993), 'Risk and firm growth: the dilemma of Nairobi's small-scale manufacturers', Discussion Paper No. 291, University of Nairobi, Institute for Development Studies, Nairobi.

McCormick, D. (1996), 'Small enterprise development: a network approach', in D. McCormick and P.O. Pedersen (eds), *Small Enterprises: Flexibility and Networking in an African Context*, Longhorn Kenya, Nairobi.

McCormick, D. and R. Atieno (1996), 'Private enterprise development in Africa: methodology for research', University of Nairobi, Institute for Development Studies, Nairobi.

McCormick, D. and R. Atieno (1997), 'Firm linkages: importance for industrial structure and performance', University of Nairobi, Institute for Development Studies, Nairobi.

McCormick, D., M.N. Kinyanjui and G. Ongile (1997), 'Growth and barriers to growth among Nairobi's small and medium-sized garment producers', *World Development*, **25** (7), pp. 1095–1110.

Mead, D.C. (1994), 'Linkages within the private sector: a review of current thinking', FIT Working Paper No. 3. Amsterdam: FIT/TOOL.

Meyanathan, D.S. and R. Munter (1994), 'Industrial structures and the development of small and medium enterprise linkages: an overview', EDI Seminar Series, The World Bank, Washington, DC.

Mitchell, J.C. (1969), 'The concept and use of social networks', in C.J. Mitchell (ed.), *Social Networks in Urban Situations: Analysis of Personal Relationships in Central African Towns*, Manchester: Manchester University Press, pp. 1–110.

Mwaniki Associates, ApproTEC, Kenya Women Finance Trust and Improve Your Business, Kenya (1997), 'Market research and variability analysis of enterprise opportunities in the agribusiness subsector', USAID Micro-private Enterprise Development Project (Microped) Agribusiness Subsector Component, US Agency for International Development, Nairobi.

Nadvi, K. and H. Schmitz (1994), 'Industrial clusters in less developed countries: review of experiences and research agenda', Discussion Paper No. 339, Institute of Development Studies, Sussex.

North, D.C. (1990), *Institutions, Institutional Change and Economic Performance*, Cambridge: Cambridge University Press.

October, L. (1996), 'Sectors, clusters and regions: a study of the Cape clothing industry', Working Paper No. 2, Development Policy Research Unit, University of Cape Town, Capetown.

Parker, J.C. and T.R. Torres (1994), 'Micro and small enterprises in Kenya: results of the 1993 survey' (final draft), GEMINI study, USAID and K-REP, Nairobi.

Pedersen, P.O. (1996), 'Flexibility and networking: European and African context', in D. McCormick and Poul Ove Pedersen (eds), *Small Enterprises: Flexibility and Networking in an African Context*, Nairobi: Longhorn Kenya, pp. 3–17.

Pedersen, P.O., A. Sverrisson and M.P. van Dijk (1994), *Flexible Specialisation: The Dynamics of Small-Scale Industries in the South*, London: Intermediate Technology.

Piore, M, and C.F. Sabel (1984), *The Second Industrial Divide: Possibilities for Prosperity*, New York: Basic Books.

Rasmussen, J. (1992), 'The local entrepreneurial milieu: enterprise networks in small Zimbabwean towns', Research Report no. 79, University Roskilde.

Scherer, F.M. (1980), *Industrial Market Structure and Economic Performance*, 2nd edn, Boston: Houghton Mifflin.

Snodgrass, D.R. and T. Biggs (1996), *Industrialisation and the Small Firm: Patterns and Policies*, San Francisco and Boston: International Centre for Economic Growth and Harvard Institute for International Development.

Teitel, S. (1993), 'Technology acquisition, operation, and development in selected Kenyan manufacturing establishments', Regional Program on Enterprise Development, Africa Technical Department, Draft Report, The World Bank, Washington, DC.

Whitley, R. (1992), *Business Systems in East Asia*. London: Sage.

Williamson, O.E. (1975), *Markets and hierarchies: analysis and antitrust implications*, New York: Free Press.

Williamson, O.E. (1985), *The Economic Institutions of Capitalism*, New York: Free Press.

Winch, G. (1996), 'Contracting systems in the European construction industry: a sectoral approach to the dynamics of business systems', in R. Whitley and P.H. Kristensen (eds), *The Changing European Firm: Limits to Convergence*, London: Routledge.

12.   The role of a research and development institute in the development and diffusion of technology

B. Bongenaar and A. Szirmai

This chapter analyses the role of a major research and development organization in the development of technology for and the diffusion of technology to the industrial sector of Tanzania. The research and development organization in question is the Tanzanian Industrial Research and Development Organization (TIRDO). An important aim of TIRDO is to adapt technology to local circumstances and transfer it to domestic industrial firms. The technology projects of the institute are usually fairly small-scale in nature. They make use of domestic resources and try to substitute for imported products. On the basis of an in-depth analysis of a large number of technology projects of this organization, the chapter tries to identify the factors contributing to or hampering the successful development and diffusion of technologies in the context of a developing economy.[1]

THEORETICAL BACKGROUND

The theoretical rationale for funding public research and development organizations is market failure. Given the semi-public nature and positive external effects of research and development (R&D), the volume of private investment in R&D will tend to be suboptimal. In the context of a low income economy, this is compounded by imperfect information, lack of skilled personnel and financial resources in the private sector. This chapter examines whether a public research and development institute can fulfil its functions, through successful development and diffusion of appropriate technologies.

We present a simplified scheme of the technology development process to structure the empirical analysis of the technology development project. The scheme involves two basic assumptions. The first is that a research and development institute in a low-income economy will not develop technology from scratch, but rather will use and adapt existing technology to fulfil technological needs: it innovates rather than invents,[2] it focuses more on specific techniques than on wider technologies. The second assumption, based on the charter of TIRDO, is that the target group of the research and development organization consists of domestic industrial enterprises.

Identification ⟶ Acquisition ⟶ Adaptation ⟶ Selection ⟶ Technology ⟶ Implementation
and selection   of   of firms   transfer   innovation
of technology   techmology

Figure 12.1   Phases in the technology development process

Figure 12.1 presents the six main phases in the model of technology development: identification and selection of technologies, acquisition of technology, adaptation, selection of firms, technology transfer to firms, and implementation of innovations. These steps have to be executed for each technology development project and will be analysed separately.

The phases are analytical rather than purely sequential. In one sense, the phases do represent a logical sequence in time. Identification precedes acquisition and acquisition precedes adaptation. In a similar fashion, selection of firms precedes transfer of technology and transfer precedes implementation. However, the selection of firms may precede identification of technology and technology transfer and implementation involves further adaptation. Also there are relationships of circular causation from 'later' phases, to 'earlier phases' (feedback) and from earlier to later phases, and activities in different phases can – and often should – be undertaken simultaneously. Therefore the scheme should primarily be seen as an analytical device, rather than a full-blown theoretical model.

R&D is only one of the aspects of more complex models of technological change and innovation (Malecki, 1991: 114–17). This chapter examines the innovation process from the perspective of the research institution. We do not study the determinants of innovative behaviour by organization or of their adoption decisions. We only examine how the R&D institution develops technology and tries to transfer it to industrial organizations.

IDENTIFICATION AND SELECTION OF TECHNOLOGY

The two main concepts in the identification and selection phase are: *assessment of needs* and *appropriateness*. In order for a technology to be adopted by the target group of industrial firms, there has to be a need for it.

These needs, in turn, are based on the needs of the customers of the target group: consumers and other industries (UNIDO, 1991: 167).

If information about needs is a necessary condition for innovation, a technology development institute should assess the needs of industry at an early stage in the technology development process. To assess the needs of larger groups of enterprises, the organization can make use of formal needs assessments or informal needs assessments. The *formal needs assessment* consists of an initiative of the development institute to analyse the market need for a type of technology. A drawback of this approach is that it requires substantial investments in market research by the institute, for this sole purpose. *Informal needs assessment* refers to the assessment of technology needs through regular contacts with the firms of an industry. The industry provides the product market knowledge that is the basis for assessing technology needs. In such an innovation network, a situation can be created in which all actors involved benefit from the network. The quality of an informal needs assessment depends on the frequency and intensity of contacts and the size of the network (Wissema and Euser, 1988: 19–29). A distinct advantage of such assessment efforts is that they also make contributions to several other phases of the technology development process.

Appropriateness refers to the evaluation of effects of technologies within the wider societal context, both in the short run and the long run (Riedijk, 1987: VIII). The chosen technology should be appropriate in terms of local market conditions, local resources, labour supply and quality of workforce, environmental and geographic conditions, cultural features and national objectives and policies (Van Egmond, 1995: 10, 1993: 56; UNIDO, 1991: 167). The chosen technology should be appropriate both from the perspective of the welfare of the people directly involved and socially appropriate from the perspective of collective welfare.

Another aspect frequently mentioned in the context of appropriateness is *technological distance*. This is defined as the technological sensitivity to differences in pertinent social, economic and physical circumstances. Westphal and Evenson (1993: 5–6) link the technological distance to the wider concept of the technological capabilities of a country. The greater the technological distance, the more difficult the transfer of technology becomes (see also Caniëls, 1999; Van der Straaten *et al.*, 1992).

A further variable affecting the appropriateness of a technology is *adaptability*. Adaptability refers to the question of whether the research and development organization has the capabilities to engage in a given technology development process (Mourik *et al.*, 1991). In the process of technology selection, criteria such as financial risks, technical risks, the levels of investment required and the availability of the necessary capabilities and know-how have to be assessed from the perspective of the research and development organization itself.

Figure 12.2 summarizes the relationships between the concepts discussed above. The first step in the selection of technology is the formal or informal identification of needs. In this step a technology is selected that is directly linked to a specific project. This project is linked with the needs of an industry.[3] In the second phase, the selection process focuses on the most appropriate techniques within a wider technological framework.[4] The concept of appropriateness tries to cover all the above-mentioned aspects: social, economic and physical appropriateness, technical distance and adaptability by the research and development organization. As mentioned, the appropriateness refers to the desirability of the technology for solving certain problems and its suitability to physical, social, economic and technical aspects of the industrial environment. Adaptability refers to the time required, and the resources and capabilities needed for the acquisition, adaptation, diffusion and implementation of the technology as compared with the capabilities (financial, knowledge, equipment) of the R&D organization.

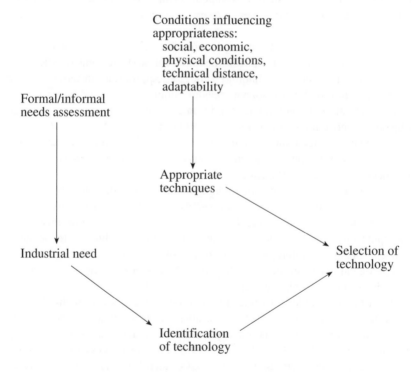

Figure 12.2   Identification and selection of techniques

ACQUISITION OF TECHNOLOGY

Technology development as analysed in this chapter involves the adaptation of already existing technologies. This implies that the technology needs to be acquired before the adaptive activities of the R&D organization can commence. The technology will normally be found on the international technology market, a market characterized by extreme imperfectness and a weak and dependent position of developing countries (Van Egmond, 1993: 86).[5]

The cost of technology depends on the manner and the package in which it is transferred. There are two kinds of costs: (UNCTAD, 1972: 24–7): *direct costs* associated with the purchase, development and use of a technology and *indirect* hidden costs associated with restrictions on the use of the technology. Five categories of *technology flow* can be distinguished: free flow of technology, flows associated with the purchase of products, sponsored flows, flows embedded in commercial contracts and flows through explicit technology acquisition contracts (Van Egmond, 1993: 81–4).

Central to the choice between flow mechanisms is the concept of *unpacking*. Unpacking involves the knocking-down of a technology into its components, and the separate purchase of every component, if possible from different suppliers (Van Egmond, 1995: 20). The R&D organization will have a stronger bargaining position if it can unpack a technology (UNCTAD, 1978: 11). It has more choice with regard to the channel through which the technology will be acquired (Van Egmond, 1993: 104–14). An unpacked technology can be acquired through simple direct transactions, with free price-setting. Other advantages of the unpacking strategy are the increase of opportunities to build up technological capabilities, more control over the technology transfer, and the decrease of technological dependency.

Unpacking is not a simple strategy. The degree of unpacking in technology acquisition depends on the unpacking capabilities of the R&D institute and the unpackability of the technology involved. *Unpacking capabilities* involve the capability to understand, divide and combine the technology. Furthermore, an unpacking strategy requires sufficient knowledge of the technology market to source the different elements from suppliers, and the ability to pick the transfer mechanism that is most advantageous, based upon (socioeconomic and financial) criteria of interest (UNCTAD, 1978: 33).

Unpackability depends not only on the organization's capabilities but on the *unpacking possibilities* of the technology. The unpackability of a technology is determined by a set of characteristics including age, embodiedness of technology, accessibility, freedom of transfer and the extent to which technology has been studied. The international technology market does not always allow for the unpacking of a technology. Especially with new technologies, or technologies that concern core elements of the suppliers' industrial sector, it may be impossible to use an unpacking strategy (Van Egmond, 1995: 20). Old, widely studied, publicly available technologies, not embodied in expert knowledge are most suitable for an unpacking strategy.

The direct outcomes of the technology acquisition process include: the costs of a technology, the type of technology transfer deal and the type of flow channel used. The most favourable outcome should result in low direct and hidden costs, and direct technology transfer transactions without conditions attached, through public or sponsored channels. The relevant relationships are summarized in Figure 12.3.

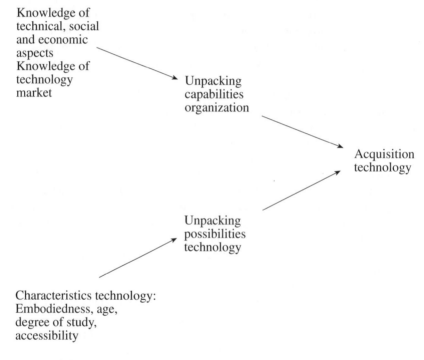

Figure 12.3   Acquisition of technology

ADAPTATION

The purpose of adaptation is to make a technology more appropriate to local conditions. The adaptation phase is an extremely important phase in the transfer of technology to developing economies (Van Straaten *et al.*, 1992; Dar, 1990: 137). Many innovations fail due to inadequate attention to differences in the socioeconomic and physical conditions in the originating and target environments.

The degree of care in selecting appropriate technologies in the selection and acquisition phases affects the degrees of adaptation required. The more effort that is put into the selection of an appropriate technology, the less effort will be needed in the adaptation phase. But even very carefully selected and acquired technologies will never be appropriate in every respect. They are always in need of further adaptation.

A technology is developed in a specific society, under specific conditions and for specific goals. The technology must be redesigned when the circumstances alter, which normally is the case with international technology transfer. The basic goal of the adaptation process is to compensate for the differences between environmental conditions before and after the technology transfer. Therefore, the adaptation process depends on the *characteristics of the origination environment* of the technology and the *characteristics of the target environment.*

In the adaptation phase, the participating technical staff is the main input. However, staff members cannot operate without non-technical capabilities within the team. Market knowledge, process control knowledge and knowledge of the social and economic implications of the technology are also essential for successful adaptation of technology (Mourik *et al.*, 1991: 111). Therefore the *capabilities of the adaptation team* and its external partners are of considerable importance. First, they provide the knowledge for the identification of the target and originating environmental conditions.[6] Second, they provide the knowledge needed for implementation of the adaptations.[7]

Figure 12.4 represents this phase in the technology development process. This figure includes three variables: the characteristics of the target environment, appropriateness of the acquired technology to the target environment[8] and the capabilities of the adaptation team and the external parties involved in the adaptation process.

SELECTION OF FIRMS

The interest of the R&D institute lies in successful transfers to firms of technologies developed at the institute. Therefore, it should select firms from the perspective of achieving the highest possible success rate in the transfer of the adapted technology. The selection process also involves the process of getting firms interested in an innovation and persuading some of them to consider adopting it.

Pack (1987) emphasizes that the successful functioning of a technology within a firm depends on the firm's ability to incorporate the technology in its

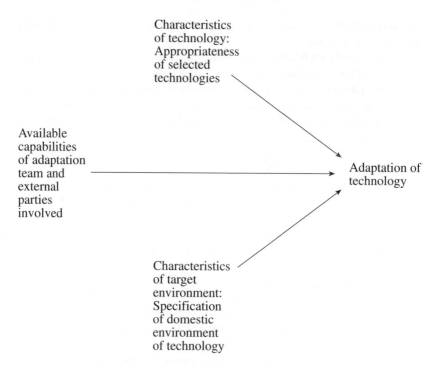

Figure 12.4   Adaptation

organization. The selection of firms should thus depend on the R&D institution's assessments of the technological, organizational, information processing, managerial and educational capabilities necessary to incorporate a new technology into the organization (see also Laseur, 1989, 1991).

Most industrial firms do not make innovation decisions easily. Firms need to be supported in making their innovation decisions. In a model of innovation decisions, Rogers (1983: 163–72) identifies two phases which determine the innovation decisions of firms: the *knowledge phase* and the *persuasion phase*. In the knowledge phase, a decision making unit (DMU) is exposed to the existence of the innovation and gains some understanding of how it functions. In the persuasion phase, the DMU develops a favourable or unfavourable attitude towards the innovation, based upon the information available to it. The acquisition of knowledge in the knowledge phase is influenced by the characteristics of the firms in question. Decision making in the persuasion phase is influenced by perceived characteristics of the innovation.

To influence these processes, various *communication instruments* can be used (Wissema and Euser, 1988: 75). In the knowledge phase, the communication channels should focus on characteristics of the DMU, its innovativeness and its communication behaviour. During the persuasion phase the DMU's perceptions of the characteristics of the innovation can be influenced in order to create more positive attitudes towards the innovation. Communication instruments include informal communication with opinion leaders in networks and the use of change agents (Rogers, 1983: 318).

The R&D institute can focus specifically on innovative firms, which are prone to adopt an innovation at an early stage. In the persuasion phase, the R&D institute can make use of financial and non-financial incentives and it can approach gatekeepers. Gatekeepers are key figures within a firm, who have frequent (internal and external) informal contacts, are interested in new developments and are recognized as such by other members of the organization. They can serve as a bridge between the R&D institute and the firm for the diffusion of knowledge. In general, the more effort that is invested in supporting firms in their innovation decisions, the greater the number of firms available for selection.

Factors affecting the success of technology transfer include the relative importance of hardware, human skills and information, the possibilities of substitution between them, the organizational requirements of the technology and the nature of co-operation between transferee and transferor. The better the match between the capabilities of the selected firm and the requirements of the technology, the greater the chances of successful transfer in the next phase. Of course, the match also depends on the competence and care with which the technology selection process of phase 1 has been performed.

The submodel for the firm selection phase is presented in Figure 12.5. It combines the actual selection of firms for technology transfer with the heightening of innovation awareness of firms, and persuading firms of the advantages of innovation.[9] On the left-hand side of the figure, one sees instruments that heighten firms' awareness of the possibilities of innovation and get them interested in an innovation. The instruments include communication methods, networking and the use of change agents. A distinction is made between general instruments, which draw the attention of firms to the need for innovation and the potential role of the research and development institute, and specific communication instruments tailored to the characteristics of the innovation and the characteristics of the firms in the target group.

In the middle of the figure, one finds instruments of persuasion, such as incentives for firms and approaching gatekeepers. To persuade the interested firms to engage in innovation, the R&D organization should play an active role. Again a distinction is made between general instruments and specific instruments. Specific instruments aim at persuading or convincing one or more promising firms to adopt the technology.

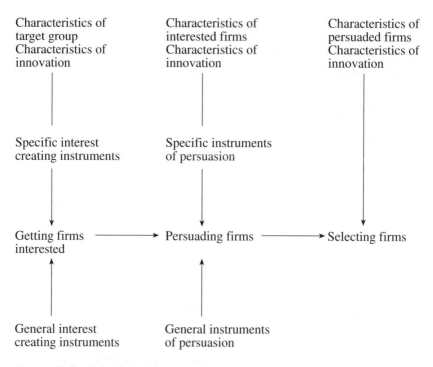

Figure 12.5   Selection of firms

On the right-hand side of the figure, one finds the actual selection of firms to which a technology will be transferred. The aim of the selection process is to select the firms offering the greatest chances of success in the diffusion of the new technologies. The selection decision depends on assessments of the capabilities of the interested firms in relation to the characteristics of the innovations. A specific innovation will require specific capabilities within its direct environment. Firms that already have many of the required capabilities will need less capability building for successful innovation. Consequently, these firms will offer better opportunities for a successful transfer of the innovation in question.

TECHNOLOGY AND KNOWLEDGE TRANSFER

During the technology transfer phase, the technology must be transferred to the selected firms, who have decided to adopt it. The transfer of hardware consists of a simple transaction of machinery and goods. Written information (infoware) needs time to be understood, but in itself it is easy to transfer.

Special attention must be paid to the transfer of knowledge (humanware) via training, instruction, learning and education. The transfer of human knowledge and learning involves longer learning periods, and is essential to the functioning of the technology (Laseur, 1989: 82). The difference between existing knowledge capabilities and the knowledge requirements of the technology, determines the required time and effort for the transfer process.

A full model of technology transfer should include all aspects of technology. However, the transfer of knowledge requires most time and effort. Therefore, Figure 12.6 represents the knowledge transfer aspects of

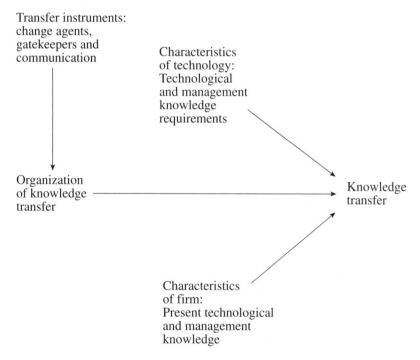

Figure 12.6   Technology and knowledge transfer

technology transfer. Two aspects are important in this model: the knowledge gap and the organization of the knowledge transfer. The knowledge gap is determined by discrepancies between the knowledge required for the innovation, and the existing knowledge within the firm. A small knowledge gap simplifies the transfer process. The organization of the transfer refers to the instruments used: communication instruments, change agents and gatekeepers.

IMPLEMENTATION AND DIFFUSION

In the implementation phase, special attention must be paid to problems arising during the implementation of the innovation and its diffusion to managers, engineers and production workers within the organization. In this phase the tacit knowledge necessary to make a technology function in a given environment has to have a chance to develop.

Change agents may play a positive role in this phase. The knowledge and technology transferred has to be effectively diffused throughout the organization and built into a functional system. During the implementation of an innovation, further adaptation or re-invention may be necessary. Rogers uses the term re-invention to describe the phenomenon that an innovation has to undergo during changes in design in the introduction phase (Rogers, 1983: 16). The more flawed the process of adaptation, the greater the need for re-invention. The process of re-invention needs support from outside, since it is not likely that firms will have sufficient knowledge and experience concerning design activities (Dar, 1990: 140).

A successful implementation of an innovation has the following characteristics: the knowledge concerning the innovation should be diffused to all people involved, the innovation should be operative, and the expectations of both the firm and the R&D institute should be realized. The stronger the support of the R&D institute for the introduction of a new technology, the greater the chance of successful implementation.

THE RESEARCH AND DEVELOPMENT ENVIRONMENT

R&D in Tanzania is mainly conducted within government organizations. Ever since the Arusha declaration in 1967, the Tanzanian government has emphasized the need for an increasing share of manufacturing in national income. A weak technological research and development base was seen as one of the reasons for slow growth of the manufacturing sector (Kahama, 1982: 8). To tackle this problem, the government aimed at creating 'centres of excellence' in research development. However, government spending on R&D is modest. Since 1986, the share of R&D in expenditures has been declining, though policy statements called for increased efforts. In 1988/9, the share of R&D expenditures in total expenditures was 1 per cent of government expenditures, against 1.1 per cent in 1978 (Mlawa and Sheya, 1990: Table 3.4).

As a result, R&D institutes did not receive sufficient funding for their activities and many institutes have had to scale down their activities. Usually, budgets were sufficient only for operational expenses such as wages. Hardly any funding was available for the R&D activities themselves. Some institutes succeeded in getting some form of external support or generated funds by offering consultancy, training and technical services to enterprises. Usually, the income thus generated is modest (Mlawa and Sheya, 1990: 14).[10]

The Tanzania Industrial Research and Development Organization (TIRDO) started its operations on 1 April, 1979. The basic functions of the organization were to carry out applied research, to provide technical services to industry and to manage a system of documentation and information designed to enhance industrial production. With funding from the UNDP, the EEC and the World Bank laboratories and facilities were created between 1980 and 1990. TIRDO has three departments which provide the services of the organization and execute the R&D projects:

- The industrial technology department. The main tasks of the department are the analysis of chemical samples, chemical engineering, food technology, processing activities and cleaner production consultancy.
- The engineering department. Its main tasks are mechanical engineering in projects, mechanical engineering services, electrical instrumentation repair and energy services.
- The information department. Its tasks are providing internal library services, information services to industry, publication of TIRDO documents and the execution of extension services.

The aim of TIRDO is to promote the manufacturing of industrial goods and to stimulate the use of local resources. Potential clients include both small- and medium-scale and large-scale enterprises. According to its statutes, TIRDO's activities include: the training of technical personnel, development and adaptation of technologies, servicing domestic industries, monitoring technological developments, co-ordinating the execution of R&D and the promotion of new technologies. Due to insufficient resources, and an overlap in goals with other organizations in Tanzania, TIRDO's activities are more limited in practice. They focus on (TIRDO, 1993b: 2):

- Consultancy studies for industry. The carrying out of feasibility studies for its own and other products to analyse economic viability of new products or processes.
- Execution of technical (R&D) projects. The execution of technical development projects and showing the technical viability of the adapted processes or products.
- Information supply to industry. Supplying specific technical information to industry.
- Technical services for industry. Offering analytical service, repair and

maintenance of instruments and equipment (electronic and mechanical), welding services, material testing services and energy auditing.

The budget of TIRDO comes from: treasury funding, project capital grants, payments for services to entrepreneurs and other income from rents and sales of products. The growth of the budget has not always been sufficient to compensate for annual inflation. Especially in the first few years of operation, and at the beginning of the 1990s, the growth of nominal budgets did not keep up with inflation. Payments for services in total TIRDO income has increased from 35 per cent in 1989 to 60 per cent in 1994. In 1995 TIRDO employed 128 staff members, of which 26 were university graduates.

Field Research

Between 1979 and 1996, 25 technology development projects were executed by TIRDO (Bongenaar, 1997: Appendix C). Using the summarized analytical framework, 12 of these projects were examined in this study. The first author of this paper spent eight months at TIRDO. Two projects – national dyes and caustic soda – were investigated in great detail. Research methods included repeated open interviews with project officers and document research. Another ten projects were examined with the help of a standardized questionnaire completed by the project leaders, again supplemented by documentary research.[11] With the exception of three projects (castor oil, satellite receivers and turkey oil), all projects were well documented. We will now discuss the different analytical phases of technology development, making use of the framework.

The Projects

The 12 projects included in this study are:

- Natural Dyes Project: an investigation into the possibilities for the use of natural dyes in Tanzanian industry. The project was executed between 1981 and 1990. The goals for the project were to conduct laboratory tests on procedures and techniques and give small-scale demonstrations on the extraction and use of these natural dyes.
- Caustic Soda Project: a research project focusing on the possibilities of local production of caustic soda by Tanzanian industry. The project was started in 1984 and ended in 1994, when the project was stopped after the creation of a pilot plant. Initially, the project focused on the batch production of caustic soda. Later it focused on continuous production of caustic soda. The goals for the project were to identify the procedures

for the production of caustic soda, to design an appropriate production plant, and to develop and demonstrate domestic commercial production using locally available resources.

- Aluminium Sulphate project: a project on the production of aluminium sulphate for the use in local water purification. The project started in 1988 and ended in 1993. It was shelved due to the lack of interest of the NUWA (the Tanzanian water company), the organization for which the investigation was started. The goals for the project were to identify and adapt processes for the production of aluminium sulphate, and to demonstrate the possibilities of using locally available resources.
- Dehydrated Castor Oil project: investigation of the production of Castor Oil using local castor seeds, for the use in, for example, the textile industry. The project was stopped due to a lack of materials and interest from both entrepreneurs and TIRDO management. Goals for the project were to identify and adapt the process for the production of dehydrated castor oil.
- Activated Carbon project: a research project into the production of activated carbon using local waste materials, used within the food and beverages industries. The project was executed between 1992 and 1994, until it was shelved due to a lack of results from the laboratory investigation. Goals for the project were to identify and adapt the process for the production and to demonstrate the quality of the locally produced activated carbon.
- Pectin project: a project investigating the production of pectin using local waste materials for use by the food manufacturers in Tanzania. The project was executed between 1989 and 1992, and was stopped due to the insufficient quality of the produced pectin and the lack of funding. The goals for the project were to identify and adapt the process for the production of pectin and to demonstrate the quality of the pectin.
- Refractories project: investigation of the production of refractories using local materials. Refractories are widely used in all industries involving heating processes and heating facilities. The project was executed between 1988 and 1993, and was shelved due to the lack of outside funding. The goal for the project was to develop a process using specific available raw materials.
- School Chalk project: a project on the production of chalk using Morogoro Ceramic Ware waste gypsum and precipitated calcium carbonate from the caustic soda pilot plant. The project started in 1990, and was still going on in 1996. Goals for the project are the identification and adaptation of a process for the production, and the demonstration of its technical and financial viability.
- Wood Adhesive project: research into the production of wood adhesives

using cashew nut shells. After initial research was finished, the project was extended with research into effective, locally available and safe preservative against insects and fungal decay for wood products. Research was started in 1989, and was still continuing in 1996. Though there was national and international interest for the project, no diffusion took place to industry. Goals set for the project are the identification and adaptation of a process for the production using cashew nut shells, identification of local and natural available fungicides, and the demonstration of the technical and financial viability of the production of the wood adhesives and fungicides.

- Solar Thermal Systems project: research project of thermal energy for drying (as main purpose). Within the project, the investigators try to combine specific needs of users with specific solar systems available. The project started in 1991, and was still not officially ended in 1996, though no further activities were being undertaken due to a lack of funding and lack of commitment from entrepreneurs. Goals for the project were to design, produce and stimulate the use of local systems of thermal drying.

- Satellite Receiver project: project for the local design of a satellite receiver for TVs. The project was started as a follow-up to a satellite dish project. The project started in 1995, and was still going on in 1996. The goal was to produce simple receivers, producible with the equipment of the organization.

- Turkey Red Oil project: a project on the production of turkey red oil using locally available castor seeds, used within the textile industry to dissolve dyes. The project was shelved due to lack of funding and lack of interest from the target group. Goals for the project were to identify and adapt a process for the production of the oil.

Some of the TIRDO projects explicitly focus on small-scale enterprises (natural dyes project), others explicitly on large enterprises (continuous production of caustic soda). In most cases the technologies involved are rather small-scale, and both small-scale and larger enterprises are targeted. As will be explained below, there is little detailed information on target groups, because this aspect of TIRDO's work has not received sufficient attention.

Technology Identification and Selection

For ten of the 12 projects examined, the initiative is taken by a member of the organization or one of its governing bodies.[12] Industrial firms only play a marginal role in the process of project selection. There are hardly any attempts at systematic *needs assessment*. The identification of a project is most frequently motivated by import-substitution considerations (mentioned in nine out of 12 cases) and the availability of indigenous raw materials (mentioned in ten cases). In four cases, pressure from the management of the institute to produce a 'viable' proposal is mentioned as a motive. In three cases only, is the initiative (partly) the result of contacts with (representatives of) industry.[13]

During the whole selection process entrepreneurs are hardly involved. At best, entrepreneurs are contacted by the investigator for technical information concerning the use of certain goods, materials and techniques within its production processes, both in terms of quality and quantity.

Project proposals are normally written by the principal researchers. They are responsible for the definition of the proposal, and they evaluate the technology and project as well. The quality of the proposals differs considerably due to the lack of standards for the writing up of projects. In some cases, the principal researcher got other members of the organization involved, such as members of the information department, but this is not the rule.

All proposals give a short description of the technology involved, and occasionally discuss alternative technologies. The adaptability of the technologies by TIRDO (is TIRDO able to conduct the research?) is normally investigated. Based upon the complexity and the type of technology and the capabilities of the organization, the time, equipment and funding needed to master and adapt the technology are estimated. All proposals specify the tasks to be executed within the project. Normally only technical tasks concerning development, production and testing are included.

Appropriateness is hardly ever systematically investigated. Based on characteristics of the technology, the expected effects are assessed by the principal researcher. It is rare for an economist, an entrepreneur or a social group from outside TIRDO to be involved in the assessment of appropriateness. Normally, only positive effects are mentioned; negative effects are simply ignored. Aspects of government policies and economic criteria such as import substitution, foreign exchange earnings and tax earnings, are regularly considered. For some projects, socioeconomic aspects such as income distribution and job opportunities are mentioned in the evaluation. Financial implications, for example the earning and investments for future entrepreneurs, are sometimes evaluated.

If a pilot plant is within the scope of a project, a division is made within the proposal (in the older projects the pilot plant is specified as a separate project). Since TIRDO does not have the budget to develop technologies itself, budgets are specified in terms of donor contributions and TIRDO contributions (with TIRDO providing the staff for a project). After the approval of the projects by the council of TIRDO, the proposals are used to secure funding from donor agencies. The projects only start on a full scale after funds have been made available; laboratory research normally starts earlier.

ACQUISITION OF TECHNOLOGY

The technologies involved in the projects have some typical *characteristics*. The technologies are mostly old, always over five years of age, already studied world wide, and never of an advanced nature. In two cases, the technology was even not innovative for Tanzania. In the case of the caustic soda project, some components of the technology were found in the domestic economy. But this is an exception. In all other cases, acquisition of foreign technology is the rule. Normally, the aim of the project is process innovation. The technologies are mostly embodied in knowledge; knowledge concerning the process involved, its relation with the available materials and the desired output. Information needed for the project focuses on the process description, and information on the control of the process. Equipment consists of relatively simple locally available or locally producible equipment. In the acquisition phase, it is primarily technical staff who are involved.

Table 12.1 summarizes the technology transfer mechanism used in the acquisition phase. Two important sources of knowledge are TIRDO's information department and public libraries. Foreign and domestic R&D institutes are also regularly used for the acquisition of knowledge and information, through training and documentation. The involvement of foreign or local companies is relatively low. When it occurs it is of a non-commercial nature.[14] Regarding the *technology flow mechanism*, free flow is by far the most important.

Table 12.1   Suppliers of technology and flow mechanisms for transfer

Technology supplier	Times used	Flow mechanism	Relative importance
Information department	9	Free flow	71%
Libraries	6	Sponsored flow	14%
Foreign companies	1	Flow accompanied with products	10%
Local companies	2	Commercial technology acquisition	4%
Foreign R&D institutes	3		
Local R&D institutes	2		
Other	1		

Notes:
$n = 12$;
Importance of each flow mechanism measured on scale 1–5;
Relative importance based on average scores per mechanism.

Usually, the organization does not bargain with technology suppliers concerning the conditions for technology transfer, except in the case of acquisition of equipment. Costs for the acquisition of the technology usually seem to be low.[15] Twice, larger expenditures were made for the setting up of pilot plants. A relatively small part of total project costs for the organization are spent during acquisition. Costs identified include expenditures on travel, reproduction, and in some cases on equipment. Equipment, only acquired if funding is available, is mostly acquired locally. TIRDO tries to use or adapt local designs for its specific purposes. Only complex equipment, such as measuring equipment, valves and motors, is purchased from foreign suppliers. The project team approaches several suppliers, and selects on the basis of both technical and price specifications provided by prospective suppliers.

Concluding, it seems that the organization acquires technology effectively, using an unpacking strategy. The technologies are acquired from different sources and mostly through free-flow channels. The technologies involved are suitable for this approach: old, well studied and embodied in knowledge and information. The organization has the capabilities to unpack the technology. Costs of this phase are relatively low, compared to total project costs. Bargaining activities are involved in the acquisition of equipment.

Adaptation

TIRDO's main interest in new technologies lies within this phase. The purpose of the adaptation phase, is to make a technology appropriate for its environment. TIRDO's primary aim in this phase is the adaptation of a technology to locally available raw materials. This has always been the main goal for projects executed by the chemical department. Aspects of the technological environment (available knowledge and equipment), the social environment (special social benefit groups) and the economic environment (financial implications), are sometimes mentioned as secondary goals of the adaptation process. The adaptive criteria tend to be related to physical aspects of the technology and reflect the capabilities and areas of interest of the project team. These interests are chiefly technical in nature.

Most staff involved in the adaptation phase come from within the organization. Besides the project team other departments are sometimes involved, especially during the pilot plant stage. The first part of the research, the laboratory investigation, is normally executed by the project team itself. Eighty per cent of the involved staff are chemical and mechanical engineers. Within the organization non-technical involvement in the adaptive work is very low. In two-thirds of the cases, actors from the environment (companies and other institutes) are involved in the work. This contribution is normally limited to the testing of materials. Only R&D institutes co-operate in the execution of the work itself.

Table 12.2   Success of the adaptation process

Project	Result met expectations		Shelved	Budget overrun	Time overrun
	Technical	Non-technical			
Activated carbon	6	3	Yes	No	No
Aluminium sulphate	5	3	Yes	No	No
Castor oil	5	1	Yes	No	No
Caustic soda	8	4	No	Yes	Yes
Natural dyes	6	2	No	No	Yes
Pectin	4	2	Yes	No	Yes
Refractories	5	3	Yes	No	No
School chalk	7	4	No	Yes	Yes
Solar systems	6	4	Yes	No	Yes
Turkey red oil	6	1	Yes	No	No
Wood adhesives	9	5	No	No	No
Average	6.1	2.9			

Note: Project results meeting technical and non-technical expectations both scaled from 1–10, $n = 11$. In the case of shelved projects, the question whether results met expectations referred to the partial results. See Appendix A, variable IV for details.

The success of an adaptation is measured in terms of the extent to which the output of the project meets the expectations of the involved staff. We distinguish technical and non-technical expectations. Table 12.2 presents the scores on these items for the different projects. Whether a project has been shelved or whether its goals have been realized within the projected time and budget, is also indicated.

As indicated in Table 12.2, the realized technical result often meets prior expectations. Insuperable technical problems hardly ever occur, except during pilot plant construction. However, consideration of non-technical factors makes the success of a project less clear-cut. Many researchers expect that there will be interest for the technology developed on the part of industrial enterprises and donors (industries are more interested in profitability, while donors are interested in the direct applicability). In practice, however, projects are often shelved due to lack of interest on the part of donors and industry.

In sum, TIRDO usually executes the adaptations from a narrow technical point of view. From this technical viewpoint, the participation of staff is sufficient, the selection of aspects for adaptations is in line with the staff's capabilities and the results are good. However, due to this one-sided input of capabilities, the technologies are not sufficiently adapted in a broader sense. Financial, economic and social aspects are not included in this phase, and the technologies are not appropriate for domestic industry.

Selection of Firms

This paragraph focuses on one of the activities most underrated by TIRDO's management: the 'selling' of a technology to local industry. Within the R&D organization there is still widespread belief that sooner or later adequate technologies should and will sell themselves.

Only a few projects reach the phase where TIRDO searches for entrepreneurs interested in adopting the innovation. Most projects are shelved before this phase is reached. Only in five projects have diffusion activities actually taken place (natural dyes, caustic soda, school chalk, wood adhesives and solar systems). In three other projects (aluminium sulphate, pectin and refractories) some promotional activities have taken place during an initial stage of the project.

We divide the selection activities into activities to interest entrepreneurs in an innovation and activities to persuade entrepreneurs to adopt the innovation. Table 12.3 summarizes the different methods used. To create interest in the projects, TIRDO uses a combination of general and selective communication instruments. Selective communication instruments are preferred by the

Table 12.3   Interest creating activities and instruments for persuasion

(a) Methods for initial interest		(b) Methods for persuasion	
Method	Times used	Method	Times used
Publication	2	Free consultancy	2
Radio & TV	2	Technology ownership	1
Trade fairs	3	Support in loan securing	2
Workshops	3	Financial stimuli	
Direct communication through extension officer	5	Private guidance	2
Direct mailing	3	Tailor-made (re)design	4
Other	2	Result insurance	2
		Pilot plant implementation	2

Note: $n = 8$.

organization. The target group of firms is based upon the expected use of certain goods within their current production processes.[16] For two projects, the school chalk and the wood adhesives project, a market survey has been performed to analyse a target group for the innovation.

Some activities are undertaken to persuade the enterprises to accept an innovation, by reducing entrepreneurs' uncertainties. The tailor-made design of production systems based upon the specific needs of the entrepreneurs is mentioned in four projects. One method, though not specifically mentioned, is subsidizing the use of a technology. The R&D organization does not try to recover the total development costs of a technology, only charging direct costs and (usually) some fixed fee for development costs.

The number of interested firms differs considerably across the projects. The number of instruments TIRDO uses to interest and persuade also differs from project to project, and a relation between the instruments used and number of firms expressing interest seems evident. As indicated, the total activities for technology diffusion are modest. The organization does not put enough effort into interesting and motivating entrepreneurs. So far, no firms have been persuaded to adopt an innovation. One may conclude that TIRDO's execution of the selection phase is not very effective.

Transfer and Implementation

In the survey study, the transfer and implementation phases have not been formally included, as no project had progressed up to the stage that the innovation was actually being transferred to firms in the target group. For the two case studies investigated in more detail, natural dyes and caustic soda, some remarks regarding transfer and implementation were made by persons involved. These remarks focus on the plans that the R&D organization had formulated for the transfer of the innovations. However, at the time of writing no transfer had actually been realized.

For example, in the case of the caustic soda project the TIRDO staff did indicate what the implications of technology transfer would be. They described the equipment and knowledge prerequisites for transfer in general terms. (for example '... are expected to have "feeling for chemicals".'). There was interest on the part of firms, a pilot plant was in operation and one entrepreneur seemed to be willing to adopt the technology. However, the worsening economic climate and decreasing prospects of protection of domestic industry, prevented the entrepreneur from following up on his interest.

A few remarks are in order concerning two instruments which are of importance for the diffusion of technology in the last three phases of technology development projects: the use of change agents and making use of contacts within industrial networks. Change agents are normally not used in TIRDO projects. Only in one case, the School chalk project, could a kind of change agent be identified: one member of the project team focused on supporting all entrepreneurs with the different aspects of the innovation decision.[17]

Contacts with firms and individuals within a well-developed industrial network can contribute positively to the selection of a technology for development and the subsequent success in the diffusion of the innovation.[18] The involvement of networks in TIRDO's projects turns out to be low. Direct influence of domestic industry on project content and on activities of project teams is lacking. Though there are some contacts with industrial firms in most of the projects investigated, the scope of these contacts is limited.

General Characteristics of the Technology Development Process

As there is not a single instance of transfer of technology to enterprises, it is not possible to measure the overall effectiveness of the transfer and implementation phases in terms of successful adoptions. Table 12.4 summarizes five important variables characterizing the four evaluated phases of the technology development process: (I) assessment of existing needs and (II) appropriateness in the technology identification and selection phase; (III) care exercised in acquisition; (IV) success in adaptation; and (V) use of diffusion instruments in the firm selection phase. Table 12.4 also presents a rough proxy variable for project success (VI) based on the interest expressed by entrepreneurs in an innovation and the stage that the negotiations concerning the innovation have reached. The variables are based on the survey returns. The scaling of the variables is briefly described in Appendix I and in more detail in Bongenaar (1997). The scaling procedures are rough and should not be given any precise mathematical interpretation. Nevertheless, they provide useful summary indicators of activities in different phases of the technology development process.

Only the acquisition phase has an average score of more than 6. Two variables have very low scores: the assessment of existing needs (I) and the variable relating to the diffusion activities in the firm selection phase (V). This indicates that the main problems in project execution are concentrated within these two phases. Both phases refer to the interactions between the institute and its environment and indicate that this interaction does not take place as often and as intensively, as required.[19]

Inspection of the individual projects indicates that their scores in the different phases tend to be related. 'Good' projects tend to score well on most variables. The school chalk, wood adhesives and solar systems are examples of such projects. The castor oil, activated carbon and refractories projects are

*Table 12.4   Main variables for success of the technology development
process in different phases*

Project	Assess existing needs	Appropriate	Acquisition	Adaptation	Activities for diffusion	Success project
	I	II	III	IV	V	VI
Aluminium sulphate	3	6	8	4	1.5	2
Caustic soda	2.5	6	6	4	10	7
Natural dyes	2	5	7	6	1.5	6
Castor oil	1.5	1.5	5	3	-	1
Activated carbon	3	5	7	5	-	1
Pectin	2	6	6	3	1.5	2
Refractories	3	4	5	4	1	3
School chalk	2	7.5	7	6	8.5	8
Wood adhesives	3.5	7.5	8	7	6	7
Solar systems	4	7.5	7	5	1.5	7
Satellite receivers	1.5	5	8	-	-	1
Turkey red oil	7.5	4	6	4	-	2
Average[a]	3	5.4	6.7	4.5	3.9	3.9

Note: [a] Calculated with respectively $n = 12$, $n = 12$, $n = 12$, $n = 11$, $n = 8$, $n = 12$. The variables are roughly scaled from a negative pole of 1 to a positive pole of 10.

examples of 'bad' projects. This suggests that the inter-phase relationships are also very important. Nevertheless, irrespective of the project, specific phases of the technology development process tend to have much lower scores than the other phases.

CONCLUSIONS

The Research and Development Organization TIRDO is successful to the extent that members of the organization succeed in developing technologies that meet their expectations in a technical sense. Relative success in the technical sphere, however, has not led to the diffusion of the technologies to the target group, as originally intended.

To start with positive findings, both the acquisition and the technical adaptation activities are fairly successful. The acquisition of technology is performed reasonably well by TIRDO. Technologies involved in the technology development processes are normally old, and processes are described in publicly accessible information. The technical staff members involved are well educated in the field of their technical specialization and the information department of the organization is experienced in the search for information on the international market. The technologies acquired are unpackable and the acquisition teams have the capacity to unpack technologies. As for the output of the adaptation phase, in most projects the implemented adaptations functioned according to the expectations of the organization, and the projects were regarded as technically successful. One could well argue that the experience with acquisition and adaptation of technologies in TIRDO has contributed to the building up of technological capabilities within the institute. These technological capabilities are of potential value in future stages of industrial development.

Nevertheless, successful technology development requires more, both in terms of efforts and in terms of outcomes. The selection of projects is usually not based on adequate need assessments of domestic industry. Needs, if indicated in a project, refer to possible uses of the intended output of the technology and are based upon national indicators and policy documents. They are seldom related to specific requests from industrial firms. Initiatives for the identification of technologies tend to be taken by members of the TIRDO staff, rather than by the target group. The organization should take measures to intensify communication, networking activities and linkages with industry and should formulate procedures to translate the needs of industry into viable projects.

The organization hardly evaluates the appropriateness of technologies for the Tanzanian environment. To this end, three main actions should be taken: laying down fixed procedures for the evaluation of projects, involving non-technical staff in the evaluation process and using these evaluation results in management's decision making.

The absence of involvement of non-technical personnel in projects can be noted in several phases of technology development. This results in a one-sided view of technology. In addition to technical expertise, economic, social and communicative expertise is needed in all phases of project execution.

TIRDO makes little use of instruments to interest entrepreneurs and to persuade them to adopt an innovation. The lack of activities in this phase is partly due to the institution's assumption that good technologies should sell themselves. On the basis of the analysis in this chapter, the organization should focus on intensifying diffusion activities both in terms of quantity and quality. Finally, the organization should try to learn from past experiences, and to use systematic evaluations of completed projects to improve the execution of future projects.

One possible explanation for the observed lack of success in technology transfer is a general lack of innovativeness of Tanzanian industrial enterprises, struggling to survive in a difficult environment. During the period studied, many parastatals were being privatized, industrial production was stagnating and there were serious financial constraints which hampered innovativeness. Small scale enterprises, in particular, lacked the financial and human resources to innovate. The innovativeness of enterprises was not the focus of this investigation, though it is obviously a relevant factor. However, the research reported on in this chapter strongly indicates that lack of success in technology diffusion is also related to the lack of sufficient activities to align TIRDO's activities to the expectations and needs of domestic industrial organizations.

Research and development institutes should regard the marketing of the technologies as an essential element of research and development work. Marketing activities should commence before a project is initiated, and should continue to influence the work during the complete span of a project. Technologies should not be regarded as successful on their own merits, but should be judged by the extent to which they succeed in serving even a technologically conservative industry's needs and expectations. Therefore, the R&D organization should step up its efforts to extend its industrial network. Weakly developed industrial networks and insufficient linkages between research institutes and domestic industry are factors with an overall negative influence on different aspects of the innovation process (c.f. Meeus and Oerlemans, 1993). In the execution of projects, the organization should seek co-operation with domestic industry and with other (local) technical and non-technical institutes.

Most of these recommendations will not necessarily require supplementary funding. More important are changes in mentality of management and staff. Instead of tending to regard domestic industry as backward and uninterested in (local) technologies, one should investigate why firms failed to adopt the technologies developed within the organization.

Several of the issues and problems analysed in this chapter are of wider relevance for technology development in research and development institutes in developing economies. Though our limited data do not allow for strong inferences, our results are consistent with findings in the literature. The importance of industrial networks, needs assessments, appropriateness of technologies and marketing are mentioned in many studies, as essential to the successful diffusion of innovations. Giving higher priorities to these aspects of technology development could lead to a more efficient and effective use of resources invested in the research and development sector.

NOTES

1. This chapter is based on the M.Sc. thesis of B. Bongenaar, 'Analysing technology development', Eindhoven, March 1997. This thesis was based on eight months of fieldwork at TIRDO. We thank TIRDO and its former director Dr G. Njau for the opportunity to execute this research project. We should like to note the impressive degree of openness on

the part of the staff of TIRDO, to outside examination of their projects. The aim of this chapter is not to offer easy criticism by uninvolved outsiders, but to contribute to the understanding of the factors, which may contribute to or hamper the success of technology development. This chapter provides a theoretical elaboration of an earlier version to be published in Szirmai and Lapperre (eds), *The Industrial Experience of Tanzania*, MacMillan, 2000. We thank Leon Oerlemans and Henny Romijn for useful comments.

2. Invention is the output and the process by which a new idea is discovered or created. An innovation is an idea or object perceived as new by a group (Rogers, 1983).
3. At this stage the selection of the project is the main issue. Thus, the caustic soda project at TIRDO aims at producing caustic soda. The specific way of producing this commodity is secondary.
4. In Figure 12.2 we do not make a precise distinction between selection of technology and selection of techniques, in order not to complicate the figure too much. The reason for this is that in the subsequent steps of the analysis the acquisition and transfer of the techniques involves not only the techniques themselves, but the know-how and understanding required to operate them (see also note 3 above).
5. TIRDO projects do not involve the acquisition of domestic technologies.
6. This also is one of the main reasons for the need for co-operation of the target group and non-technical members in the adaptation phase.
7. By means of changing elements of the technology or by appending new elements.
8. Originally, the model included the specification of the original environment of the technology as a variable. However, often no specific environment of origin could be identified and sometimes different parts of a technology had different origins. Therefore the final model for this phase uses the appropriateness to characterize the technology, rather than its environment of origin.
9. It is clear that creating interest and persuading firms overlaps with the first phase of identification and selection of technology, in which the needs of the target group are identified. Although raising interest /and awareness is discussed here in the context of the selection phase, this activity can be undertaken throughout the whole technology development cycle. It is even preferable to undertake these activities at early stages in the cycle.
10. Income from services in the R&D sector estimated at 15 per cent of total income, external assistance at 30 per cent of total income.
11. For more detailed discussion of the technical aspects of the projects, their output and the research findings, see Bongenaar (1997).
12. Members were obliged to come forward with project proposals.
13. Contacts occur resulting from contract work and extension visits.
14. No costs being charged for acquisition, or knowledge being provided without profit.
15. Specific cost calculations for acquisition could hardly be made due to a lack of data.
16. For example, for caustic soda production, TIRDO expected the producers of soap to use the technology in their production process; for wood adhesives, the producers of particle board.
17. A Dutch student temporarily involved in the project.
18. Other positive effects, in acquisition and adaptation of the technology can be expected as well.
19. This notion also arose when discussing the organization and the Tanzanian R&D sector. It therefore is likely that this problem is general for the other R&D institutes as well.

REFERENCES

Bongenaar, B. (1997), 'Analysing technology development, part I: evaluating the role of the Tanzania research and development organization', Eindhoven, M.Sc. Thesis, Technology and Development Studies, Eindhoven University of Technology.

Caniëls, M. (1999), 'Regional growth differentials', Ph.D. Thesis, University of Maastricht.

Dar, U. (1990), 'Management of technological change – an overview', UNIDO, *Management of Technological Change: Issues and Case Studies from India*, UNIDO, chapter XIV.

Egmond-de Wilde de Ligny, E.L.C van (1993), 'International technology transfer to developing countries', Lecture notes no. 1649, Technische Universiteit Eindhoven, Eindhoven.

Egmond-de Wilde de Ligny, E.L.C van (1995), 'International technology transfer to developing countries', Summary of ITT lectures 1994–1995, ITDS/EUT, Eindhoven.

Kahama, C.G. (1982), 'Tanzania professional centre 2nd inter professional conference on priorities in national development: executive summary', University of Tanzania, Dar-Es-Salaam.

Laseur, W.J.J. (1989), *Technologie Investeren overzee*, Groningen, Meppel.

Laseur, W.J.J. (1991), *Managing Technology Transfer*, The Hague: Thieme.

Malecki, E.J. (1991), *Technology and Economic Development – The Dynamics of Local, Regional and National Change*, Harlow: Longman Science & Technical.

Meeus, M.T.H. and L.A.G. Oerlemans (1993), 'Economic network research: a methodological state of the art', in P. Beije, J. Groenewegen and O. Nuys (eds), *Networking in Dutch industries*, Leuven: Garant.

Mlawa, H.M. and M.S. Sheya (1990), 'Profiles of R&D institutions in Tanzania – managing the interface amongst scientific and technological research, public policy and productive structures', Secretariat of the future actions committee of management of science and technology for development (MANSCI).

Mourik, C. van, E.M. van der Ouderaa and C.G. Hage (1991), *Management van Research en Development*, Deventer: Kluwer.

ND I, 'Natural dyes project file I', collection of approximately 100 notes, reports and documents, TIRDO, July 1981–May 1984.

ND II, 'Natural dyes project file II', collection of approximately 70 notes, reports and documents, TIRDO, May 1984–November 1990.

Pack, H. (1987), *Productivity, Technology and Industrial Development*, Washington, DC: World Bank.

Riedijk, W. (ed.) (1987), *Appropriate technology for developing countries*, Delft: Delft University Press.

Rogers, E.M. (1983), *Diffusion of Innovations*, Third edition, New York: The Free Press.

Straaten J. van der, *et al.* (1992), *Technology Transfer and Development – A Contribution to Policy Making*, Amsterdam: Tool.

TIRDO (1989), *Ten Years of the Tanzania Industrial Research and Development Organization (TIRDO) 1979–1989*, TIRDO.

TIRDO (1993), *Operational Guidelines and Procedures for the Extension Services – Manual*, TIRDO.

TIRDO (1993b), *Draft TIRDO Five-year Plan 1993/94–1997/98*, TIRDO.

TPC (1992), *Meetings of the Technical Programme Committee*, vol 1–22, TIRDO.

United Nations Conference on Trade and Development (UNCTAD) (1972), *Guidelines for the Study of Transfer of Technology to Developing Countries*, New York: United Nations.

United Nations Conference on Trade and Development (UNCTAD) (1978), *Handbook on the Acquisition of Technology by Developing Countries*, New York: United Nations.

UNIDO (1991), *Manual for the Preparation of Industrial Feasibility Studies*, Vienna: UNIDO.

Westphal, L.E and R.E. Evenson (1993), 'Technological change and technology strategy', Development Economics seminar, paper no. 93-1/4, The Hague.

Wissema, J.G. and L. Euser (1988), *Samenwerking bij technologische vernieuwing - De nieuwe dimensie van het management van innovatie*, Deventer: Kluwer bedrijfswetenschappen.

APPENDIX A: CONSTRUCTION OF THE VARIABLES

The variables I–VI in Table 12.4 are composite variables. The score of each project is the average of the composite variable scores calculated from the questionnaires completed by the principal project researchers, and a questionnaire completed by the first author, based upon his analysis of the project files. For more details see Bongenaar 1997, appendix B.

I. Assessment of existing needs (scale 1–10)
The composite variable score is the average of scores on three variables, each scaled from 1 to 10.
- Initiative taken by the organization versus initiative taken by industry (Scale 1–10; 1: TIRDO – 10: industry)
- Initiative motivated by expressed needs of firms or motivated from within the organization (Scale 1–10; 1: no needs assessment – TIRDO internal need assessment – government – 10: expressed needs)
- Degree of influence of target group in this phase (scale 1–10; 1 no influence; 10 maximal influence)

II. Appropriateness (scale 1–10)
The composite variable score is the sum of scores for two variables:
- Extensiveness of the investigation of appropriateness, measured in terms of the number of appropriateness criteria mentioned (scale 0–5; number of criteria mentioned divided by 4, maximum number mentioned 20)
- Indicated appropriateness of the technology, measured by average indicated appropriateness of the technology on a maximum number of 20 criteria of appropriateness (scale 1–5, after rescaling of average scores to a 1–5 range)

III. Careful acquisition of technology (scale 1–10)
The composite variable score is the sum of scores for two variables:
- Unpackability: the possibilities of unpacking a technology (scale 1–5; 1: difficult to unpack – 5: easy to unpack).
The unpackability scale scores are the average of the scores on the following three items: age of technology (1: young – 5: old), familiarity of technology (1: hardly studied – 5: widely studied) and accessibility (1: mainly private – 5: mainly public).
- Unpacking capabilities: the capabilities of the project team to unpack a technology reflecting technical capabilities and non-technical capabilities (scale 0–5, after rescaling of scores to a 0–5 range).

IV. Degree of success in adaptation (scale 1-10)

The composite variable score is the average of two variables:

- Project result fulfilled technical expectations (scale 1–10; 1: Did not fulfil expectations – 10: Completely fulfilled expectations). These scores are based upon the scores of eight items, with a scale of 1-4, which are averaged and rescaled to a 1–10 range).
- Project result fulfilled non-technical expectations (scale 1–10, 1: Did not fulfil expectations – 10: Completely fulfilled expectations). The score of this variable is based upon 8 items with a scale of 1-4, averaged and rescaled to 1–10.

V. Use of diffusion instruments (scale 1-10)

The composite variable score is the sum of scores for two variables:

- Use of awareness creating instruments in a project, to create awareness of the technology amongst members of its target group (initial interest) (scale 0–5, number of instruments used divided by maximum number of instruments, rescaled to 0–5)
- Use of persuasion instruments used in a project, to persuade members of the target group to adopt a technology (scale 0–5, number of instruments used divided by maximum number of instruments, rescaled to 0–5)

VI. Success of the project (scale 1-10):

This variable reflects the judgement of the investigator concerning the degree of interest of firms in an innovation (1 no interest expressed by any firm – 10 adoption by at least one firm). The score is in turn based on:

- The number of firms showing some interest in an innovation
- The stage of negotiations reached regarding an adoption decision.

13. Social capital and technological innovation processes in the South

Árni Sverrisson

The purpose of this chapter is to explore the idea of social capital, which is economically useful social connectivity, and its potential for understanding technological innovation in small enterprise clusters or enterprise collectives in the South. The chapter draws on field research carried out by the author over a number of years in different African countries and literature describing other experiences there and elsewhere,[1] under different research contracts, which are gratefully acknowledged.

The concept of social capital provides us with an opportunity to sharpen the focus of earlier findings based on network analysis and clustering concepts (Van Dijk and Rabellotti, eds, 1997). Although social capital is obviously related to modes of networking which in turn often presuppose spatial clustering, the concept of social capital opens interesting avenues for exploring how economic development is shaped by social contexts. More specifically, the concept of social capital, in distinction from more general ideas about networks and clusters, poses issues of how social networks are managed; how connections are accumulated, rationalized, and eventually devalued; how network connections established for other reasons take on economic significance; and how economic connections achieve social significance. The assumption frequently implicit in discussions about networks in clusters, that these are more effective the denser, more intense and more frequently observed they are, is thereby questioned. Perhaps a little less but more focused networking and somewhat sparser but more effective clusters are more successful in terms of local innovation and development?

Technological innovation is a form of entrepreneurship. Much of the discussion which follows is therefore focused on entrepreneurship and innovation as a particular instance of that activity. It follows from Schumpeter's (1934: 66) definition of entrepreneurship, that is, combining existing resources in new ways, people, machines and materials, that social connectivity is important to this process. However, what exactly does this mean for innovation in the South? Some tentative answers are provided in this chapter, with the help of the social capital concept.

The idea of social capital has been popularized by *inter alia* Francis Fukuyama (1996), and was earlier developed by, for example, Burt (1992) and Bourdieu (1984). In the first section, these three different theories of social capital are summarized. In the second section, innovation processes are discussed from the vantage point provided by the concept of social capital. The third section outlines how types of innovation in the South are influenced by different forms of social capital, and in the fourth section, the issues that arise from the earlier discussion are summarized in the form of a preliminary model.

It is important to establish one distinction at the outset, between, on the one hand, economic transactions in general and, on the other hand, the varied interaction specific to innovation processes. There is a large and growing literature on the ways in which different forms of social capital facilitate economic transactions and the organization of economic activities more generally, but there is much less on the effects social capital has on innovation processes, however understood, and this is particularly the case with innovation processes in the South. It is of course possible to pose causal link between general prosperity and innovation, according to which innovation creates prosperity or, alternatively, prosperity creates an economic environment congenial to innovative activity. However, in this chapter more direct mechanisms through which social capital facilitates or hinders innovation will be in focus. Innovation will be understood as the activity of bringing novel technologies into social contexts where they were not before, leading to new products, better quality of old products or lower production costs. It is in other words the diffusion end of the innovation process which is discussed here, with a particular emphasis on small enterprises in the South and the problems they face. Process, product and organizational innovations will be considered, but the emphasis will be on new manufacturing technologies (process) rather than new consumer products or new division of labour, although the three, of course, often go hand in hand in Southern contexts.

As noted by Sabel and Zeitlin (1997) and Pacey (1990) transplantation of technologies rarely happens in the form of uncritical import and implementation. Instead, there is conscious reflection and selection of what is appropriate according to local definitions of the situation. Technologies are, as it were, re-innovated each time they are brought into different social contexts. New ways of organizing maintenance, new applications and new ways of organizing work with these technologies and new competence in operating them under local conditions have to be found to make local innovation based on 'technology transfer' work. The question is: can theories of social capital contribute significantly to a better understanding of this process?

FORMS OF SOCIAL CAPITAL

In this section three different theories of social capital are summarized. Fukuyama poses a form of social capital, which does not belong primarily to individuals, but rather is a characteristic of social collectives and, in his case, entire societies. This concept is best explained by recapitulating Fukuyama's historical hypothesis. Some societies are characterized by a general and spontaneous sociability, which is manifested in a strong civil society and high propensity and low obstacles to co-operating with relative strangers. In other words, trusting strangers is the norm. The paradigmatic case is the United States, at least earlier if not now, where all kinds of voluntary civic and religious organizations were, according to Fukuyama, stronger and more numerous than elsewhere. Japan and Germany are additional examples. Other societies are rather characterized by strong family ties and suspicion of strangers – an extreme case of this is found in Southern Italy where according to Putnam (1993) trust is limited to nuclear families. China is another example, and Chinese communities outside China are also distinguished by the importance of family ties and kin-based organization. Another example is France, where family ties are held to be strong and civil society weak.

From this it follows that the formation and maintenance of large-scale organizations is easier in the USA and Japan than in China or France, or rather these organizations can develop without active state intervention and under private ownership. In contrast, large-scale organizations in China or France, and other countries similarly endowed, can only arise through state initiatives. Large-scale organizations are, in Fukuyama's view of the world, the main vehicles of progress and prosperity, and, therefore, unavoidable. However, when they are state owned they are less effective than when privately owned. Hence, countries with weak civil societies in the sense indicated above, which lack general sociability in contrast to family-based solidarity and trust, will prosper less than the others.

This hypothesis can be criticized on several counts, some of which are too obvious to merit explication. However, what I want to point out is rather the useful part of the argument, namely that prevalent forms of sociability influence economic life, preferred forms of organization and to some extent, therefore, innovation processes. It is of course possible to stand Fukuyama on his head and maintain that countries with strong family ties are more likely to thrive through flexible strategies and small organizations, but I doubt if such an argument would do justice to the historical facts. Rather, if the prevailing conventions of interaction include assumptions that everyone, and not just friends and kin, will keep promises, deliver on contracts, and abstain from taking unfair advantage of each other when they can, this should be helpful, whether the prevailing organizational form is small organizations or large ones (Humprey and Schmitz, 1996).

Interpreting Fukuyama's hypothesis in this way gives us a handle on macro-level circumstances which shape sociability. Societies in which the government's relation to the citizenry are in the form of censorship, restrictions on travel and trade and similar measures, and where isolation of communities from one another because of this is manifest, such societies are not likely to generate spontaneous sociability of the kind that leads to close co-operation among relative strangers. Hence, economic life will in all likelihood be characterized by short-term considerations and localized co-operation, and organization of long-term relationships including credit and major co-operative projects will be correspondingly difficult. At the same time, not every relationship in a country needs to fit the prevailing pattern – islands of trust among relative strangers are created through urbanization, educational experiences and iterative transactions. Once this is accepted it follows that in a country individuals will be unequally endowed with social capital depending on where they are and whom they deal with.

Bourdieu provides us with a concept of social capital, which enables us to systematically study such differences among people and social positions in the endowment of social capital. Based on his studies of French society, he distinguishes between three types of capital, that is economic, cultural or symbolic, and social. I will abstain here from reviewing Bourdieu's entire theoretical structure, and focus on the last type of capital. For Bourdieu, this consists in the social connections or links which a person has and can be mobilized for various purposes. Hence, at any point in time, it is more than just the connections which are active and manifest at that time: there are always latent connections established at some point which, should the need arise, can be activated. One instance of this is when information is needed about something out of the ordinary, such as when a person is out looking for a job (Granovetter, 1974) or is considering a technological innovation.

This type of social capital is *inter alia* based on family connections, but not exclusively. Family connections one is born with, as it were, and these connections influence one's opportunities. However, any connections accumulated over a lifetime are social capital in this sense, a source of access to information and other resources not otherwise available. It is also easier to accumulate social capital if one already possesses a good measure of it according to Bourdieu's way of thinking. All connections are not equally valuable. Well-placed persons tend to connect to other well-placed persons, which opens access not only to these persons but also to their contact networks in turn. Such well-placed persons may be wealthy or educated or both, but not necessarily. The whole point of distinguishing between different forms of capital is to devise independent indicators of social position, which can explain patterns of power and domination. Power can be based on education, sociality or money, each or all.

Burt (1992) also distinguishes between three forms of capital, that is, financial capital, human capital and social capital. Social capital is the connections any actor maintains with other actors. Essentially, he therefore puts in focus the same sources of power and success as does Bourdieu. However, while Bourdieu sees capital as a set of possibilities attendant on social position, or in other words, a latent network, Burt focuses on actual and manifest connections maintained by an actor here and now: in a sense his social capital is his social position. Maintaining this capital entails a cost or effort, however measured, and in return actors gain access to resources by which they can offset that cost and effort. If that is not the case, the relationship is redundant and actors will discontinue it, if they do not have some exogenous reasons for doing otherwise.

It follows that maintaining many connections of the same kind is not economical, according to this point of view. Buying some input from many suppliers does not make sense if one supplier is enough. Talking about the same thing with many different people only makes sense as long as this adds new information. In practice, as field researchers know, the novelty of information gained decreases rapidly after a few encounters. Conversely, creating new relationships where none existed before makes sense insofar as the effort of establishing and maintaining them is less than the 'profit' and this is particularly likely if an actor combines through himself two networks which can be supportive of each other in some way if they are connected but which are connected only through him. Duplicating existing connections, in other words, is not likely to lead to anything. Hence, Burt's conception leads logically to an emphasis on middlemen and go-betweens who, moreover, monopolize the connection or try to do so: machinery importers immediately come to mind.

As can be seen Burt's approach is better suited than Bourdieu's for analysing ordinary business networks (which is how he has applied it) and its value outside that context is debatable, because 'rational' strategies are likely to be counterproductive. Writes Burt: 'Judging friends for efficiency is an interpersonal flatulence from which friends will flee' (1993: 82). Hence, if Bourdieu is able to show us important ways of contextualizing economic transactions and innovation processes, which open interesting ways of analysing the social composition and innovation potential of local communities in terms of, *inter alia*, social capital, Burt is more helpful when it comes to understanding the strategies of individual economic actors in the terms of immediately observable network structures.

His simple but elegant propositions – redundant relations will be cut off, unique links are most giving – highlight two aspects of strategic networking which are often forgotten. When an actor decides to co-operate with someone, he is usually deciding not to co-operate with one or several other candidates, either because they have nothing to offer or because they do so on unfavourable terms. Further, opportunities for profitable networking usually present themselves in the form of an absent connection. On both counts, abstaining from and unmaking connections on the one hand and identifying opportunities for novel connections in the universe of absent ones on the other, we see that latent connections or at least actors' perceptions of them are the basis of strategy, but in ways very different from that proposed by Bourdieu. Lastly, the relevance of each approach depends on the extent to which general social or more strictly economic considerations apply, and that in itself varies from one local context to another, and perhaps also from one person to another.

In this section we have established that social capital can be seen as a general asset available to all members of a society on more or less equal terms, as an amorphous and spontaneous capacity of association. It can also be seen as position-dependent and structured and therefore not available to everyone on the same terms. Thirdly, it is possible to create social capital instead of just using whatever is at hand, enacting more or less explicit strategies.

The different theories do not exclude each other. It is quite possible to see the creation and management of social capital in the sense proposed by Burt happening within the constraints posed either by the general presence of amorphous sociability *à la* Fukuyama, or by the positional structure of sociability posed by Bourdieu. Further, even if the presence of general and amorphous sociability is assumed, this does not exclude the possibility that the actual use made of this asset varies within a society according to the parameters suggested by Bourdieu or some other relevant factors. However, rather than delving further into the logic of social capital in general let us turn to the consequences different forms and quantities of this asset have in innovation processes.

INNOVATION, SOCIAL NETWORKS AND SOCIAL CAPITAL

The presence or possession of social capital influences innovation primarily by facilitating or precluding particular network constellations which are conducive to or obstacles to innovation processes. Innovative action tends to be formed by active reflection of the kind rarely found in connection with routine economic transactions (Allen, 1983; Scranton, 1997). It is more akin to the foregoing deliberations, for example firm acquisitions and major investment programmes, both of which can also be parts of an innovation process. Therefore, analysis in terms of social capital and networks is limited to defining opportunities, or sets of opportunities: it gives us no certainty or even strong predictions that actors will behave in particular ways.

The innovation process can be divided into the following phases:

1. Analysing the immediate business environment
2. Acquiring information about possible technologies
3. Deciding on the acquisition of particular technologies
4. Acquisition of particular technologies
5. Implementation of particular technologies

This simplified presentation of the process is intended to help us to identify different networks involved in acquiring and implementing a particular technology, such as, for example, a numerically controlled lathe, and to identify how social capital in some of the senses discussed above influence it.

Let us start at the beginning: a machine is available somewhere in the world which could be used to solve some of the problems faced by proprietors of small- and medium-sized workshops somewhere in the South. Our starting point is the analysis made by each proprietor of the current situation in this locality from his/her point of view, and by pairs, groups, associations and the entire collective together. This constant reflection process needs to be taken into account in any analysis of industrialization alternatives (Sabel and Zeitlin, 1997), but what I want to emphasize here is the networked and collective character of it. People talk to each other about things that matter to them, and that is how they learn to think about them.

As Meyer-Stamer (2000) has documented, such interaction need not be intense or frequent, and if we are not careful, we might end up confusing similarities in decision making which are occasioned by similar situations of the decision makers with similar decisions made on the basis of consensus developed through discussion (Burt, 1987). Hence it is important to employ a concept of social capital which makes it possible to distinguish the one from the other, that is, to analyse if concrete information has been transmitted through the links observed.

This being said (and keeping the oats from the wheat may be demanding in practice) we can see that observations about trust in general or social capital in the form of spontaneous sociability can explain some of the propensity for colleagues to talk, which can be and is observed in varied contexts. However, in almost every case we can also observe that this spontaneous sociability is constrained, formed, and facilitated, in short, structured, by the particular historical contexts we find presented in case studies from different times and places. Further, it is a remote possibility that everyone in a particular locality at a particular time will agree on a general analysis of the situation, or that everyone will draw similar conclusions for themselves. Thus the analysis leading to a decision that something needs to be done about the current technology in use (rather than say, suppliers, workers, partners, customers, the location, the government or life in general) depends rather on the way a proprietor or manager fits into this structure than any general circumstances surrounding him or her. It depends as much on their evaluation of suppliers, workers, partners, customers, and so on, as on any technical considerations *per se*, that is, on their evaluation of the usefulness and appropriateness of the actual social capital which they possess. In a sense this is the essence of Bourdieu's idea of social capital, insofar as it pertains to the matter at hand. The connections one has and how one uses them creates one's possibilities to orient oneself in the world: the better placed one's contacts, the more reliable is the information and more pertinent is the analysis they provide as an input into one's own reflections. But there are limitations: people who are connected to people with scarce resources, be they money, power, nobility or learning, will learn to orient themselves among them and according to their views of the world, as adapted to particular circumstances. If the resources possessed by someone's contacts are of the kind available to most, such as labour power, the time of the day, or elementary working skills, the information gathered will be accordingly common property and the resulting analysis will reflect that. Most of us, and that includes innovators in the South, find ourselves somewhere between the two extremes, but exactly where we are on the scale and how we connect to people with scarce resources, largely defines the possibilities for innovative activity.

Further, particular pieces of social capital may actually become obstacles to new ways of relating to the world. This is Fukuyama's argument: when family ties are prominent and non-family viewed with suspicion, large-scale organizations cannot form spontaneously, leading to government intervention and hence, less prosperity. Therefore, dissolution of family loyalties in economic matters is an important component of progress (Hydén, 1987). From the point of view of innovation a slightly different argument applies. Although families and kin are important in forming general world views they are rarely exceptionally good sources of economic and technical information. Whether family connections are good for innovative prospects therefore depends on whether your family belongs to the exceptions or not. Similar arguments could be applied to, say, ethnic or caste cleavages, but I will abstain here. Suffice it to say that there are a large number of economic worlds where ethnic, racial or caste categories are among the organizing principles (the Indians in Kenya and the white minority in Zimbabwe being the ones best known to me). In these worlds innovation takes place although generalized or spontaneous sociability is not much in evidence in the societies concerned. If anything these worlds are islands of segregated networking with tenuous and far from trustful relations to the surrounding society. But participation in them creates privileged access to people with scarce resources, including business information and technological knowledge, and, therefore, they work - if not very well.

It may seem difficult to keep the process discussed above separate from the process of acquiring information about possible technologies, as such technological advances and improvements which are there and known will always enter into any reflections on the current situation in the business. The point where such deliberations turn into more active consideration of possible technological change can, however, be identified as when this type of solution is preferred above or in conjunction with other possible ones. A proprietor of a small furniture workshop who faces increasing orders can, for example, try subcontracting for some components or entire pieces, in the latter case turning himself into a merchant, or increase his employment of (casual) workers, before he seriously starts thinking about new machinery as a way of responding to the situation, and if no one else in his location has brought in machines as yet and everyone is using hand tools, the idea of machinery may not seem so obvious in the first place. I have discussed this situation in detail elsewhere (Sverrisson, 1993) and will limit myself to pointing out that this choice depends *inter alia* on the general orientation of the proprietor. It is sometimes assumed that firms always aim at expansion but among proprietors of small enterprises in the South, survival orientations are often found, and may be prevalent in particular locations and this in turn influences attitudes to innovation.

Once the step is taken to consider technical novelties, new networks come into play, and those existing take on a new aspect. Thinking about machines means thinking about fewer, not more workers, but at least some of these fewer workers would need to be able to handle the machine. Neighbouring proprietors, who earlier might help in meeting excessive demand (and potentially creaming off some of it for themselves) and who would therefore be owed money, now become potential benefactors of a new machine, who might hire the use of it in some fashion, and therefore owe money. Customers who earlier came willingly because of low price may not be willing to pay more to help defray the cost of new machinery - other customers who prefer the finish achieved by mechanical means over 'hand-made' may take their place. Materials and inputs might change as well, and suppliers who were previously suitable therefore have to be replaced. In short, the decision to actively seek a technological solution to the problem of increased demand can potentially change the entire network of a workshop proprietor, and hence, devalue his existing social capital. In addition to the financial risks, there are, in other words, social risks, which are, moreover, less amenable to calculation.

The networks through which information about possible technologies is gained must by definition take our innovator outside his or her location, and in many cases in the South, such networks must be constructed from scratch. Let us reduce this problem, for the purpose of this argument, to finding out about available machines within some relatively well-defined category (for example wood lathes) and the pros and cons of constructing them locally. There are a number of questions that need to be answered, such as the capacity needed, price, import regulations and duties, and so on. Who has the answers and how to reach them? Again, referring to generalized sociability and trust can only answer such questions in the most general way, but the divide in terms of propensity of association which I (and others) have observed elsewhere between proprietors linked to the global capitalist economy and those who operate mainly within local economic cultures needs to be bridged somehow for technological information to be transmitted successfully (Sverrisson, 2000). Hence, the problem here is the structure of social capital rather than its eventual presence or absence, and further, it appears from the varied case studies now available that active intervention of some kind of broker or through a 'bridging' mechanism is needed to overcome this problem. This can be in the form of commercial links as those created by people who import and sell machinery, or through varied development projects which provide machines.

In the former case financing problems may be insurmountable, and in the latter case the reflection process described above is rather conducted within the project than in a community of businessmen, often leading to inappropriate selections based, for example, on what is available in the country footing the bill. However, in both cases we can see that it is the pattern of relationships, that is, the form of social capital, rather than its presence or absence as such, which poses serious obstacles.

Hence, in the end it may be necessary to resort to local sources and local technical competence and therefore, local social capital, simply because this is the only way to gather relevant and specific information, in order to concretize a general idea about mechanization, wherever that originates. The observed result is often the construction of simplified versions of technologies (Takeuchi, 1991; Sverrisson, 1997). Locally made wood lathes are for example ubiquitous in Africa. However, even then, minimal technical information is needed, but it can be acquired in many different ways. Whatever is offered commercially can be analysed, technologies offered through development projects can be critically deconstructed, and earlier experiences elsewhere can also be a source of critical technical information.

Once the decision is made, the soundness of such reflections is put to the test. First, the concrete networks through which acquisition takes place must deliver and the proprietor adjust his activities accordingly, in order to be able to pay commercial importers or local machine makers, cope with (or evade) corollary demands (on accounting procedures for instance) made by development projects, and so on. There is a difference between the previous phase where information was sought and this one, where actual relationships are established. In the former the social capital available is mobilized and eventually supplemented, and the resulting information processed. In the latter case an opportunity arises to develop this capital more actively and in particular to develop relationships that connect local operators to global technological processes. Acquisition means after all that a business transaction of some kind takes place (except in the instances where the new technology is constructed entirely within the workshop in question) which often lasts some time, for example while a machine is being paid off, a loan paid or a project runs. In the case of local construction, interaction continues while the design is negotiated, during actual construction, installation and testing, and until the last payment is made and even beyond that because of maintenance and repair, which, one could add, may not be altogether pleasant occasions on which to meet. Hence, the possibility of continuing this relationship is opened up, repeating the transaction with yet another new technology, now much easier to acquire, because the acquisition network is already there and can provide relevant information.

A similar argument applies to the implementation process. New, suppliers, customers, workers, and so on, open up different possibilities: if the older social capital is devalued, new capital can be developed in its place. The technology itself brings with it its own potential social capital, as it were, opening doors earlier closed and making connections previously valued redundant. If a furniture workshop previously needed five skilled carpenters, the introduction of a combined carpentry machine can reduce this number to one, who does the work with the help of two apprentices. If the proprietor earlier spent all his time sweet-talking poor customers into buying his products cheaply, he may now be able to deal with people who like mechanized finish and prompt delivery without worrying about the cost. Alternatively, machines may make production and therefore products cheaper and save marketing time in the process, even make special salespeople redundant for a while or transfer the effort from salesmanship to advertising – getting around the word about the good prices. Such examples could be multiplied. Technological innovation, just as it changes the forms of financial and human capital, likewise transforms social capital (Sandee, 1995). In sociological terminology we would talk about the change in role sets attendant upon technological change, which in turn leads to networks of a very different character (Barley, 1990).

Once a technology has been adopted in a locality all this is changed. It is well known that first adopters are not always the most successful, they make the mistakes that later adopters can avoid, if information spreads within the community, which again is a function of the form of social capital prevailing there. If local conventions of interaction include fairly free sharing of technical information, others will be able to follow the first adopter fairly quickly. The same holds of course if observation makes such information flows unavoidable because of the layout of workshops, for example, whatever the interaction conventions, but open workshop layouts are not likely in secretive communities.

What this means in weeks and months depends on the circumstances. Once a woodworking machine is introduced in a locality, every carpenter there can potentially rent it (or the use of it) or buy its services in one way or another, and learn for himself about its benefits, if any. As soon as the customers have caught on and learned to expect such benefits, new adopters can follow. The process is likely to be quicker for novelties such as new designs, the adoption of which does not imply establishing acquisition networks; emulation facilitated by local networks is enough (King and Aboudha, 1991). The main point here is, that after the ice is broken, the main source of information and inspiration to adopt a technical novelty is usually the local network of proprietors and technical personnel itself. The perceived quality of information gained through this route depends on the kind of connections each individual proprietor and/or technician has to his/her colleagues, who are usually also the competition.

The presence of generally trustful relations in the sense proposed by Fukuyama may help us understand why such situations occur more frequently in some societies than others. However, it should be remembered that such information, even if its sources are distributed throughout a network, are usually transmitted through particular members, with whom the receiver has a specific relationship based on earlier co-operation, for example in fulfilling a particularly demanding order, or through family connections, or because of spatial proximity, or whatever. It is these relations, and the informed judgement of the knowledge transmitted through them, which *inter alia* explains whether an innovation is adopted by a particular proprietor (Burt, 1992; Mizruchi, 1993) rather than some ethereal quantity such as 'trust'.

TECHNOLOGICAL INNOVATION IN THE SOUTH

Technological innovation is often assumed to be absent in the South, indeed, this absence is a defining characteristic of underdevelopment according to some ways of thinking. However, a closer look reveals a more nuanced picture in which acquisition of multi-purpose, flexible, machinery and imitative adaptation appear in the foreground. Both are suited to overcoming the scarcity of capital and small, local, markets prevalent in these countries.

Hence, I will focus this section on the following question. What kinds of social capital facilitate/hinder the development of networked innovation processes rooted in flexibility considerations, imitative or otherwise?

First, let me note that the kind of spontaneous sociability discussed by Fukuyama can well facilitate networked production and corresponding innovation, either in the form of a flexible production apparatus or in the form of specialized units in closely knit networks. There is at least no evidence to my knowledge that the presence of spontaneous sociability has adverse effects on any co-operative venture whatsoever although naive trust could (and does sometimes) rob inventors or innovative pioneers of some or all of the benefits of their lead. It is only when governments or other agents privilege this type of sociability over others in economic life, that the adverse effects on networked production materialize and large-scale organizations prevail (Scranton, 1997).

Turning to other forms of social capital, the available evidence is contradictory. There are any number of testimonies to the fact that many ventures in the South are financed and staffed through family connections, that clustering facilitates the building of non-family business links and that social position in the official hierarchy as well as ethnic or caste considerations are powerful influences on whom you interact with on a regular basis and whom you only deal with at arm's length. Economic transactions are, accordingly, structured by the prevailing mixture of social capital in particular locations. However, what all this means for innovation processes is not so straightforward.

In order to get a little closer to a solution of this problem, we can explore how social capital structures innovation opportunities, that is, how are connections established which facilitate the construction of technological artefacts or their transplantation from one social context to another? First, family connections. We tend to think of family as close-knit and residing close to each other, and therefore, such connections tend to keep people to the old routines. However, this is a truth with modifications. Family connections often facilitate migration, often for educational purposes, and migration brings people into contact with new and unexpected things. Family connections which cross the urban–rural divide or even the global North–South divide are therefore potential innovation opportunities. Ghanaians abroad help their relatives start companies and purchase machines for that purpose, to name an example from my own work (Sverrisson, 1997), and the role of family connections in bringing new immigrants to the United States possessing state of the art knowledge and skills has been documented by Scranton and others. Using family money or family staff helps reduce uncertainty in many volatile business environments creating the opportunity to take the risks involved in pursuing new product lines or in developing new methods of production. One person I once interviewed in Kenya had three lieutenants, each entrusted with the daily running of a part of his operation so he could concentrate on developing it. All were his wives, but could have been his sons or in-laws, given a different family structure.

Such connections do not always promote innovation, however. In Zimbabwe, where most rural families have one or more members working in town, local craft production suffers from the competition from urban producers facilitated by frequent travel to and from the countryside: shopping in urban areas for use in rural areas is the rule for many products. Many small entrepreneurs feel that family responsibilities are burdens rather than assets, and commonly enough they constitute a drain on the company funds, siphoning away resources for investment, which could be used for innovative purposes, or they may saddle the company with incompetent kin when more competent staff could create possibilities for development (Trulsson, 1997). Hence, we can see that family are useful for innovation when they bring in something new or reduce risk, but only then.

Similar arguments apply to other forms of ascribed or inherited social capital. Thus, for example, a large number of innovative ventures have been based on access to the networks of government officials in Africa, facilitating everything from the acquisition of import permits to access to foreign aid projects, and both family and more extended kin connections are also operative in this context (Trulsson, 1997). However, rent-seeking and corruption rather than innovative behaviour are equally, if not more common. Caste-based relations have facilitated innovative practices among shoe merchants in Agra, but have equally hindered the diffusion of such practices to everyone in the area, leading to a strong technological dualism and underdevelopment of the area as a whole (Knorringa, 1995).

Connections established through earlier careers can facilitate exchange of information and therefore innovation later on, and reduce the risk of starting new ventures. I have met carpenters and metalworkers who familiarized themselves with power tools and machinery in parastatal corporations, vocational training institutions, a variety of private firms and in prison, and later built on this technical experience, but also on the connections made earlier with prospective partners and customers in developing their own ventures. This form of social capital which is accumulated rather than ascribed tends to be more effective because redundant relationships can be cut off fairly easily, which is not the case with close kin. On the other hand, dealing with well-known people can reinforce the propensity to continue on the same track, rather than to develop something very different. If one starts a company by dealing with customers one learned to know as a foreman at another company, the likelihood is that one will continue to deal with them in the same way as earlier, rather than spring any surprises on them (Halimana and Sverrisson, 2000).

If we consider the forms of social capital related to geographical proximity or clustering, this can be quite powerful as I have described elsewhere, for example in the Timber Market area in Accra (Sverrisson, 1997). The division of labour and consequent task specialization among carpenters in this area has undoubtedly facilitated the mechanization of the carpentry trade, but in the form of specialized enterprises which turn, plane, cut joints and so on mechanically, rather than in the form of general mechanization. Clustering, however, also fosters imitative practices. It is hard to keep a new trick from your neighbours, who therefore catch up quickly on any novel design or production method (King and Aboudha, 1991). Hence, the division of labour within a cluster seems to be the engine of innovation rather than clustering *per se*, but once an innovation takes root, its benefits are quickly transferred to everyone through subcontracting, observation and similar practices. If no innovations take root, because of an underdeveloped division of labour, isolation from the rest of the world or some other reason, such as excessive exploitation of the cluster by middlemen or cut-throat competition for the scarce money of poor customers, imitative practices have the opposite effect: they create collective stagnation (for example Visser, 2000).

Social capital in the form of connections through middlemen to larger and more demanding markets can also be a powerful basis for innovation, and certain theories of European industrialization see this as the key to the expansion of manufactures in the pre-industrial era, which in turn created the prerequisites of the industrial revolution (Kriedte *et al.*, 1981). This aspect has been drawn out *inter alia* by Sandee and Rietveld (2000). But as they and others have also shown, extended trade can also fortify existing structures of exploitation, perpetuate traditional practices and lower producer margins, thereby hindering innovation and risk-taking more generally, a major reason why informal producers in small African towns tend to sell their products directly to consumers. Also, as I have had the opportunity to observe in Ghana, increased possibilities for import trade and large profit margins can strangle local production and therefore, local innovation. At the local level, deregulation of restrictions on trade can divert capital and labour from production to trade, eventually leading to even stronger prevalence of hawking activities in the informal sector. Hence, development of trade as the specialized activity of making connections between producers and consumers may increase prosperity, at least temporarily, and, for some, enhance the opportunities for technological innovation.

Hence, we are left with the conclusion that generalized social capital in the form of spontaneous sociability (or trust) does not in itself explain why innovation occurs, and can even less explain why particular forms of innovation occur and not others. Further, distinguishing between different forms of social capital following Bourdieu, and examining the most common forms of position-dependent social capital still leaves us without adequate explanation of how opportunities for innovation are created. Different forms of social capital can under fortuitous circumstances facilitate innovation, but the same forms can under other circumstances become obstacles to innovation processes.

This leaves us with two directions in which we can search for solutions to our original problem. One direction is the general connectivity prevailing in a particular society, but in a form different from that posed by Fukuyama. There is no reason to doubt that the social fragmentation and legal restrictions on travel and trade characterizing both the societies of the South and Soviet-type societies everywhere has had a negative influence on innovation processes by creating obstacles to information flows. The other direction is the action of particular entrepreneurs, who manage, with the help of forms of social capital, to innovate in circumstances which for others present mainly obstacles or at least an occasion to continue as before and avoid the risk inherent in technological innovation. This latter direction takes us towards Burt's conception of social capital.

INNOVATION AND STRATEGIC ACCUMULATION OF SOCIAL CAPITAL

As outlined above, the creation, maintenance and accumulation of social capital, according to Burt, is the result of strategic action by entrepreneurs. From an innovation perspective this means that entrepreneurs who are able to create the type of links identified above as necessary for innovation, will take the lead; others are not likely to do so. This implies, *inter alia*, effective screening of information through relevant contacts, and not wasting time and effort on contacts who have nothing to tell. The form of innovation, moreover, will depend on the form of these links, that is, on how social capital is structured, which in turn depends on circumstances in the locality in which an innovator is active. They can be established by means of family connections, or political connections, or by some of the chance encounters which any professional life in the South or elsewhere constantly throws upon everybody's shores (Granovetter, 1974). Hence, in most localized contexts in the South, a prudent proprietor will avoid cutting any links which cost little or nothing, lest they turn out to be valuable later on. Yet, indiscriminate socializing is equally impracticable there as elsewhere. Success therefore depends on the capacity to manage network connections properly, balancing cost in the present against future returns. It is also necessary to give business considerations their proper due and not too much more, amidst competing concerns, such as family obligations, general decency and integrity, 'keeping face', honour and the demands of chieftancy, that is the socially constructed and expected generosity common in recently reciprocal economies (Hydén, 1987; Trulsson, 1999), all depending on where the fledgling innovator finds himself. Ability and opportunity do not guarantee success, however, in innovation any more than any other activity. From studies of great innovations we can glean the conclusion, that success often depends on a specific combination of circumstances and a good measure of politicking and luck, although more general circumstances also enter the picture (for example Hughes, 1987).

In lieu of a conclusion it is therefore possible to suggest the elements of a three-level model of innovation which includes:

- Macro-level: General connectivity of a society based on prevailing interaction conventions
- Meso-level: Possibilities for selective networking based on position, power, location, functional complementarities, experience, associations, etc.
- Micro-level: Abilities, opportunities, constraints, risk-taking and specialization of potential entrepreneurs/innovators

It can be expected that general connectivity enhances the probability of innovative activity. Measuring this is not straightforward, however. Using a proxy, such as for example the prevalence of civil society organizations, as suggested by Fukuyama's argument, would introduce cultural biases which are difficult to control (Bulmer and Warwick, 1993).

The model would also suggest that the possession of social capital, which is easily transformed or dispensed with (acquired rather than ascribed, say, business connections) facilitates innovation. Social capital which is more inert (ascribed rather than acquired, say, close kin) doesn't facilitate innovation apart from exceptional cases. The relative importance of each in conducting business in a particular location or among particular groups would explain in part the probability of innovation. In this regard, the distinction between innovation and growth is particularly important. It is well known that family networks, as well as tribal, clan, ethnic, religious, and other networks facilitate the starting of new enterprises and their expansion, although at a certain point this type of network may become a constraint. This, however, should not be confused with the issue of whether they facilitate innovation within some enterprise collective.

Further, complementarities (and therefore division of labour) among enterprises in a location would increase the probability of innovation, and similarities among enterprises in types of activity (that is, similar location in the production chain) would decrease the probability of innovation. The implication here is that in collectives where enterprises specialize and therefore have much to do with each other, innovation is both more feasible because direct competition is less, and easier, because of larger margins. In cases where competition is more intense and profit margins as well as other types of redundancy are low, imitation is more likely than innovation, according to the argument pursued here. Technological upgrading in such cases would rather be the result of the exit of less sophisticated enterprises rather than the effect of an innovation dynamism *per se*.

However, matters are complicated by the occurrence of network clusters which limit the reach and utility of particular types of social capital. Such clusters are areas of the local enterprise network within which connections are more dense than in the collective as a whole. If such clusters exists, there will also be areas of the network which are sparsely connected, and which can, in effect, be invisible walls between groups in what appears to be one enterprise collective. Sometimes, as in the case of the Indians in Kenya and the Europeans in Rhodesia/Zimbabwe, such invisible walls are not very difficult to trace. In other cases where the walls are not directly linked to directly observable attributes, they remain hidden until dug up by network analysis. Hence, a social capital model would have to include a component accounting for different topologies of connectivity rather than just differences in the number of connections entrepreneurs have.

Lastly, variation in individual characteristics and strategies including the actual ways in which individual entrepreneurs/innovators handle family relations, their hedging strategies and so on would have to be accounted for. It is an interesting issue in itself whether innovation is primarily created through generation of abundant opportunities which can be identified at the meso-level, or if it is the acute utilization of the existing opportunities, even if they are few and far between, which results in innovation.

The strategy suggested here can therefore be summarized as follows: Because macro-level social capital, that is the social capital possessed by entire societies (countries) is difficult to measure, it is assumed to be constant. The social capital of enterprise collectives, that is the meso-level social capital can, however, be measured in various ways. It is of course also possible to compare meso-level social capital in collectives in different countries. Therefore it seems reasonable to focus research efforts on this level. The individual or micro-level social capital, for which a large number of standard measures exist already, should, in principle, be able to account for the rest of the variation in innovative capability, however measured.

Whether such a model would have more or less explanatory power than other possible ones based on, say, human capital (education), financial capital (money), both of which are relatively easy to measure, or intangibles such as trust, remains to be seen. However, all theories of social capital assume that it is but one resource that entrepreneurs and innovators can use in their activities, and introducing it into the discussion serves the purpose of developing explanations of the hitherto unexplained rather than entirely superseding earlier theories.

NOTE

1. This research is funded by SAREC, the research division of the Swedish International Development and Cooperation Agency (SIDA).

REFERENCES

Allen, R.C. (1983), 'Collective invention', *Journal of Economic Behaviour and Organisation*, **4**, pp. 1–24.

Barley, S.R. (1990), 'The alignment of technology and structure through roles and networks', *Administrative Science Quarterly*, **35**, pp. 61–103.

Bourdieu, P. (1984), *Distinction: A Social Critique of the Judgement of Taste*, London: Routledge & Kegan Paul.

Bulmer, M. and D.P. Warwick (eds) (1993), *Social Research in Developing Countries: Surveys and Censuses in the Third World*, London: UCL Press.

Burt, R.S. (1987), 'Social contagion and innovation: cohesion vs. Structural equivalence', in *American Journal of Sociology*, **92**, May, pp. 1287–335.

Burt, R.S (1992), *Structural Holes: The Social Structure of Competition*, London: Harvard.

Burt, R.S. (1993), 'The social structure of competition', in Richard Swedberg (ed.), *Explorations in Economic Sociology*, New York: Russel Sage Foundation.

Fukuyama, F. (1996), *Trust: The Social Virtues and the Creation of Prosperity*, London: Penguin.

Granovetter, M.S. (1974), *Getting a Job: A Study of Contacts and Careers*, Cambridge, Mass.: Harvard University Press.

Halimana, C.M. and Á. Sverrisson (2000), 'Enterprise networks in transition: light engineering industries and structural adjustment in Zimbabwe', in Á Sverrisson and M.P. van Dijk (eds), London: Macmillan.

Hughes, T.P. (1987), 'The evolution of large technological systems', in W.E. Bijker, T.P. Hughes and T. Pinch (eds), *The Social Construction of Technology: New Directions in the Sociology and History of Technology*, London: MIT.

Humprey, J. and H. Schmitz (1996), 'Trust and economic development', Institute of Development Studies Discussion paper 355, Brighton.

Hydén, G. (1987), 'Capital accumulation, resource distribution and governance in Kenya: the role of the economy of affection', in M.G. Schatzberg, *The Political Economy of Kenya*, New York: Praeger.

King, K. and C. Aboudha (1991), 'The building of an industrial society: change and development in Kenya's informal sector 1970–1990', Occasional paper No. 30, Centre of African Studies, Edinburgh University, Edinburgh.

Knorringa, P. (1995), *Economics of Collaboration in Producer-Trader Relations: Transaction Regimes between Market and Hierarchy in the Agra Footwear Cluster, India*, Amsterdam: Vrije Universiteit.

Kriedte, P., H. Medick and J. Schlumbohm (1981), *Industrialization before Industrialization*, Cambridge: Cambridge University Press and Paris: Editions de la Maison des Sciences de l'Homme.

Meyer-Stamer, J. (2000), 'Adjusting to an open economy: a case study of three industrial clusters in Santa Catarina/Brazil', in Á. Sverrisson and M.P. van Dijk (eds).

Mizruchi, M.S. (1993), 'Cohesion, equivalence and similarity of behaviour: a theoretical and empirical assessment', *Social Networks*, **15** (3).

Nadvi, K. (1994), 'Industrial District Experiences in Developing Countries', in UNCTAD, *Technological Dynamism in Industrial Districts: An Alternative Approach to Industrialization in Developing Countries?* Geneva: United Nations.

Pacey, A (1990), *Technology in World Civilization*, Oxford: Basil Blackwell.

Pedersen, P.O., Á. Sverrisson and M.P. van Dijk (eds) (1994), *Flexible Specialization: the Dynamics of Small-Scale Industries in the South*, London: Intermediate Technology Publications.

Putnam, R. (1993), *Making Democracy Work*, New York (see chapter Parilli).

Sabel, C. and J. Zeitlin (1997), *World of Possibilities: Flexibility and Mass Production in Western Industrialization*, Cambridge: Cambridge University Press.

Sandee, H. (1995), *Innovation Adaption in Rural Industry: Technological Change in Roof Tile Clusters in Central Java, Indonesia*, Amsterdam: Vrije Universiteit.

Sandee, H. and P. Rietveld (2000), 'Innovation adoption in rural industry cluster: A comparison of a roof tile and copper handicraft clusters in Indonesia', in Sverrisson and van Dijk (eds).

Schmitz, H. (1996), 'Small shoemakers and Fordist giants: tale of a supercluster', Institute of Development Studies Discussion Paper no. 331, Brighton.

Schumpeter, J.A. (1934), *The Theory of Economic Development: An Inquiry into Profits, Capital, Credit, Interest, and the Business Cycle*, Cambridge, Mass: Harvard University Press.

Scranton, P. (1997), *Endless Novelty: Specialty Production and American Industrialization, 1865-1925*, Princeton: University Press.

Sverrisson, Á. (1993), *Evolutionary Technical Change and Flexible Mechanization: Entrepreneurship and Industrialization in Kenya and Zimbabwe*, Lund: University Press.

Sverrisson, Á. (1997), 'Enterprise networks and technological change: aspects of light engineering and metalworking in Accra', in van Dijk and Rabellotti (eds).

Sverrisson, Á. (2000), 'Economic cultures and innovation processes: The social embeddedness of industrial development' in Sverrisson and van Dijk (eds).

Takeuchi, J. (1991), *The Role of Labour-Intensive Sectors in Japanese Industrialization*, Tokyo: United Nations University.

Trulsson, P. (1997), *Strategies of Entrepreneurship: Understanding Industrial Entrepreneurship and Structural Change in Northern Tanzania, Department of Technology and Social Change*, Linköping: University.

van Dijk, M.P. and R. Rabellotti (eds) (1997), *Enterprise Clusters and Networks in Developing Countries* (Eadi Book Series no. 20), London: Frank Cass.

Visser, E.J. (2000), 'Structural Adjustment and Cluster Advantages: a Case from Peru', in Sverrisson and van Dijk (eds).

PART V

Conclusions and Recommendations

14. Enterprise co-operation, technology partnerships and S&T policies for the promotion of innovation for SMEs

Meine Pieter van Dijk

Different case studies in this book have shown that local technological development is important for promotion of innovation for SMEs. The local adaptation capacity should be developed further. Governments and donor organizations should go from an approach stressing the transfer of technology to one stressing the development of such a local capacity to develop and adapt technology, possibly with assistance provided in the framework of development co-operation. Private firms would be the major actor, besides universities and local research and development organizations. They have most of the technical and practical skills available in the country. Large-scale and multinational companies can also play a role, in particular in the case of strategic alliances focusing on producing locally internationally competitive products.[1] UNCTAD (1998) also stresses the importance of interfirm agreements to enable firms to meet the challenges of the new international competitive environment.

In this chapter we will take a development perspective: how to stimulate the development of local technological capability to help the development of small and medium enterprises in developing countries. Different types of enterprise co-operation were analysed in the previous chapters. In Chapter 6 they ranged for example from co-operation between large international and small and medium local enterprises in Zimbabwe to co-operation between small enterprises in Ghana and Burkina Faso. Also examples of science and technology (S&T) policies to promote innovation and the development of a local technological development capacity were given. In this chapter conclusions will be drawn concerning enterprise co-operation and science and technology policies for this type of capacity building and innovation diffusion.

A number of new ways to promote technology development and innovation diffusion for SMEs has been mentioned in this book. In this chapter we will discuss three in more detail: technology partnerships, enterprise co-operation and national science and technology policies. The concept of national systems of innovations has been suggested by neo-Schumpetarian researchers such as Freeman (1987) to point to what may be necessary for innovation. The importance of the concept is that it is broader than just pointing to some laboratories or research institutes. It stresses the synergetic effects of all the institutions active in the field. The question is whether the development of a national system of innovation would be necessary for technology adaptation and innovation diffusion for small enterprise development.

TECHNOLOGICAL PARTNERSHIPS: THE MECHANISMS

It is important to look at the mechanisms of technology transfer, the local capacity to adapt and develop technologies and the degree to which government, private sector associations and donor organizations can influence the process. The type of actors involved does influence for example the nature of the agreement and the results to be expected. Partnerships may concern different sectors and can receive support from different sources. Licensing and franchising are alternatives for technology partnerships.

The question is to what extent the process of technology transfer and adaptation can be influenced. Donor organizations certainly play a role; however, government and private sector organizations should also play a role, facilitating the transfer and specifying clearly what kind of technology is needed. Sometimes specialized institutions or chambers of commerce can play that role. The private sector has its own ideas what kind of supporting policies are needed for developed countries' enterprises to invest in developing countries. ERT (1993) mentions for example:

- The need to re-evaluate development assistance, since too often political criteria influence the allocation of aid;
- A GATT code for investments, resembling the OECD Code on the liberalization of capital movements;
- There should be rules for the treatment of foreign direct investments in regional agreements;
- There should be a global competition policy;
- Regulation of domestic financial markets;
- Investment insurance schemes;
- Deregulation concerning sectorial access and licensing requirements;
- No restrictions on foreign ownership and foreign exchange transactions;
- Protection of and remuneration for intellectual property;
- No protectionism or other restrictions on foreign trade.

DIFFERENT TYPES OF ENTERPRISE CO-OPERATION

Enterprise co-operation can be classified on the basis of the sector (industry, mining, energy, communications, finance and insurance business, trade, environment, and so on). In certain sectors technology partnerships are actively promoted. The need for up-to-date technology is very clear in sectors like telecommunication, mining and energy. In other sectors the market is important and a reason for co-operation, while sometimes the required investments are huge – an argument to co-operate with other enterprises.

The UK has launched a programme for another type of partnership: the technology partnership initiative. This programme makes available environmentally friendly technology to third world countries by linking up British producers with third world consumers of such technology. There are also many examples of public–private partnerships and of private–private partnerships between firms in developed and developing countries. Other possibilities would be public–public and private–private partnerships with partners coming from developed and or developing countries.

Third world governments sometimes actively promote investments from one country in other countries in the region. Bangladesh considered it could learn a lot for example from other developing countries in the region. Programmes would be established with these countries, concerning for example shrimps (Indonesia); Vietnam wants closer co-operation in textile, jute and shrimp sectors; Indian investors urged to take part in industrial projects; and the Thai Bangladesh Joint commission to push private sector development.[2]

AN EXAMPLE: THE SCIENCE AND TECHNOLOGY POLICY AND INNOVATION IN BANGLADESH

The science and technology policy of a country may influence technology development and innovation diffusion as will be illustrated for Bangladesh, where efforts were made to stimulate technology capacity building through policies and projects.[3] The perspective taken is that technological capacity needs to be developed from below, building on the level of skills of the workers, the training capacity in the country and the available mechanisms for innovation diffusion. Science and technology policies can also have a beneficial impact on the development of local technological capability.

Most technology used in Bangladesh is still imported. Export-oriented industries want the most modern technology at least for the core of their activity, to remain competitive on the world market. It is quite possible that the handling of raw material or of the final product still happens in a very labour-intensive way. Entrepreneurs in Bangladesh complain that it is not easy to copy or further develop new technologies, which contain all kinds of digital instruments.

The Bangladesh Chamber of Industry and Commerce may advise its members on the technology to buy in the case of imported technologies. The main criteria used by the Chamber are: it should be the latest technology and the most efficient one! The Export Promotion Bureau claims the technology choice is made completely by the investors. However, the Bureau has a matching grant fund to share the total cost with the investor. For example technical assistance by Italians in the leather sector is paid from the fund. The United Nations Development Programme (UNDP) has assisted with experts from the International Trade Centre (ITC), and the World Bank has funded an export development fund located in the Bangladesh Bank, which can be used for credit in foreign exchange for imports of raw materials.[4] In a second phase it is hoped that the project will finance spare parts and machinery (Huq *et al.*, 1993). The Board of Investment has also been active and organized for example an investment conference in 1994. How much foreign investment (and with it which technology) came forward is not very clear. For 1994 the figure of US$ 200 million was mentioned. This is as much as India received in 1993 (corrected for a seven times larger population).

There are also examples of local innovations, although they are not always completely commercial yet.[5] We came across locally developed instant tea and the use of green jute for pulp, to produce paper. Researchers complained that it is difficult to get these technologies accepted outside the agricultural sector, where there are no extension services for that purpose, like for example in the agricultural sector. The science and technology policy of Bangladesh could contribute to the development of local technological capability. The country has nine universities and about 58 research and development organizations. The importance given to science and technology is proven by a document dating from 1985, which has never been revised. The Ministry for Science and Technology has been reinstalled and there is a National Council for Science and Technology (NCST), which meets regularly and discusses issues like local capacity for technology adaptation. The Ministry for Science and Technology is actually working on a paper that will be submitted to the NCST concerning long-term planning of science and technology. Budget-wise the ministry is not very important, however.

Several factors are inhibiting the growth of the private sector in Bangladesh. One can disagree about whether political instability is important; the private sector certainly complains about the lack of infrastructure (for example: 'inadequate power to inhibit industrial growth', FBCCI Newsletter May 1994). Secondly, the productivity of labour is low in Bangladesh. Labour is often unionized, or used by different political parties for strikes. Others emphasize the heavy bureaucracy and the lack of more sophisticated industrial activities in Bangladesh.

More importantly, it was found that in the eyes of the private sector there is no real technology policy in Bangladesh. Originally science and technology was mainly a responsibility of the government. In the liberalization process the private sector, and in particular the specialized research institutes started playing a more important role.[6] Consequently, the process of technology transfer and adaptation clearly differs in the formal export-oriented industrial sector, the local small and medium enterprises and the non-governmental organizations (NGO) sector, as will be illustrated now.

A number of donors are active in the local small and medium sector enterprises and in this sector a local technological capacity has been built up. Small enterprises copy imported tools and machines and most of the spare parts. In the small and medium enterprise sector the capacity to copy machines and spare parts is well developed, in particular in the private mechanical workshops. In the private formal sector one large machine tools factory also tries to produce as many tools locally as possible.

In the NGO sector there are many projects for income generating activities of poor people. In this sector appropriate technologies are often introduced and sometimes the local technological capacity is developed to produce these technologies and maintain them. Examples are biogas equipment, improved handlooms, energy saving technologies and the introduction of crop rotation.

The fact that the science and technology policy of 1985 has not been updated reflects that the government has other priorities, such as food production, industrialization and the development of the social sector. Much of the research and development is taking place in sector specific institutions, such as the jute and rice research institutes. Very little or no research and development is carried out in the industrial sector in Bangladesh. Recommendations would need to be elaborated for different industrial sectors in Bangladesh. In the export processing zones the foreign investor chooses the technology. Local knowledge of the design or fabrication process is very limited.

The challenge for the industrial sector in Bangladesh is to increase the value added of its products. In the garment sector it is estimated that at present the value added is only 20 per cent.[7] Some consider foreign direct investment (FDI) as the front runner and main vehicle of technology transfer in Bangladesh and seem to be happy with it, neglecting the potential of the local technological system and of appropriate science and technology policies. The development of the garment sector is very much linked to the quota of exports to Europe and the United States. In the future Bangladesh may have to compete with the most effective producers in the world. Given that they have to import most of the cloth it will be difficult to be an efficient producer. One alternative is to increase trade in the region. This alternative is greatly stressed and applies for Africa as well.[8]

The science and technology policy of Bangladesh is outdated and the country is more occupied with the effects of the Uruguay Round of GATT than with formulating its science and technology policy. Technology will come with foreign investment and the way to make foreign investment in developing countries more attractive is to provide more up-to-date information to potential investors. In practice technology partnerships are often a necessary condition for entering markets in developing countries. Government policies can enhance partnering by facilitating the development of local technological, managerial and organizational capabilities (UNCTAD, 1998).

THE ROLE OF SCIENCE AND TECHNOLOGY POLICIES FOR LDCS IN GENERAL

From studies on Ethiopia, Tanzania, Bangladesh and Nepal, summarized in UNCTAD (1995) some conclusions can be drawn concerning the need to influence the science and technology policies of developing countries in general to promote innovation for local SMEs. For the developed countries the OECD carries out such reviews of their science and technology. UNCTAD should play a similar role for developing countries. The recommendations will be presented under the headings: review of science and technology policies, receiving assistance for formulating such policies, identifying the role of government, paying attention to institutions and the needs of small entrepreneurs, farmers and the poor.

1. The Need to Review Present Science and Technology Policies

Some countries do not have a science and technology policy, or where they do it is not implemented. An evaluation should be undertaken, preferably by independent experts, to try to assess to what extent the science and technology policy reflects the priorities of the country, is being implemented and has been successful in achieving its objectives. Points of attention could be:

a.   How broadly or narrowly has the policy been defined?
b.   How were the needs and priorities defined and are they still valid?
c.   Has attention been paid to implementation and has the policy been implemented successfully?
d.   What has been the role of foreign assistance in implementing the policy?

e. Have policies been elaborated at the meso- (sectoral, regional and institutional) level?
f. Have the basic needs of the population been adequately addressed (see also section 5 below)?

2. The Need for Assistance in Formulating Comprehensive Science and Technology Policies

A review as suggested under section 1 may reveal the need to formulate different types of science and technology policies in LDCs. The differences between these science and technology policies and those of a more traditional nature could be of four types:

a. Science and technology would be defined more broadly than usual. Instead of limiting its scope to the natural and physical sciences, attention would also be given to the social sciences.
b. Instead of concentrating on research and development, attention would also be paid to the issue of dissemination of research and development results and the use made of them.
c. The needs of the users would be taken more into consideration (see section 5 below).
d. Instead of concentrating on academic research, the importance of including the roles of primary and secondary education and of vocational training would be stressed. It may be necessary to change the content of these forms of education and training. In vocational training the innovative mentality of the students may have to be stimulated, so that they become more dynamic entrepreneurs at a later stage.

Least developed countries should receive technical assistance to evaluate their present policies and to formulate more comprehensive science and technology policies. Countries making the transition to a more market-oriented economy will face a number of specific problems, which would need to be taken into account.

3. Identification of a Different Role for the Government

It is not the government that will develop new approaches to technological capacity building. The government can facilitate market processes, but cannot replace private initiative, organizations and partners.

In the case of science and technology policies, East Asia can be taken as an example. Governments can create the conditions for the development of the economy, but this requires a new role for the state in the economy. Instead of controlling and directing, the state would be creating the appropriate conditions for the development of certain sectors and activities. The major elements would be:

a.   Consultations with the private sector.
b.   Concentration by Governments on providing infrastructure, education and training and an appropriate macroeconomic framework.
c.   Account to be taken in the science and technology policy of the resources of the country and the results of the consultation process with the private sector (see point a. above) with respect to the future development of the economy.

4.   Pay Attention to the Meso Level when Implementing Science and Technology Policies

Science and technology policies need to be elaborated at the sectoral, regional and institutional level. In the larger countries in particular the number of different (sub) sectors, the number of provinces (or states) and the number of institutions involved may be very large.

Projects tend to be at the macro level, while in fact implementing policies is more difficult than formulating them. It requires considering the institutional capacity of the different actors concerned, making funds available, and assuring that there is co-ordination among the different institutions involved.

5.   Identify Science and Technology Needs of Farmers, Small Entrepreneurs, Women and the Poor

The identification of the science and technology needs poses problems in every country. Taking into account the problems of poor people particularly is difficult. Too often a small group, belonging to the upper layers of society, determines the priorities. Consequently many countries have either no science and technology policy or else only very specific ones. In this connection the question that must be asked is to what extent science and technology policies have contributed to the satisfaction of the basic needs of the population.

Too much emphasis was given in the past to small enterprise development through credit and technical assistance. The risk is a large number of small enterprises producing the same product at ever smaller margins. Rather technology adaptation and innovation diffusion should have been emphasized, using the existing technology development institutions as much as possible. The EU has taken this line in its development assistance to the former communist countries in Eastern Europe.

6. Projects could be Started in the Following Fields

a. Evaluation of science and technology policies of LDCs.
b. Support for the formulation of science and technology policies aimed at addressing the basic needs of the population.
c. Projects furthering the implementation of science and technology policies.
d. Assistance to governments in periods of transition in defining a new role for the government in the development process.
e. Identification of the science and technology needs of the population.

A partnership is a shared learning experience. To allow the learning to take place in a systematic way research institutes need to be involved and those parts of the private and public sectors involved need to take a more open approach to this kind of shared learning process.

NOTES

1. How are strategic alliances different from old-fashioned joint ventures (UN, 1990)? There are gradations between traditional contracts at one extreme and mergers or acquisitions at the other. Strategic alliances are in the middle and should clearly be distinguished from joint ventures. Global competition forces companies to work with others to develop new capabilities ranging from technology development to new marketing and distribution skills.
2. Other examples of such regional co-operation projects were mentioned in the Federation of Bangladeshi Chambers of Commerce and Industry (FBCCI) Newsletter (May 1994).
3. Van Dijk (1995) studied for UNCTAD how to build up and reinforce the local technological capacity in two Least Developed Countries (LDCs), Bangladesh and Nepal. The emphasis was on identifying forms of technology co-operation that exist and on listing options for developing countries to develop such forms of technology co-operation.
4. In the framework of the UNDP-financed Tokten project a number of Bangladeshi scientists living abroad visited the country for a certain period to work on a specific subject (for example the problem of dealing with used polythene bags). The project has been stopped.
5. Discussion was held with the Bangladesh Atomic Energy Commission and the Bangladesh Council for Scientific and Industrial Research (BCSIR). We did not visit the Jute Research Institute, the Rice Research Institute, the association of garment producers and the one for leather producers.
6. As one of the people interviewed remarked: 'People do not look at Science and technology as a tangible instrument that has real value'.
7. Having India as a neighbour has its disadvantages. India tended to flood the market with industrial products. The country has not opened its borders to the same extent as Bangladesh and seems to treat neighbouring countries as satellites as far as trade is concerned.
8. For example in the FBCCI Newsletter, May 1994: Myanmar for enhanced trade (suggestion to create Free Trade Zone in the Bangladesh–Myanmar border).

REFERENCES

Bramezza, I. (1996), *The Competitiveness of the European City and the Role of Urban Management in Improving the City's Performance*, Rotterdam: Tinbergen Institute, No. 109.

Dijk, M.P. van (1995), 'Investment in technological capacity building in Bangladesh and Nepal', in UNCTAD (1995), pp. 39–61.

Dijk, M.P. van (1998), *Financial Flows and Capital Markets in Emerging Asian Economies, Sources for Urban and Private Sector Development*, Rotterdam: Euricur.

ERT (1993), *European Industry: A Partner of the Developing World*, Brussels: European Round Table of Industrials.

Freeman, C. (1987), *Technology Policy and Economic Performance, Lessons from Japan*, London: Pinter Publishers.

Huq, M., K.M. Nabiul Islam and N. Islam (1993), *Machinery Manufacturing in Bangladesh*, Dhaka: UPL.

OECD (1991), *Managing Technological Change in Less-advanced Developing Countries*, Paris: OECD.

Pietrobelli, C. (1996), *Emerging Forms of Technological Co-operation: The Case for Technology Partnership*, Geneva: UNCTAD.

Singer, H. (1977), *Technologies for Basic Needs*, Geneva: ILO.

UN (1990), *Joint Ventures as a Channel for the Transfer of Technology*, New York: United Nations.

UNCTAD (1995), *Technological Capacity Building and Technology Partnership, Field Findings, Country Experiences and Programs*, Geneva: UN.

UNCTAD (1998), 'Report on the expert group meeting on the impact of government policy and government /private action in stimulating inter-firm partnerships regarding technology, production and marketing', Geneva: UNCTAD.

15. Innovation and small enterprise development in developing countries: some conclusions

Meine Pieter van Dijk and Henry Sandee

Our aim was to study what innovation means for the development of small enterprises in developing countries. Innovation adoption and technological change in small enterprises are frequently discussed without agreement on their main characteristics and features. There is a need for a framework to put order in all the different studies, classifications, definitions, and concepts that are used while studying this topic. Therefore we have opted for a broad definition of innovation, which includes the diversity of experiences with technological change and small enterprise development.

After discussing the broad definition, we discuss in this chapter how to view the experiences with innovation adoption given all the recent attention to local technological capability and capacity for small enterprise development. We prefer using the concept of technological capacity for this final chapter as it is somewhat broader than capability (see also Romijn's contribution). The technological capability literature is concerned with long-term development processes and is interested in whether innovation adoption will become an ongoing process rather than remaining a one-time event. In the latter case small enterprises may adopt new technology but it does not necessary imply that they are embarking on a trajectory of indigenous technological upgrading. This is a particularly relevant issue for clustered small enterprises, widely discussed in this book, as there is ample evidence of agglomerations of small producers in developing countries adopting innovations. Innovation adoption offers scope for joint action and learning processes that may enhance upgrading of technological capacities.

Subsequently we discuss in detail incremental versus radical innovations in the case of micro and small enterprises. Finally, this concluding chapter assesses the process of innovation adoption and diffusion. We mentioned in our first chapter that innovation adoption does not come about spontaneously but that it is a process in which distinct phases can be distinguished and different actors may take the lead. We will report on the similarities and differences in innovation adoption and diffusion processes among small enterprises in different stages of the innovation process and depending on which actor takes the lead.

A BROAD DEFINITION OF INNOVATION

Sverrisson in Chapter 13 notes that technological innovation is often assumed to be absent in the South. This absence is in fact a defining characteristic of underdevelopment according to some ways of thinking. However, a closer look in the different chapters of this book reveals for micro and small enterprises a more balanced picture in which acquisition of multi-purpose, flexible, machinery and imitative adaptation appear in the foreground.

For that reason Van Dijk suggests in Chapter 6 a broader definition, calling an innovation in the case of micro and small enterprises studies, 'all the researcher did not expect'. It may mean making a slightly different product, slightly better, using different raw material, economizing on the use of energy, improving design, financing in a new way, and so on. One can also see that innovation is sometimes related to the production technology, but also to the availability of new materials, advanced electronics or the larger efficiency of certain efficient smaller-scale technologies, which have become available. Innovation frequently concerns imitation of production techniques, designs, management forms, marketing strategies, and so on that are already in use elsewhere. However, as Romijn suggests in Chapter 2 at the local level such imitation processes still constitute an act of creativity, and it can be viewed as an innovation within the particular context within which it is newly introduced. Also Qualmann (Chapter 8) reports that African small enterprise consists mainly of 'adaptive imitators' rather than innovators. Small entrepreneurs' innovations concern introduction of *locally* new designs, *locally new* adaptations of technology, and so on.

Parrilli in Chapter 7 also notes that in the context of a very poor developing country such as Nicaragua, innovation is a big word. This industry is still at the handicraft level: low productivity, limited mechanization, working for the local market and using family workers. In this case, it is hard to talk about innovation as production of 'absolutely new' products, processes or ways of doing things. It would be better to talk about imitation and learning about developments elsewhere.

Sandee (1995) found for the roof tile industry that there are differences among clusters of small enterprises in moulds used for printing tiles. Small adjustments are made in accordance with local technological capacities and experiences. Clusters deserve special attention because of the possibilities for small enterprises to adopt innovations jointly. Clustering facilitates adoption of technology with so-called 'indivisible elements' that cannot be adopted successfully by individual firms because it is too costly or risky. An example is adoption of clay mixers by small roof tile enterprises. Technological progress in the roof tile industry embodies the adoption of a package that consists of new moulds, new printing methods using presses rather than hand-printing, and power-driven mixers to improve the quality of clay for printing. Mixers are expensive and cannot be used in a commercially viable way by individual adopters. Joint usage of the mixer becomes a prerequisite for successful innovation adoption and it is highly facilitated by clustering of small enterprises.

Sverrisson explores the idea of social capital, which is economically useful social connectivity, to understand technological innovation in small enterprise clusters or enterprise collectives in the South. He also looks at technological innovation as a form of entrepreneurship. In his Chapter 13, he focuses on entrepreneurship and innovation as a particular instance of that activity. Innovation is understood as the activity of bringing novel technologies into social contexts where they were not before, leading to new products, better quality of old products or lower production costs. In other words he points to its role at the diffusion end of the innovation process, discussed by Sverrisson, with a particular emphasis on small enterprises in the South and the problems they face.

DEVELOPMENT OF TECHNOLOGICAL CAPACITY IS IMPORTANT

Although ever more technology is available in the global economy, the further development of local technological capacity is very important. It allows independent technological choices and leads to the capacity to adapt, improve and generate new technologies. Adoption of locally new technology does not necessarily mean that small producers will be in a position to improve the technology gradually over time and will eventually be able to make more radical improvements in the longer run. An ongoing (sustained) process of adoption of incremental and radical innovations is dependent on the development of such capacities of small firms and their business environment.

In the previous chapters the importance of the development of technological capability and capacity has been shown several times. It has also been observed that there are usually pioneers in a cluster of small enterprises who start experimenting with new ideas. Such ideas may enter the cluster through visits to other areas or visits by traders, suppliers, customers, and so on, to the cluster. However, Sverrisson remarks that first adopters are not always the most successful, they make the mistakes that later adopters can avoid, if information spreads within the community, which is a function of the form of social capital prevailing there. What does this mean for the development of technological capacity within clusters of small firms? Pioneer adopters play an important role in introducing locally new technology to the cluster. Their efforts will be characterized by trial and error. It contributes to the development of their capacities through learning by doing. Later adopters may avoid their mistakes and adopt the right designs, methods, or equipment right from the beginning. This leads to productivity gains for later adopters *vis-à-vis* pioneers but their position may be less favourable from the viewpoint of local technological capacity upgrading as they have not been through a process of trial and error. Interestingly, clusters of small firms may have the 'best of both worlds' due to the fact that there are both pioneers and efficient later adopters working side by side.

Romijn in Chapter 2 starts out to study what makes firms learn and finds that there is a process of capability building within small firms which has positive effects. The learning process is incremental and evolutionary with internal efforts to master the production and repair of machinery and equipment, search for relevant technological information, and so on. Also Clancy in Chapter 4 notes that acquisition and upgrading of technological capacities is a slow process. She adds that learning requires an explicit effort to produce changes in processes, procedures and organizational arrangements. Learning processes in clusters of small firms do not have to be internal to the firm but may be spread over firms in the clusters. However, it is of importance that such learning processes and subsequent development of technological capabilities are internal to the cluster.

The concept of learning is used for regions (Morgan, 1997), while Storper (1993) argues that innovation requires both technological and organizational learning. In all cases agglomeration of activities tend to provide the basis for these learning processes. Sometimes the total is referred to as the innovative milieu (Maillat, 1995), which is a very explicit reference to the ability of a production system to generate innovation processes. Technical assistance aimed at innovation adoption needs to take account of the complexity of such learning processes that require much more than the usual one-shot interventions to foster innovation adoption. Technical assistance aimed at innovation adoption is not effective when there is no access yet to those market channels that are interested in the new product. Assistance is more relevant in dynamic clusters where there is demand for technical and financial assistance to accommodate growth processes that were initiated by buyers and producers. Thus assistance needs to be geared to those small firms and clusters where learning processes are under way and where producers are already in the process of upgrading their technological capabilities. Albaladejo in Chapter 10 stresses the importance of designing support services on the basis of the indigenous capacities of local firms and the process of inter-enterprise learning. Support in dynamic clusters should be designed differently compared with more dormant clusters to adjust it as much as possible to existing local capacities.

In order to understand innovation adoption by small enterprises it is vital to examine local technological capacities. Innovation adoption will have a more long-term impact on small enterprises if it leads to learning processes that stimulate firms to embark on a trajectory of growth and upgrading. In the case of clustered small enterprises we need to make a distinction between enhancement of technological capacities at the firm level and at the cluster level. An individual firm may not be able to enhance its technological capacities but the cluster in which it is located may well be on a trajectory of sustainable growth.

We conclude that small enterprises imitate and adapt rather than invent and innovate. Innovation adoption by small enterprises boils down to both incremental and radical improvements that bolster productivity. These improvements are generally based on experiences of firms elsewhere that have adopted specific innovations already. In general, however, there remains the need to adjust innovations to the local needs and circumstances.

INCREMENTAL AND RADICAL INNOVATIONS

We find it most useful to make a distinction between incremental and radical innovations because it is closest to the daily practice of starting up and expanding small businesses. Small entrepreneurs are continuously making small improvements. Such incremental innovations take place within most small enterprises, although some are more successful in generating improvements than others. Radical innovations concern discrete leaps in productivity generated by the use of new technology. We have seen in this book that such radical changes require a range of adjustments in both production and marketing.

Clancy presents another example of gradual innovation in Chapter 4. She found that in the small-scale briquetting sector in India, innovation concerns chiefly using new technology rather than producing it. Clancy found mainly evidence of process innovations such as creating adjustments that gave rise to efficiency improvements.

Incremental innovations also take place virtually everywhere although there are differences in intensity and impact. Radical changes are more important and small firms need them if they are to remain competitive in a changing world. Radical changes occur on a limited scale only as they require substantial investments and ability to take risks.

The distinction between incremental and radical innovations is also relevant for a discussion on local technological capacities. It shows us that such capacities are upgraded gradually over time. However, there are limits to what can be achieved by incremental changes. Upgrading of capacities will also lead to radical innovations especially when small entrepreneurs themselves are not spectators but actors in the process. The challenge for support organizations is to promote more radical innovations rather than incremental ones, which have a greater chance of taking place spontaneously.

DIFFERENT STAGES IN THE INNOVATION PROCESS

Based on our assessment of the various contributions to this book we find that for small enterprises, innovation adoption and diffusion is a process taking place in different stages:

a.   New technologies continually become available and later on they become accessible for producers at a specific location, but they nearly always involve equipment, machinery, etc. that is already in use elsewhere.
b.   New technology is introduced by (clusters of) small firms on their own accord (probably incremental innovations, usually producer driven) or it is suggested by buyers or support agencies. In the case of new technology with indivisible elements, successful introduction requires collaboration among small enterprises.
c.   Technology is adjusted to local needs and circumstances. Small producers do this individually but in clusters; pioneer adopters may play leading roles in assisting neighbouring producers to adapt the technology to local conditions.
d.   Subsequently, the new technology is used by an increasing number of local producers (diffusion) while further economies of scale and scope may be achieved when firms divide tasks among themselves in accordance with individual strengths and weaknesses of their own businesses. Further small adjustments may take place.

Sverrisson provides a similar overview of phases in the innovation process. He explains that there is a need for actors to analyse the business environment prior to innovation decisions and this also encompasses acquiring information on the technology that best fits their needs and budgets. Subsequently, a choice has to be made on the acquisition of particular technologies that will lead to their acquisition and implementation. Sverrisson then carefully analyses this process, to conclude that technological innovation, just as it changes the forms of financial and human capital, likewise transforms social capital. Thus successful innovation adoption and diffusion among small enterprises requires changes in both direct production and marketing arrangements. It also requires changes in the relations among producers and between producers and other actors. Innovation may lead to the formation of new networks that are necessary to render adoption successful. In sociological terminology we would talk about the change in role sets attendant upon technological change, which in turn leads to networks of a very different character (Barley, 1990).

DIFFERENT ACTORS PLAY A ROLE IN THE INNOVATION PROCESS

The various contributions in this book have shown that different actors may play key roles in introducing and diffusing innovations among small enterprises. Many innovation processes are not driven by the small producers themselves but by other actors. Buyers (for example, traders) and support agencies (institutions) turn out to be very important potential agents of change as well. Therefore, it is relevant to make a distinction between producer-driven, buyer-driven, and institution-driven innovation adoption processes for small enterprise development. We will briefly illustrate the distinction below because this distinction is also relevant when we want to understand to what extent innovation adoption contributes to the enhancement of technological capabilities in small enterprises.

Knorringa speaks of a process of endogenous technology upgrading capability and studies it in the context of clusters at different levels of development. He compares the process of upgrading in clusters that are driven by different actors. First, local producers may play the key role in cluster development processes. This is most useful for the enhancement of local capacities as small producers may share the risks, costs and experiences associated with innovation. This is the example of producer-driven innovation.

In the case of producer-driven innovation a distinction was made in learning by doing, social learning and collaboration in clusters. The latter is also the subject of Knorringa's chapter. He analyses the capability of combinations of actors in specific clusters to implement and build on incremental innovations, because he considers that as a rule they do not initiate radical innovations. Van Dijk in Chapter 6 also stresses learning, referring to the endogenous growth theory, which stresses the importance of economies of scale and endogenous labour-saving developments. Innovation is a combination of an innovative mentality, skilled labour and multi-purpose equipment as suggested by the flexible specialization paradigm (Pedersen *et al.*, 1994).

Secondly, traders, buyers or big firms, all located outside the cluster, may also take the lead in the development of a cluster. In this case, there is the imminent danger that much of the benefits of innovation accrue to 'outsiders' and innovation may not lead to substantial upgrading of technological capacities. McCormick and Atieno notice that firms contract out specialized activities ranging from security services to technology-intensive manufacturing of component parts. By doing so they benefit from the skills accumulated in these other enterprises. Subcontracting is an important linkage mechanism through which clustered small enterprises are linked to bigger firms. Subcontracting may have a mixed impact on the development of local technological capacities of small firms. On the one hand, it may contribute to strengthening capacities whenever the contract arrangements would allow small firms to develop complete products in which they can put much of their creativity. On the other hand, subcontracting may also be detrimental to the enhancement of technological capacities if small firms focus on production of specific parts only, with little opportunity for learning.

Helmsing indicates in Chapter 5 that the capacity of enterprises to innovate does not only depend on firm-level characteristics, but also on market structure and local conditions. He examines to what extent the local structure is conducive to co-operation and innovation and focuses his research in Zimbabwe on the role of science and technology centres and intermediary support organizations for this purpose. Independent business services, which could have contributed to an innovative milieu, have hardly been developed in the city where he did his research, Bulawayo, after the economic crisis that raged in Zimbabwe. Helmsing's study and also the contribution of Bongenaar and Szirmai in Chapter 12 are examples of the difficulties that government institutions face in fostering innovation adoption by small enterprises. Institution-driven innovation processes rightly aim at adjusting technologies that have proven to be successful elsewhere in local conditions. However, such institutions do not always succeed in identifying commercially viable innovations, and, subsequently, innovation adoption fails as it is not picked up by the small-scale producers.

POLICIES THAT LEAD TO INNOVATION

Bongenaar and Szirmai present a case study of innovation adoption and diffusion in the African context. Their study of a government agency in Tanzania involved in industrial research and development shows the processes of acquisition and adaptation of *existing*, and often imported, technology to local circumstances. Subsequently, the agency stimulates innovation adoption and diffusion of technology within the manufacturing sector. The agency is concerned primarily with adaptation of existing technology to local circumstances rather than the creation of new technology as the main thrust of innovation within the small enterprise sector. Its methods appear to be rather similar to the upgrading strategies of small-scale entrepreneurs themselves who do not invent but adapt, imitate, and adjust technologies that have proven to be successful elsewhere. However, the case of Bongenaar and Szirmai illustrates an important difference between such innovation processes that are generated by government agencies *vis-à-vis* small-scale entrepreneurs and buyers.

Different chapters have described different policies leading to innovation, or the factors conditioning the technology adaptation and adoption process. In general, the importance of learning recurs and hence of any policy stimulating producers and their workers to learn. As mentioned in the text in many countries the development of a business support system provides a contribution to this learning process, because it takes place partially in institutions designed to support the micro and small enterprise sector.

Albaladejo gives a useful example from Spain on how to develop service centres for small enterprise development. Successful centres are responsive to the industry's demands, react to the needs of the customers, and are primarily intermediate agents that facilitate and strengthen processes of change in small enterprises that are already on their way. This is an important lesson for the improvement of service centres in developing countries: successful centres should build upon local technological capabilities and support change processes initiated by the small-scale enterprise sector. Furthermore, support centres may play a role in bringing small producers closer to potential (niche) markets, which may trigger off their interest for innovation.

In the different chapters a number of suggestions have been made concerning ways to stimulate innovation and innovation diffusion (also Freeman, 1987). The different authors stress different mechanisms. For example McCormick and Atieno stress the role of linkages, Bongenaar and Szirmai the role of R&D institutes and Sverrisson the role of social capital.

CONCLUSION

The conclusion is that innovation takes place all the time through incremental improvements in production processes and products. In this sense it is a cumulative process. Technologies lead to learning, which leads to improvements. Innovation among small enterprises through radical changes takes place on a much more limited scale. It is of importance though because of its substantial contribution to small enterprise development. In a number of chapters we noted that hardly any radical technological development or innovations take place over prolonged periods. This occurs during an economic recession (Helmsing and Qualmann) when the economic outlook is negative, and also in the absence of institutional support that is crucial to trigger off change (Parrilli). Moreover, there are situations where collaboration among small producers is a prerequisite for innovation but such joint action does not get off the ground (Sandee). Helmsing also concluded that not all firms respond to external changes in innovative ways. He introduces this distinction between defensive and innovative firms, to conclude that the latter are the minority in his study.

Technologies are, according to Sverrisson, re-innovated each time as they are brought into different social contexts. New ways of organizing maintenance, new applications and new ways of organizing work with these technologies and new competence in operating them under local conditions have to be found to make local innovation based on 'technology transfer' work. Technological development and innovation are rightly considered crucial for micro and small enterprises because they need to be competitive in an evermore global economy. More research will remain necessary to shed light on the process, but at least we have some support from more recent economic and sociological theories, from a number of case studies, such as the ones reported on in this book, and from experiments with policies and programmes to stimulate technological development and innovation.

REFERENCES

Barley, S.R. (1990), 'The alignment of technology and structure through roles and networks', in *Administrative Science Quarterly*, **35**, pp. 61–103.

Freeman, C. (1987), *Technology Policy and Economic Performance, Lessons from Japan*, London: Pinter Publishers.

Maillat, D. (1995), 'Territorial dynamic, innovative milieus and regional policy', *Entrepreneurship and Regional Development*, **7**, pp. 157–65.

Morgan, K. (1997), 'The learning region: institutions, innovation and regional renewal', *Regional Studies*, **31** (5), 491–503.

Pedersen, P.O., A. Sverrisson and M.P. van Dijk (eds) (1994), *Flexible Specialization, The Dynamics of Small-scale Industries in the South*, London: IT Publications.

Sandee, H. (1995), *Innovation Adoption in Rural Industry: Technological Change in Roof Tile Clusters in Central Java, Indonesia*, Amsterdam: Vrije Universiteit.

Storper, M. (1993), 'Regional "worlds" of production: learning and innovation in the technology districts of France, Italy and the USA', *Regional Studies*, **27** (5), pp. 433–55.

Index

Trulsson, P. 125, 126, 135, 293, 296
Tunisia 30

United Kingdom 226, 306
United Nations 38
  Development Programme 261, 307
  UNCTAD 127, 135, 303, 309
United States 135, 144, 153, 282, 292,
    308
  Agency for International Development
    99
  Food and Drug Administration 52
unpacking 253
  capability 253–4
  possibilities 253–4
Utterback, J.M. 124

vertical level 157–9
Vietnam 306
Visser, E.J. 294

Warwick, D.P. 296
Watanabe, S. 20, 24, 29, 34, 36, 37, 38
Webster, L.M. 168–9
Weijland, H. 48, 50
Westphal, L.E. 17, 251
Whitley, R. 224
Williamson, O.E. 169–70, 223, 228
Winch, G. 226
Winter, S. 170
Wissema, J.G. 251, 256

Wittgenstein 4
wood products industry 173, 174, 175,
    188, 189
World Bank 112, 128, 166, 168, 169,
    261, 307

ZECO Engineering Ltd 98
Zeitlin, J. 58, 211, 281, 286
Zimbabwe 5, 303
  Business Herald 134
  Central Statistics Office 98–9
  Directory of Brand Names and
    Products 99
  garment industry 102, 104, 106
  Institute of Housing and Urban
    Development Studies 98
  Institute of Social Studies 98
  Matabeleland Chamber of Industries
    99
  National Chamber of Commerce 99
  National University of Science &
    Technology 97, 112, 115
  social capital and technological
    innovation 287, 293, 297
  technological capability 24, 25, 29,
    33, 34, 37, 38
  Venture Capital Company 116
  see also Bulawayo; Burkina Faso,
    Ghana and Zimbabwe
ZIMTRADE 115
Zucker, L. 150